Roman Society

in the Last Century

of the Western Empire

ROMAN SOCIETY

IN THE LAST CENTURY

OF THE WESTERN EMPIRE

by SAMUEL DILL

 THE MERIDIAN LIBRARY

Published by MERIDIAN BOOKS, INC.   *New York*

Samuel Dill

Samuel Dill was born in County Down, Ireland, in 1844. After serving as a tutor at Oxford, he became Professor of Greek at Queen's College, Belfast. The Universities of Dublin and Edinburgh awarded him honorary degrees, and Oxford named him an Honorary Fellow. He died in 1924. He is the author of *Roman Society from Nero to Marcus Aurelius* (already published in The Meridian Library, ML1), *Roman Society in Gaul in the Merovingian Age,* and the present work.

Second Revised Edition
The Meridian Library Edition first published September 1958
First printing August 1958

Library of Congress Catalog Card Number: 58—13570

Manufactured in the United States of America

PREFACE TO SECOND EDITION

THIS second edition of a work, which has met with such
a generous reception both from the educated public and
from learned critics, has not been fundamentally altered.
It is possible that materials, so fragmentary and gleaned
from so many sources, might here and there have been
arranged in an order more satisfactory to the critical
reader.   On the other hand, it is not improbable that
something of the freshness of the original impression
derived from the authorities might be lost in an effort to
obtain a more perfect sequence.   At the same time the
opportunity of a reprint has been used to make a good
many minor changes.   An occasional looseness of expression has been amended; statements which seemed too
strong or incautious have occasionally been toned down;
and some slips as to fact, or the form of proper names,
have been corrected.   A few additional references have
been inserted in the notes, especially to Friedländer's
Sittengeschichte Roms, which, although it deals only with
the society of the first and second centuries, may be
instructively used for purposes of comparison with the

society of the later Empire. Lastly, a table of the more important dates of the period has been added, with the object of facilitating the perusal of a book in which some knowledge of the general history is necessarily assumed.

6th July 1899.

PREFACE

A FEW words of preface seem to be necessary to explain
the object of this book, and the limits within which the
writer has wished to confine it. It is perhaps superfluous
to say that nothing like a general history of the period
has been attempted. That is a task which has been
already accomplished by abler hands. The subject of
this work is mainly what it professes to be, the inner life
and thoughts of the last three generations in the Empire
of the West. If external events are referred to, it is only
because men's private fortunes and feelings cannot be
severed from the fortunes of the State.

The limits of the period covered by this study of
Roman society have not been arbitrarily chosen. The
last hundred years of the Western Empire seem marked
off both by momentous events, and, for the student of
society, by the authorities at his command. The commencement of the period coincides roughly with the
passage of the Gothic hordes across the Danube, the
accession of Gratian and Theodosius, the termination of
the long truce between paganism and the Christian
Empire, and the reopening of the conflict which, within
twenty years, ended in the final prohibition of heathen

rites. It closes, not only with the deposition of the last shadowy Emperor of the West, but with the practical extinction of Roman power in the great prefecture of the Gauls. Perhaps even more obvious are the lines drawn by the fullest authorities for our subject. The earliest extant letters of Symmachus, which describe the relations of the last generation of great pagan nobles, belong to the years 376–390. The literary and political activity of Ausonius coincides with the same years, and from his poems we derive an invaluable picture of a provincial society in the reigns of Gratian and Theodosius. A searching light is thrown on the same generation by some of S. Jerome's letters, by the *Saturnalia* of Macrobius, and by many Inscriptions. At the other end of our period we are almost equally fortunate in our information. The works of Apollinaris Sidonius of Auvergne are a priceless revelation of the state of society, both in Rome and in Gaul, from the accession of Avitus till the final triumph of the Visigothic power.

Nor is there wanting a certain bond of union among these and other scattered materials when they are closely scrutinised. At the beginning of the period, Roman society is indeed sharply divided in a determined religious struggle, and the sharpness of the contrast is rendered more decided by the increasing fervour of asceticism. But at the hottest moment of the conflict there was a mass of scepticism, lukewarmness, or wavering conformity, between the confines of the opposing creeds. The influences which inspired that attitude had not spent their force at the close of the fourth century. When the terrors of the anti-pagan laws had produced an outward submission, the Christianity of many of the noble and lettered class seems to have been far from enthusiastic. The discipline of the schools was a powerful rival of the Church. Men who had had that training were steeped in the lingering sentiment of paganism, and looked with distrust, or even with contempt, on the severer form of Christian renunciation. One can scarcely doubt that Sidonius, in his early manhood, and some of his friends down to the fall of the Western Empire, would have been far more at home in the company of Symmachus or Flavianus than in that of S. Paulinus of Nola.

It would, of course, be impossible to treat of society in such a period without some reference to those who devoted themselves to the higher ideals of the Christian life. But they belong rather to the future. Our interest in these pages must be concentrated on those whose greatest pride it was to preserve and transmit the traditions of the past. The main purpose of this work is to give some account of that worldly society which, in its ideals, tone, and external fortunes, had undergone but little change between the reign of Gratian and the dethronement of Romulus Augustulus.

The period is an obscure one, and the materials are widely scattered. The difficulty of arranging them in an orderly view is not slight; and the writer is painfully conscious that a critical eye may easily discover omissions and faults of treatment. His only claim is that he has made an honest attempt to answer a question which has often presented itself to his own mind— How were men living, and what were their thoughts and private fortunes, during that period of momentous change ?

It only remains for the author to express his warmest thanks to his old pupil and friend, the Rev. Charles Plummer, Vice-President and Librarian of Corpus Christi College, Oxford, for the kind care with which he has gone over the proof-sheets.

4th October 1898.

TABLE OF DATES

EMPERORS OF THE WEST

Reign of Valentinian I. .	. . . . .	364-375
,, Valentinian II.	. . . . .	375-392
,, Gratian .	. . . . .	375-383
,, Theodosius I. .	. . . . .	379-395
,, Honorius	. . . . .	395-423
,, Valentinian III.	. . . . .	425-455
,, Maximus	. . . . .	455
,, Avitus .	. . . . .	455-456
,, Majorian	. . . . .	457-461
,, Severus .	. . . . .	461-465
,, Anthemius	. . . . .	467-472
,, Olybrius .	. . . . .	472
,, Glycerius	. . . . .	473
,, Julius Nepos .	. . . . .	474-475
,, Romulus Augustulus	. . . .	475-476

KINGS OF THE VISIGOTHS

Reign of Alaric .	. . . . . .	395-410
,, Ataulphus	. . . . . .	410-415
,, Wallia .	. . . . . .	415-419
,, Theodoric I.	. . . . . .	419-451
,, Thorismond	. . . . . .	451-453
,, Theodoric II. .	. . . . .	453-466
,, Euric .	. . . . . .	466-485

Birth of D. Magnus Ausonius	. . . .	*circ.* 310
,, S. Martin .	. . . . .	,, 316
,, Ammianus Marcellinus	. . . .	,, 330
,, Sext. Petron. Probus. .	. . .	,, 334
,, Virius Nicomachus Flavianus	. . .	,, 334

CONTENTS

BOOK I

THE TENACITY OF PAGANISM

CHAPTER I

THE PAGAN ARISTOCRACY AND THE CONFUSION OF PARTIES

CHAPTER II

THE LAST CONFLICTS OF PAGANISM WITH THE CHRISTIAN EMPIRE

CHAPTER III

S. AUGUSTINE AND OROSIUS ON THE CAPTURE OF ROME

CHAPTER IV

SOME CAUSES OF THE VITALITY OF THE LATER PAGANISM

BOOK II

SKETCHES OF WESTERN SOCIETY FROM SYMMACHUS TO SIDONIUS

CHAPTER I

THE INDICTMENT OF HEATHEN AND CHRISTIAN MORALISTS

CHAPTER II

THE SOCIETY OF Q. AURELIUS SYMMACHUS

CHAPTER III

THE SOCIETY OF AQUITAINE IN THE TIME OF AUSONIUS

CHAPTER IV

THE SOCIETY OF APOLLINARIS SIDONIUS

The family of Apoll. Sidonius—His career—Publication of his letters—
Great changes in the interval between Ausonius and Sidonius—Yet
the condition of the upper class remains unaltered—Sidonius tells
little of the middle and lower classes—His interest centres in his own
order—Its exclusive tastes — Minute faithfulness with which he
describes his own society—Monotony of its life—His wide circle of
acquaintance—The ideal of the Roman noble as sketched by Sidonius
—Pride of birth—High birth considered even in episcopal elections—
Imperial office generally sought for its external distinction—Yet
there must have been a number of men possessing high administrative
capacity to fill the prefectures, etc.—Duties of the Pretorian prefect
—But many Gallic nobles were becoming farmers on a large scale—
Instance of Syagrius—A country squire on good terms with the
Germans—Extent of senatorial estates—That of Ausonius at Bazas,
about 1000 acres—The *villa* a little community in itself—Description of it—The arrangements of a great house—Avitacum—Great
houses fortified—Roads unsafe—Mode of travelling—Country house
visits—Voroangus and Prusianum—Daily life at a country house—
Position of women — They are treated with great respect — Few

BOOK III

THE FAILURE OF ADMINISTRATION, AND THE RUIN OF THE MIDDLE CLASS, AS REVEALED BY THE THEODOSIAN CODE

CHAPTER I

THE DISORGANISATION OF THE PUBLIC SERVICE

General view of the social and administrative disorganisation of the period
—The government with the best intentions strove to find a remedy
—The sense of responsibility expressed by the later emperors—The
rhetorical tone of the later legislation—The hereditary guilds of Rome
—The *corporati* bound to their functions, but constantly trying to evade
them—Failure of the corn-supply through desertion or evasion on the
part of the *navicularii*—Different modes of evasion—Wholesale desertion in 455—Disorganisation in the army—Frequent enactments *de re
militari* in Stilicho's time—Failure of recruits—Money accepted from
the great proprietors instead of men—Aversion to military service—
Self-mutilation to escape it—Frequency of desertion—Concealment of

CHAPTER II

THE DECAY OF THE MIDDLE CLASS AND THE AGGRANDISEMENT OF THE ARISTOCRACY

BOOK IV

THE BARBARIANS AND THE FUTURE OF THE EMPIRE

CHAPTER I

THE GENERAL CHARACTER OF THE INVASIONS

CHAPTER II

ROMAN FEELING ABOUT THE INVASIONS AND THE FUTURE OF
THE EMPIRE

CHAPTER III

RELATIONS OF ROMANS WITH THE INVADERS

Subject of this chapter : the relations of Gallo-Romans with the invaders
from the first appearance of the Visigoths in Gaul till their conquest

of Auvergne in 474—The *Eucharisticos* of Paulinus Pellaeus—He was
a grandson of Ausonius—General character of the poem—Paulinus
has little interest in public affairs, yet his poem has a great value—
It is the sole authority for the temporary occupation of Bordeaux by
the Visigoths in 414—Their movements from 412 till 414—They support Jovinus and then overthrow him—Ataulphus at Narbonne—His
marriage with Placidia, the sister of Honorius—How Ataulphus came
to occupy Bordeaux, and proclaim Attalus as Emperor—Paulinus
obliged to accept the office of Count of the Largesses—The Goths
leave Bordeaux—Paulinus loses everything and flies to Bazas, which
is besieged by the Goths—A servile revolt breaks out in Bazas—
Paulinus determines to appeal for aid to the king of the Alans, who
is serving with the Goths—Strange interview—The Alan king
deserts the Goths, who decamp—The subsequent fortunes of Paulinus
—He thinks of becoming a monk—Falls into poverty—Fate of his
sons—In his old age receives unexpectedly from an unknown Goth
the price of some portion of his estates at Bordeaux—Light which the
Eucharisticos throws on the attitude of the Goths to Rome—Fluctua-
tions of Gothic policy in the lifetime of Apollinaris Sidonius—They
sometimes support the Empire, sometimes they are at war with it—
Auvergne long left in peace—Family of Sidonius on friendly terms
with Theodoric II.—Sidonius also on good terms with the Burgundians—Their settlement at Lyons—Chilperic *magister militum*—
The Burgundians a kindly race, but their personal habits offend the
taste of Sidonius—Change in the attitude of the Visigothic power on
the accession of Euric—Causes of this—Roman maladministration—
Euric an intolerant Arian — His encroachments — Overthrows the
Breton troops in Berry—Assails Auvergne—Gallant defence made
by Ecdicius, brother-in-law of Sidonius—Moral influence of Sidonius
He fortifies the courage of the people by solemn religious services—
The Rogations introduced by Mam. Claudianus of Vienne—Embassy
of Epiphanius to Euric—Negotiations of the four bishops—They
surrender Auvergne to Euric—Indignant protest of Sidonius—How
Euric treated the Catholics—Sees left vacant—Churches falling into
ruins—This policy subsequently mitigated, probably through the
influence of Leo, Euric's Roman minister — Count Victorius, a
Catholic, appointed governor of Auvergne—Sidonius banished for a
time to the fortress of Livia—Leo obtains his release—His stay at
Bordeaux—His flattery of Euric and the queen—He is restored to
his diocese—Attitude of the Gallo-Roman nobles to the Germans—
Some seclude themselves and fortify their houses—Yet they had
probably not much to fear except from irregular bands—Some take
service under the German king as administrators—Why they were
needed—Position and character of Leo, the secretary of Euric—The
tribe of delators—Their sinister arts described by Sidonius—While
the Germans wished to maintain order, there are signs of suspicion

BOOK V

CHARACTERISTICS OF ROMAN EDUCATION
AND CULTURE IN THE FIFTH CENTURY

Subject of this book : the culture of pagan tradition—Attitude of the
Church to the ancient literary culture—By many Churchmen in the
West it was long viewed with suspicion — Hellenism hostile to
Christianity—But in the fourth century the Church determines to
use the ancient discipline for its own purposes—Attitude of SS.
Jerome and Augustine—S. Jerome's love of learning—" Spoiling the
Egyptians "—Ancient forms of literature applied to sacred subjects
—Juvencus—Proba—The two Apollinares—No hard and fast line
between classical and mediaeval literature—Singular permanence of
the school tradition—Example in the case of Ennodius of the time of
Theodoric — His declamations on hackneyed themes — Failure of
original power after the Silver Age—Singular barrenness of three
centuries—Deadening effect of academic conservatism—Its pagan
spirit—Opposition between Hellenism and serious Christianity—
Example in the conversion of S. Paulinus—His correspondence with
his old professor Ausonius shows the gulf between the ascetic and the
academic spirit of the time—Influence of imperial authority and
patronage in perpetuating the school system—Academic endowments
under the Empire—Julian claims control over academic appointments
—The stipends of professors fixed in 376—Position and emoluments
of professors as described by Ausonius—Some of the rhetors men of
wealth and high social standing — Profession of letters greatly
honoured — Literary enthusiasm of the aristocracy, especially in
Gaul—The great schools of Gaul from the earliest times—Marseilles,
etc.—The literary renaissance of the fourth century—Its centres
were Trèves and the schools of Aquitaine, especially Bordeaux—
Fame of Bordeaux in the Roman world—The subjects of academic
study—Jurisprudence at Arles and Narbonne—Philosophy decaying
in the fourth century—Platonists in the time of Sidonius—But

BOOK I

THE TENACITY OF PAGANISM

CHAPTER I

In spite of ‚the moral force which ensured the future to
the Christian faith, its final triumph was long delayed.
Religious conservatism is, of all forms of attachment to
the past, probably the most difficult to overcome. It
has its seat in the deepest and most powerful instincts of
human nature, which, when they have once twined
themselves around a sacred symbol of devotion, are only
torn away after a long struggle. But this form of
attachment is peculiarly obstinate when it is identified,
as religion has so often been, with patriotic reverence for
the glory of an ancient state, which in the omens of its
birth, the election of its magistrates, the daily work of
peaceful administration, or in the stress of war, and the
exultation of conquest, has for many ages recognised the
same divine sanction and help. Superstitious fancy, or
the seductive charm of sacred festivals, may keep the
vulgar constant to the old faith; but the class which in
high office has been specially charged with the safety of
the State, and which, by a chain of real or imagined
ancestry, is more closely identified with its career, is
penetrated with a deeper conservatism than that of the
common herd. Antiquarian and literary culture also
reinforce religious sentiment, or replace it, when it has

decayed. Even the sceptical epicurean, to whom all faiths are alike, will prefer that which has the refined charm of immemorial possession, and which has received an added dignity and glory from the magic touch of genius, and the reverence of heroic characters.

For nearly a hundred years the emperors had intermittently denounced the practice of the rites of heathenism. Yet the edict [1] which closes the long series of anti-pagan laws shows, by the fierceness of its tone, and the severity of the penalties with which it threatens the offender, that the spirit of paganism was not yet crushed. In the very years in which Theodosius was issuing the laws which were to extinguish the ancient superstition, men were reviving a prophecy that the religion of the Cross was about to reach its final term,[2] and the most solemn pagan rites were publicly celebrated.[3] At the close of the fourth century the majority of the Senate were little touched by the Christian faith,[4] although the wives and daughters of some of them had adopted its most ascetic form. Staunch adherents of paganism still held the Urban or Pretorian prefecture in the reign of Honorius. They might still meet, apparently with no thought of the imminent triumph of the Church, to hear one of their number expound the sacerdotal lore of Rome,[5] and another set forth the Stoic or Alexandrian interpretation of the myths, or the command of augural science possessed by Virgil. Their great poet, as if he were writing in the age of Augustus, could invite the Christian Emperor Honorius to survey the shrines of the gods,[6] which still in all their old splendour surrounded the imperial palace

[1] *Nov. Th.* tit. iii.

[2] *S. Aug. de Civ. Dei*, xviii. 53. See Seeck's *Symmachus*, cxviii.

[3] *C.I.L.* vi. 512.

[4] Seeck's *Sym.* liv. ; Zos. iv. 59.

For the opposite view cf. Prud. *c. Sym.* i. 566 ; Ambros. *Ep.* 17, 10 ; Rauschen, *Jahrbücher der Chr. Kirche*, p. 119.

[5] Macrob. *Sat.*

[6] Claudian, *de Sex. Cons Hon.* 44,

with a divine guardianship. Another pagan poet,[1] who had been prefect of the city, a quarter of a century after the death of Theodosius, could pour contempt on the Christian profession, and rejoice at the sight of the villagers of Etruria gaily celebrating the rites of Osiris in the springtime. Magic and divination of every form had long been under the ban of the State. Yet a prefect of Honorius proposed to employ the Tuscan sorcerers,[2] who offered the aid of their arts against Alaric, and Litorius, fighting against a successor of Alaric in Gaul, consulted the pagan seers before his last battle, under the walls of Toulouse.[3] In the last years of the Western Empire, the diviners of Africa were practising their arts among the nominal Christians of Aquitaine.[4]

Long after the external rites of heathenism had been suppressed, the pagan tone and spirit retained its hold on men's imaginations. The obstinate, unchanging conservatism of the Roman character never displayed itself more strikingly than in the age when Roman institutions were tottering. That race, so tenacious of the past, yet so bold and aggressive, always strove to disguise fundamental changes, and to retain the charm of old associations under altered circumstances. In this, as in other respects, the Church carried on the tradition of pagan Rome. The prejudices and attachments of a thousand years, which might be proof against the fervid dialectic of S. Augustine, were gently trained by pious arts to turn to other objects of love and devotion.[5] She followed the advice of the great pontiff, to break the idols and consecrate the churches. The cycle of the Christian year was in many points adapted to the pagan calendar. The cult of saints and martyrs was established at the very altars where incense had been offered

---

[1] Rutil. Namat. i. 440, 375.
[2] Zos. v. 41.
[3] Prosp. *Chron.* 439.
[4] Apollin. Sidon. *Ep.* viii. 11.

[5] For a specimen see S. Paulin. Nol. *Carm.* 27, 548 - 580 ; the principle of accommodation is stated in S. Aug. *Ep.* 47, § 3.

to Mars or Bacchus.[1]   At Naples, lamps burning before
the image of the Virgin took the place of those before
the family gods.[2]   The worship of the Virgin mother
weaned the Sicilian peasant from the worship of a
goddess of less immaculate fame.

Many a literary noble of Aquitaine in the fifth
century was probably as really pagan as the peasant
who bowed before the old altar on Mount Eryx. His
grandfather in the days of Ausonius may have conformed
to Christianity; some of his friends might have sold
their lands, and followed S. Paulinus to Nola or S.
Jerome to Bethlehem; but he himself was often as
little of a Christian as the men who, three generations
before him, had pleaded with the Emperor to leave the
Altar of Victory in the Senate-house.   Like Ausonius,
he might pay a cold and perfunctory homage to Christ,[3]
and visit the neighbouring town for the Easter festival;
but the whole tone of his thoughts and life was inspired
by the memories of the heathen past.   With no belief in
the old gods, he was steeped in the literary spirit and
culture of paganism.   The Roman schools had moulded
him far more than the teaching of the Church.   The
unbroken academic tradition of eight hundred years,
coming down from the age of the great sophists, was a
tremendous force; and it was a force which repelled
all novelty, and all idealism which looked to the future
rather than to the past.   All the literature on which he
had been nourished was created in the atmosphere of
paganism, and teemed with mythological allusions.   His
teachers were saturated with Hellenism, which to the
end maintained a cold and distant attitude to Christian
devotion.   From his earliest years his gaze was turned
to the great deeds of Roman heroes who had worshipped

---

[1] Ozanam, *La Civ. au Vme siècle*,
i. 231.
[2] Maury, *La Magie*, p. 152.

[3] Auson. *Ephem.* ii. 15 ; *Ep.* 10,
17 ; *Idyll.* 11, 88.

Mars and Jupiter,[1] who had read the fate of their campaigns in the flash of lightning or the flight of birds or the entrails of the victim at the altar, who had consulted the Chaldaean seer about their objects of ambition or their hour of death.[2] If he could not rival the achievements of these great sons of Rome, he could still add his name to the Fasti in which theirs appeared. He could maintain the stately forms of the past, and the literary and antiquarian tradition which he regarded as the finest essence of the national life.

In the final stand which paganism made against imperial edicts and the polemic of the Church, many different forces were arrayed. Sensuality and gross superstition in the degraded masses clung to the rites of magic and divination, to the excitement of the circus, and the obscenities of the theatre. And these base influences long maintained their hold. But it would be a grave mistake to suppose that the old faith rested only on ignorant superstition and sensuality, or on the hard formalism of the old Roman mythology. For many generations the cults of Eastern origin, the worship of Isis,[3] of the Great Mother, and Mithra, had satisfied devotional feelings which could find little nourishment in the cold abstractions of old Roman religion, or the brilliant anthropomorphism of Greece. The inscriptions of the fourth century reveal the enduring power of these Syrian or Egyptian worships.[4] They cultivated an ecstatic devotion, and gave relief to remorse for sin.

---

[1] S. Augustine had a genuine admiration for great Romans of the early ages, *e.g.* Regulus, *de Civ. Dei*, i. c. xv. Cf. S. Jerome's *Ep.* 60, § 5, quid memorem Romanos duces quorum virtutibus quasi quibusdam stellis Latinae micant historiae ?

[2] The grandfather of Ausonius was himself an astrologer. *Parent.* iv. 17 :

tu coeli numeros et conscia sidera fati callebas, studium dissimulanter agens.

S. Aug. had consulted the books of astrologers (libris genethliacorum deditus) in his youth. *Conf.* iv. 3.

[3] See Réville, *Rel. unter den Sev.* i. c. 2 and 3, pp. 52, 59, 76.

[4] *C.I.L.* vi. 512, 749-754, 499-504. Cf. Renan, *M. Aurèle*, p. 579 ; *infra*, p. 64.

They had their mystic brotherhoods and guilds, with an initiatory baptismal rite.[1] They had their rules and periods of fasting and abstinence from all the pleasures of sense. They had a priesthood set apart from the world with the tonsure and a peculiar habit. And, in initiation to their mysteries, a profound impression was made on the imagination and feelings of the novice. The baptism of blood, of which many a stone record remains, was the crowning rite of the later paganism, relieving the guilty conscience, and regarded as a new birth.[2] It can hardly be doubted that, while these cults may not have supplied the moral tone and discipline, which was the great want in all heathen systems, they stimulated a devotional feeling which was unknown to the native religions of Greece and Rome. There was, moreover, in this later pagan movement, penetrated as it was by syncretism, a decided tendency to monotheistic faith.[3]   Praetextatus held the most prominent place among the last generation who openly worshipped Isis, Mithra, Hecate, and Magna Mater.[4] Yet, in the *Saturnalia*, he is put forward to explain that, under the many names of the Pantheon, it is the attributes of one Great Power which are really adored.[5]

The inner monotheism of the loftier minds in paganism was the fruit of a millennium of the freest and most disinterested philosophic movement in history. More than five centuries before Christ, Greek speculation had lifted men's minds to the conception of a mysterious Unity behind the phantasmagoria of sense.[6]   In the fifth century after Christ, Macrobius, at once Pagan and Neoplatonist, holds fast to the doctrine of the Infinite

[1] Apul. *Met.* xi. c. 23 ; Tertull. *de Baptismo*, c. 5, nam et sacris quibusdam per lavacrum initiantur, Isidis alicujus et Mithrae. Cf. Juv. vi. 522 ; Porphyr. *de Abst.* iv. p. 367.

[2] Prudent. *Peristeph.* x. 1021.
[3] Réville, ii. c. 10, p. 285.
[4] *C.I.L.* vi. 1779.
[5] Macrob. *Sat.* i. 17.
[6] Arist. *Met.* i. 5, Ξενοφάνης . . τὸ ἓν εἶναί φησι τὸν θεόν.

One,[1] from whom, by a chain of successive emanations,
the Universe proceeds.   If this lofty conception of the
Divine Nature often lent itself to the support of systems
which seemed to degrade and fritter away the central
idea of pure religion the philosophic supporter of
paganism was ready with an explanation.   He would
have said the Infinite can neither be known nor expressed
by finite powers.   Yet the human spirit instinctively
turns with reverence to the Father of all spirits, and, in
its helplessness, can only find utterance for its yearnings
in symbolism of word or act.   Plato sought an image of
the Infinite Good in the Sun.[2]   Common worshippers
adore it under the names of Jupiter, Apollo, Isis, or
Mithra.[3]   The Great Reality can by any human soul be
only dimly conceived, and expressed only in a rude
fragmentary way.   We see the Divine One in religious
myths " as through a glass darkly."   Yet, if we purge
mythology of the gross fancies of rude ages, the myths
may be used as a consecrated language of devotion.
They are only faint shadows of the Infinite One, from
which we are separated by an impassable gulf ; yet they
represent the collective thought and feeling of the past
about God.   They are only symbols, but a religious
symbol is doubly sacred when it has ministered to the
devotion of many generations.   In some such way the
philosopher reconciled himself to the ancient worships.
Yet although, like Longinianus,[4] a correspondent of S.
Augustine, he might believe that the ancient sacred rites
had a real value, he believed also that the one " great,
incomprehensible, and ineffable Creator" was to be
approached only by the way of piety, truth, and purity
in word and deed.

Philosophy and the mysticism of the East had given

---

[1] Macrob. *Com. in Som. Scip.* i.
17, 12.
[2] *Rep.* bk. vi. p. 508 ; cf. *Hellenica*,
p. 176.

[3] Plut. *de Is.* c. 67 ; cf. Vacherot's
exposition of the creed of Porphyry,
École d'Alexandrie, ii. pp. 111, 112.
[4] S. Aug. *Ep.* 234.

a new life to the religion of Rome. But old Roman
patriotic feeling was perhaps the most powerful support
of paganism in its final conflict with the Church. Men
like Symmachus, Flavianus, and Volusianus were often
sceptics at heart. They may have believed vaguely in
some Divine Power, and were ready to admit that He
might be approached by many ways; but their real
devotion was to Roma Dea,[1] the idealised genius of the
Latin race, with its twelve centuries of victorious warfare
and skilful worldwide organisation. In every step of
that marvellous career, their ancient gods had been their
partners. The forms of its ancestral religion were inex-
tricably intertwined with the whole fabric of the State.[2]
Imbedded in law, language, literature, the deepest
instincts of the people, her ancient worship seemed
inseparable from the very identity of Rome. The true
Roman, even though his religious faith might not be very
deep or warm, inherited the most ancient belief of his
race that the gods of a city were sharers in all its
fortunes. Apostasy from them was identified with a
languid patriotism. and was regarded as the cause of
public calamities.[3] The complete and literal acceptance
of the Christian faith seemed to mean a refusal to perform the duties of citizen or soldier, a scornful abandonment of the old traditions of culture, even a loss of faith
in the mission of Rome.[4]

In that age, as in our own, there were widely different
conceptions of the meaning of the Christian profession.
There can be little doubt that there was a vast mass of
interested and perfunctory conformity to the religion
which had become the established religion of the State.
The philosophic scepticism and worldly tone of the
cultivated pagan were often not much altered when he

[1] Claudian, *de Bell. Gild.* 46 ; *de Bell. Get.* 50 ; Rutil. Namat. i. 47-132.
[2] Sym. *Rel.* 3, ergo Romanae re-ligiones ad Romana jura non per-tinent ?
[3] *Ib.* 3, sacrilegio exaruit annus.
[4] Auson. *Ep.* xxv. 44-74.

transferred his nominal allegiance from his ancestral gods to Christ.   There was a worldliness and easy self-indulgence in the higher rank of nominally Christian society, which moved alike the indignation of the ascetic and the good-humoured ridicule of the pagan observer.[1] But a large and growing class took the claims of Christ more seriously.   To carry out to the letter the precepts of the Sermon on the Mount, in the midst of a society penetrated with individualism and easygoing sensuality, seemed a hopeless attempt.[2]   The aspiration after Christian perfection could be satisfied only by a with-drawal from the contamination of the world, and a complete renunciation of the duties of citizenship.   This spirit has by some modern historians been made respon-sible for the resignation of the defence of the Empire to barbarian mercenaries, for the decay of industry and wealth, for the decline of letters and art, and the darkness of a thousand years.[3]   And there is some of the religious literature of that period which gives a colour to part of this indictment.   In the very years when the great invasions were desolating the provinces of the West, and when the hosts of Radagaisus and Alaric were threatening the heart of the Empire, S. Paulinus wrote a remarkable letter to a soldier who felt himself drawn to the higher Christian life.[4]   In this epistle the ascetic ideal is expounded with a breadth and absence of qualification which shock and amaze the modern reader.   The evangelical counsels of perfection are construed in the sternest and most uncompromising fashion.   Christian

[1] Hieron. *c. Johann. Hierosol.* 8, miserabilis Praetextatus qui desig-natus consul est mortuus, homo sacrilegus et idolorum cultor, solebat ludens beato papae Damaso dicere : "facite me Romanae ecclesiae epis-copum et ero protinus Christianus." As a comment on this *mot* of Prae-textatus read the reflections on the conflict for the papal seat in 367 in Amm. Marc. 27, 3, 14.

[2] S. Paulin. Nol. *Carm.* x. 33, 316 ; cf. Renan, *M. Aurèle*, p. 627.

[3] Renan, *M. Aurèle*, pp. 595, 603, la vie humaine est suspendue pour mille ans.

[4] S. Paulin. *Ep.* xxv.

obedience is boldly represented as inconsistent with the
duties of citizenship and the relations of family life.
The love of father or mother, of wife or child, the desire
for riches or honour, devotion to one's country, are all so
many barriers to keep the soul from Christ.   There is
not a word to indicate that a Christian life, worthy of
the name, could be made compatible with the performance
of worldly duties.   The rich are condemned for ever, in
the words of prophet or evangelist.[1]   The soldier is a
mere shedder of blood,[2] doomed to eternal torment.[3]
There is no possibility of serving both Christ and Caesar.
This was the way in which secular life was regarded by
the voluntary exiles who followed S. Jerome, in the last
years of the fourth century, to the convents at Bethlehem,
or who retired to the Syrian or Egyptian deserts, the
islands of the Tuscan Sea, and the hermitages in the
woods of Gaul.   Such a movement might well seem to
an old-fashioned Roman as a renunciation, not only of
citizenship, but of all the hard-won fruits of civilisation
and social life.   If this was the highest form of Christian
life, as its devotees proclaimed it to be, then Christianity
was the foe, not only of the old religion, but of the social
and political order which Rome had given to the world.
It is hardly to be wondered at that the monks were
execrated alike by the mob[4] and by the cultivated pagan
noble.[5]

Yet it would be a mistake to suppose that in general
society the line between the two camps was sharply drawn.
As a matter of fact, there was on either side a large
wavering class, half-hearted, sceptical, or formalist.   We

[1] S. Paulin. *Ep.* xxv. § 2, et iterum
per prophetam ait, "Exterminati
sunt omnes qui exaltati fuerant
auro et argento."   In Evangelio
quoque clamat . . . "vae vobis
divitibus," etc.
[2] *Ib.* § 3, mortis minister est.

[3] *Ib.* § 1, quod si maluerimus
Caesari militare quam Christo . . .
ad Gehennam transferemur.
[4] Hieron. *Ep.* 39, § 5, quousque
genus detestabile non urbe pellitur?
non lapidibus obruitur?
[5] Rutil. Namat. i. 440.

know, on the testimony of Libanius,[1] that there were
many sham converts to Christianity, whose conformity
was due either to fear or motives of selfish ambition.
Such men were ready to return to their old faith as
lightly as they had conformed to the new. Apostasy to
heathenism became so frequent that Gratian and Theodosius felt bound to restrain it by severe legislation.[2]
The upper class were for generations far more united by
the old social and literary tradition that they were
divided by religious belief. There were friends of
Sidonius living at the close of the Western Empire who
were at heart as pagan as Symmachus who saw paganism
finally proscribed.[3] In truth, the line between Christian
and pagan was long wavering and uncertain. We find
adherents of the opposing creeds side by side even in the
same family at the end of the fourth century. Mixed
marriages (*imparia matrimonia*) were evidently not
uncommon. Any one acquainted with the life of S.
Jerome will remember Paula, the great Roman lady, who
was the leader of the aristocratic exodus to the Holy
Places.[4] She gave up all her vast wealth to maintain
the religious houses which she founded at Bethlehem.[5]
Her whole soul was absorbed in the study of the
Scriptures, and in the thought of the life to come.[6] Yet
Paula was united in early youth to a noble named Julius
Toxotius,[7] who boasted of his descent from Aeneas, and
who refused to abandon the worship of his ancestors.
Their son, the younger Toxotius, who, at any rate in his
youth, was also a staunch pagan, was married to Laeta,[8]
another devout friend of S. Jerome, to whom he addressed
a letter on the proper education for a Christian maiden.

[1] *Orat. pro Templis*, ed. Reiske, p. 176.
[2] *C. Th.* xvi. tit. 7 ; cf. Gode- froy's note to xvi. 7, 1 ; Rauschen, *Jahrbücher*, p. 153.
[3] Apollin. Sid. *Ep.* viii. 9 ; viii. 11.
[4] Hieron. *Ep.* 108.
[5] *Ib.* § 30, testis est Jesus, ne unum quidem nummum ab ea filiae relictum.
[6] *Ib.* § 26.
[7] *Ib.* § 4 ; Thierry's *S. Jérome*, pp. 26, 27.
[8] *Ib.* 107, § 1.

Laeta herself was the offspring of a mixed marriage.
Her mother was a Christian, and her father was one of
the most distinguished chiefs of the pagan aristocracy,
Publilius Caeonius Albinus.[1] The affectionate relations
of this household seem to have been quite undisturbed
by the difference of creed` among its members.   S.
Jerome speaks of Albinus in a friendly tone as a most
learned and distinguished man, and sketches a pleasant
picture of the old heathen pontiff listening to his little
grand-daughter singing her infant hymns to Christ.
Albinus, like many of his class in that day, was plainly
tolerant in matters of religion; yet he was a colleague of
Symmachus in the pontifical college, and he figures in the
Saturnalia of Macrobius as a great master of the antiquarian lore of old Rome.[2]

In general society the cultivated sceptic or pagan
appears to have often maintained a friendly intimacy
even with the most uncompromising champions of the
Church.   The correspondence of S. Augustine reveals the
singular freedom and candour with which the great
religious questions of the time were debated between the
cultivated members of the two parties.   Among the
friends of the great bishop was Volusianus, brother of
that Laeta to whom we have just referred.[3]   Volusianus,
although he is said to have been afterwards converted,[4]
was at this time, if not a decided pagan, like his father
the pontiff, at any rate little disposed to accept the
fundamental tenets of the Christian faith.   He seems to
have lived in a circle which debated not only the old
philosophical questions, but those doctrines of the Christian
creed which present the greatest obstacles to the reason.

[1] His restoration of a ruined
Capitol at Thamugad in Numidia
is commemorated in an inscription
of the time of Valentinian and
Valens, *C.I.L.* viii. 2388 ; cf. *C.I.L.*
viii. 6975, which contains the dedication by him of a chapel to Mithra;
cf. Macrob. *Sat.* i. 2, 15 ; Hieron.
Ep. 107, § 1.
[2] Macrob. *Sat.* i. iii.
[3] S. Aug. *Ep.* 132 ; cf. Seeck's
Sym. clxxix.
[4] Baron. *Annal. Eccl.* v. 728
(quoted in Seeck's *Sym.* clxxix.).

At one of these gatherings[1] the difficulties of the
miraculous conception of Christ, and of the Incarnation
of the omnipresent Ruler of the Universe in a single
human form, subject to all the changes, wants, and limi-
tations of humanity, were raised.   And Volusianus, in a
letter full of deferential admiration for Augustine's
character and learning, asks for some light on these
puzzling questions.   In another letter,[2] Marcellinus, who
was a friend of both, submits, on behalf of Volusianus,
some other problems as to the apparent inconstancy of
the Deity in abrogating the Jewish law which He had
Himself given, and the possibility of obeying the precepts
of the Sermon on the Mount in the government of a
dominant state.   On both sides there is an urbanity and
an absence of partisan heat, which show the strength of
the ancient culture in the fierce conflict of beliefs.   The
same tone is conspicuous in the correspondence of the pagan
philosopher Longinianus and Augustine.[3]   Their letters
seem to show that the two men were on terms of friendly
intercourse, and although Longinianus cannot give a
satisfactory answer to the question, " What think you of
Christ ? " a devout monotheism supplied some common
ground with the Christian bishop, who deals in a singularly gentle tone with the philosopher's lingering and
vaguely expressed attachment to ancient mystic rites.
Augustine's letter to Lampadius on fatalist superstitions
displays even more startling tolerance.[4]   Yet Lampadius
was a devotee of the pagan belief in astrology and divination.   He was Pretorian prefect in the short-lived government established in 409 by the old senatorial party,[5] with
Attalus as emperor and Alaric as master of the forces,
which was the last attempt of the old pagan spirit to
regain the sceptre.

[1] S. Aug. *Ep.* 135.   [4] *Ib.* 246.
[2] *Ib.* 136.   [5] Zos. vi. 7.
[3] *Ib.* 233, 234, 235.

In the circle of Symmachus, which is better known to
us than any other of that time, there is a striking inter-
mixture of pagan and Christian, with a reticent suppres-
sion of all differences on religious questions.   Q. Aurelius Symmachus was the chief of the pagan aristocracy,
the most gallant defender of the old religion in its last
struggles for toleration.   His ancestors had held the
highest office since the days of Constantine,[1] and he himself had added fresh lustre to the honours of his house.
He was regarded as the finest product of the literary
tradition of Rome,[2] an *arbiter elegantiarum* whose critical
judgments were infallible, the greatest orator of the
Senate.   Probably, like so many of his class for ages, he
was a sceptic whose inner creed was a vague monotheism.
But he cherished a sentimental, or a statesmanlike,
attachment to the ancient forms of the Roman religion.
The fortunes and the dignity of Rome were in his eyes
inseparably linked with her guardian deities.[3]   The
grandeur and beneficence of her career were for ever
associated with the religion of the old Fabii, Decii, and
Scipios.   There are, indeed, but few direct references to
religion in his private letters, none to Christianity or the
internecine war of faiths which was raging around him.
Like Claudian and Macrobius, he seems to shut his eyes
to the spiritual revolution which in his closing years was
sending the world of Western Europe on a new orbit.
To the very end of the legal existence of paganism, he
maintained the same tranquil, old-world tone about
religion.   He records the meetings of the Sacred College,
and the recurrence of the festival of Magna Mater.   He
mentions in his letters terrifying prodigies,[4] such as the
consul suffectus being thrown from his car, somewhat in

[1] Seeck's *Sym.* xl.
[2] Auson. *Idyll.* x. ; *Ep.* xvii. ;
Prudent. *c. Sym.* i. 632 :

  O linguam miro verborum fonte fluen-
    tem,

Romani decus eloquii, cui cedat et ipse
Tullius . . .

Ambros. *Ep.* 18, 2.
[3] Sym. *Rel.* 3.
[4] *Ep.* vi. 40 ; i. 49 : ii. 34.

the manner of the early annals.   When the Vestal
Virgins prayed for leave to erect a statue to Vettius
Agorius Praetextatus,[1] the man who "possessed the
deepest knowledge of sacred things," probably the best
and most devout pagan of that age, and a dear friend of
Symmachus, he resisted the proposal, partly on the
ground of propriety, partly as a violation of ancient
usage.   Personally the most kindly and humane of men,
he demanded of the prefect that an erring Vestal should
be surrendered to pontifical authority, to be punished in
the cruel old Roman fashion.[2]   He once or twice laments
the growing neglect of the ancient worship,[3] and prays
the gods to pardon it, although he cannot help feeling
that it is sometimes due to an unworthy subservience to
the feelings of the Court.   It seems as if Symmachus
was incapable of imagining that the Roman State could
ever finally disown the gods in whom the men of her
great ages had believed.

Yet the correspondence of Symmachus shows that he
lived on terms of friendly and even affectionate intimacy,
not only with nominal Christians, but with determined
foes of the old religion.   In the list of his friends, indeed,
almost every shade of belief or of indifference is represented ; and there is no better way of understanding the
religious condition of that time than to study some of the
men with whom the great pagan noble was intimate, from
Praetextatus the heathen mystic, to S. Ambrose the great
champion of Catholic orthodoxy.

Praetextatus was probably the truest representative of
the last generation of paganism.   The inscriptions which
commemorate his virtues and distinctions are a proof
of the space he filled in the eyes of contemporaries.[4]

---

[1] *Ep.* ii. 36.
[2] *Ib.* ix. 147.
[3] *Ib.* i. 51, nunc aris deesse
Romanos genus est ambiendi.

[4] *C.I.L.* vi. 1779, 2145. The
latter refers to a monument erected
to him by the Vestals.

He was proconsul of Achaea in the reign of Julian,[1] and,
after a long retirement of fifteen years,[2] he held the
Pretorian prefecture in the reign of Theodosius, and was
designated for the consulship in 385, when he died in
his sixtieth year. Praetextatus combined all the
qualities which then constituted the ideal of the Roman
noble. He was devoted to letters, had emended MSS.,[3]
and translated Aristotle. His house is the scene of the
learned conversations of the *Saturnalia.*[4] As a statesman, he resisted the law of Valentinian I. against
nocturnal rites,[5] which seemed intolerable to his provincial subjects in Greece. When he was prefect of the
city he gained universal popularity,[6] without offending
any party, although he had the difficult duty of maintaining order when, in the furious struggle for the papal
throne, the rival factions of Damasus and Ursinus were
slaughtering one another on the pavement of the
churches.[7] On his death, even S. Jerome,[8] who consigns
nim to outer darkness, agrees with Marcellinus that he
received the tribute of a universal mourning from the
populace of Rome. Praetextatus was the most learned
theologian and the most enthusiastic devotee in the ranks
of the last pagan nobles. His monument describes him
as augur, priest of Vesta, priest of the sun, curial of
Hercules, devoted to Liber and the Eleusinian deities,
neocorus, hierophant, pater patrum, cleansed by the rite of
the Taurobolium.[9] His wife, Fabia Aconia Paulina, was
his partner in all sacred things, and was famous in the
Roman world for her religious eminence. It is noteworthy that Praetextatus is almost the only one of his
friends to whom the reticent Symmachus mentions the

---

[1] Amm. Marc. xxii. 7, 6.
[2] Seeck's *Sym.* lxxxviii.
[3] Sym. *Ep.* i. 53 ; cf. Seeck,
xxxvii.
[4] Macrob. *Sat.* i. 1.
[5] Zos. iv. 3.

[6] Amm. Marc. xxvii. 9, 8.
[7] *Ib.* xxvii. 3, 12.
[8] *Ep.* 23, ad cujus interitum
urbs universa commota est.
[9] *C.I.L.* vi. 1779.

subject of religion,[1] although even the pious Praetextatus seems to have sometimes forgotten his sacerdotal duties in the repose of his country-seat in Etruria.[2]   When, as Urban prefect, Symmachus announced his death to the Emperor,[3] he described Praetextatus, with the assent of the whole people, as a model of all private and public virtue.

Another name among the pagan friends of Symmachus deserves special mention.   Virius Nicomachus Flavianus, a member of the great Anician house,[4] was son of a man who, after long obscurity, rose to prominence in the pagan reaction of Julian.   Flavianus was a young man of twenty-seven when Julian came to the throne, and along with Venustus his father,[5] and his cousin Symmachus, obtained a provincial governorship.   For twelve years of the reign of Valentinian I. Flavianus was in retirement; but in the reign of Gratian, he, along with Symmachus, shared in the extraordinary ascendency which the circle of Ausonius enjoyed for some years. Flavianus received the vicariate of Africa, Hesperius, the poet's son, being proconsul of the province at the same time.   After the manner of the pagan or indifferent governors of the age,[6] Flavianus showed indulgence to the heretics of his district,[7] and incurred a rebuke from the orthodox Emperor.   In the reign of Theodosius he regained the favour of the Court, and was made prefect

---

[1] Sym. *Ep.* i. 47, 48, 51.

[2] *Ib.* i. 45.

[3] *Ib.* x. 10.

[4] The Symmachi also belonged to it ; cf. Seeck, cii., and the Stemma on p. xl.

[5] Amm. Marc. xxiii. 1, 4, Venusto vicariam commisit Hispaniae. This is the Venustus of Macrob. i. 5, 13, Flavianus—mirando viro Venusto patre praestantior.

[6] Cf. the efforts of the Priscillianists to have their cause brought

before a friendly governor in Spain, Sulp. Sev. *Chron.* ii. 49.

[7] S. Aug. *Ep.* 87, § 8, to a Donatist bishop, describes Flavianus as " partis vestrae homo." Cf. *C. Th.* xvi. 6, 2, addressed to Flavianus in 377, ordering him to suppress Anabaptism ; and xvi. 5, 4, 378, to Hesperius, in which the continuance of heretical worship is attributed to "dissimulatio judicum." But the date of the law is doubtful. Cf. Godefroy's notes and Seeck's *Sym.* cxiv.

of Italy in 383, his two sons also being elevated to governorships of provinces. After a brief interval, he once more rose to favour and held the prefecture in 391.[1] But his career was drawing to a disastrous close. Although he wielded such power under the Emperor who finally proscribed the heathen ritual, Flavianus was an obstinate reactionary in religion. He became the heart and soul of the brief pagan restoration under Eugenius. He obtained the restoration of the altar of Victory to the Senate-house,[2] and of their endowments to the sacred colleges. By lavish hospitality, and promises of official advancement,[3] he tempted weak-kneed or indifferent Christians to desert the cause of Theodosius and the Church. All the arts of ancient divination were brought into play by the greatest living master of the science.[4] And a prophetic verse was recalled or invented which foreshadowed the end of the Christian superstition three hundred and sixty-five years after the Passion.[5] The reckoning seemed to tally exactly with the crisis of events. But the gods proved false to their faithful champion; the illusions of the past only led Flavianus and his party to their doom. Amid the tempest which raged over the battle on the Frigidus and gave the victory to Theodosius, Flavianus *more majorum* died by his own hand. He had staked all on the success of the pagan cause and lost. Yet, strange to say, his memory was respected, and even honoured, by the victors. His confiscated estates were afterwards restored to his sons.[6] The Emperor in a message to the Senate deplored the loss to the State and to himself. Nearly forty years

---

[1] See Seeck's note, 579 ; Rauschen, *Jahrb.* pp. 150 and 337. Rauschen controverts Seeck's view (*Prol.* cxvii.) that Flavianus was praef. praet. in 389.

[2] Paulin. *vit. Ambros.* c. viii. § 26.

[3] See the *Carm. Paris.* (a poem discovered at the end of a MS. of Prudentius) quoted by Seeck, cxviii.

[4] Sozom. vii. 22, τὰ μέλλοντα ἀκριβοῦν λογιζόμενος ἐπιστήμῃ παντοδαπῆς μαντείας.

[5] *De Civ. Dei*, xviii. 53, 54.

[6] Sym. *Ep.* iv. 19.

after the battle on the Frigidus the Emperors Valentinian
and Theodosius did justice to the virtues and distinction
of Flavianus in a monument which is still extant.[1]   A
master of augural lore, a learned historian, and a
philosopher, he was one of that band who, when
paganism and letters were perishing, united in a single
love the literature and the religion of the past.[2]

Several of the great German chiefs, who wielded
such power in that age, were among the most intimate
friends of Symmachus.   Of these some boldly adhered to
the religious practices of their ancestors without any
hindrance to their advancement.   Others conformed to
the Church, with more or less intensity of faith.   With
Stilicho, the autocrat of the early years of Honorius,
Symmachus was naturally on the most friendly footing.
We can well believe that there would be strong bonds of
sympathy between the chief of the party who claimed
toleration for paganism, and the statesman who strove to
find a *modus vivendi* between Roman and Goth, Catholic
and Pagan, and who incurred the anathemas of the
bigots of both parties, of Rutilius Namatianus[3] and of
Orosius.[4]   Richomer, another friend of Symmachus, a
Frank chief of the highest character, who never
abandoned his ancestral faith,[5] is a remarkable example
of the religious confusion of the time.   He was on terms
of the most friendly character with Libanius, the last of
the Hellenists, and yet he rose to be consul and magister
militum under a prince engaged in extirpating heathenism.[6]
He was a personal friend of Arbogastes and Eugenius, the
chiefs of the pagan reaction of 394 ; yet he was designated
to command the cavalry of Theodosius against them when

[1] *C.I.L.* vi. 1783.

[2] Peter's *Gesch. Litt. über die
Röm. Kaiserzeit*, ii. 32 ; cf. i. 137 ;
Seeck's *Sym.* cxv. ; Macrob. *Sat.*
i. 5, 13.

[3] *Itin.* ii. 41.

[4] Oros. vii. 38.

[5] Liban. *de Vita Sua*, i. p. 136,
ἱεροῖς τε καὶ θεοῖς προσκείμενος.   Cf.
Ep. 785, 926.

[6] See the authorities collected in
the *Prosopographia of the C. Th.* ed.
Ritter.

he was overtaken by death.[1]   Another Frank, Bauto,
whatever his own religion may have been,[2] took care to
have his daughter, the future Empress Eudoxia, brought
up a devout Catholic.

Among the correspondents of Symmachus there are
Christians of many shades of conviction, from the great
Bishop of Milan to the trimmers who were ready to
acquiesce in a pagan restoration under the shadowy
authority of Attalus.   The Ambrosius of the letters of
Symmachus is almost certainly the illustrious saint
and pastor who, by the force of genius and character,
wielded a greater power than any other man in the
last struggle of paganism with the Christian Empire.[3]
The man who confronted fearlessly the Arianism of
Justina,[4] and who forced Theodosius to do penance for
the massacre of Thessalonica,[5] threw the whole energy of
a powerful nature into the conflict, so long wavering and
doubtful, which gave the final victory to the Church
before he died.   When Symmachus, as deputy of the
Senate, appealed to the Emperor to restore to their house
of assembly the altar of Victory, the most venerable
symbol of the pagan Empire, S. Ambrose resisted the
proposal with all the arts of a rhetoric, trained, like that of
his opponent, in the ancient schools.[6]   The two men
were the chosen champions of the opposing hosts, and
they fought with an equal energy of sentiment or conviction.   But although they were so sharply opposed in
matters of religion, they were connected both by blood
and culture.   Symmachus writes to the bishop in the
tone of an assured and unruffled friendship.[7]   In one

[1] Zos. iv. 55.
[2] Seeck, *Sym.* cxl., makes him a
Christian on the strength of a singular participle in one of S. Ambrose's
Epistles.   Cf. Rauschen, *Jahrb. der
Christ. Kirche unter dem K. Theod.*
p. 204, n. 4 ; S. Ambros. *Ep.* 57.
[3] Seeck's *Sym.* cxxviii. ; Ambros.

de Sat. Excessu, i. 32.   But cf.
note in Migne's ed.
[4] Paulin. *vita S. Ambr.* c. iv.
§ 12.
[5] *Ib.* c. vii. § 24.
[6] *Ib.* c. viii. § 26 ; Sym. *Rel.* 3.
[7] Sym. *Ep.* iii. 33, 34.

letter he even claims his good offices on behalf of a man
who had served under the usurpation of Eugenius.   S.
Ambrose on his side speaks of Symmachus in a tone of
respect for the sincerity of his pagan zeal, and admiration
for the skill of his rhetoric.[1]

There are one or two other decided Christians in the
list, such as that Vincentius, who, while prefect of Gaul,
strove to cultivate the friendship of S. Martin.[2]   But
most of the other so-called Christian friends of Symmachus
had little in common with the enthusiasm of S. Ambrose.
Some of them belonged to that large class of waverers
and sceptics to whom a religious profession was only a
means of safety or of ambition.   The most distinguished
friend of Symmachus in the high official world was
Sextus Petronius Probus.   Descended from a long line
of consuls,[3] Probus was regarded as the greatest glory of
the Anician house.[4]   Proconsul of Africa in his twenty-
second year, he held the Pretorian prefecture four times,
in one case for a term of eight years, and was colleague
of the Emperor in the consulship of 371.   His rank and
virtues are commemorated in many inscriptions, and in a
poem of Ausonius addressed to Probus,[5] when he wielded
at Sirmium a power second only to that of the Emperor.
His wife and his sons were devoted Christians ;[6] his grand-
daughter Demetrias took the vow of virginity.   Yet
Probus himself was only baptized on his deathbed.[7]   And
Ammianus Marcellinus more than hints that love of
wealth and power was his strongest passion.[8]   Caecilianus,
who bore a great part in the negotiations with Alaric, was
a great friend of S. Augustine as well as of Symmachus.[9]

---

[1] Ambros. *Ep.* 57, 2, functus est
ille partibus suis pro studio et cultu
suo.

[2] Sulp. Sev. *Dial.* i. 25, 6.

[3] Seeck's *Sym.* xci. ; *C.I.L.* vi.
1752, 1753, 1756.

[4] Hieron. *Ep.* 130, § 3.

[5] *C.I.L.* vi. 1751-6 ; Auson. *Ep.*
xvi. ; cf. Amm. Marc. xxvii. 11, 1.

[6] Prudent. *c. Sym.* i. 551 ; Hieron.
Ep. 130, § 3.

[7] *C.I.L.* 1756, senior donatus
munere Christi.

[8] Amm. Marc. xxx. 5, 4-7.

[9] Aug. *Ep.* 151, § 14.

But he appears to have been a rather lukewarm Christian; for the saint remonstrates with him for being content at his age to remain a catechumen.

On a lower level than Probus and Caecilianus are two men, among the familiar friends of Symmachus, who had an ephemeral distinction in the years of Alaric's invasion. Their attitude to religion represents that of many of their contemporaries. The Jovius of the letters of Symmachus is probably the believer in chance and the superstitions of astrology whom S. Paulinus laboured to convert from his errors.[1] Yet he began his public career by overturning the temples of heathenism at Carthage.[2] He is praised by Symmachus for his high principle and virtue;[3] but the account which the historian gives of his career seems to convict him either of fickleness or treachery. He was a personal friend of Alaric, and, on the fall of Olympius, the leader of the Catholic reaction, Jovius succeeded him,[4] and resumed the tolerant religious policy of Stilicho, along with an attempt to conciliate Alaric by conceding some of his demands. Having failed to obtain the Emperor's assent to his views, he suddenly took up an attitude of determined hostility to the Gothic chief.[5] Yet within a very short time we find Jovius in the office of Pretorian prefect under Attalus,[6] the puppet emperor whom Alaric had set up. In the breach between Attalus and his patron, Jovius deserted Attalus, as he had deserted Honorius.[7] The believer in mere chance, as the ruling force in the universe, seems, on the more charitable hypothesis, to have allowed his own life to be governed by it. There is only a faint glimmering of any higher principle in his career, when occasionally he showed a certain faith in the Gothic power.

Another great figure in the events of those puzzling

[1] S. Paulin. Nol. *Ep.* xvi.
[2] Aug. *de Civ. Dei*, xviii. 54.
[3] Sym. *Ep.* viii. 30 ; ix. 59.
[4] Zos. v. 46, 47.
[5] *Ib.* v. 49 ; Sozom. ix. 7.
[6] Zos. vi. 8.
[7] Olympiod. *Frag.* 13.

years was Priscus Attalus.[1]   He was of Asiatic origin.
His father had a great literary reputation, was the friend
and correspondent of Libanius, and rose to high office.[2]
Attalus possessed the superficial literary and rhetorical
arts which were then in vogue; he could deliver elaborate
orations, write pretty verses,[3] and accompany them on
the lyre.   As to religion, he was a Hellenist, with no
faith either in the old system or the new, but with a
sentimental attachment to the past.[4]   Yet his brilliant
accomplishments gave him a foremost place in the
senatorial ranks, and when the city was hard pressed by
Alaric he was one of the envoys chosen to lay before the
Emperor at Ravenna the miseries of the capital.[5]   The
mission failed; but Attalus accepted the office of count
of the sacred largesses,[6] and shortly afterwards that of
prefect of the city.   When Alaric, so long mocked by the
mingled weakness, perfidy, and insolence of the court at
Ravenna, seized the magazines at Ostia, and ordered the
Senate, as the price of their safety, to depose Honorius
and elect a new chief of the State, their choice fell on
Attalus.[7]   And surely there was never a more curious
spectacle than when the sceptical Hellenist received
baptism at the hands of an Arian bishop,[8] to please his
Gothic masters, while he gave his sanction to reactionary
dreamers like Lampadius and Tertullus, who revived for
a moment the arts of divination and the pagan ceremonies
of the old Republic.

These men, of such various shades of enthusiasm or
indifference, appear to have lived together in perfect
amity.   The urbane senator, in whose friendship they
are united for the study of the historian, seems to have
found no more difficulty in his relations with Ambrose

[1] For the authorities as to his
career see Seeck's *Symmachus*, clxx.
[2] Amm. Marc. xxviii. 4, 3.
[3] Olympiod. *Frag.* 24.
[4] Sozom. ix. 9.

[5] Zos. v. 44.
[6] *Ib.* v. 44 and 45.
[7] *Ib.* vi. 7.
[8] Sozom. ix. 9.

and Probus than with Flavianus or Praetextatus. They were all during the life of Symmachus united in the service of the State. Pronounced pagans held the prefecture or the consulship under Theodosius and Honorius, and were even their trusted counsellors.[1] It was not till 416 that they were formally excluded from office.[2] Many of these pagan officials had for years in their hands the enforcement of laws against superstitions or heresies with which they themselves sympathised. In the long truce between the hostile camps, the pagan, the sceptic, even the formal, lukewarm Christian, may have come to dream of a mutual toleration which would leave the ancient forms undisturbed. But such men, living in a world of literary and antiquarian illusions, knew little of the inner forces of the new Christian movement. The chiefs of the Church were of a very different mould from the chiefs of the Senate.

[1] Symmachus was consul in 391; Flavianus was prefect of Italy in 391; his son was proconsul of Asia in 383 (Rauschen, p. 148); Richomer was consul in 384 (Rauschen, p. 172). Macrobius, author of the *Saturnalia*, was probably Praef. Praet. of Spain in 399, Procos. of Africa in 410, and Praepositus S. Cubiculi in 422 (*C. Th.* xvi. 10, 15; xi. 28, 6; vi. 8). But there is some doubt. Cf. Godefroy on xi. 28, 6, n. 6; Jan, *Prol. ad Macrob.* v. vi.; Teuffel, *Rom. Lit.* ii. p. 453; Peter, *Gesch. Litt.* i. 142. Rutilius Namatianus was prefect of the City in 414 (*Itin.* i. 157). His father, Lachanius, had been Consularis Tusciae (*ib.* i. 579).

[2] *C. Th.* xvi. 10, 21, qui profano Pagani ritus errore seu crimine polluuntur, nec ad militiam admittantur, nec Administratoris vel Judicis honore decorentur.

CHAPTER II

THE LAST CONFLICTS OF PAGANISM WITH THE CHRISTIAN EMPIRE

THE sixteenth book of the Theodosian Code contains a series of twenty-five edicts against the practice of pagan rites. It begins with a curt command that superstition shall cease and "the insanity of sacrificial rites shall be abolished."[1] It closes, more than eighty years afterwards, with denouncing the penalty of death against any who still presume to take part in "the damnable practices" so long forbidden by the State.[2] It is true that in the edict of 423 the Emperor seems sanguine that heathenism is almost extinct,[3] and he somewhat mitigates the penalties against those "who are still entangled in the accursed worship of daemons." There is even a curious note of toleration in the law of the same year,[4] which imposes a heavy fine on any person offering violence to Jews or pagans who lived in quietness and outward obedience to the law. But this clemency was probably misunderstood. In country places, sometimes with the connivance of indifferent officials, the old temples were still frequented, and

---

[1] *C. Th.* xvi. 10, 2, cesset superstitio ; sacrificiorum aboleatur insania.

[2] *Ib.* xvi. 10, 25.

[3] *Ib.* xvi. 10, 22 and 23, paganos qui supersunt, quanquam jam nullos esse credamus, legum jamdudum prescripta compescant.

[4] *Ib.* xvi. 10, 24.

sacrifices were still offered more than fifty years after
the death of the great Theodosius. The fierce tone of
the Novella of 439 proves that legislation had not
yet finally subdued the obstinacy of old superstition.
The closing enactment in the Code, against the obstinate
and hated remnant, is the most vehement of all.[1] In
that strange rhetorical tone of the later Code, the
infuriated Emperor, after referring to the almost
ostentatious contempt of pagans for "the thousand
terrors of the laws," asks "why the springtime has
resigned its wonted charm, why the summer with its
scanty harvests mocks the hopes of the toiling husband-
man, why the rigours of winter have condemned the
fruitful soil to barrenness?" It must be the vengeance
of Nature for continued impiety. The violated majesty
of the Heavenly Power demanded expiation and revenge.
Probably the timid devotees, who still clung to their
rustic altars, found the explanation of these calamities in
the impiety of the Emperor. But here, so far as open
pagan ritual is concerned, the conflict with the Empire
closes. The final triumph over the devotional attachments of a thousand years was reserved for the dialectic
or the accommodating arts of the Church.

The secret of the long conflict is not to be sought
exclusively in the obstinacy of immemorial custom, and
the conservatism of a race wedded to ancient usage.
The truth is, that in the period of transition the laws
were administered for the most part by officials belonging
to the pagan or wavering class. But, above all, the
imperial government for a long time was only half-
hearted in the war against the old religion of the State.
The policy of Constantine and his successors, till the
reign of Gratian, was, in spite of appearances, one of
practical toleration to the legitimate practice of pagan

---

[1] *Nov. Theod.* tit. 3. The law is directed against Jews, Samaritans,
heretics, and pagans.

worship in the West.[1] It is true that Constantius, Valentinian I., and Valens made the practice of the arts of divination, astrology, and magic a political crime,[2] and strove to repress them with a ruthless determination. But from 356 to 381 there is no law in the Code directed against public heathen rites. In the interval they were either authorised or connived at. Symmachus and his colleagues still hold the meetings of the pontifical college ; the feasts of Magna Mater are still celebrated ; the Vestals still guard the eternal fire. Even Gratian did not expressly abolish the heathen worship, although on his accession, for the first time, he declined to accept the pontifical robes, and withdrew from the sacred colleges their estates and endowments.[3] His most serious assault on the old religion was the removal of the statue and altar of Victory from the Senate-house.[4] The figure of Victory, originally brought from Tarentum, was regarded as the sacred symbol of Roman greatness. From the days of Augustus it had stood over the altar at which twelve generations of senators had seen their sittings opened with sacrifice, and at which they had sworn allegiance to the chief of the State.[5] The Senate which contained such attached pagans as Praetextatus, Symmachus, and Flavianus, and which almost certainly at this time had a majority opposed to the innovation,[6]

---

[1] Cf. Boissier, *La Fin du Pag.* ii. pp. 271, 296 ; Rauschen, *Jahrbücher der Christ. Kirche unter dem K. Theod.* p. 127, die Opfer dagegen, auch die blutigen, blieben im Westreiche bis zum Gesetz des Theodosius vom 24 Feb. 391 erlaubt : *C. Th.* xvi. 10, 10.

[2] There is a controversy as to the laws between 341 and 356, interdicting pagan worship. The most probable conclusion seems to be that, if they were issued, they were not rigorously enforced. Duruy, vii. 297 ; cf. Maury, *La Magie*, pp. 110-114.

[3] Zos. iv. 36, τῶν οὖν ποντιφίκων κατὰ τὸ ξύνηθες προσαγαγόντων Γρατιανῷ τὴν στολὴν ἀπεσείσατο τὴν αἴτησιν. For doubts about this statement see Rauschen, *Jahrb. der Chr. K.* p. 120, n. 4.

[4] Sym. *Ep.* x. 3 ; cf. Seeck's *Sym.* liii. liv.

[5] Gregorovius, *Rome in the Middle Ages*, i. 67.

[6] Cf. Seeck, *Sym.* liv. ; cf. the account of the Senate's opposition to Theodosius in Zosimus, iv. 59 ; and on the other hand the boast of Prudentius, *c. Sym.* i. 566. Ambros. *Ep.* 17 affirms that the Christians

resolved to petition the Emperor to rescind the decrees.
But the Christian party, through Damasus and Ambrose,
succeeded in preventing the deputation from even
getting an audience.[1] The events which immediately
followed seemed a judgment of the gods on their enemies.
Gratian fell by the assassin's hand, leaving no heirs;
and a terrible famine wasted the provinces which were
the granaries of Italy.[2] The pagan party took fresh
courage, and in 384 their two greatest chiefs, Praetextatus
and Symmachus, were raised, the one to the prefecture of
Italy, the other to that of the city.[3] Praetextatus
signalised his tenure by obtaining a decree for the
prevention of the spoliation of temples,[4] and to require
the restitution of works of art which had been abstracted
by private persons. Once more the Senate formally
resolved to petition the Emperor to repeal the law of
Gratian. And Symmachus, as the head of the deputation, was entrusted with the task of stating their views.
The speech which he composed for the occasion is still
extant,[5] and is invaluable as the last formal and public
protest of the proscribed faith. It is penetrated at once
by the spirit of sceptical tolerance, and the spirit of old
Roman conservatism. "Each nation," says Symmachus,
"has its own gods and peculiar rites. The Great
Mystery cannot be approached by one avenue alone.[6]
But use and wont count for much in giving authority to
a religion. Leave us the symbol on which our oaths of

were in a majority. But, if so,
why did they not prevent the
appeal to the Emperor? and why
were even the Christian members
of the Consistorium in favour of
yielding? Cf. Rauschen, p. 119,
n. 10, who deals in a rather
arbitrary way with the evidence;
cf. Boissier, ii. 315; Gibbon, c. 28.

[1] Ambros. *Ep.* 17, 10, misit ad
me Sanctus Damasus . . libellum
quem Christiani senatores dederunt,
etc.

[2] Sym. *Rel.* 3, secuta est hoc
factum fames publica.

[3] See the references to the *C. Th.*
in Seeck, lv.

[4] Sym. *Rel.* 21.

[5] *Ib.* 3.

[6] Uno itinere non potest perveniri ad tam grande secretum; cf.
a similar liberal tone in the letter
of Maximus to S. Augustine, *Ep.*
16, § 4

allegiance have been sworn for so many generations.
Leave us the system which has so long given prosperity
to the State. A religion should be judged by its utility
to the men who hold it. Years of famine have been the
punishment of sacrilege. The treasury should not be
replenished by the wealth of the sacred colleges, but by
the spoils of the enemy." And the venerable form of
Rome is introduced, in a piece of powerful rhetoric,
pleading for reverence for her many centuries of life,[1] for
leave to follow her immemorial customs and traditions,
and the faith which had kept the Gauls and Hannibal at
bay. According to S. Ambrose, the oratory of Symmachus
had a powerful effect even on the Christian members of
the Consistory.[2] Nor does the great bishop disguise
his own admiration for its skill and power. But once
more its arts and energy gained a victory for the
Church.

Yet, in spite of intervals of imperial displeasure,
Symmachus and his kinsman Flavianus continued to
hold high place. Flavianus was Pretorian prefect in
391, and in the same year Symmachus rose to the
consulship. Once again Symmachus was commissioned
by the Senate to ask for the restoration of the altar of
Victory. But Theodosius was thoroughly mastered by
the powerful will of S. Ambrose, and the chief of the
pagan party was hurried from the imperial presence, and
set down at the hundredth milestone from Milan.[3]
Another effort, and the last, was made in 392. The
Consistory again would have yielded, but the young
Valentinian stood firm, although this time S. Ambrose
was absent from the field.

The law which definitely prohibited pagan worship in
the West was published in the year of the consulship of

[1] Romam nunc putemus adsistere
atque his vobiscum agere sermonibus
. . . reveremini annos meos. . . .

[2] Ambros. *Ep.* 18, 2 ; *de Obit.
Valent.* 19.
[3] Prosper. *de Promiss. et Praedict
Dei*, iii. c. 38 ; S. Ambros. *Ep.* 51.

Symmachus.[1] Down to 391, notwithstanding the determined attitude of Gratian, the legitimate practice of the
ancient rites in the Western provinces was little interfered
with.   But the law of Theodosius and Valentinian II.
forbids absolutely the offering of sacrifices, and even the
visiting of temples.   Heavy fines are imposed on
governors and officials of every degree who shall infringe
the law, or connive at its infringement. The law of 392
is addressed to a prefect of the East, but it is evidently
intended for the whole Roman world.   It is of the most
sweeping and uncompromising character.[2]   No one, however highly placed in respect of birth, fortune, or office,
is to presume to disobey it.   The most private worship
of the household gods, by incense, lights, or garlands, is
interdicted.[3]   And every other mode of heathen worship
is forbidden in a long and exhaustive enumeration.   All
governors, defensors, and curials of cities are bound under
heavy penalties to see to the observance of the law.

Yet the victory of the Church was not so secure as
the confident tone of legislation might seem to proclaim.
In the very year when the first of these laws was
published a votary of Mithra within the walls of Rome
received "the new birth to eternal life" through the
cleansing rites of the Taurobolium.[4]   Even more significant is the fact that many persons of rank and dignity
were deserting the Christian fold, and lapsing into
Jewish or Manichaean or pagan superstitions.   There is
no more remarkable chapter in the Code than that which
deals with apostasy.[5]   Constantine and Constantius had
found it necessary to threaten severe penalties against

[1] *C. Th.* xvi. 10, 10.
[2] *Ib.* xvi. 10, 12, nullus omnino,
ex quolibet genere, ordine hominum,
dignitatum, vel in potestate positus,
vel honore perfunctus, etc.
[3] Vel secretiore piaculo, Larem
igne, mero Genium, Penates nidore
veneratus, accendat lumina, im-

ponat tura, serta suspendat.
[4] *C.I.L.* vi. 736, arcanis perfu-
sionibus in aeternum renatus taurobolium crioboliumque fecit. The
names of the consuls are made out
to be those of 391, Tatianus and
Symmachus.
[5] *C. Th.* xvi. tit. 7.

those who forsook Christianity to join the Jews or Manichaeans.[1] The law of the elder Theodosius in 381 is the first in the Code directed against the tendency of nominal Christians to relapse into heathenism.[2] Between 381 and 396 the Code contains six enactments, denouncing in tones of increasing severity those who have profaned their baptism and betrayed the faith of Christ by a return to idolatry, and withdrawing from them the rights of bequest or inheritance.[3] Apostates of rank and dignity are to be degraded and branded with perpetual infamy,[4] and all hope of restoration by penitence is refused to the renegade. Thirty years later, Valentinian III. thought it necessary to repeat the previous edicts, and even to add to their emphasis.[5]

That men should abandon the religion of the State in the face of such trenchant legislation is a proof, not only of the force of old religious associations, but also of a certain confidence that the cause of paganism was not yet hopeless. Nor was the confidence altogether unreasonable. The men who, in the foremost place and station, still clung obstinately to the faith of their ancestors, Symmachus, Flavianus, or Praetextatus, had seen the reign of Constantius. In their early youth they had beheld the Church torn by fierce conflicts, in which Christian charity and common humanity were forgotten in a controversy about what to them seemed barren verbal subtleties. They had seen the bishops of rival sects anathematising one another, and men of lofty character driven into poverty and obscure exile for years,

---

[1] *C. Th.* xvi. 8, 1 and 7; cf. xvi. 7, 3. See Godefroy's Paratitlon.

[2] *Ib.* xvi. 7, 1. See Godefroy's note on this law. Cf. Rauschen, *Jahrbücher der Chr. Kirche*, p. 153. He denies, apparently without sufficient grounds, the conclusions of Godefroy.

[3] *C. Th.* xvi. 7, 4, testamenti non habeant factionem; nulli in hereditate succedant; a nemine scribantur heredes.

[4] *Ib.* xvi. 7, 5, de loco statuque dejecti perpetua urantur infamia. Notice that this is addressed to the arch-pagan prefect, Virius Nicomachus Flavianus, in the consulship of his friend Symmachus.

[5] *Ib.* xvi. 7, 8.

while the military and administrative force of a government, nominally Christian, lent itself to satisfy the
rancour of theological hatred. They might well feel, with
the honest pagan Ammianus Marcellinus,[1] that no savage
beasts could equal the cruelty of Christians to one
another. On the other hand, their own religion, down
to 391, had, in many respects, enjoyed practical toleration. Every one was still free to worship in his own
fashion. There was no interference with conscience or
the expression of opinion. Seven Christian emperors had
accepted the pontifical robes on their accession.[2] In the
year 356 Constantius, on his visit to Rome, had shown
extraordinary interest in the religion of old Rome.[3] He
had allotted priesthoods, and granted funds from the
treasury for the sacred ceremonies. Attended by the
Senate, he had gone the round of the ancient temples,
and shown a sympathetic curiosity in their legends and
antiquities. The pagan revival of Julian, brief and
illusory as it was, may well have encouraged hopes of a
more enduring restoration. When he granted universal
toleration, recalled the martyrs of the Arian persecutions,
and preached peace and goodwill to an assembly of
bishops, he seemed to give paganism or Hellenism for the
moment a position of moral superiority. Yet Julian
himself discerned keenly the real weakness of paganism
in the absence of a dogmatic system and moral discipline,
and he strove to supply them.[4] Charity and the pastor-
ate of souls must no longer be a monopoly of the
Galileans. The priest was to instruct his people, instead
of merely performing a part in theatrical ceremonies
before the altar. The cruelties of the amphitheatre and
the obscenities of the stage were no longer to be coun-

[1] Amm. Marc. xxii. 5, nullas
infestas hominibus bestias ut sunt
sibi ferales plerique Christianorum
expertus ; cf. xxi. 16, 18, for the
historian's opinion of the theological disputes of the time.
[2] *Ib.* xvi. 10 ; Sym. *Ep.* x. 54.
[3] Sym. *Rel.* iii.
[4] Jul. *Ep.* 52 ; *Fragm. Ep.* in
Hertlein's ed. i. pp. 387, 389, 391.

tenanced by true votaries of the Sun-god. A man who had lived through such a period, and who had, under Christian emperors, with impunity served as pontiff and been consecrated publicly in the Taurobolium, might well doubt whether the power, so often asserted and so constantly defied, was destined finally to triumph.

The murder of Valentinian II. by the hand or machinations of Arbogastes,[1] and the elevation of Eugenius to the purple, seemed for a moment to offer a chance of realising such dreams. Buried in his country seat, and professing to be satisfied with rural pleasures, Flavianus was really a man of great ambitions. In spite of his paganism, he was a favourite at the court, and rose to the highest offices. Yet under all his apparent epicurean indifference, or his study of imperial favour, Flavianus nursed, more than any of his contemporaries, the dream of restoring the religion and spirit of ancient Rome. We cannot help imagining him a man who suppressed, under a crust of half melancholy, half contemptuous pessimism, the fire of an energy which in earlier times might have done great service to the State. A fascinating charm, which disarmed theological antipathy, united to a burning hatred of the Christian *régime*, commanding ability combined with hopeless illusions, are probably the secret of his strange and tragic career. He threw himself into a movement which seemed for a moment to promise the chance of a real pagan reaction. Eugenius, a Christian in name, was a Hellenist in culture,[2] and readily sanctioned the repeal of the anti-pagan laws. At the instance of Flavianus,[3] the altar of Victory was once more restored to its place, the expenses of heathen rites were once more borne by the

---

[1] Zos. iv. 54; Socr. v. 25; Sozom. vii. 22. Cf. Rauschen, *Jahrbücher der Chr. Kirche*, pp. 362-363, for a discussion of the authorities.

[2] *Ib.* iv. 54; cf. Seeck's *Sym.*

cxviii. ; Sozom. vii. 22, Εὐγένιος δέ τις οὐχ ὑγιῶς διακείμενος περὶ τὸ δόγμα τῶν Χριστιανῶν.

[3] Paulin. *vit. Ambros.* § 26.

State, and all the curiosity of divination was allowed free
play.   Two years were spent in preparations for the
conflict on which so much depended.   On both sides the
leaders strove to fortify the courage of their party by
prophecy or oracle.   Theodosius sent one of his eunuchs
to consult a solitary of great age and famous sanctity in the
depths of the Thebaid.[1]   Flavianus was no less active in
securing supernatural assurance of the success of his
cause, and an oracle was circulated,[2] which seemed to
predict the final overthrow of the Christian faith in the
very year of the impending struggle.   As consul of 394,
he celebrated the festivals of Isis and Magna Mater
under the eyes of the usurper.[3]   The pagan party were
full of hope and confidence.   When Arbogastes and
Eugenius quitted Milan to meet the army of Theodosius,
they boasted that they would return to stable their horses
in the Christian basilica.[4]   Within a few days these
hopes were crushed in the battle on the Frigidus.
Flavianus by a voluntary death refused to witness the
victory of the cause he hated, or to accept the probable
clemency of the conqueror.   The triumph of Christianity
seemed complete and final.   Serena, the wife of Stilicho,[5]
one of the generals of Theodosius, in the presence of the
last Vestal Virgin, took the necklace from the throat of
the Great Mother, and placed it on her own.   The
sacrilege was, to pagan minds, within a few years terribly
avenged.[6]

Even yet the pagan cause evidently did not seem to
its adherents to be hopelessly lost.   In spite of the defeat
of Eugenius, the mass of the Senate were still obstinately
attached to the faith " which had kept the city unravaged
for a thousand years." [7]   And one of the last acts of

[1] Claudian, *in Eutrop.* i. 312.
[2] Aug. *de Civ. Dei*, xviii. 53.
[3] Rufin. *Hist. Eccl.* ii. 33 ; *Carm.
Paris.* ; cf. Rauschen, *Jahrbücher*,
p. 368.

[4] Paulin. *vit. Ambros.* § 31.
[5] Zos. iv. 57.
[6] *Ib.* v. 38.
[7] *Ib.* iv. 59 ; but cf. Rauschen,
p. 299, n. 4.

Theodosius was to convoke the conscript fathers and appeal to them to abandon their errors, and to accept the faith which promised absolution from all sin and impiety. According to Zosimus, the homily produced no effect, and the Emperor had even to listen to arguments in favour of the ancient religion of the State.[1]

In the year following the victory over Eugenius, Honorius and Arcadius found it necessary to repeat their father's prohibition of all heathen rites.[2] But the student may easily discover in this law the cause which made such constant iteration necessary. It is directed specially against governors of provinces and their officials, who condoned offences against previous edicts.[3] Neglect on the part of the inferior officers to carry out the Emperor's commands is now made a capital offence.[4] Theodosius had shown a similar distrust of his subordinates in the law of 392.[5] And it appears again and again in the legislation of this period. In the province of Africa the leaders of the Church complained of the slackness of the provincial officers in giving effect to the penal laws against paganism.[6] We may compare the difficulties of the Emperor in securing obedience to his laws against heathen rites with the apparently insuperable obstacles which the government had to encounter for a hundred and fifty years, in its efforts to purge the corruption of the financial service.[7] In both cases, the prohibitions are repeated with wearisome frequency, and pointed by threats of the severest punishment. But the Emperor was met by a dead weight of official resistance or negligence, which apparently rendered legislation almost nugatory. The provincial governor and his staff

---

[1] Zos. iv. 59, μηδενὸς δὲ τῇ παρακλήσει πεισθέντος, κ.τ.λ.

[2] *C. Th.* xvi. 10, 13.

[3] *Ib.* xvi. 10, 13, sciant autem moderatores provinciarum nostrarum et his apparitio obsecundans, etc.

[4] *Ib.* xvi. 10, 13, insuper capitali supplicio judicamus officia coercenda.

[5] *Ib.* xvi. 10, 12.

[6] Aug. *Ep.* 91, § 8 ; cf. 97.

[7] See book iii. c. 2 of this work.

were often in sympathy, or in league, with the offenders.
A knowledge of the history and opinions of the official to
whom the law is addressed will often explain the reason
of the necessity for its repetition.   For instance, the law
of 391,[1] against the apostasy from the Christian faith of
persons of high birth or official rank, is addressed to
Flavianus, then Pretorian prefect, the man who, within
three years, was to be a leader in the great pagan reaction under Eugenius.   A law of 409[2] directed another
Pretorian prefect, Jovius, to take the severest measures
against those renegades who were adopting the superstition of the Heaven-worshippers.   It may well be doubted
whether Jovius, who, if he had any serious policy or faith,
believed in the tolerant policy of Stilicho, and in astrology,
was likely to display much zeal in enforcing the will of
the Emperor against such heretics.

On the other hand, the pagan sentiment or the taste
of many officials sometimes influenced the Government to
restrain the fanatical Vandalism which, both in the East
and the West, was making havoc of the temples and their
treasures of art.   It was probably the pagan author of the
Saturnalia who evoked the edict of 399,[3] forbidding the
destruction of such masterpieces in Spain and Gaul.   In
the years which followed the death of Theodosius, there is
a marked effort to check the desecration of the ancient
shrines by greed or fanaticism.   S. Jerome and S. Augustine exult over the ruin of the temples of the false gods.[4]
And there is no doubt that the destructive energy of men
like Theophilus of Alexandria,[5] S. Martin of Tours, and
Marcellus in Syria, had many imitators.   But the

[1] *C. Th.* xvi. 7, 5.

[2] *Ib.* xvi. 8, 19.   On these Coeli-
colae *v.* Godefroy's note, t. 6, p. 258.

[3] *Ib.* xv. 10, 15.

[4] Hieron. *Ep.* 107, § 1, auratum
squalet Capitolium.   Fuligine et
aranearum telis omnia Romae templa

cooperta sunt; Aug. *Ep.* 232, § 3,
videtis certe simulacrorum templa
partim sine reparatione collapsa,
partim diruta, partim clausa, etc.;
cf. Gregorovius, pp. 58-60.

[5] Sulp. Sev. *vit. S. Mart.* c. 13;
Sozom. vii. 15; cf. Godefroy's note
to *C. Th.* xvi. 10, 16.

emperors had no wish to see the demolition of costly and beautiful buildings.[1] They might still be used as places of public meeting and resort, or consecrated to Christian worship. The tumultuous gatherings, headed by monks, which wrought such deplorable havoc in the East, were prohibited by Arcadius;[2] and there is evidence that governors of taste and sentiment seconded the imperial will. The Christian poet Prudentius makes Theodosius recommend to the Senate the preservation of the temple marbles, as monuments of national greatness and masterpieces of art.[3] In the reign of the younger Theodosius nearly 300 temples of the gods were still standing, although their ornaments and plates of gold had been torn off to swell the ransom demanded by Alaric. Many works of art were buried and forgotten, in the terrors of persecution or invasion.[4] But in the time of Honorius, and even in that of Justinian, immense numbers of them were still preserved, both in the open spaces of the city and in the halls of the nobles.[5]

From the death of Theodosius till 408, although the religious conflict was fierce, it was controlled to some extent by the moderating influence of Stilicho. It is not our purpose to disentangle the perplexed story of those puzzling and disastrous years. On the one side were the bishops, backed by some of the great nobles and the officers, Roman or barbarian, of the elder Theodosius, the party which had already won a great, though not yet decisive victory. On the other was the mass of the senatorial class, with a crowd of Arians, Jews, Manichaeans, and philosophic freethinkers, who, though divided in

---

[1] *C. Th.* xvi. 10, 15, volumus publicorum operum ornamenta servari ; cf. xvi. 10, 3.
[2] *Ib.* xvi. 10, 16.
[3] *Contra Sym.* i. 501. Inscriptions show that in 483 statues of Minerva were restored by the Urban prefect. *C.I.L.* vi. 526, 1664.

[4] Gregorovius, i. 78, n. 3.

[5] In the time of Justinian, 3785 statues remained in the city. Gregorov. i. 79 ; cf. *Notitia Occid.* c. iv. The curator statuarum was an officer under the Praef. Urb. ; see Böcking's ed. p. 201.

religious belief, were united by old patriotic associations, or by the hatred of a menacing theocracy. Stilicho, who was left guardian of the young emperors, was, or gave himself out to be, the depositary of the last wishes of Theodosius on the religious problem of the time. He interpreted his commission to be one of toleration,[1] to hold the balance even between the opposing factions. In the year 395 an amnesty was proclaimed,[2] and the brand of ignominy, attached to the party of Eugenius, was obliterated. Ancient pagan festivals in Africa received legal sanction.[3] The judicial power of the episcopate was limited,[4] and the Senate, which was the stronghold of pagan sentiment, was accorded an authority which it had not enjoyed for many ages. Yet the anti-pagan laws still in theory retained their force, and the crowd of pagans and heretics were, at least nominally, kept in bounds.[5] Amid the fury of party feeling and fanaticism, the cool, and probably sceptical, statesman succeeded in satisfying neither Christian nor pagan, and was finally execrated by both alike.[6] The ominous advent of Alaric and Radagaisus stimulated still further the war of religions. Then began that melancholy strife of sophistry, as to the efficacy of the old gods or the new to protect and prosper their worshippers, which was only closed by the genius of S. Augustine. Every fluctuation of fortune was eagerly seized upon, and skilfully used, to discredit or to glorify Jupiter or Christ. What we are chiefly concerned to notice is the force and fervour of pagan sentiment at this time. Never in the early days of Rome was superstition apparently more rampant. At the first tidings of the coming of the Gothic hosts, all the old omens of the days of the Samnite and Carthaginian wars reappear.

---

[1] Ambros. *de Obit. Theod.* 5.
[2] *C. Th.* xv. 14, 12.
[3] *Ib.* xvi. 10, 17. Cf. Godefroy's note.
[4] *Ib.* xvi. 11, 1 ; cf. xvi. 2, 12, 23, 41.
[5] *Ib.* xvi. 5, 37, 38, 39.
[6] Rutil. Namat. ii. 41 ; Oros. vii. 38 ; cf. Rauschen, *Jahrbücher der Christ. Kirche*, p. 558.

The terror of the time can still be felt thrilling in the verses of Claudian. Men talked of dreams, of strange flights of birds, of comets and eclipses, of showers of stones, and unearthly sounds in the silence of the night.[1] They watched the settling of swarms of bees, and turned the leaves of the Sibylline books of fate.[2] They recalled the flight of the twelve vultures which had crossed the gaze of Romulus, and, in defiance of chronology, abridged the years portended by their flight.[3] When Radagaisus with his host of 200,000 Goths descended from the Alps, the old pagan feeling defied all restraint, and the cries of its panic and regret reached the ears of the Bishop of Hippo.[4] The most terrible invader who had ever appeared in Italy, men said, was a diligent votary of his strange northern gods; and the sons of old Rome were deprived of the help of their ancient deities, to whom they were now forbidden to offer a grain of incense. Meanwhile the feeling of suspicion towards Stilicho was deepening into hatred on the Christian side. The clergy did not find in him the facile instrument of persecution that they desired. They exalted the piety and virtues of the weak and worthless Honorius at the expense of the man without whose guidance Honorius was a mere cipher.[5] They circulated the myth, which was accepted also by the pagan Rutilius,[6] that Stilicho had let loose the hordes of barbarism on the Empire, with the deep purpose of re-establishing the pagan religion, and that his son Eucherius

---

[1] Claud. *de Bell. Get.* 227-247.

[2] *Ib.* 231 :

quid carmine poscat
fatidico custos Romani carbasus aevi.

[3] *Ib.* 265 :

tunc reputant annos, interceptoque volatu
vulturis, incidunt properatis saecula metis.

[4] Aug. *de Civ. Dei*, v. 23, nobis apud Karthaginem dicebatur, hoc credere, spargere, jactare paganos, quod ille diis amicis protegentibus et opitulantibus, quibus immolare cotidie ferebatur, vinci omnino non posset ab eis, qui talia diis Romanis sacra non facerent nec fieri a quoquam permitterent.

[5] Aug. *Ep.* 97 ; Hieron. *Ep.* 123, § 17, quod non vitio principum, qui vel religiosissimi sunt, sed scelere semibarbari accidit proditoris ; Oros. vii. 37, 11.

[6] Rutil. Namat. ii. 46.

was to be the Julian of another religious reaction.[1]   The
great general and statesman was charged with slackness
and perfidy in his campaigns against Alaric.[2]   The
victory at Pollentia was attributed to supernatural aid, in
spite of the sacrilegious violation of the holy time of
Easter.   With reckless inconsistency the men who
lauded the Christian clemency and reverence of Alaric,
vilified Stilicho's policy of conciliation as treachery and
weakness.[3]   On the other hand, the old Roman party still
more heartily detested the man who had borne a part in
the victory over Eugenius,[4] and who relied on those
German captains and soldiers who were now the main
defence of Rome.   The ignoble triumph of the motley
combination which overwhelmed Stilicho has been often
told, and need not be repeated here.   The hypocritical
Olympius,[5] who owed his first rise to Stilicho, attained a
brief ascendency, amid the blessings and congratulations
of the dignitaries of the Church.[6]   And the Church took
an ample revenge for the interval of clemency.   The last
endowments of the old religion were withdrawn,[7] the
images of the gods were pulled down, the temples were
either confiscated or destroyed, the banquets and games
were prohibited.   All enemies of the Catholic faith were
banished from the imperial service.[8]   The feigned enthusiasm of Olympius obtained for the bishops that civil
jurisdiction which had been strictly limited by Stilicho.[9]
And, to ensure the victory, the bishops themselves were

[1] Oros. vii. 38, § 1.
[2] Ib. vii. 37, 2, taceo de Alarico
rege cum Gothis suis saepe victo,
saepe concluso semperque dimisso.
[3] Ib. vii. 39 ; de Civ. Dei, i. 1.
[4] Zos. iv. 57, 59 ; Rutil. Namat.
ii. 41.
[5] Zos. v. 32, ἐν δὲ τῇ φαινομένῃ
τῶν Χριστιανῶν εὐλαβείᾳ πολλὴν ἀπο-
κρύπτων ἐν ἑαυτῷ πονηρίαν.—Cf.
Olympiod. § 2, μιαιφόνῳ καὶ ἀπαν-
θρώπῳ σπουδῇ 'Ολυμπίου ὃν αὐτὸς τῷ
βασιλεῖ προσῳκείωσε τὸν διὰ ξίφους

ὑπέμεινε θάνατον.
[6] Aug. Ep. 96, temporali vero
felicitate ad aeterna lucra te pru-
denter usurum minime dubitamus.
Written in 408 to Olympius.
[7] C. Th. xvi. 10, 19.
[8] Ib. xvi. 5, 42.   This mischievous
enactment, which deprived Rome of
the services of some of her best
soldiers, is referred to in Zos. v. 46.
It was issued within three months
after the death of Stilicho.
[9] Ib. xvi. 10, 19 ; xvi. 2, 39.

charged with the congenial duty of enforcing the laws, which the milder or less conscientious lay-governor had often allowed to sleep.[1]

Another short-lived and impotent pagan reaction occurred in 409, when Alaric, with the approval of the Senate, set up a rival emperor to Honorius in the person of the dilettante Attalus.[2] The leading members of this government belonged to the pagan party. Lampadius, the Pretorian prefect, was an avowed believer in divination and its kindred arts, and had been honoured with a letter from S. Augustine on the subject of this superstition.[3] Marcian, the prefect of the city, had, during the brief ascendency of Eugenius, been guilty of apostasy.[4] Tertullus, the consul of 410, was a declared pagan of the old school, who did not hesitate, in addressing the Senate, to express a hope that the ancient pontificate would be revived in himself.[5] The treacherous or fickle Jovius, whom Attalus raised to the prefecture,[6] was a free-thinker of the type common in those days of fluid convictions.[7] Under such patronage, the Chaldaean fortune-tellers and diviners, who had been banished by so many emperors, renewed their activity.[8] For the first time since the days of Constantine, the *Labarum* disappeared from the

---

[1] The African bishops in October of 408 sent a deputation to demand the enforcement of the laws against pagans and heretics, and S. Augustine backed up their demands by a private letter to Olympius (*Ep.* 97). At the same time the pagans, on the death of Stilicho, clamoured for the repeal of these laws, on the ground that they had emanated from Stilicho. That they were not vigorously enforced during Stilicho's ascendency seems implied in the words : omnia quae in Donatistas, Manichaeos, sive Priscillianistas, vel in Gentiles a nobis decreta sunt non solum manere decernimus, verum in executionem plenissimam effectumque deduci (*C. Th.* xvi. 5, 43). Stilicho's death took place 10 Kal. Sep. 408 ; the laws excluding pagans from the army, and enforcing penalties against heretics, are dated 18 and 17 Kal. Dec. 408. See Godefroy's note to *C. Th.* xvi. 10, 19.

[2] Zos. vi. 7.

[3] Aug. *Ep.* 246.

[4] He was procos. of Africa in 394. See *Carm. Paris.* 78, quoted by Seeck, *Sym.* n. 588.

[5] Oros. vii. 42.

[6] Zos. vi. 8.

[7] Paulin. Nol. *Ep.* 16.

[8] Sozom. ix. 8, μάντεσι δέ τισιν ὑπαχθεὶς, οὔτε Ἀλαρίχῳ ἐπείσθη.

coins.[1]   Attalus, in a speech of ornate rhetoric,[2] charmed
the Senate with the picture of a reunited empire of both
East and West, and held out the hope of a speedy restoration of the festivals and temple services of their ancestors.
It was the last attempt of the old pagan spirit to assert
itself openly in the Empire of the West.   It was made
with the support of a German and Arian chief.   Attalus
had, in deference to Alaric, received baptism at the hands of
Sighe-Sar, an Arian bishop.[3]   Yet he was for the moment
the head of a party, some of whom dreamed of a return
to the tolerant policy of Constantine or of Valentinian I.,
with the support of the Gothic power; while others may
have even nursed the hope that the hated faith was already
doomed.   Attalus was a worthy representative of such
illusions.   And the great chief, who had been his sole
stay, was within a few months laid to rest in the secret
grave in the bed of the Busentus.[4]

    With Stilicho probably fell his friend and brilliant
eulogist, the poet Claudian.   He had, beyond a doubt, a
high place in that society, of which he is the sole literary
glory.   Yet it is curious that, about the history of the
last man of letters, who has something of the manner and
inspiration of the great age, so little is known.   He had,
in his days of prosperity, assailed in a biting epigram[5]
the cupidity of an Egyptian compatriot, who rose high in
the imperial service, and became Pretorian prefect after
Stilicho's death.[6]   We can only conjecture the fate of the
poet, from an epistle addressed to this dignitary,[7] imploring his mercy by an appeal to the examples of pity consecrated in Grecian legend.   Claudian's great crime was
that, in the words of Orosius, he was " a most obstinate

---

[1] Eckhel, *Doctr. Num.* (quoted
in Thierry's *Alaric*, p. 413).

[2] Zos. vi. 7 ; Sozom. ix. 8 and 9.

[3] Sozom. ix. 9.

[4] Jordan. *de Reb. Get.* 30.

[5] Claud. *Epigr.* 30 :
insomnis Pharius sacra, profana rapit.

[6] *C. Th.* xv. 14, 13. Cf. Seeck's
Sym. clxxxvi. n. 944 ; Teuffel, ii.
440, § 6.

[7] *Ep.* 1.

pagan." What his religious convictions really were we
can never know. Probably his deepest religious attachment was to *Roma dea*, the "mother of arts and arms,"
who has gathered the vanquished into her bosom, who
has given her citizenship to the world, whose dominion
shall have no end.[1] Born on the banks of the Nile,[2] he
was yet a Roman of the Romans, and had a mingled
hatred and contempt for the new Rome on the Bosphorus,
with its mushroom and effeminate civilisation.[3] The
verve of Juvenal reappears in his bitter raillery of the
eunuch minister of the Eastern Empire, and of the cring-
ing servility of the Byzantine nobles.[4] It is little wonder
that Claudian was the favourite of the Roman Senate,[5]
still pagan to the core, and profoundly jealous of the
Eastern capital. His powers were lavished on the achievements of Stilicho, whose policy was to humour the Senate
by a politic deference to its antiquated prerogatives.
Serena, Stilicho's wife, was his great friend and patroness,[6]
and is said to have arranged a wealthy match for the
poet. On all this circle he expends the traditional ornament of Greek and Roman mythology. Nor does he
hesitate to do the same for the Christian princes, Theodosius and Honorius, who were pledged to the extirpation
of Paganism. There is hardly a hint in Claudian that
the Roman world has officially adopted a faith hostile to
all his pagan dreams. He appears placidly unconscious
of the great revolution, and recalls Honorius to the
Penates of the Palatine,[7] as if Rome was still the Rome
of Augustus.

A few years after the eclipse of Claudian, we have a

[1] Oros. vii. 35, 21, poeta eximius
sed paganus pervicasissimus ; Aug.
de Civ. Dei, v. 26 ; Gesner's Prol.
to Claud. v. ; Rauschen, *Jahrbücher
der Christ. Kirche,* pp. 555-9 ; cf.
Claud. *de Cons. Stil.* iii. 136-160 ;
de Bell. Get. 50 *sqq.*
[2] Claud. *ad Gennad.* 3, et nostro

cognite Nilo ; cf. *Ep.* 1, 56.
[3] Claud. *in Eutrop.* ii. 326-341.
[4] *Ib.* ii. 137.
[5] See an inscription dedicated
praegloriosissimo poetarum — petente Senatu, *C.I.L.* vi. 1710.
[6] Claud. *Ep.* 2.
[7] Ib. *de VI*[o] *Cons. Honor.* 407.

glimpse for a moment of another pagan man of letters, who is now little known, but who is the last genuine representative of the old pagan tone in literature. Rutilius Namatianus was one of the Gallic aristocracy who had remained untouched by the great Christian enthusiasm aroused by S. Martin. His father [1] had held high imperial office, and he himself [2] had been Urban prefect in 414,[3] only six years after the trenchant law had been published, which condemned to final ruin the temples and images of the old gods. He had lived in intimate friendship with the greatest Roman nobles; and the fragment of his poem which we possess comes to us as a solitary revelation of their deeper feelings. It is the tale of his homeward voyage to Gaul in the year 416,[4] when he was reluctantly compelled, by the ravages which his paternal estates had suffered from the invaders,[5] to leave the city, to whose gilded fanes he looks back with religious veneration and patriotic regret.

The poem has great interest from a purely literary point of view. But we are at present concerned only with the author's attitude to the opposing creeds. Brief and fragmentary as it is, it discloses more of the inner pagan sentiment of the aristocratic class than the much more voluminous poetry of Claudian. Claudian's paganism is more purely literary; it has the air of an unchallenged supremacy. He writes as if he belonged to the age of Virgil, as if Christianity had never existed. On the religious conflict of his time he shows the calm reticence of Symmachus or Macrobius. He is either too full of Roman pride to recognise the new faith, or too cultivated

---

[1] Rutil. Namat. i. 595; cf. 575 *sqq.* He had been consularis Tusciae, and Praef. Urb. (*C. Th.* vi. 26, 8).

[2] *Ib.* i. 157, 473.

[3] *Ib.* i. 157-160, 473; cf. *C. Th.* xiii. 5, 38, which is addressed to Albinus, Praef. Urb. in 416.

[4] This is inferred from Rutil. Namat. i. 135:

quamvis sedecies denis et mille peractis
annus praeterea jam tibi nonus eat

(*i.e.* 1169 A.U.C.). The capture of Toulouse is mentioned in i. 496.

[5] Rutil. Namat. i. 25:

praesentes lacrimas tectis debemus avitis.

to hate it. Rutilius is a man of different mould. He lets us see plainly the working of his own mind on religious subjects, and the feelings of his class towards those who rejected the old religion of their country. That such a poem should have been published under the Christian empire, and that its author should have held the highest office, is a startling proof of the persistence of the old Roman practical toleration of freedom of thought.

Rutilius is faithful to the old religion, but he is not its slave.[1] Sometimes he will uphold the literal truth of a myth. Sometimes he will use the language of Euhemerism or Deism. He displays in fact that mixture of scepticism and credulity, of conformity and free thought, which characterised the cultivated pagan for many ages before his time. But there is no hesitation in the tone in which he speaks of the enemies of Paganism. In some scathing lines,[2] he gives vent to the concentrated hatred which was felt by his caste for the memory of Stilicho. The impious traitor, who burnt the Sibylline books and, for his own selfish ends, laid open the hearth and citadel of the Empire to the tribes of the North, is consigned to the lowest depths of Tartarus. Nothing could surpass the almost brutal contempt which Rutilius feels for the Jews,[3] with one of whom he had an encounter in his wanderings; for their obscene rite of initiation, for the listless sloth of their Sabbath, spent in commemoration of a God who was weary of his work of creation.[4] But when he speaks of " the conquered race that crushes its conquerors,"[5] there can be little doubt that he has in view the religion which was crushing out his own. The islands of the Tuscan Sea, which he passed in his voyage,

---

[1] Rutil. Namat. i. 255 ; cf. i. 73.

[2] *Ib.* ii. 41.

[3] *Ib.* i. 384-398 :
humanis animal dissociale cibis.

[4] *Ib.* :
septima quaeque dies turpi damnata
    veterno,
tamquam lassati mollis imago Dei.
[5] *Ib.* v. 398 :
victoresque suos natio victa premit.

swarmed with monkish exiles,[1] who had forsaken family
and public duty for a life of prayer and solitary asceticism.
The monks in those days were hardly judged even by
their own co-religionists.   At the funeral of Blaesilla,[2]
the daughter of a great Roman house, who had withdrawn from the world and was believed to have shortened
her life by her austerities, the mob of Rome broke into
shouts of execration against what they regarded as an
inhuman fanaticism.   The aversion to the ascetic life,
felt by the cultivated man of the world, is expressed in
more urbane form by Ausonius in his letters of expostu-
lation to S. Paulinus.   But that feeling probably never
found more pointed utterance than in the lines of Rutilius
on the hermits of Capraria.   In the eyes of the pagan
noble and Roman patriot, they are wretches who wish to
screen themselves from too observant eyes, who make
themselves miserable to avoid misery, who, while they
flee from the ills of life, are incapable of enjoying its
blessings.[3]   Rutilius had little conception of the force
and destiny of the movement which he derided.

In the practice of those arts which professed to control nature and to forecast the future, in the excitement
or obscenity of the theatre and the circus, the heathen
spirit found a shelter long after its public ritual had
ceased.

The belief in the arts of magic, divination, and astrology was probably the most living and energetic force in
the pagan sentiment of the time.   These practices had
always been suspected by Roman statesmen.[4]   The cultivation of them was condemned under the severest

---

[1] Rutil. Namat. i. 440 :
          jam se Capraria tollit.
    squalet lucifugis insula plena viris.
[2] Hieron. *Ep.* 39, § 5, dolet
(mater) filiam jejuniis interfectam.
. . .   Quousque genus detestabile
Monachorum non urbe pellitur ?
[3] Rutil. Namat. 445 :

quaenam perversi rabies tam stulta cerebri,
dum mala formides nec bona posse pati.

Cf. the reference (518) to a friend
who has become a recluse, "perditus
hic vivo funere civis erat."

[4] See Maury's *La Magie*, p. 70
sqq.

penalties by the legislation of the fourth and fifth centuries.[1] Yet it was never really suppressed, and, in its
strange terrors and seductions, it perpetuated the power
of heathenism far into the Christian ages.[2] Its fascination, both over the cultivated class and the vulgar, was
never more powerful than in the first decade of the fifth
century. There is no more singular episode, in that time
of unstable beliefs and uncertain party lines, than that in
the year 408, when some Tuscan adepts in the secret
arts offered their services to Pompeianus, prefect of Rome,
to save the city from the Goths.[3] They told the prefect
how, a short time before, they had by their spells called
down the lightning,[4] and driven the Goths away from the
walls of a beleaguered town. The prefect consulted the
pontifical books, and was evidently inclined to try the
effect of the ancient arts. But the practice of them was
sternly prohibited,[5] and a recent law had laid a special
responsibility on the higher magistrates, and on the
bishops, to enforce the prohibition. Pompeianus in his
difficulty sought the advice of Innocent, Bishop of Rome.
This great pontiff, who was also a great patriot,[6] did not
see fit to oppose his own opinion to the wishes of the
people at such a crisis, but he stipulated that the magic
rites should be performed secretly. The Tuscans, however, insisted that the ritual would only be efficacious if
publicly performed on the Capitol and in the open spaces
of the city, in the presence of the Senate. It has been
suggested that Innocent, foreseeing this, gave his consent
under a legally impossible condition, to save the Christian
cause from an outburst of popular hatred. How the
matter ended is uncertain. The Christian historian says

---

[1] *C. Th.* ix. tit. 16.

[2] Maury, pt. i. c. 7.

[3] Zos. v. 41.

[4] *Ib.* v. 41 ; Sozom. ix. 6. The
name of the place appears variously

as Neveia, Larnia, and, by njec-
tur, Narnia.

[5] *C. Th.* ix. 16, 3, 5.

[6] ὁ δὲ τὴν τῆς πόλεως σωτηρίαν
ἔμπροσθεν τῆς οἰκείας ποιησάμενος
δόξης λάθρα ἐφῆκεν αὐτοῖς ποιεῖν ἅπερ
ἴσασιν. Zos. l.c.

that the rites were performed, but that they proved un-
availing.[1] The pagan Zosimus affirms that the aid of the
Tuscans was declined. In any case, the incident reveals
the persistent force of pagan superstition.

The proposal of Pompeianus was a gross violation of
many laws, from the time of Constantine.[2] The con-
sultation of a seer, diviner, or any professor of the magic
art, was made by Constantius an offence punishable by
death.[3] A similar penalty was denounced against the
tribe of Eastern fortune-tellers by Valentinian and
Valens,[4] and, in spite of the general toleration of heathen
worship which characterised the rule of these Emperors,
a ruthless war was waged with the secret arts, which
were suspected as lending themselves to conspiracy
against the Emperor.[5] One law especially of that time,
relating to offenders of the senatorial class,[6] reveals what
was probably a real political danger. The persecution to
which philosophers and professors of Hellenism were
subjected in the reign of Valens may have had some
connection with the later Neoplatonic cultivation of
magic and dark superstitions.[7] The earlier Alexandrines
condemned the magic arts.[8] But it is well known that,
in the later stages of Neoplatonism, the power to wield
the forces of nature, and to predict the future, was more
and more openly claimed. Fasting, prayer, and mystical
elation were thought to bring the votary into communication with the supernatural powers. The influence of the
stars on the fortunes of human life, which was denied by

[1] Sozom. ix. 6; cf. Zos. v. 41.
[2] C. Th. ix. 16, 1 and 2. Constantine, however, permitted *public*
sacrifices of divination ; qui vero id
vobis existimatis conducere, adite
aras publicas atque delubra.
[3] *Ib.* ix. 16, 4, sileat omnibus
perpetuo divinandi curiositas.
Etenim supplicium capitis feret
gladio ultore prostratus, etc.
[4] *Ib.* ix. 16, 8.

[5] Amm. Marc. xxvi. 3. Zos. iv.
13 gives an idea of the grounds of
the Emperor's suspicion of these
practices.

[6] *C. Th.* ix. 16, 10, "de Senatoribus maleficii reis."

[7] Maury, *La Magie*, p. 121.

[8] Vacherot, *L'École d'Alexandrie*,
ii. p. 115, where the opinions of
Porphyry are set forth ; cf. ii. 147.

Plotinus, became an article of faith with many of his successors.[1] In the hands of Maximus and Chrysanthius, and the men who surrounded Julian, Neoplatonism lost its philosophic purity and elevation,[2] and tended more and more to absorb the more materialistic conceptions of paganism.[3] The theurgic virtues, miracle and magic, overshadowed the detached and lofty idealism of the earlier Alexandrines. S. Augustine,[4] with his keen practical sense, strikes at this degraded Platonism as the very heart of the heathen position, and particularly at its doctrine of daemons, which was the foundation of the belief in incantations and magic. The daemons were the powers acting as mediators between the gods, who dwell apart in the highest heaven, and mortal men.[5] Along with certain divine qualities, the daemons have all the passions of humanity;[6] they are irritated by neglect, or soothed and propitiated by gifts and sacrificial rites.[7] From them comes the knowledge of the future by augury and dreams, and the power to command the elements, by occult arts, songs, incantations, and potions. The noteworthy thing is that, in condemning this baleful superstition, the Christian often showed that he had quite as much faith in daemonic

---

[1] Macrob. *Somn. Scip.* i. 19, 27, et Plotinus . . . pronunciat nihil vi vel potestate eorum hominibus evenire.

[2] Vacherot, ii. 145, where the logical development of the belief in magic arts, etc., is traced from the fundamental principles of the school; Plotinus and Porphyry recoiled from these consequences. But the doctrine of the universe, as a "sympathetic whole" bound together by affinities, inevitably led to theurgy on the one hand and magic on the other (Vach. ii. 147).

[3] *Ib.* ii. 148; cf. Eunap. *vit. Iamblich.* p. 13 (Boissonade's ed.), where Iamblichus is said to have risen 10 cubits from the earth during prayer (cf. p. 15). In the life of Maximus, an image of Hecate breaks into smiles under the influence of incantation (p. 51).

[4] *De Civ. Dei*, viii. 14 *sqq.*

[5] Vacherot, ii. 127; Maury, *La Magie*, p. 87.

[6] *De Civ. Dei*, viii. 14, habent enim cum diis communem immortalitatem corporum, animorum autem cum hominibus passiones.

[7] *Ib.* viii. 16, dicit (Platonicus) ad eos pertinere divinationes augurum, aruspicum, vatum atque somniorum, ab his quoque esse miracula magorum.

powers as the pagan had.[1] Constantius threatens with
death those who dare to disturb the elements, or to call
forth the spirits of the dead by magic spells.[2]   S.
Augustine regarded these beings as spirits banished from
heaven for unpardonable sin, who, by diabolic deceit, had
persuaded men to give them divine honours.[3]

The law of 409, ordering the expulsion of the
Mathematici from Rome, and all cities of Italy, was
probably suggested by Pope Innocent,[4] to prevent a
repetition of that painful scene of superstitious observance
at which he may have had to connive.   But the threats
of Honorius,[5] while they may have driven many of the
crowd of diviners and sorcerers into remote country
places, utterly failed to extinguish the superstition, and
men even in high station long continued to practise the
forbidden rites with impunity.   The leading members of
the government, established by the order of Alaric, were
devoted to the black arts.   Attalus, the new Emperor,
was ready to accept a nominal Christianity; but he
belonged to the crowd of sceptics, whose only real faith
was in Hellenism and astrology or magic.   When
Alaric wished to send troops over to Africa in order
to crush Heraclian, the adherent of Honorius, Attalus
relied more on the promises of diviners,[6] who told him
that he could become master of Africa without a conflict, than on the counsels of a serious statesmanship.
Lampadius, the Pretorian prefect in this singular government, was, as we have seen, the friend and correspondent

[1] Maury, p. 99 ; Friedländer, iii.
p. 458.   The Christian doctors were
only following the Hebraic tradition on this subject.

[2] C. Th. ix. 16, 5, multi magicis
artibus ausi elementa turbare, vitas
insontium labefactare non dubitant,
etc.

[3] De Civ. Dei, viii. 22, quia de
caeli superioris sublimitate dejecti
merito inregressibilis transgres-

sionis in hoc sibi congruo velut
carcere praedamnati sunt.

[4] Ib. ix. 16, 12 ; Zos. v. 41.

[5] C. Th. ix. 16, 12, non solum
urbe Roma, sed etiam omnibus
civitatibus pelli decernimus.

[6] Zos. vi. 7, ταῖς δὲ ἐπὶ τοῖς
μάντεσιν ἐλπίσιν ἑαυτὸν ἐκδιδοὺς καὶ
ἀμαχητὶ περιποιήσεσθαι Καρχηδόνα
καὶ τὰ περὶ Λιβύην ἅπαντα πεπεισ-
μένος, κ.τ.λ. Sozom. ix. 8.

of S. Augustine, who laboured to convert him from his belief in astrology.[1] The mass of the Roman aristocracy, with the illustrious exception of the great Christian house of the Anicii,[2] rejoiced in the advent to power of this strange alliance of Arian Christianity, dilettante Hellenic culture, and Chaldaean superstition. Doubtless, as we shall see in a later page, there was a purer and more respectable element in the force of the last pagan reaction. There was a real patriotic feeling, a real religious devotion, and a philoscphic theology, which, however arid and, to our minds, uninspiring, yet enabled the nobler sort to maintain their hold on the faith of the past, while they put out of sight its grosser elements. But the baser form of ancient superstition was probably the most tenacious and energetic. No penal legislation could eradicate the belief, held alike by the most educated and the most ignorant, that there was a lore which could control the operations of nature, and compel the future to unveil its secrets. In the very year when the last of the anti-pagan laws was published, Litorius, the lieutenant of Actius, in his conflict with the Visigoths, was led to his destruction under the walls of Toulouse by trusting (to use the words of the Chronicle) "in the responses of seers and the monitions of daemons."[3] Only a year or two before the fall of the Western Empire,[4] Lampridius, an accomplished man of letters at Bordeaux, and one of the most admired and trusted friends of Sidonius, the bishop of Auvergne, consulted a troop of African sorcerers as to the hour of his death.

In the cruel sports of the arena and the impurities of the stage the Christian Fathers for ages recognised that paganism had its strongest and most enduring hold on the people. S. Cyprian said that "idolatry was the

---

[1] Aug. *Ep.* 146.

[2] Zos. vi. 7.

[3] Prosp. *Chron.* ad a. 439, dum

aruspicum responsis et daemonum significationibus fidit, pugnam cum Gothis imprudenter conseruit, etc.

[4] Sid. *Ep.* viii. 11.

mother of games." Diana presided over the hunting
scenes, the god of war was the patron of the gladiatorial
combats.[1] When the bloody strife had closed, a figure,
representing the powers of the under world, gave the
finishing stroke to the wretches who were still lingering.
The Romans, under the most Christian Emperors
Theodosius and Honorius, were still gloating over
spectacles which their ancestors established to do honour
to the *manes* of departed relatives.[2] The amphitheatre
gave a sort of consecration to the old savage instinct for
cruelty, as the theatre gratified the pruriency of low
desires. It is difficult for us to conceive the fascination
which those awful holocausts of human life exercised, not
only on characters hardened by voluptuousness, but on
the cultivated and humane.[3] A philosophic friend of
S. Augustine,[4] who was half inclined to be a Christian,
and who on principle detested such spectacles, once
allowed himself to be drawn into the fatal circle. At
first he resolved to close his eyes to the ghastly horrors
of the scene. Presently, at the applause raised by some
crisis in the conflict, his eyes opened and would not be
withdrawn. The fumes of the carnage seemed to
intoxicate his senses; he lost his identity, and became
one of the bloodthirsty crowd. He went away eager to
return.

Men can find a justification for any established
institution, and these cruel displays were defended, even
by good and eminent men,[5] as the virile amusements of a
warlike race, accustoming it to make light of death. No
such defence was possible in the last years of the Empire,
when the Roman army was recruited and officered by

[1] Tertull. *de Spectaculis*, 9, 10 ;
Apol. 15, 12 ; cf. Friedländer, ıı. p.
216.
   [2] Suet. *Jul.* 26 ; Valer. Max. ii.
4, 7 ; Liv. *Epit.* 16.
   [3] Plin. *Panegyr. Traj.* 33, visum
est spectaculum inde non enerve

nec fluxum, nec quod animos
virorum molliret et frangeret, sed
quod ad pulcra volnera contemp-
tumque mortis accenderet.
   [4] Aug. *Conf.* vi. 8.
   [5] Plin. *Traj.* 33 ; Cic. *Tusc.* ii.
17, § 41.

Germans; and when Romans would mutilate themselves,[1] and bury themselves in any retreat to escape military service.[2] Yet this nerveless and effeminate mob had been indulged by successive emperors with these revolting atrocities. Even the greatest and best princes had to satisfy the cravings of a proletariat, which probably had more of "the ape and tiger" than any that ever existed. Trajan, with the approval of the humane Pliny, had, after his Dacian victories, sent down 10,000 gladiators into the arena.[3] M. Aurelius, in the performance of social duty, gave gladiatorial shows himself,[4] and attended them, though in a prefunctory and reluctant fashion. But the people were offended when he turned away to read or pen despatches in the amphitheatre; and when he enrolled the gladiators for the Marcomannic war,[5] men said, with a sneer, that he had diminished the pleasures of the people in order to convert them to philosophy. The Emperor Constantine, in the year of the Council of Nicaea, restrained, by an ambiguous edict,[6] this cruel amusement in the Eastern Empire. But in the West it went on almost unchecked. Valentinian, indeed, forbade Christians to be condemned to the gladiatorial school as a punishment for crime.[7] And, in 367, members of the Palatine service were also exempted from this fate.[8] But the elder Theodosius did not abolish the inhuman spectacle,[9] when he interdicted the peaceful worship of the pagan temples. In the last years of the fourth century[10] Symmachus had, at great

---

[1] *C. Th.* vii. 13, 10, "de Murcis"; cf. Amm. Marc. xv. 12, 3.

[2] *C. Th.* vii. tit. 18 *passim.*

[3] Dion Cass. lxviii. c. 15, καὶ μονομάχοι μύριοι ἠγωνίσαντο.

[4] Capitolin. *M. Ant.* 6; cf. Capitolin. *Ant. P.* c. 12; Vop. *Aurel.* c. 33.

[5] *M. Ant.* 23, quod populum sublatis voluptatibus vellet cogere ad philosophiam.

[6] *C. Th.* xv. 12, 1, cruenta spectacula in otio civili et domestica quiete non placent.

[7] *Ib.* ix. 40, 8.

[8] *Ib.* ix. 40, 11; cf. xv. 12, 2.

[9] See Godefroy's refutation of Baronius on this subject, in the note to xv. 12, 1.

[10] On the date, see Seeck's *Sym.* lxxii. The games did not take place till 401.

trouble and expense,[1] arranged for a gladiatorial combat
at the games which were to celebrate his son's prætorship.
But the band of Saxons who had been brought from the
shores of the Baltic to grace the festival, refused to
gratify the mob of Rome by a public exhibition of their
fighting powers, and preferred a quiet death in their
cells.   In the year 404, the inauguration of the sixth
consulship of Honorius was to be celebrated by the
customary sacrifice of life.   Prudentius pleaded with the
Emperor to abolish the ghastly rite,[2] as his father had
stopped the sacrifice of animals at the altar.   The poet's
prayer was answered, not by the will of Honorius, but by
the martyrdom of the heroic monk, who flung himself
into the arena, and died amid the curses of the mob,
whose cruel pleasures he had dared to interrupt.

But even when the cruelties of the arena were
abolished, the circus and the theatre maintained for a
long time their dangerous attractions.   The Roman passion
for these spectacles was of marvellous intensity.   The
austere pagan, Ammianus Marcellinus,[3] relates that, at a
time when famine was threatening, and when foreigners,
including the "professors of the liberal arts," were
ordered to withdraw from the city, three thousand dancing
girls were allowed to remain.   Long after the time of
which Ammianus wrote, the passion for the lubricity of
the stage defied all the authority and moral influence of
the Christian Church.[4]   Orosius and Salvianus regarded
the theatre as a more serious danger than even the invasions of the barbarians.   S. Augustine had to complain
that the African churches were often emptied by the attractions of these spectacles.   Sidonius, late in the century,[5]

[1] Sym. *Ep.* ii. 46.
[2] *Contra Sym.* ii. 1124 :
ille urbem vetuit taurorum sanguine tingi ;
tu mortes miserorum hominum prohibeto
    litari.
[3] Amm. Marc. xiv. 6, 19.
[4] Salv. *de Gub. Dei*, vi. § 88.

[5]. Sid. *Carm.* xxiii. 264 *sqq.*, esp.
v. 286 :
seu Ledam quis agit Phrygemque
    ephebum
aptans ad cyathos facit Tonanti
suco nectaris esse dulciorem.

Cf. Tertull. *de Spect.* 10, 17.

describes the doubtful exhibitions of mythological pantomime as if they were still in full life and vigour.

The whole of the imperial legislation with regard to
actors shows at once the degradation of the Roman stage
and the stubborn attachment of the people to the
indescribable enormities perpetrated in the name of art.
The worst social curse of the Lower Empire, the hereditary character of nearly all callings, had left perhaps its
deepest brand on the actor's profession. Treated as the
vilest of mankind, yet the indispensable minister to the
pleasures of the people, he was chained to his calling
from generation to generation.[1] The Church fought one
of its noblest battles to release these unhappy slaves of a
cruel voluptuousness; and the hand of S. Ambrose is
distinctly seen in some of the laws issued during his
great episcopate.[2] The bishops of Africa, where the
allurements of the theatre were most powerfully felt,[3]
never failed to press the claims of humanity and morality
on the stolid Honorius. But their efforts seem to have
been ill rewarded, for, in 413, the Emperor orders the
" Tribune of Pleasures " at Carthage to recall to their
wretched trade the actresses who had, by " imperial kindness," been previously released.[4] From the time of
Valentinian I. (371) the Church had indeed gained a
great victory.[5] The actress who, *in articulo mortis*, asked
for, and received, the last sacraments, was not to be
dragged back again, in case of recovery, to her hateful
life. But the operation of the law is guarded by careful
provisions to prevent a feigned conversion depriving the
people of an attractive artiste.[6] Even the law, which was
probably extorted by the energy of S. Ambrose in 380,
provides that actresses, who have not professed Christianity,

---

[1] *C. Th.* xv. 7, 4 ; *v.* Godefroy's
Paratitlon and notes ; cf. Wallon,
L'Esclavage, iii.

[2] See Godefroy's note to *C. Th.*
xv. 7, 4.

[3] Salv. *de Gub. Dei,* vi. § 69.

[4] *C. Th.* xv. 7, 13.

[5] *Ib.* xv. 7, 1.

[6] See Godefroy's note, t. v. p. 412.

shall have no release. And the law of 381 commands that if an actress, by professing Christianity, has secured her emancipation, but has relapsed into vice, she shall be recalled to theatrical servitude for ever; and the cold, cruel, hardness of the language of this law shows an inhuman contempt for a class whom society doomed to vice, and punished for being vicious.[1] It would be amusing, if it were not painful, to notice the care with which the Emperor regulates the dress of actresses,[2] with but little care for their morals, unless they can steal into the Church by means of the sacraments. The Emperor's sense of dignity, or perhaps a lingering consciousness of divinity, causes him, in 394,[3] to banish all pictures of theatrical performers from the neighbourhood of his own "sacred" statues. But the theatre and the circus were too dear to the people to be crushed by any authority but the growing power of the Church. And even the Church found it a hard task to crush them. Salvianus is rhetorical and he has a *parti pris*. But on matters of notorious fact his testimony must be accepted. And he assures us that Christians were indulging in the madness of the circus and the wantonness of the theatre, when the arms of the Vandals were ringing round the walls of Carthage and Cirta; and that the applause of the spectators was mingled with the groans of the dying and the battle-cries of the besiegers.[4]

---

[1] *C. Th.* xv. 7, 4, given at Milan; see Godefroy's note. *Ib.* xv. 7, 8, detracta in pulpitum sine spe absolutionis ullius ibi eousque permaneat donec anus ridicula, senectute deformis, nec tunc quidem absolutione potiatur, cum aliud quam casta esse non possit; cf. Rauschen, *Jahrbücher der Christ. Kirche*, pp. 68, 91.

[2] *C. Th.* xv. 7, 11, his quoque vestibus noverint abstinendum quas Graeco nomine a Latino Crustas vocant, etc.; cf. xv. 7, 12, his illud adjicimus ut mimae publico habitu earum virginum quae Deo dicatae sunt non utantur.

[3] *Ib.* xv. 7, 12.

[4] *De Gub. Dei*, vi. §§ 69, 71, fragor, ut ita dixerim, extra muros et intra muros praeliorum et ludicrorum, confundebatur vox morientium voxque bacchantium . . .

CHAPTER III

HITHERTO we have been occupied with the efforts of legislation, often baffled for more than a hundred years, to suppress the open practice of heathen rites. Persecution of any opinion or religious practice, however false, by sheer force, is not a pleasant subject of contemplation to the modern mind. And it is with a feeling of relief that we turn from the threats of exile and death in the anti-pagan laws, to the more potent efforts of Christian dialectic to conquer the ingrained moral and intellectual habits of so many generations of pagan devotion. We may think that in this controversy rhetoric sometimes does duty for logic, that the reasoning is often sophistical, that the facts of history are coloured and perverted to serve a controversial purpose. Yet it is a great advance in a religious struggle, when the appeal is to reason rather than to mere force; and we may well believe that the *City of God*, and even the treatise of Orosius, had an influence on many pagans who were obdurate in the face of threatening edicts. The Emperor might compel a perfunctory conformity to the will of the State; S. Augustine probably won many a wavering, restless spirit to the ideals of the Church which was to dominate the future.

The capture of Rome by Alaric produced a profound effect on the minds both of Christian and pagan.[1]

---

[1] For its effect on Christians see S. Jerome's *Ep.* 126, § 2, Ezechielis   volumen olim aggredi volui . . . sed in ipso dictandi exordio ita

Following so soon upon the confiscation of the temples and sacred revenues by Honorius, it gave fresh poignancy to the feelings of numbers who were still attached to the old faith, who had suffered in fortune by the invasion, and many of whom had fled into remote exile.[1] The bitterness of the religious conflict was intensified, and the causes of the unexampled catastrophe became the subject of the last great controversy between the opposing creeds. From the time of M. Aurelius, the pagan controversialists were in the habit of attributing public calamities to apostasy from the national faith.[2] On the occurrence of a famine or pestilence, the mob broke into threats and execrations against the Christians. The war of sophistry had gone on, with ever varying subtlety, according to the fortunes of the Empire at the time. The true Roman was inclined to judge a religion by its material results.[3] His gods were expected to be of use to their worshipper, who purchased their help and favour by sacrificial gift and observance. He could not understand the Christian theory,[4] that calamity might be sent by Heaven for the good of the sufferer. Hence, he naturally attributed the growing troubles of the Empire to neglect of the ancient rites; and, when the last unimaginable horror came,—the sack of the city, which he fondly believed to be destined to endless dominion, the votary of the old gods found an irresistible argument against the pestilent superstition which had first suppressed his worship, and so soon afterwards had, by its impiety, brought the imperial city to the dust.

It is perhaps difficult for us to conceive the impression

animus meus occidentalium provinciarum, et maxime urbis Romae vastatione confusus est, ut, juxta vulgare proverbium, proprium quoque ignorarem vocabulum: diuque tacui, sciens esse tempus lacrimarum.

[1] Hieron. *Ep.* 128, § 4, proh nefas,

orbis terrarum ruit. . . . Urbs inclyta et Romani imperii caput uno hausta est incendio. Nulla est regio quae non exules Romanos habeat.

[2] Tertull. *Apol.* 40.
[3] Zos. iv. 59 ; Sym. *Rel.* 3.
[4] *De Civ. Dei*, i. 8.

which the capture of Rome made on both the heathen
and the Christian world.   Even the rude barbarian,
bred on the Danube or amid the forests of Thuringia, felt
a strange awe of that city, so distant, yet so omnipresent
in its power, which to his imagination, in her world-wide
dominion and marvellous vitality, was a superhuman
force.   We know how Alaric, while he felt himself
drawn on by an irresistible spell to sack the Eternal
City, still almost trembled at the prospect of success,[1]
and how, as he drew near Rome, his Goths were scattered
in panic by the lightnings that shot round the walls of
Narnia.[2]   The barbarian was impressed chiefly by the
power of Rome in imposing her laws on the world.   But
to the Roman, whether Christian or pagan, she was also
the heir of Greece, the seat of culture and letters, of all
humanising influences for more than five centuries.   She
was to Prudentius and Orosius, as well as to Claudian
and Rutilius, the beneficent power which had been the
mother of peaceful arts, which had made of so many
warring races one country, which had spread peace and
order wherever her eagles flew.[3]   And the belief in her
eternity had become an unquestioned article of faith.
The uniformity of law, language, and administration,
which spread with such quiet power over all geographical
barriers, seemed to have become part of the order of
nature, as irresistible and as enduring as the laws of the
material world.

To the minds therefore both of Christian and pagan,
the news of the capture of Rome by Alaric came as a
great moral shock.   In the sack of the city Christians
had fared no better than unbelievers.[4]   Their houses had

[1] Sozom. ix. 6 ; Socr. vii. 10 ; cf.
Claud. *de B. Get.* 507.
[2] Zos. v. 41.
[3] Prudent. *contra Sym.* ii. 640 ;
Oros. v. 2, 1 ; Claud. *de Cons.
Stilich.* iii. 154 ; Rutil. Namat. i.

63, 83, 133 ; cf. S. Jerome's outburst on hearing of the capture of
Rome, *Ep.* 127, § 12, capitur urbs
quae totum cepit orbem ; cf. Friedländer, ii. p. 4.
[4] *De Civ. Dei*, i. 9.

been burnt or pillaged, their daughters violated;[1] many of the churches had been despoiled of their sacred treasures.[2] The faith of many Christians was rudely shaken. But far more crushing was the effect of the calamity on those to whom Rome was the hearth of the old religion, attachment to which was identified with patriotism. They had again and again warned the Emperor of the danger of forsaking the gods under whose protection Rome had enjoyed such long prosperity. Now their fears and warnings had been terribly confirmed. "Rome had perished in the Christian times." The State had forfeited the protection of the gods, or was suffering from their anger. The cultivated epicurean, who had little sympathy with either pagan or Christian enthusiasm, contributed his doubts to the cause of the ancient religion. If he believed in any gods at all, he did not believe that they interfered in the affairs of men. But as a patriotic Roman, he may have thought the new spirit of Christian renunciation, which made men indifferent to the earthly commonwealth, and in a world of fierce passions and wild forces acted up to the ideal of the Sermon on the Mount, was responsible for the national humiliation.[3]

The province of Africa was still, in spite of its long Christian tradition, a stronghold of heathen superstition[4] or cultivated scepticism,[5] which not all the eloquence and energy of S. Augustine,[6] backed by the persecuting force of the State, had been able to overpower. The invasion of Alaric and the capture of the city drove crowds of the Roman aristocracy to seek a refuge in the towns of Africa.[7] It may readily be imagined how,

[1] *De Civ. Dei*, i. 16.
[2] As to the precise amount of damage done see Gregorovius, *Rome in the Middle Ages*, i. 159.
[3] Cf. the letter of Marcellinus to S. Augustine, *Ep.* 136, § 2.
[4] Aug. *Ep.* 232 ; cf. *C. Th.* xvi. 10, 20.

[5] Aug. *Ep.* 16, 234.
[6] *Ib.* 97 ; cf. *Ep.* 93 ; note 1, p. 43 of this book.
[7] See the description of the way in which they were received by Count Heraclian in Hieron. *Ep.* 130, § 7.

when they arrived with their excited tales of the desecration of the imperial city by the Goths, grief and indignation broke forth, how old hatred, terrified into silence,
would be kindled once more, how sceptical acquiescence
in the new *régime* would have its old doubts revived.
Volusianus, one of the great family of the Albini,[1] a son
of that old heathen pontiff described by S. Jerome, and
himself a pagan of the gentler sort, was in 412 in a
company in which the discords of philosophy and the
claims of Christianity were canvassed.   In particular
Volusianus proposed the question,[2] whether the precept
about turning the other cheek to the smiter could be
reconciled with the policy of a dominant state, whether,
in fact, Christianity was not the cause of the decadence
of Rome.   The discussion was reported to S. Augustine
by Marcellinus, a friend of Volusianus, and drew from
the bishop an elaborate reply.[3]   The letter in which
Augustine strove to remove the doubts of Volusianus and
his friends has a great interest as containing the germ of
the famous work which Augustine commenced in the
following year.[4]   The Gospel, he says in effect, is not
opposed to war waged justly and mercifully.   So far
from its doctrines being hostile to the stability of the
State, if they were practised by public servants and
citizens of every degree, they would prove the salvation
of the State.   The decay of the Roman commonwealth
began long before the coming of Christ in the decay of
the old Roman morality, in the spread of venality and
licence, which are described in scathing terms by heathen
moralists and satirists.[5]   Whither, he asks, might not
this tide of human depravity have borne us if there had
not been planted above it all the Cross, by clinging to

---

[1] Seeck's *Sym.* clxxix. ; Hieron.
Ep. 107, § 1.
[2] Aug. *Ep.* 136, § 2.
[3] *Ib.* 138, § 16.
[4] Ebert, *Lit. des Mittelalters*, i.
223. Its composition occupied the
years 413-426 ; cf. Aug. *Retract.* ii.
43, 1.
[5] He quotes Sall. *B. Jug.* c. 35,
O urbem venalem, etc.

which we might save ourselves from being swept into the abyss ?   In this morass of vice, this decay of the ancient discipline, there was need for authority from on high to bring home the lesson of voluntary poverty, chastity, benevolence, justice, concord, real piety, all the brightness and strength of virtue ; and that not merely for the virtuous conduct of this life, nor to secure complete harmony in the earthly commonwealth, but also to obtain eternal salvation and admission to a celestial commonwealth which shall know no end, to whose citizenship we are joined by faith, hope, and charity. So, as long as we are strangers and sojourners, we must endure, if we cannot amend, those who wish to establish the State on the foundation of an impunity of vice; whereas the early Romans founded and gave it greatness by their virtues.   They did not indeed possess a knowledge of the true God, to guide them to the Eternal City. Yet did they hold fast to a certain inbred probity, which might suffice to establish the earthly city, and give it glory and safety.   God thus desired to show in the wealthy and glorious empire of Rome how much availed the civic virtues, even without true religion, in order to make men understand that, when that was added, men might become citizens of another state, of which the king is truth, the law is love, and eternity the bourn.

The *City of God* dedicated to Marcellinus, was begun in 413, and not finished till 426,[1] four years before the author's death.   It has some of the faults which we might expect from what S. Augustine tells us of the distractions of his daily life;[2] but its vastness of range and conception gives us the measure, not only of the writer's genius, but of the force of the enemy to be overthrown.   All that wealth of learning and subtlety of

---

[1] *Retract.* ii. 43.

[2] *l.c.* quod opus per aliquot annos me tenuit, eo quod alia multa intercurrebant, quae differre non oportet et me prius ad solvendum occupabant ; cf. Possid. *vit. Aug.* c. 19, and *Serm.* 302, quoted in Hurter's ed.

disquisition would not have been wasted by a busy and
practical man in trampling out the embers of an exploded
superstition.   So far as the work is polemical, it is an
assault, in the first place, upon the political view of the
Roman religion, and, in the next, on the philosophical
attempt to rehabilitate it.   The circumstances which
suggested the work are described in its opening pages,
from which we can easily revive the debates which the
humiliation of the great city excited.   The fall of Rome,
exclaims S. Augustine, due to Christianity ?   Why, the
conqueror was a Christian, and respected the altars of
the Christian basilicas;[1] whereas your great poet describes Priam slaughtered at the shrine, which could not
protect him.[2]   Why have the Christians suffered as well
as the pagans, do you ask ?[3]   Because suffering is a
different thing to a Christian and a pagan.[4]   To the one
it is grievous, to the other it may be joyous, a chastisement for his good.   The history of Rome is full of crimes
and calamities which the gods have either caused or
permitted.   How have the old gods guarded Rome ?[5]
Do the memories of the Caudine Forks and Cannae, and
many another day of calamity and despair, suggest no
doubts about their power or will to guard her ?   The
truth is that the old religion did not give real prosperity,[6]
for it contained elements which were fatal to character
and happiness.   And conquest, unsupported by justice,
may be only brigandage on a large scale.[7]   Yet here S.
Augustine seems guilty of a patriotic inconsistency.   He
is, after all, a true Roman at heart.   He is proud of the
great past of Rome, and of the qualities which had given
her her place in the world.[8]   God made choice of the

[1] *De Civ. Dei*, i. 1 ; cf. Oros. vii.
39.
[2] *Ib*. i. 2.
[3] *Ib*. i. 9.
[4] *Ib*. i. 10.
[5] *Ib*. iii. 17.
[6] *Ib*. iv. 26.

[7] *Ib*. iv. 4, remota itaque justitia
quid sunt regna nisi magna latro-
cinia ? cf. iv. 3, 15 ; iii. 10 ; cf.
Oros. v. 1, 4.
[8] *Ib*. v. 15, his omnibus artibus
tamquam vera via nisi sunt ad
honores imperium gloriam . . .

Latin race to establish an empire which should weld the
nations of the world into one people. The Latin race
chose honour and dominion for its portion, and they had
the reward which their purely civic virtue deserved.
But the heathen daemons had never brought good to
Rome, as they had never warded off evil from her.
They aided the cruel Marius to reach a seventh consulship;[1] they allowed the pious Regulus to be put to the
extremity of torture.[2]   If they did not save the city
from being taken by the Gauls,[3] when Roman virtue was
at its highest point, why should we fancy that the
neglect of their rites has caused the capture by the
Goths ?   And yet S. Augustine attributes to these
daemons vast powers for evil, while he will not allow
them any power for good. They promised success to
Sulla,[4] but they never, with their powers of prevision,
tried to avert his crimes. Their power or example
corrupted the ancient virtue of the Roman people by
legends,[5] which were lessons in cruelty and lust. Their
worship has created the horrors of the amphitheatre and
the stage.[6]   In their name the empire of Rome has been
swelled to an unwieldy bulk by incessant wars. During
the centuries from the peaceful reign of Numa to the
accession of Augustus, a single year in which the gates
of war were closed is noted as a miraculous event.[7]

While Augustine was engaged in preparing this final
assault on paganism, his fifth book being completed,[8] a
young Spanish priest arrived at Hippo about 414. His
native country was being devastated by the Sueves and

imperii sui leges imposuerunt multis
gentibus . . . Perceperunt mer-
cedem suam ; cf. v. 21.

[1] *De Civ. Dei*, ii. 23.

[2] *Ib* i. 15.

[3] *Ib*. ii. 22, sed tamen haec numi-
num turba ubi erat, cum, longe
antequam mores corrumperentur

antiqui, a Gallis Roma capta et
incensa est ?

[4] *Ib*. ii. 24.

[5] *Ib*. ii. 6 ; cf. iv. 27, prava
docent, turpibus gaudent.

[6] *Ib*. ii. 25 ; cf. ix. 6, ix. 3.

[7] *Ib*. iii. 9.

[8] *Ep*. 169, § 13 ; cf. § 1 of the
same letter, and *Ep*. 166, § 2.

Vandals.[1] He escaped from their snares or violence, and
sought a refuge in Africa, which as yet was considered
safe from the invaders. S. Augustine was struck with
his zeal, readiness, and enthusiasm, and determined to
engage him in a historical composition which should
serve as a kind of supplement to the *City of God*. The
task which was assigned to Orosius was to refute, by an
examination of history, the pagan assertion that the fall
of Rome was a consequence of her abandonment of her
old religion.[2] Rome has been taken by a barbarian chief,
said the pagans; her prosperity has for the first time met
with a disastrous check. Under her old gods she had an
unbroken career of success, resulting in the establishment
of equal laws, and a serene and bountiful civilisation
among scores of peoples who in former ages were degraded
and desolated by continual feuds. It is only a few years
since the religion of the Nazarene was made binding on
all Romans; and within fifteen years from the death of
Theodosius, the destroyer of the ancient faith, the hitherto
inviolate seat of Roman government has been desecrated.
" Rome has perished in the Christian times."

The work of Orosius had a great popularity in the
Middle Ages,[3] and from some modern critics it has received
too flattering notice as the first attempt to found a philosophy of history. This description of it can only be
accepted, if by the words " philosophy of history " is
meant an arbitrary and uncritical handling of the facts to
suit an *a priori* theory, or a temporary theological purpose. Orosius himself would hardly have claimed for
his work any such character. His researches were not
very profound. His authorities are probably limited to
the Bible, Livy, Tacitus, Suetonius, Justin, Eutropius, and

[1] Idat. *Chron.* ad a. 410, debacchantibus per Hispanias barbaris,
etc. ; Oros, iii. 20, 5, 6.
[2] See the Prol. of Orosius.

[3] King Alfred had Orosius translated into Anglo-Saxon. The MSS.
from the seventh century are numerous, *v.* Teuffel, ii. p. 475.

perhaps S. Jerome's version of Eusebius's Chronicle.[1] He
was not writing for a remote generation, with a theory of
human evolution which would stand the test of scientific
criticism. He was a man of his own age, thoroughly
convinced of his thesis before his researches began,
thoroughly practical, and not over-scrupulous. He cares
nothing for the inner springs of historical movements, so
far as they are merely human. The chain of natural
causes has no interest for him. His eye is fixed on the
external fortunes and vicissitudes of the great races who
have occupied the stage of history. It is fixed also
rather on their calamities and reverses than on anything
which might mitigate the tale of "mourning, lamentation,
and woe," which has been the portion of the human race
before the coming of Christ. His business was to collect
in an ordered narrative from the annals of the past, before
the final triumph of the Cross, all the tales of misery
from war, famine, and pestilence that the human race had
suffered, all that was startling and desolating in floods
and volcanic fires, all the horrors of monstrous crime.
He is convinced that the carnage and ravages of war, the
stress of plague and dearth, the convulsions of nature,
were more tremendous in the pagan times.[2] Nature herself, like the temper of the Goths,[3] has grown milder with
the advent of a purer faith among men! In the process
of proving his thesis, Orosius treats mere legend with the
same respect as authentic history. The exploits of the
Amazons [4] are as useful for his purpose as the invasion
of the Gauls of Brennus. In the long catalogue of
deadly wars he magnifies the numbers of the slain, and
seems almost to exult in the carnage of pre-Christian

---

[1] He mentions other writers, but
probably only at second hand. He
knew little of Greek authorities :
cf. Mörner, *de Oros. vita*, p. 50, and
Peter's *Die Geschichtliche Litt. über
die Röm. Kaiserzeit*, ii. 158, 255.

[2] Oros. iv. *Praef.* The world in
414 is as it were only nocturnis puli-
cibus titillatus !

[3] *Ib.* ii. 14, 3 ; ii. 19.

[4] *Ib.* i. 15, 4.

battlefields.   He has seldom a word to say of the objects
for which the victims fell.   The glories of peaceful times
have no interest for his determined, historical pessimism.
There is not a word of the splendour of the age of
Pericles.[1]   Demosthenes is only referred to as an orator
purchased by Persian gold.[2]   It is difficult to conceive
that such a collection of the gloomiest episodes in history
or myth, selected for a single controversial purpose which
is everywhere apparent, should have influenced any mind
in the learned and cultivated circle of the pagan friends
of Symmachus.

Orosius constantly complains of the double exaggeration by which the pagans magnified the prosperity and
glory of past ages, and the disasters of their own day.[3]
The charge is probably true.   The immediate effects of
the invasion may have easily been painted in too sombre
colours.   The capture of Rome so disordered men's
imaginations, and awoke such bitterness of party-feeling,
that a calm estimate of the facts was hardly possible.
Orosius, however, is guilty of the grossest exaggeration
on the other side.   In his retrospect he surveys the
history of the world from the creation, with a determination to see nothing that does not lend itself to his controversial purpose.   It is characteristic of the peculiar
method and fairness of this work that, in painting the
bloody wars of the regal period,[4] the name of Numa is
never mentioned.   The sack of the city by Brennus [5] was
far more terrible and destructive than her capture by
Alaric.   Hardly a Roman senator escaped the violence of
the Gauls.   Hardly one lost his life at the hands of the
Goths.[6]   In old times Sicily was constantly laid waste

---

[1] Pericles is mentioned once as
general, along with Sophocles, i. 21,
15 ; cf. a somewhat similar and
amusing reference to the great age
of Greece in Prosp. *Chron.*

[2] Oros. iii. 16, 1.

[3] *e.g.* i. 21, 17 ; iv. *Praef.*

[4] *Ib.* ii. 4 ; Mörn. p. 37.

[5] Oros, ii. 19.

[6] *Ib.* ii. 19, 13, ibi vix quemquam inventum Senatorem, qui vel
absens evaserit, hic vix quemquam

by the convulsions of nature and the ravages of war. In
the present quiet and prosperous times, even Etna, which
once spread ruin in field and city, sends up only a column
of harmless smoke to remind the world of its former
energy.[1]   Rome was founded in bloodshed, and her career
has corresponded to the omens of her birth.   There is
hardly a break in the monotonous tale of incessant wars,[2]
until the universal peace of the reign of Augustus was
given to the world by the coming of Christ.   In like
manner, the fall of Athens, the overthrow of Spartan
supremacy, the conquests of Philip and Alexander,[3] are
described with a determined exaggeration of the slaughter
and misery which they caused.   The absurdity, perhaps,
culminates, when Orosius inveighs against those who
complain that a cowardly brigand (it is thus that Alaric
is described) has outraged a single corner of a world
which is enjoying generally a secure tranquillity![4]   The
author occasionally shows some flashes of insight into the
position of Rome, and her relation to the barbarian races,
to which we shall refer in another chapter.   But as to
the main drift of his book it is difficult to acquit him of
a deliberate distortion of the facts of history.

These two works, of such unequal merit, are noticed
here chiefly for the purpose of showing the latent force
of the pagan sentiment which they were intended to
disarm and silence.   Both S. Augustine and Orosius are
fully conscious of the magnitude of their task, and of the
strength of the enemy.   It was not the ignorant superstition of the masses, blindly clinging to the religious usages
of their ancestors, which they set themselves chiefly to

require, qui forte ut latens perierit ;
cf. *de Civ. Dei*, iii. 29 ; Socr. *Hist.
Eccl.* vii. 10, says that many senators were tortured and slain.

[1] Oros. ii. 14, Aethna ipsa, quae
tunc cum excidio urbium atque
agrorum crebris eruptionibus aes-
tuabat, nunc tantum innoxia specie
ad praeteritorum fidem fumat !
[2] *Ib.* iii. 8.
[3] *Ib.* iii. 14 : ii. 16, 13 ; iii. 2, 10 ;
iii. 13, 11.
[4] *Ib.* iii. 20, 9, et nos perpetuae
recordationi haesurum putamus
quod plurima orbis parte secura
unum angulum fugax latro violavit.

discredit and overthrow.   The controversy began, as we
have seen, in a company of lettered men, whose smoulder-
ing doubts about the policy of the religious revolution of
Theodosius, flashed out and found expression on the
capture of Rome in 410.   Both works are addressed to
the educated class, who still clung to paganism, either as
the ancestral faith of Rome, under the protection of which
her great mission had been accomplished, or as enshrining
the venerable and imaginative symbols of the lofty and
comprehensive theory of God and the Universe, expounded
by the school of Alexandria.   The *City of God* assails the
paganism both of the patriot and the philosopher.   It is
addressed to a class capable of following the most subtle
reasoning, acquainted with the history and antiquities of
Rome, or saturated with the metaphysics of Plotinus and
Porphyry.   The treatise of Orosius is addressed only to
the anxious patriot, and it has none of the depth and
range and subtlety of S. Augustine's great work.   Yet
even Orosius could hardly have been read by any one
who had not been trained in the higher discipline of the
Roman schools.

From this point of view the controversy has a profound interest for the historian.   It is true that the voices
of the champions of paganism reach us only, as it were,
by echoes from the pages of their assailants.   Hardly a
word has come to us directly from that crowd of philosophic sceptics, conservative dreamers, or devotees, who
called forth the full strength of the great bishop of Hippo.
It is admitted that the *City of God* dealt a deathblow at
the cause of paganism, and, by its learning and dialectic,
completed the work of anti-pagan legislation.   Its occasional sophistry, which may irritate the modern reader,
would probably, in the heat of conflict, be as damaging
to the enemy as its sounder arguments.   If its appeals
to history to show the helplessness of the gods to protect
their worshippers from evil fortune often seem to us

unfair and weak, its exposure of the moral evil in the ancient cults is irresistible. The absence of the moral influence in paganism, and the corruption of Roman character by the games and festivals which were sanctioned or enjoined by the old faith, is S. Augustine's most powerful reply to the argument that Rome owed her material success to her gods. Julian saw the moral helplessness of the system, to which he gave a momentary and illusive revival in the years when S. Augustine was an infant. But Julian's life was short, and it may be doubted whether, if it had been longer, his efforts to effect a moral and philosophic renovation of paganism could have given real life to that which was rotten at the root.

Yet, when we look merely at the narrower issue, on which the momentous controversy began, there is a strange feeling of pathos in reading the often sophistical recriminations as to the supernatural causes of a world-wide convulsion. The ancient majesty of the imperial city had been violated, and the magic of that great name was vanishing amid agonies of regret. Some of the fairest provinces of the West had been occupied by the German invaders. Four years after the completion of S. Augustine's great work, the Vandals will have overrun Roman Africa, and the saint's last hours will be disturbed by the roar of battle under the walls of Hippo.[1] The mutual recriminations of Christian and pagan as to the religious causes of the great catastrophe may to some seem small and frivolous, in comparison with the interests which were at stake; to others perhaps rather coarse and materialistic in their conception of the office and value of religion. We have been trained to seek for the causes of the fall of Rome in the exhaustion of the municipal class under fiscal burdens, in bad and cruel administration, in the decline of public spirit and courage. Some

[1] Possid. *vit. Aug.* c. 29.

historical critics, even those bred in the traditions of the
Catholic Church, are almost ready to take the pagan side
in the quarrel, and to find the causes of the collapse in
the ascetic spirit, which, by contemning wealth and
refusing to bear the burdens of civil society, undermined
its economic and political stability.[1] The controversial
part of the *City of God* will probably have the fate of all
polemics inspired by the needs or passions of the moment.
But its spiritual and constructive side, which lies beyond
the scope of this work, will be a permanent possession of
the race. It lifts the eye from the mundane level on
which the relative material advantages of opposing creeds
are balanced or fiercely contrasted. Eternity is not
promised by the Christian's God to anything earthly.
The spiritual city alone does not pass away. It has no
frontiers, it draws its citizens from all races and peoples,
it embraces all the faithful on either side of the river of
death. *Fundamenta ejus in montibus sanctis.*

[1] Renan, *Marc. Aurèle*, p. 603.

CHAPTER IV

SOME CAUSES OF THE VITALITY OF THE LATER PAGANISM

THE dialectic of S. Augustine is regarded as having completed the overthrow of the pagan cause. Yet his assaults are directed against the old State religion of Rome, rather than against those cults of Egypt and Syria [1] which had, for more than two centuries, practically overshadowed the religion of Numa.[2] From a controversial point of view S. Augustine was right. Although the native gods of Latium no longer inspired much devotion, they were the recognised protectors of the old Roman state. Their cults were intertwined with the whole fabric of public and private life. Even the Christian emperors, till the time of Gratian, assumed the office of Pontifex Maximus. The old sacred colleges still met for ceremonial functions in the reign of Theodosius.[3] The festival of the Lupercalia, which was traced back to the Arcadian Evander, was, with all its coarse and savage ritual, celebrated down to the last years of the fifth century.[4]

In the fourth century the ancient religion of Latium, while revered and defended as the symbol of national greatness by the conservative patriot, supplied little nutri-

---

[1] He refers, however, to the cult of Mater Deum, i. c. 5.
[2] But the old rites and festivals, e.g. the Lupercalia and Ambarvalia, were sedulously kept up ; cf. Réville, *Rel. unter den Sev.* p. 26.

[3] Sym. *Ep.* i. 51.
[4] Gibbon, c. 36. Cf. Virg. *Aen.* viii. 343. It was revived by Augustus (Suet. *Octav.* c. 31). Luperci are found in Inscriptions of Mauretania, *C.I.L.* viii. 9405, 9406.

ment for the devotional cravings of the age. The old
Roman theology was a hard, narrow, unexpansive system
of abstraction and personification, which strove to represent in its Pantheon the phenomena of nature, the relations
of men in the state or the clan, every act and feeling and
incident in the life of the individual. But, unlike the
mythologies of Hellas and the East, it had no native
principle of growth or adaptation to altered needs of
society and the individual imagination. It was also
singularly wanting in awe and mystery. The religious
spirit which it cultivated was formal, timid, and scrupulous.[1] It was bound up with the everyday business and
practical life of society. Its sacred colleges were not,
except in the case of the vestals, set apart from the
world; they were simply a kind of magistracy for the
exact performance of certain sacred rites and functions.
When the ceremony was over, the celebrant returned to
ordinary civic life. The old Roman worship was business-
like and utilitarian.[2] The gods were partners in a contract
with their worshippers, and the ritual was characterised
by all the hard and literal formalism of the legal system
of Rome. The worshipper performed his part to the
letter with the scrupulous exactness required in plead-
ings before the praetor.[3] To allow devotional feeling to
transgress the bounds prescribed by immemorial custom
was "superstitio."[4] Such a religion was little calculated
to satisfy generations who had come under the spell of
Greek philosophy and the mysticism and ecstatic devotion
of the East.

The conservative and patriotic spirit which, as in the
case of Symmachus and Flavianus, clung to the old

[1] Boissier, *La Rel. Rom.* Introd.
c. 2 ; Preller, *Mythol. Rom.* (Dietz),
Introd. i.

[2] Boissier, *Rel. Rom.* i. pp. 21,
22 ; Mommsen, *Rom. Hist.* i. 182 ;
cf. Cicero's definition of pietas (*de*

Nat. Deor. i. 41), as justitia adversum deos.

[3] Preller, p. 102 ; Boissier i. 14
sqq.

[4] Boissier, i. p. 23.

national faith, as inseparable from the safety and dignity
of Rome, was undoubtedly a serious obstacle to the final
triumph of Christianity.   But he would ill interpret the
religious history of the time who should confine his
attention to the official paganism.   The paganism which
was really living, which stirred devotion and influenced
souls, was that neither of Latium nor of Hellas.   It came
from the East—from Persia, Syria, Egypt—the homes of
a conception of religion which was alien to the native
spirit both of Greece and Rome.[1]   These Oriental cults
satisfied emotional cravings, which found no stimulus for
devotion in the arid abstractions of the old Latin creed,
or in the brilliant anthropomorphism of Greece.   They
aroused and cultivated, often to a dangerous degree,
intense and ecstatic feeling.   In their mysteries, if they
did not teach a higher morality, they raised the worshipper
above the level of cold, conventional conformity, and
satisfied in some way the longing for communion with
the deity, and assurance of a life beyond the grave.
They had their modes of appeasing the troubled conscience
by expiation, by ascetic abstinence, by the baptism of
blood.   In the sacred corporations,[2] such as the Isiaci
and Pastophori, they provided, what was the great want
of the times, social help and mutual encouragement, the
stimulus or the consolation of common interests and
enthusiasms.   Whoever will cast his eyes over the inscriptions of the closing years of the fourth century will
be struck by the number of dedications to deities of foreign
origin—to Isis, the Sun, Magna Mater, and Attis, above
all, to Mithra.   He will find on these tablets some
of the greatest names among the Roman aristocracy,
a Clodius Hermogenianus,[3] a Flavianus,[4] a Venustus,[5]

---

[1] Boissier, *Rel. Rom.* i. pp. 396
sqq. ; Réville, *Rel. zu Rom. unter
den Sev.* c. ii. ; Duruy, *Hist. Rom.*
v. 739 ; Friedländer, iii. p. 444.

[2] Renan, *M. Aurèle*, p. 577 ;

Boissier, i. 417.

[3] *C.I.L.* vi. 499, *a.p.C.* 374.

[4] *Ib.* vi. 501, *a.p.C.* 383.

[5] *Ib.* vi. 503, *a.p.C.* 390.

a Volusianus,[1] a Vettius Agorius Praetextatus.   If he
looks into the inscriptions of the provinces, he will discover that these worships have been carried by Roman
travellers or soldiers to Gaul,[2] Spain, Britain, to remote
camps on the edge of the African desert, or on the Rhine
and the Danube.   He will notice on many of these
monuments that the person commemorated has held
sacred office in a great number of these cults, that he has
been priest of Mithra the unconquered, priest of the Sun,
priest of Isis, and that he has performed the Taurobolium.[3]
He will observe with interest that there is a tone of
moral and devout feeling which he had not expected to
find in a pagan epitaph.   The famous monument erected
by Fabia Aconia Paulina to her husband Praetextatus,[4]
after recording his many secular and sacred honours, and
celebrating his birth, learning, and culture, speaks of his
contempt for these transient distinctions, and the hope
of a blessed reunion after death.   And Paulina is fervent
in her gratitude for the love and confidence with which
her husband has made her a partner in all sacred things.
Praetextatus, in a companion inscription, commemorates
his wife as the sharer of his inmost secrets, devoted to
the temple service, a friend of the gods, pure in mind and
body, benevolent to all.

These cults, which were the vital centre of the last
generation of paganism in the West, had found their way
to Rome long before the imperial period.   The Eastern
conquests of the Republic made the maintenance of old
Roman exclusiveness impossible.   In a city which was
the meeting-place of so many races, it was hopeless for

---

[1] *C.I.L.* vi. 512, *a.p.C.* 390 ; cf.
ib. 736, 755.

[2] *Ib.* xii. 405, 1311 (Mater deum),
xii. 2706, 1535 (Mithra), xii. 734,
1562 (Isis).   The Taurobolium
appears in an immense number of
Gallic inscriptions in *C.I.L.* xii. ;
cf. Renan, *M. Aurèle*, p. 579.   See

the provincial inscriptions to Mithra
collected in Cumont's *Monuments
figurés relatifs aux Mystères de
Mithra*, i. pp. 129-171.

[3] Cf. several of the Inscr. referred
to, and particularly *C.I.L.* vi. 504.

[4] *C.I.L.* vi. 1778-79.

the most vigilant conservatism,[1] however much inspired
with a suspicion of exotic modes of devotion, finally to
shut them out. The attempt was made again and again,
and as often defeated. Foreign traders, foreign slaves,
travellers, and soldiers returning from long campaigns
in distant regions, were constantly introducing religious
novelties which fascinated the lower class, always the
most susceptible of religious excitement, and then penetrated to the classes of culture and privilege. The Great
Mother of Pessinus found a home at Rome in the second
Punic war.[2] The Pastophori of Serapis were established
as early as the days of Sulla.[3] After repeated attempts
on the part of the government to exclude Egyptian
worships,[4] the triumvirs, in 42 B.C., founded a temple of
Isis and Serapis in the Campus Martius.[5] The worship
of Mithra, the solar cult which was destined to be the
most formidable rival of Christianity in its last struggle
with heathenism, was introduced in 70 B.C. after the
overthrow of the Cilician pirates by Pompey.[6] Under
the Flavian dynasty the religions of the East had special
prominence.[7] But the Eastern cults had their great
triumph in the age of the Antonines, and under the
Oriental princes of the third century. A considerable
number of dedications to Sol Invictus, Serapis, and
Mithra belong to the reigns of M. Aurelius and Commodus.[8] Antoninus Pius erected a temple to Mithra at
Ostia;[9] and Commodus had a fancy to be initiated in
the Isiac mysteries, and actually took the tonsure of that

---

[1] Boissier, *La Rel. Rom.* i. p.
384.

[2] Liv. xxix. 10.

[3] Preller, p. 479.

[4] *Ib.* p. 479. Cf. the picture of
the Egyptian gods arrayed against
the Roman at Actium, Virg. *Aen.*
viii. 698:

omnigenûmque deûm monstra et latrator
　　Anubis, etc.

[5] Dion Cass. xlvii. 15.

[6] Plut. *Pomp.* c. 24, ὧν ἡ τοῦ
Μίθρου καὶ μέχρι δεῦρο διασώζεται
καταδειχθεῖσα πρῶτον ὑπ' ἐκείνων
(*i.e.* τῶν πειρατῶν).

[7] Suet. *Vesp.* c. 7.

[8] Cf. *C.I.L.* vi. 723-727, 740,
746, 354, viii. 2630.

[9] Réville, p. 81.

worship.[1] Caracalla and Alexander Severus both added
to the splendour of the temple service of Isis.[2] Aurelian,
whose mother was a priestess of the Sun, attributed his
victory over Zenobia to the god's favour, and built a
stately temple for him at Rome, enriched with the spoils
of Palmyra.[3]

The Egyptian cults, and pre-eminently that of Isis,
had an immense influence on the Roman mind during
the whole imperial period. Isis was a deity with many
functions and many attractions.[4] She was the goddess
of the springtime and of the fruitfulness of nature. She
was the guardian of those whose life is on the sea. She
had a special care of women in the troubles of mother-
hood. She lighted souls into the world beyond death.
The ceremonies of her worship, which in many respects
show a singular rapprochement to those of the Catholic
Church, had a powerful effect on the imagination and the
feelings. There is a sacerdotal class set apart for spiritual
functions and the guidance of souls, and distinguished by
the tonsure and a peculiar dress.[5] There are baptismal
rites of initiation, for which ascetic abstinence is a
necessary preparation. In Egypt, on the very ground
which in the fourth and fifth centuries was to be the
home of Christian monks, there was long before them the
ascetic life of the cloister devoted to the worship of
Serapis.[6] The ritual has many traces of our modern
ideas of devotion, and foreshadows in some respects that

---

[1] Lamprid. *Com.* c. 9, sacra
Isidis coluit ut et caput raderet et
Anubin portaret.

[2] Id. *A. Sev.* c. 26 ; Ael. Spart.
Carac. c. 9.

[3] Flav. Vop. *Aur.* c. 4, 31, 39 ;
Zos. i. 61.

[4] Preller, p. 477 ; Réville, *Rel.
unter den Sev.* p. 53.

[5] Apul. *Met.* xi. c. 10, antistites
sacrorum . . . candido linteamine

cinctum pectoralem adusque vestigia strictim injecti . . . capillum
derasi funditus, vertice praenitentes.
Cf. Plut. *de Is. et Osir.* 4 ἐφ' ὅτῳ
τὰς τρίχας οἱ ἱερεῖς ἀποτίθενται καὶ
λινᾶς ἐσθῆτας φοροῦσιν.

[6] Chaeremon, quoted by Porphyr.
de Abstin. (*Frag. Hist. Gr.* iii. p.
497), ἀπέδοσαν ὅλον τὸν βίον τῇ τῶν
θείων θεωρίᾳ καὶ θεάσει . . . λιτότητα
δὲ ἐπετήδευσαν καὶ καταστολήν,
ἐγκράτειάν τε καὶ καρτερίαν.

of the Catholic Church. There are matins and vespers
to rouse the goddess or to lay her to rest, at which white-
robed priests officiate.[1] Women receive a prominence
which was denied them under the old religion, and their
devotion to the ritual of Syria and Egypt was a social
characteristic of the early Empire [2] as it was of the closing
years of paganism in the West.[3] There was indeed much
in these cults calculated to have a special charm for
female sensibility. It is a common characteristic of some
of the most popular of them that the interest centres on
a divine death and resurrection. There is the alterna-
tion of the passionate sense of loss with the passionate
joy of recovery, and the emotions, as in the mysteries of
an earlier time, were probably stimulated by striking
scenic effects. The cold, calm, rigidly formal religion of
old Rome has given place to ecstatic devotion, and the
sense of sin and error finds relief in penitential discipline
and solemn cleansing.

In the last struggles of paganism with the Christian
Church, the cult which exercised the most powerful
attraction was that of Mithra.[4] It gave expression to
the growing tendency to monotheism,[5] and to the craving
for moral support, purification, and comfort through
religion, which became more and more imperious in the
third and fourth centuries. It was at first a sun-worship
of Persian origin. But its early character was greatly
altered by syncretism, by accretions from other, especially
Phrygian, worships, and by natural development to meet
the devotional and moral wants of the times. The

---

[1] Apul. *Met.* xi. 20.

[2] Juv. vi. 489, 528 ; *C.I.L.* xii.
1532, 3061 (Narbonne), viii. 2630
(Numidia). Devotion to Isis in
the time of Catullus and Tibullus
seems to have been compatible with
very loose morals. Catull. x. 26 ;
Tibull. i. 3, 23. Cumont, i. 178,
denies that women were admitted
to the mysteries of Mithra.

[3] *C.I.L.* vi. 1779, 1780.

[4] Réville, *Rel. unter den Sev.* pp.
74 *sqq. ;* Preller, p. 490 ; Duruy,
vi. p. 146, vii. 48 ; Renan, *M.
Aurèle,* p. 576.

[5] See the centralisation of many
worships in the temple of the Sun
attempted by Elagabalus, Lamprid.
c. 3 ; cf. c. 7.

worship of the Sun was the central force in Julian's attempt to remedy the dogmatic and moral weakness of paganism.   In the fourth century the ancient god of light has become the supreme Power,[1] who is all-seeing, all-pervading, who is the lord and giver of life, the cleanser from sin, the protector of the miserable, the conqueror of evil daemons and death, who assures to his faithful worshippers the hope of immortality.   The monuments of Mithra have been found all over the Roman world,[2] in all the regions of Italy, in Spain, Africa, and all the provinces bordering on the Danube and the Rhine, in Gaul, and in Britain.   Nothing is more familiar than the group in which the young warrior, wearing a Phrygian cap and short tunic, and mantle blown back by the wind, kneels on the back of a bull and buries his poniard in its throat, surrounded by the mystic beasts and the two Dadophori.[3]   His worship was conducted in underground grottoes, brilliantly lighted and adorned with symbolic figures.   The symbolism of his ritual has exercised and puzzled the ingenuity of modern archaeologists.[4]   Probably it conveyed many meanings to the devotee; but the central idea in the end seems to have been that of a Power who conquers the spirits of darkness, leads souls from the underworld, and gives peace by purification.   The ritual was complicated and impressive.   There was a kind of baptism of neophytes, confirmation, consecration of bread and water, cleansing of the tongue with honey, and other ablutions.   The great festival of the god was celebrated

---

[1] Réville, p. 88 ; Cumont, *Monuments figurés, etc. de Mithra*, Textes Orientaux, i. pp. 1-6. Cf. Porphyr. quoted *ib*. pp. 39, 40, 41. In his interesting book on *Neoplatonism*, p. 56, Dr. Bigg says that the religion of Mithra was " the purest and most elevated of all non-Biblical religions."

[2] Preller, p. 496 ; *C.I.L.* viii.

8440 (Sitifis in Mauretania), 9256, xii. 1535 (Gallia Narb.) 2706, v. 807, 809 (Aquileia), 4283.   Cf. Cumont, i. pp. 87-171.

[3] See the representation of the Vatican group in Duruy, v. p. 748 ; cf. Cumont, ii. iii. passim.

[4] Réville, pp. 89, 90-94 ; cf. the materials accumulated in Cumont, ii. and iii.

on the 25th of December.[1] His mysteries created a
powerful bond of union, and in this respect satisfied one
of the most urgent needs of society under the later
Empire. The initiated formed a close guild or corporation presenting many points of resemblance to Freemasonry.[2] The novice had to submit to a series of
severe ordeals and ascetic exercises, prolonged fasting,
flagellation, passing through water and flame. There
were many degrees of initiation bearing fantastic titles,[3]
and culminating in the dignity which bore the title of
Pater. Whatever the real moral effect of initiation may
have been, there can be no doubt that it developed a
warm devotion and faith in that future life which it
promised to the pure worshipper.

The most impressive rite in Mithra-worship was the
baptism of blood, called the Taurobolium. This ceremony
was apparently a sacramental repetition of the symbolic
slaughter of the bull by the god himself. It was
originally part of the Phrygian ritual of the Great
Mother, and is connected with her name on many
monuments;[4] but, after the religious fashion of the
times, it had been absorbed by the cult of the Sun. The
earliest trace of the Taurobolium in the West is found
on a Neapolitan monument of the last years of Hadrian's
reign.[5] It spread far and wide through the provinces,
and traces of it are found near Lyons as early as
184 A.D.[6] The ceremonial has been described in a well-

---

[1] Réville. p. 95. But cf. Cumont,
i. p. 68 n.

[2] Preller, p. 497 ; Réville, p. 97.
On the ordeals of initiation, see
Cumont, i. p. 27.

[3] Hieron. *Ep.* 107, § 2, 'ad
Laetam,' where the titles of them
are given, Corax, Gryphus, Miles,
Leo, Perses, Heliodromus, Pater ;
v. Cumont, i. 18, n. 1. See the
title Pater in 504, 1778 of *C.I.L.* vi.

[4] Réville, p. 66 ; *C.I.L.* vi. 505,
506, 508, iii. 5524, xii. 357, 1222,
4325.

[5] Boissier, *Rel. Rom.* i. p. 412.

[6] *C.I.L.* xii. 1782. This taurobolium lasted from the 20th to the
23rd of April. At Orange (in
Gallia Narbonensis) an inscription
was found commemorating a taurobolium pro salute Imp. M. Aurel.
Commodi, *C.I.L.* xii. 1222. A
taurobolium of 245 A.D. in Gall.
Narb. was performed for the imperial house on 30th Sept. xii. 1567 ;
cf. viii. 5524, 8263 (African Inscr.).

known passage of Prudentius,[1] and the inscriptions of his age frequently refer to it.[2]   The penitent was placed in a trench covered over with planks having apertures between them.   A bull was led on to this platform, and with due ceremonial,[3] conducted by the priests, was slaughtered so that the blood streaming from its throat might bathe the votary below.   It was esteemed a matter of great importance that not a drop should be wasted, and the subject of the rite used all his efforts to enjoy the full benefit of the sacred flood.   The ceremony was a long and costly one, attended by great crowds, with the magistrates at their head.   Its effects were supposed to last for twenty years, when it was often repeated.[4]   It was believed to work some sort of spiritual cleansing and reform, and the man who had enjoyed such a blessing left the record of it on stone, often concluding with the striking phrase, *in aeternum renatus.*[5]

This religion was the focus of the real devotion of the last age of paganism.   It was supported with defiant zeal by some of the greatest senatorial houses, and offered the most stubborn resistance to the anti-pagan laws.   The dedications to Mithra are most numerous [6] in the very years when the Christian Empire was destroying his grottoes.   M. Renan has declared his belief [7] that, if the growth of Christianity had been checked by some mortal weakness, Mithraism might have become the religion of the Western world.   With a true instinct, the Christian controversialists, from the second century, recognised in this cult the most dangerous spiritual foe

---

[1] Prud. *Peristeph.* x. 1011. See a sketch of the scene in Duruy, v. 743.

[2] *C.I.L.* vi. 499, 504, 509, 511.

[3] *Ib.* xii. 1782, 1567.

[4] *Ib.* vi. 512 (iterato viginti annis expletis), 502.

[5] *Ib.* vi. 510.

[6] *Ib.* vi. 751, 752, 753, 754, 1778, 510, 500, 504, 511. These inscr. belong to the years 376-387 ; cf. Hieron. *Ep.* 107, § 2, ante paucos annos propinquus vester Graccus cum praefecturam gereret urbanam nonne specum Mithrae . . . subvertit, fregit, excussit. This refers to the year 376.   But cf. note *g* in Migne's ed. col. 868.

[7] *M. Aurèle*, p. 579.

of the Church, and ascribed its similarity to Christian ritual to the malign ingenuity of daemcns.[1] In its expiation for sins by bloody baptism, its ascetic preparation for the holy mysteries, its oblation of the consecrated bread, its symbolic teaching of the resurrection, they might well see a cunning device of the Evil One to find a false resting-place for souls who were longing for the light.

Whether such worships as we have been describing aroused or satisfied a genuine devotional feeling in our modern sense, is a question which it is difficult to answer. But the thoughtful student will probably hesitate before he answers in the negative. The gulf which separates us from the world of heathen imagination is so wide, the influence of custom and old association in matters of religion is so powerful, that we may easily do injustice to the devout sentiment of paganism. Grotesque or barbarous religious symbols, even those tainted in their origin with the impurity attaching to nature-worship,[2] often sloughed off their baser elements, and, with the development of a more sensitive morality,[3] and a higher conception of the divine, may have become the vehicles of a real religious emotion. What the worshipper will find in a worship depends greatly on what he brings. The same symbol or rite will have various meanings and effects to different minds. To the mind to which it is strange, it may seem to have no meaning at all. The mystery of the death of a

---

[1] Prud. *Peristeph.* x. 1008 ; Tertull. *de Cor.* c. 15 ; *de Praescrip. Haeret.* 40, Mithra signat illic in frontibus milites suos ; celebrat et panis oblationem, et imaginem resurrectionis inducit, etc. ; S. Paulin. Nol. *Poem. Ult.* 112-117.

[2] The initiation of Commodus in the mysteries of Isis and Mithra, and the devotion of Elagabalus to sun-worship make one suspicious.

But there is a long interval between these monsters and the apparently blameless devotees of the reign of Gratian ; cf. Lamprid. *Com.* c. 9 ; *Elagab.* c. 3, and *C.I.L.* vi. 1778, 1779.

[3] Note the horror with which the infamies of Elagabalus were regarded by all classes, Lamprid. *El.* c. 17 ; cf. Boissier, *Rel. Rom.* ii. pp. 419 *sqq.;* Friedländer, iii. p. 611.

divine being, his descent to the underworld, and his joyful restoration, was the central idea of many of the cults which most influenced the religious feeling of antiquity. The ritual in which that feeling found expression would to us now appear perhaps shocking, perhaps grotesque and absurd. The drama of the Eleusinian goddesses, if we could witness it, would probably be a poor and tasteless show, with no spiritual contents.[1] Yet there is no doubt that it produced a profound effect on the devotee, and Pindar gave voice to the universal sentiment of Greece when he said,[2] " Happy he who has seen the spectacle : he knows the bourn of life, he knows its divine source." Even among those who hold the same central truths of the Christian faith, how hard it is for the member of one sect to join in the ritual of another. The Puritan, accustomed to express his devotion in bare and simple forms consecrated to him by the memories of early religious emotion, is unable to conceive the awe and tenderness which the Mass excites in the devout Catholic, who has witnessed its ceremonial from infancy.

It is fortunate that we have preserved to us in the pages of Apuleius an invaluable description of an initiation into the mysteries of Isis, which, though the scene is laid in the reign of Marcus Aurelius, was probably often reproduced in the closing years of paganism.

The people of Corinth are about to celebrate the spring festival of Isis, and the opening of the busy traffic on the Aegean, by a religious procession to the shore, and the offering of a consecrated vessel to the goddess who cares for the toilers of the sea. Lucius, who has been imprisoned by evil arts in the forms of an ass, is

---

[1] Maury, *Rel. de la Grèce*, ii. p. 340 ; Lob. *Aglaoph*, i. pp. 111, 112 ; Gard. and Jevons, *Greek Antiq.* p. 283.

[2] Pind. *Frag.* 137 (Christ) ; cf. Soph. *O.C.* 1051 ; *Frag.* 753 :
ὡς τρὶς ὄλβιοι
κεῖνοι βροτῶν οἳ ταῦτα δερχθέντες τέλη
μόλωσ' ἐς Ἄιδου.

awaked by a dazzling light, and in a fit of devotion cries to the Queen of Heaven, worshipped under many names, to deliver him from his cruel fate. In answer to his prayer, there rose from the moonlit sea a divine and awful form,[1] which no words could shadow forth. Her long rich tresses were crowned with flowers, and with a radiant moonlike disc upheld by arching snakes on either side. Her robe of glistening white now changed to saffron, now flushed into rose-like flame. Her mantle of deepest darkness was bordered with the bickering light of stars. " Lo, I come," the vision said, " in answer to thy prayers, I Nature, mother of all things, mistress of all the elements, the primal birth of all the ages, supreme divinity, Queen of the world of shades, first of the inhabitants of heaven, in whom all gods have their unchanging type. . . . One Power adored by all the world under many a name and with many rites. . . . Dry thy tears and assuage thy grief : already by my providence the dawn of a saving day is breaking. Attend my solemn festival and await the touch of my priest which shall set thee free. Become my servant, and live in hope by constant devotion and steadfast purity to see my glory in the world to come."

Lucius awoke with a strange gladness in the freshness of the morning. The birds are singing under the inspiration of the spring, hymning the mother of the stars and the ages, the mistress of the universe.[2] The young foliage is rustling in the southern breeze. The sea is asleep, hardly disturbed by a ripple. The naked splendour of heaven is not veiled by a single cloud.[3] A great procession is forming, a picturesque masquerade in various character and costume. First come the belted soldier, the hunter with short tunic and hunting

[1] Apul. *Met.* xi. cc. 3-6.

[2] *Ib.* xi. c. 7, matrem siderum, parentem temporum, orbisque totius dominam blando mulcentes affamine.

[3] *Ib.*, caelum autem nubilosa caligine disjecta nudo sudoque luminis proprii splendore candebat.

spears, an effeminate figure wearing jewels and false hair.
a gladiator with helmet, sword, and greaves. Another
follows with the well-known mantle, beard, and sandals
of the wandering philosopher. A bear is borne along in
a matron's litter. An ass, with wings fastened to its
flanks, carries a feeble old man, to represent Bellerophon
and Pegasus to the laughing crowd. Women in white
robes scatter flowers along the route. Then follows a
mixed crowd of men and women and youths in snowy
vestments, bearing torches and candles, and chanting a
sacred poem to the melody of flutes. Next comes the
throng of the initiated, men and women, of every age
and rank, clad in white, and the priests with shaven
heads carrying the sacred symbols.[1] Last of all are
borne the images of the great Egyptian gods, and the pix
containing the holy mysteries.[2] On the approach of the
chief priest, Lucius was restored to humanity by a magic
garland, and the miracle is made the subject of an
address, in which he dwells on the power and the
goodness of the goddess.[3] "Behold," he says, "ye
impious doubters, and recognise your errors. Behold
one who has by the grace of Isis been delivered from
his woes." And Lucius, that his future life may be
shielded from the cruelty of Fortune, is exhorted to join
in the holy warfare and put on the yoke of a willing
service.[4] The procession, with the favoured Lucius in
their midst, soon reached the margin of the sea.[5] There
a sacred bark, resplendent with white sails and ensigns
of gold, and pictures of strange Egyptian legend, was

---

[1] Apul. *Met.* xi. c. 7, sed antistites sacrorum, proceres illi qui candido linteamine cinctum pectoralem adusque vestigia strictim injecti potentissimorum deum proferebant insignis exuvias.

[2] *Ib.* c. 11, ferebatur ab alio cista secretorum capax, penitus celans operta magnificae religionis.

[3] *Ib.* c. 15, videant irreligiosi, et errorem suum recognoscant.

[4] *Ib.*, quo tibi tamen tutior sis atque munitior, da nomen huic sanctae militiae . . . et ministerii jugum subi voluntarium.

[5] *Ib.* c. 16, navem faberrime factam, picturis miris Egyptiorum circumsecus variegatam summus sacerdos . . . deae nuncupavit dedicavitque.

consecrated with mystic ceremonies and solemn prayer.[1]
Fragrant odours filled the air, libations were poured upon
the waves.   The holy vessel, which was to win the protection of the goddess for the sailor, was launched before
a gentle breeze, and the crowd watched its voyage till it
faded in the distance.

Then opens another scene in the drama.   The procession returns to the temple.   The images and symbols
of the gods are placed in the sanctuary.   Then, standing
on the steps, the scribe summons the sacred Guild of the
Pastophori, vowed to the service of the deity, to a solemn
meeting.   He reads a prayer,[2] for the mighty prince, the
Senate, the knights, the whole people of Rome, for all
upon the sea, for the wealth and prosperity of all subjects.
And the congregation is dismissed with a solemn form,[3]
which in its Latin equivalent remains embedded in the
name of the most sacred rite of the Catholic Church.
Full of the thought of his former misery, and of the joy
of deliverance, the neophyte is lost in devotion.   He
remains in constant attendance before the image of the
loving power which has wrought his salvation.   He
makes her temple his home.   Day and night without a
pause are spent in prayer before her.   He is filled with
longing for the supreme joy of full communion which has
been promised him; yet he cannot escape from the anxious
thought that his feeble virtue may be unable to keep the
law of this spiritual service.[4]   Another vision from the
goddess quiets his distrust, and stimulates his longing.
He rushes to the temple as the offices of the early morning

[1] Apul. *Met.* xi. c. 16.

[2] *Ib.* c. 17, indidem de sublimi
suggestu, de libro, de litteris fausta
vota praefatus: Principi Magno,
Senatuique et Equiti, totoque
Romano Populo, nauticis, navibus,
quaeque sub imperio mundi nostratis
reguntur, etc.

[3] Λαοῖς ἄφεσις. Réville, *Rel.*

unter den Sev. p. 57. Cf. note in
Hildebrand's ed. p. 1051. The
right reading has probably been restored.

[4] Apul. *Met.* xi. c. 19, tamen
religiosa formidine retrahebar, quod
enim sedulo percontaveram, difficile
religionis obsequium, et caerimoni-
arum abstinentiam satis arduam,
etc.

are beginning.   The white veils of the holy image are
drawn aside.   The holy water from the secret spring is
sprinkled.   The litany of the dawn is performed at the
altars.   He is more fervent than ever, and begs the
pontiff to admit him to the crowning rite.   But the
venerable man gently moderates his too eager impatience.
The goddess holds the keys of hell and of the path of
salvation, and all must wait for the signal of her will.[1]
He who will enjoy her secret communion must die a
voluntary death, that her grace may recall him from the
very confines of death and life by a new birth, as it were,
to run a new course of salvation.   The votary must await
in patient humility the signs of her will, and meanwhile
prepare himself for the holy mysteries by long abstinence.

At last the sign comes in the silence of the night.
Lucius rises before the dawn and presents himself before
the priest who, having laid his hands on him, leads him
into the sanctuary.   After the morning sacrifice, the sacred
books, containing a liturgy in an unknown tongue, and
covered with hieroglyphic symbols, are brought out.[2]   The
neophyte after solemn prayer is bathed and baptized, and
receives secret instructions as to his further preparation.
Ten days more he spends in fasting.   And then at vespers
came the hour which was to crown his longings.   The
priest leads him clad in linen vestments into the holy
place.   What he saw and heard could never be fully
told.   All that he could tell the world was that he drew
nigh the bounds of Death, and returned across the
elemental spaces.   "At midnight he saw the sun in his

---

[1] Apul. *Met.* c. 21, nam et inferûm
claustra et salutis tutelam in deae
manu posita, ipsamque traditionem
ad instar voluntariae mortis et pre-
cariae salutis celebrari : quippe quum
transactis vitae temporibus jam in
ipso finitae lucis limine constitu-
tos . . . numen deae soleat elicere
et sua providentia quodam modo
renatos ad novae reponere rursus
salutis curricula.

[2] *Ib.* c. 22, ac matutino peracto
sacrificio, de opertis adyti profert
quosdam libros, litteris ignorabili-
bus praenotatos, partim figuris
cujuscemodi animalium, concepti
sermonis compendiosa verba sug-
gerentes, etc.

most dazzling splendour, and came into the presence of
the Powers who rule in Heaven and Hell."

The following morning, Lucius, dressed in gorgeous
robes embroidered with dragons and griffons, was exhibited
to the eyes of an admiring multitude. Yet his own
humble gratitude for the favour of the goddess was paid
in prostration before her altar and constant prayer. Nor
could he tear himself from the scene of these sacred
emotions [1] without an agony of regret.[2] His feelings, as
he left the scene of his second birth, are embalmed in a
prayer which throws a curious light on the inner spirit
of the later paganism. "Holy one, constant saviour of
the race of men, so bountiful in cherishing them, so tender
in the mother's love which thou dost bestow on the
wretched. Nor day nor night, nor shortest moment passes
unmarked by thy benefits, without the help of thy protection for men on sea and land, without thy succouring hand
outstretched to ward off the storms of life. Powers above
and powers below alike wait on thy will. Thou makest
the world to revolve, thou givest his light to the sun, thou
art ruler of the universe, thou dost tread Tartarus under
thy feet. To thee are due the harmony of the spheres,
the return of the seasons, the gladness of the gods, the
obedience of the elements. At thy bidding the breezes
blow, the clouds gather, seeds germinate and grow. Birds
which pass across the sky, beasts which wander on the
hills, serpents which lurk underground, the monsters
which swim the deep, all tremble before thy majesty.
But I am too feeble in mind to speak thy praise, too poor
in worldly goods to pay thee sacrifice ; nor have I wealth
of utterance to tell all that I feel of thy grandeur. A
thousand lips, a thousand tongues, an unbroken eternity

---

[1] Apul. *Met.* xi. c. 24, inexpli-
cabili voluptate simulacri divini
perfruebar, irremunerabili quippe
beneficio pigneratus.

[2] . . . provolutus denique ante
conspectum deae et facie mea diu
detersis vestigiis ejus, lacrimis
obortis singultu crebro sermonem
interficiens . . . et verba devorans,
aio.

of unfailing praise would not avail. What the pious
soul, though poor withal, may do, that will I perform.
The features of thy holy godhead will be treasured in the
thoughts of my inmost soul for ever more."

This may not be the expression of a modern piety.
Yet he must be a hard and unsympathetic critic who does
not catch in this prayer the ring of a genuine religious
emotion. When we read of the passionate devotion
aroused in Lucius by the Isiac rites, we begin to understand the fervour with which Aconia Paulina,[1] herself a
priestess of Isis, speaks, in the famous inscription on the
monument of Praetextatus, of her husband's contempt
for the fleeting honours of the world in comparison with
his religious privileges, and records her gratitude for his
having made her a partner in his religious life.

But there is earlier evidence than Apuleius that the
worship of Isis, though unfortunately often combined
with very lax morality, was the source of real devotional
feeling in purer souls. Three hundred years before
Aconia Paulina, the priestess of Hecate and Isis,[2] breathed
her last in her palace on the Esquiline,[3] Plutarch devoted
a long essay to the discussion of the ritual, and the
physical and moral significance of the worship of Isis
and Osiris. This treatise shows the same spiritual and
monotheistic tendency, the same elastic variety of physical and moral interpretation applied to the ancient
myths, the same rejection of impure tales of the gods by
a higher moral intuition, which are characteristic of the
last efforts of pagan theology. Plutarch's many allegor-
ical interpretations of the Egyptian myths may seem to
a modern rather wearisome. But in a passage towards
the end the very spirit of the *Phaedo* seems to emerge.
Men are disturbed, says Plutarch,[4] when they are told, in
veiled priestly allegory, that Osiris rules over the dead,

[1] *C.I.L.* vi. 1779.   [3] Seeck's *Sym.* lxxxvi. n. 386.
[2] *Ib.* vi. 1780.   [4] Plut. *de Is. et Osir.* § 78 ; cf. § 67.

by the thought that the holy and blessed God really
dwells among the bodies of those who have passed away.
"But He himself is far removed from earth, pure, stain-
less, and unpolluted by any nature that is liable to
corruption and death. The spirits of men here below,
encumbered by bodily affections, can have no intercourse
with God, save only as by philosophic thought they may
faintly touch Him as in a dream. But when they are
released, and have passed into the world of the unseen,
the pure, the passionless, this God shall be their guide
and king, who depend on Him, and gaze with insatiable
longing on that beauty which may not be spoken by the
lips of man."

The higher devotional feeling which characterised the
paganism of the educated class from the second century
was, as we can see in the passage of Plutarch, accompanied by a decided tendency to monotheism. This movement was, as we shall discover, partly due to Platonic
influences,[1] partly to the chaos of religions, in which
a few of the more commanding and attractive absorbed or
assimilated the rest, and drew men's minds to one or two
great objects of devotion. Thus in the vision seen by
Lucius, which we have described, Isis reveals herself as
a universal Power, supreme, all-pervading, worshipped
under many names.[2] "The Phrygians call me the
Mother of the Gods at Pessinus ; the Athenians Cecropian
Minerva ; I am Paphian Venus in Cyprus ; Diana
Dictynna to the archers of Crete, the Stygian Proserpine
to the Sicilians ; I am the ancient Ceres at Eleusis. To
some I am Juno, to others Hecate. Only the Ethiopians
and Arians, illumined by the sun's dawning light, and
Egypt powerful in her ancient lore, honour me with the
ritual proper to me, and call me by my true name, Queen
Isis."

In the *Saturnalia* of Macrobius, a purely pagan work

[1] Réville, *Rel. unter den Sev.* p. 42.   [2] Apul. *Met.* xi. c. 5.

of the first quarter of the fifth century, there is a passage
which applies the same syncretism,[1] in rather a crude
form, to sun-worship. " If," Praetextatus is made to say,
"the sun is the ruler of the other lights of the heavens,
and if these orbs control our destiny, the sun must then
be the lord and author of all. The lesser deities are
simply the various effects or potencies of this supreme
power.[2] The names of the gods, whom we reverence, are
only descriptions of different departments of His government, who gives life and order to the universe." And so
one deity glides into another, as we find that his name or
attribute is only, as it were, a ray of the light which
"lighteth all men." Apollo is the great power who repels
disease, and is hence called the "Healer."[3] And the
identity of Apollo with the sun-god is proved by the
epithets Loxias, Delius, Phoebus, Lycius, Nomius, or
Pythius.[4] To take one example, the epithet Pythius,
which carries in itself the myth of the slaughter of the
Python,[5] merely describes the effects of the sun's rays
on the mists of earth. Hence too Apollo is called
Hecebolus, the Far-darting. By the same method, he
is identified with Liber or Dionysus,[6] who is in the
nocturnal hemisphere what Apollo is in the sphere of
light. Indeed the very name Dionysus (Διὸς νοῦς) shows
his identity with the sun, who is the *mens mundi.*
Mercury again must be another name for the sun,[7] if
only because, in works of art, Mercury is represented
with wings, which indicate the velocity of light. So
Aesculapius must be identified with Apollo,[8] because they
have an equal claim to the sign of the serpent and to the

---

[1] Macrob. *Sat.* i. 17. This method
of dealing with the myths of course
is a very old one ; cf. Cic. *de Nat.
Deor.* ii. 23, 24, and S. Augustine's
refutation, *de Civ. Dei,* iv. 11; cf.
Lob. *Aglaoph.* i. p. 598.

[2] *Ib.* i. 17. 4, diversae virtutes
solis nomina dis dederunt.

[3] *Ib.* i. 17, 14-16.

[4] *Ib.* i. 17, 31 *sqq.*

[5] *Ib.* i. 17, 50 *sqq.*

[6] *Ib.* i. 18, 1-15.

[7] *Ib.* i. 19, 1-10.

[8] *Ib.* i. 20, 1-5.

power of divination.   Hercules,[4] the glory of Hera, the
power of the air, is the valour of the gods who crushed
the impious race that denied their divinity,   The myths
of Venus and Adonis,[2] Cybele and Attis,[3] Isis and Osiris,
receive the same physical interpretation.   In each case
the myth is the imaginative expression for the facts of
the changing seasons, or the sadness of the shortening
days, or the gloom of winter.   In each case we arrive
once more at the central worship of the sun.   Finally,
the king of the gods,[4] who goes to visit the blameless
Ethiopians, and on the twelfth day returns to Olympus,
is plainly the sun in his diurnal course, whilst the gods
who attend him are the stars which, in their rising and
setting, follow the daily motion of the heavens.

For more than three centuries syncretism and the
tendency to monotheism were in the air.   It has been
said of the pagan theology of the third century that it
is one colossal syncretism.[5]   Among the countless cults
which found a centre in the Rome of the imperial period,
there was no strife or repulsion.   They rested on myth,
the imaginative expression of men's feelings towards
nature or the mystery of life and death, not on dogma.
And the myths could be interpreted in many different
ways.   The age when each city and district had its
peculiar gods, the sectarian age of heathendom, had
passed away with the absorption of so many nationalities
in a world-wide Empire.   Travel or conquest had made
the Romans acquainted with a host of new divinities
whose attributes seemed to fill a gap in their own
system, and whose ritual stimulated devotion or aesthetic
sensibility.   Men from the provinces flocked to Rome,
bent on business, pleasure, or advancement, and prepared
to reverence the gods of the imperial city.   Julius

---

[1] Macrob. *Sat.* i. 20, 10.
[2] *Ib.* i. 21, 1.
[3] *Ib.* i. 21, 7 *sqq.*

[4] *Ib.* i. 23, 1.
[5] Réville, *Rel. unter den Sev.* p. 102.

Caesar found the deities of Gaul the same as those of
Italy,[1] and the Gauls erected altars to Jupiter and
Vulcan beside those of their own Esus and Tarvus and
Nemausus, or combined the names of a native and a
foreign deity as in that of Apollo-Belenus.[2] The Roman
soldiers were the great apostles of syncretism. Prone
as they were to superstition, exposed to constant danger
on the march or in distant quarters, the ingrained Roman
awe of the unknown divinity made them ready to invoke
the help of the guardian gods of the regions where they
found themselves, and innumerable inscriptions remain
to attest the liberality of their faith or the blindness
of their devotion.[3] The worship of each new god who
attracted the Roman seemed another avenue of approach
to that dim and awful Power, inaccessible Himself to
human voice and thought, but revealed and adored in
different manifestations of His will and attributes
(*numina*). In truth, the old Roman religious spirit,
which combined the most rigorous formalism with the
personification of abstractions, to which no myth or
dogma of any kind attached, lent itself better than any
other to universal toleration. It invented genii for
everything, for the city, the emperor, the guild, the
camp, the legion, for every act, thought, or incident of
human life.[4] Piety consisted in a scrupulous observance
of the prescribed ceremonial,[5] not in definite beliefs or
elevation of feeling. Many of its objects of devotion

---

[1] *De Bell. Gall.* vi. 17, deum
maxime Mercurium colunt. . . .
Post hunc Apollinem et Martem
et Jovem et Minervam. De his
eandem fere quam reliquae gentes
habent opinionem.

[2] *C.I.L.* xii. 3070, Jovi et
Nemauso; 4316, Herculi Ilunno
Andose; 3077; cf. viii. 9195. Jovi,
Silvano, Mercurio, Saturno, etc.,
Diis Mauris; viii. 4578, Jovi,
Junoni, Minervae, Soli Mithrae,
Herculi, Marti, Mercurio, Genio

loci, Diis Deabusque omnibus.
Jupiter and Serapis are united,
viii. 2629; Jupiter, Juno, Minerva,
Sol, Mithras, Hercules, Genius loci,
viii. 4578; cf. Friedländer, iii. p.
444 *sqq.*

[3] *C.I.L.* viii. 2623, 2639-2641
(Dis Mauris), 9195, 8435, 8834
(Iemsal is a god's name).

[4] Réville, p. 41; Preller, p. 387;
C.I.L. viii. 2529, 6945; xii. 1282.

[5] Cic. *de Nat. Deor.*, est enim
pietas justitia adversum deos.

were mere names, and the same god could be addressed
under many names, or under any name which pleased
him.[1]

The Empire, by drawing together so many peoples
with their peculiar worships, might seem to have produced a spiritual chaos.   In reality the very multitude
and variety of these religions, combined with the spiritual
tendencies of the age, by comparison, assimilation, identi-
fication, to lead to unity.   The old gods seemed to
welcome alien worships, and borrowed their symbols
and the ritual of their mysteries.   Altars to many deities
were gathered under one roof.[2]   The worshipper was
ready to accept from any cult what satisfied devout
feeling or taste and fancy.   Men made dedications to
a host of deities of every clime.[3]   They sought initiation
in all the mysteries, those of the Eleusinian goddesses, of
Isis, and Mithra.[4]   They accumulated priesthoods in
the most various cults.   If different deities had similar
symbols or functions, the tendency was to identify them,
or to subordinate the less vigorous cults under one of
greater popularity.   The masses, by a blind instinct,
sought from any quarter satisfaction for vague religious
cravings, which become more and more imperious in the
second and third centuries, for moral support and purification, for assurance of immortality.   The cultivated
and indifferent found pleasure and excitement in the
splendour or novelty of foreign ritual,[5] as a modern
sceptic may find an aesthetic pleasure in the ceremonial
of the Mass.   The general drift of serious minds was
spiritually towards more personal relations with God,
and intellectually towards a vague monotheism or
pantheism.   The many-coloured worships, which offered
their symbolism to devotion, were, to some, clues to the

[1] *C.I.L.* vi. 110, 111.   [4] *Ib.* vi. 504, 1779.
[2] Luc. *de Syr. Dea*, 35.   [5] Lamprid. *Com.* c. 9.
[3] *C.I.L.* viii. 4578, 9195, 6955.

Great Mystery, to others, distant and indistinct adumbrations of it.   The religious attitude of many devout pagans in the third and fourth centuries is probably described in a letter of Maximus,[1] a grammarian of Madaura, to S. Augustine, about the year 390.   Maximus professes his sure and certain belief in one Supreme God, the great and glorious Father.   His virtues, diffused throughout the universe, we adore under many names, since his proper name we know not.   God belongs to all religions. And hence, while we address separate parts of Him in our various supplications, we are really worshipping the whole, under a thousand names in a harmonious discord. It was the task of the Neoplatonic philosophy to crystallise in its formulae the vague fluid instincts of the mass of men, and to try to find a secret harmony in the discord.

In the three centuries between Plutarch and Macrobius the great aim of philosophy is to reach the intellectual ground of truth underlying the crowd of worships which gave expression to the religious instinct of humanity, and faith in the Unseen.   The father of this movement is the pious and cultivated sage of Chaeronea,[2] who is probably the highest and purest character ever produced in a heathen environment.   He is in philosophy an eclectic Platonist; but he is really far more a moralist and theologian than a philosopher. He believes emphatically in one great, central Power,[3] who is sometimes spoken of, in Platonic language, as the Infinite God, sometimes as the Father of all, whose wisdom and providence controls the universe.   Plutarch

---

[1] Aug. *Ep.* 16, equidem unum esse deum, summum, sine initio, sine prole naturae, ceu patrem magnum atque magnificum, quis tam demens, tam mente captus neget esse certissimum. Hujus nos virtutes per mundanum opus diffusos, multis vocabulis invocamus. This letter seems to render doubtful Dr. Bigg's denial of a real monotheistic tendency in the later paganism (*Neoplatonism*, pp. 52, 53).

[2] Réville, p. 112 ; Zeller, *Phil. der Gr.* 3rd part, pp. 141-182 ; cf. Bigg's *Neoplatonism*, pp. 88-91.

[3] *De Is. et Osir.* 67, 78 ; *de Sera Num. Vind.* 5, 18 ; cf. *de Pyth. Or.* 21 ; on the evil principle in the world v. *de Is.* 45.

has a horror of the superstition which fears the wrath of God, and of the atheism which denies His existence.[1] The gods worshipped by the various races of men are to Plutarch, as they are to Celsus and Maximus of Tyre, the subordinate representatives of the Supreme Governor, called by many names, honoured in many fashions, but all pointing the pious soul to the central object of devotion. In his doctrine of daemons Plutarch found a refuge for polytheistic worship, and an explanation of oracular inspiration. He is a distant progenitor of the Neoplatonism of the fourth century.

Neoplatonism was the great intellectual support of the pagan spirit in the last two centuries of the Empire. The germ of its doctrine was introduced into Rome in the time of the Antonines, and the force of that strange mixture of superstition with lofty speculation, which characterised the later Neoplatonism, was so enduring and intense that S. Augustine devoted to it some of the most powerful chapters of his *City of God*.[2] The rhetor, Apuleius, of Madaura, who had been initiated in all the mysteries,[3] and who posed as an apostle of Platonism, harangued great audiences both in Rome and the provinces, and fascinated them by a " Platonism half understood, mixed with fanciful Orientalism." Plotinus, the greatest of the Alexandrians, arrived in Rome in 244.[4] Crowds of senators, magistrates, and women of high rank came to listen to the obscure eloquence of the Egyptian mystic, who summoned them, in words which moved the admiration of S. Augustine, " to flee to the dear fatherland of souls, where the Father dwells." [5]

[1] But superstition, as degrading the character, he regards as the worse ; cf. *Nec Posse Suav. Viv.* 20, 21. On Plutarch's belief in genii or daemons v. Gréard's *Morale de Plutarque*, pp. 299-304 ; Friedländer, iii. p. 430 *sqq.* ; Bigg's *Neoplatonism*, p. 95.

[2] *De Civ. Dei*, viii. 14 *sqq.* ; cf. *Ep.* 138, § 18.
[3] *Apol.* 55.
[4] Porph. *vit. Plotin.* c. 3, 7, 9.
[5] *De Civ. Dei*, ix. 17, ubi est illud Plotini, ubi ait: " Fugiendum est igitur ad carissimam patriam, et ibi pater, et ibi omnia."

The success of Plotinus was so great that he had a dream of obtaining a settlement from the Emperor Gallienus and founding a city in Campania, which should realise the ideal polity of Plato.[1] Porphyry, a Syrian, the greatest of his disciples, and a declared foe of Christianity, carried on his tradition into the first years of the fourth century. With Iamblichus the Neoplatonic system underwent a great change. It abandoned the detached and disinterested mysticism of its prime.[2] The persecution of Diocletian revealed the inextinguishable force of the Christian faith, and the danger of a religious revolution. The fate of the schools was involved in that of the temples. Philosophy threw itself without reserve into the conflict. The great Alexandrines, while ready to admit a kernel of truth under the husk of mythological symbols,[3] made no profession of religious faith in them. Their successors of the age of Julian sank the philosopher in the ardent devotee,[4] believed in sacrifice and divination, and practised magic and the theurgic arts. The idealist must always contract some stains when he descends into the arena of practical life. And Neoplatonism, while nerving paganism for its last battle, lost much of the moral purity and grandeur of Plotinus. Yet an unsympathetic critic may easily exaggerate the degradation; winking Madonnas and miracles of Lourdes will not blind a candid man to the better side of Catholicism. And we should not forget that, if Julian deluged the altars with the blood of victims,[5] and countenanced the superstitious absurdities of men like Maximus, he strove to correct vices in the pagan system infinitely worse than slavish superstition. A reactionary in one sense, he was also a daring

[1] Porph. *vit. Plotin.* c. 12.
[2] Bigg, *Neoplatonism*, p. 305.
[3] Cf. Plotin. *Ennead*, v. 8, 10; vi. 9, 9; v. 1, 7; iii. 6, 19; iii. 5, 8. For his cautious view of magic
v. iv. 3, 11; cf. Porph. *de Abst.* ii. 41-43.
[4] Vacherot, *l'École d'Alex.* ii. p. 144.
[5] Amm. Marc. xxii. 12, 6.

innovator.   It was no ordinary man who dreamt of
regenerating the ancient worship by borrowing a dogmatic
theology from Alexandria, an ecstatic devotion from
Persia, a moral ideal from Galilee.   Julian exerted his
pontifical authority to elevate the priestly character and
make it a pattern to the people.[1]   The ministers of the
gods were to be regular in their devotion, pure in mind
and body, tender in relieving the poor and outcast.   They
are to avoid all tainted literature ; they must never be
seen in taverns and theatres ; and they must exhort
their flocks to be chaste, devout, and charitable.   The
worshippers of the Sun-king are to prepare themselves for
the holy mysteries by fasting and contemplation.   This
heroic attempt to breathe a new life into paganism was
doomed to failure.   But it is a narrow and hide-bound
criticism which refuses to see great qualities in the
defender of a bad cause, and which will not admit that
superstition may sometimes be united with lofty moral
ideals.

The effort of Neoplatonic philosophy to save poly-
theism in the fourth century is a curious chapter in the
history of opinion.   In spite of some serious metaphysical
differences, there might seem to be many affinities between Neoplatonism and Christianity in their common
doctrine of the unity of God, and their moral and
spiritual idealism.   On the other hand, there might
appear at first sight an irreconcilable opposition between
the Hellenic cult of nature and sense, and a system the
centre of which was the doctrine of the Infinite and
Unknowable One.   The explanation lies in the sympathetic attachment of religious and philosophic systems to
their ancestry.   Neoplatonism could no more forget its
Hellenic origin than the Christian Church could forget
its sources in the religion of Israel.   The school of

---

[1] *Frag. Ep.* ed. Hertlein, vol. ii. p. 385 *sqq.* ; *Ep.* 62 ; Duruy, vii. 341;
Vacherot, ii. 165.

Alexandria, essentially eclectic and conservative, was bound by a continuous chain of thought and feeling to the whole past culture of Hellas, of which the greatest glory in art and letters was derived from Greek legend. Plato, their great master, while he claimed that the moral sense might correct the errors of licentious fancy, never abandoned the mythology of his race.   He had used it, as he used the ancient Orphic traditions, to adorn or enforce his philosophic teaching.

Moreover, any system of philosophy which deserves the name must guard its freedom.   Paganism had no rigid system of dogma.   Formed by the rude superstitious fancy, and endlessly varied and glorified by the genius of poetry, the legends of Hellas belong to a totally different order of thought from the definitions of Christian councils. They were food for the imagination or emotions; they were never articles of faith.   From the sixth century the greatest minds, Xenophanes,[1] Aeschylus,[2] Pindar,[3] Plato,[4] had treated them with great freedom of interpretation and criticism, and Euripides had, year after year at a great religious festival, for more than half a century exerted with impunity all the subtlety of his art to lower the dignity and dim the splendour of the great figures of Greek legend.   But the Christianity of the fourth century was a system complete, well articulated, demanding entire submission of the reason.   It would not treat with philosophy even on equal terms.   Its truths must be accepted in the form in which generations of contro-versy and the decisions of councils had finally left them. If its dogmas did not square with philosophy, philosophy must yield.   A system like the Neoplatonic, with its roots in the old world, whose best thought it strove to fuse into a whole, could not come to terms with an aggressive

---

[1] Athen. xi. 462, *Frag.* l. 21 ; cf. Ritter and Preller, *Hist. Phil.* p. 82.

[2] Aesch. *Agam.* 55, 160.   See Prof. Murray's *Ancient Gk. Litera-*

ture, pp. 223, 224; cf. *Hellenica*, " Aeschylus," p. 16.

[3] Pind. *Ol.* i. 45-85.

[4] *Rep.* ii. p. 378 ; *Euthyphr.* c. 6.

religion which claimed the monopoly of truth.   In not separating itself from paganism, while it strove to interpret the myths in a higher sense, the Neoplatonists were merely treading in the footsteps of their great master. Might it not be possible to find a niche for each of these countless gods in the temple of the inscrutable One ?[1] Might not the popular religion, without any dangerous breach with the past, be reconciled with a pure theism ? Might not a warm devotion and assiduous attention to the ancient ritual be found compatible with the ecstatic vision of God,[2] who is in Himself inaccessible to prayer or sacrifice, inconceivable by imagination or the highest effort of reason ?

Neoplatonism had some advantages over Stoicism in the attempt to support or to restore the forces of paganism.   Stoicism gave philosophic expression to the religious feeling of old Rome.   But under the later Empire, as we have seen, the old gods had fallen into the shade, and cults of Eastern origin had acquired an extraordinary power and fascination.   The tendency to monotheism in some of these systems was very marked ; and the ascetic preparation for their mysteries, together with the ecstatic tone of devotion which they encouraged, had a certain attraction for the Pythagorean and Platonic schools.   The Platonist Apuleius lived in an atmosphere of magic and mystery,[3] and in his travels sought initiation in all sorts of strange cults, which stimulated emotion, or promised glimpses of the unseen world.   The later Alexandrians of the time of Julian found in sunworship the highest symbol of their esoteric doctrine.[4]

But the great means of accommodation lay in the

[1] See the exposition of the treatise "De Mysteriis" in Vacherot, ii. p. 121 *sqq.*

[2] Vacherot, ii. p. 148.

[3] Apul. *Apol.* 55, sacrorum initia in Graecia participavi, multijuga sacra et plurimos ritus et varias cerimonias studio veri et officio erga deos didici ; cf. Bigg's *Neoplatonism,* pp. 52 *sqq.*

[4] Zeller, *die Phil. der Gr.* iii. 2, p. 629 ; Julian, *Or.* iv. καὶ γάρ εἰμι τοῦ βασιλέως ὀπαδὸς Ἡλίου.

principle of emanation.[1]   It enabled the Neoplatonist to
bridge over the chasm between the one pure abstraction,[2]
absolutely simple, not to be grasped by any act of thought
nor described by any attribute, and the worlds of spirit
and sense.[3]   Each unity in the scale gives birth from its
inner essence to another more complex, and therefore
inferior.   From the purely abstract One there is a
graduated scale of being,[4] unity, mind, soul, the universe
of sense, each successively engendered out of the inner
essence of the higher and simpler form.   Into such a
system it was not hard to fit the gods of mythology.[5]
It is true that there are wide differences between the
earlier and later Neoplatonists in their attitude to the
popular religion.   Plotinus is much more of a philosopher
than a theologian,[6] and while he tries to find a hidden
meaning in the myths,[7] in an unsystematic way, he makes
no allusion to theurgy, and deals rather ambiguously
with the external forms of devotion.[8]   So, too, Porphyry,[9]
while his system enabled him to find a metaphysical
content in legend, has no sympathy with the materialism
of worship.   He holds firmly that the Supreme cannot
be approached by any avenue of sense, by sacrifice, or
formal prayer.   God is honoured most by reverent
silence and purity of heart.[10]   To become like and offer
ourselves to Him is the acceptable sacrifice.   But the
Platonists of the fourth century are much more theo-
logians than pure philosophers.[11]   The whole forces of

---

[1] For the sense in which Plotinus held this *v.* Zeller, *die Phil. der Griech.* iii. 2, pp. 451-453.

[2] *Ib.* iii. 2, p. 454.

[3] *Ib.* iii. 2, p. 549.

[4] Macrob. *Som. Scip.* i. 17, 12, gives a simple statement of the doctrine of Plotinus ; cf. Zeller, iii. 2, p. 453 ; *Ennead*, vi. 5, 4.

[5] See the elaborate system of Sallust in Vacherot, ii. p. 124 ; cf. Zeller, iii. 2, p. 557.

[6] Vacherot, ii. p. 108.

[7] Zeller, iii. 2, p. 560 ; *Ennead*, v. 1, 4, 7 ; v. 8, 13.

[8] Zeller, iii. pp. 562, 563 ; iii. 2, 563.

[9] Vacherot, ii. pp. 112-116 ; Zeller, iii. 2, pp. 599-601, where the doubts of Porphyry are expounded.

[10] *De Abstin.* ii. 34, διὰ δὲ σιγῆς καθαρᾶς καὶ τῶν περὶ αὐτοῦ καθαρῶν ἐννοιῶν θρησκεύομεν αὐτόν.

[11] Vacherot, ii. p. 119, après Porphyre la philosophie embrasse sans réserve le polythéisme.

the ancient schools were gathered up and employed to
give system and a rational basis to the old religion.   The
fictions of mythology were justified by the example of
Nature,[1] who veils her secrets from the vulgar gaze.
The Supreme One indeed, the fountain of being, must
not be profaned by human fancy.   But the lower powers
may be dimly revealed to the multitude by allegory or
fanciful tale.[2]   The world itself is a great myth, which
at once hides and reveals the mystery of the Divine.
And the philosopher proceeds to classify the myths
according to the nature of the inner truth which they
contain.[3]   Some convey the deepest theological, or, as
we should say, metaphysical truth.   For example, Saturn
devouring his children is intelligence returning upon
itself.[4]   Others of these fictions are imaginative expres-
sions of the facts of nature.   Apollo slaying the Python
is the sun drawing up the pestilential fogs of the marshes.
The names of many deities are simply names of natural
objects or powers.[5]   Juno is the air, at once sister and
wife of Jupiter, the lord of the upper sky.   Isis is the
earth, Osiris the sun, or the moist germ which fecundates.
There is a hierarchy of gods[6] corresponding to the
hierarchy of being, and to the faculties of the human
soul.   High above all is the Supreme One, the Good, to
be approached only in ecstasy,[7] an effort of the soul far
transcending any exertion of the highest reason, in which
God is the object of an immediate vision or intuition,
and the sense of personality is lost and swallowed up in
the rapture of union with the Divine.   Then there are
the gods of the intelligible world, transcending the world
of sense, and having no point of contact with it.   Lower

[1] Vacherot, ii. p. 121.
[2] Macrob. *Som. Scip.* i. 2, 7-19,
sciunt inimicam esse naturae aper-
tam nudamque expositionem sui,
etc. Cf. the views of Proclus in
the fifth century, Zeller, iii. 2, p.
744.

[3] Zeller, iii. 2, p. 628 ; cf. Bigg's
Neoplatonism, p. 306.
[4] Vacherot, ii. p. 122.
[5] *Ib.* ii. p. 123.
[6] *Ib.* ii. p. 126; Zeller, iii. 2, p.
628.
[7] *Ennead,* vi. 7, 34, 35.

in the scale there are the powers of the sensible universe, creating, life-giving, and preserving. Lastly there are the daemons and heroes,[1] more nearly akin to the world of sense, and acting as intermediaries between it and the sphere of pure intelligence, in which reside those powers, far above the region of the sensible, who cannot come to us, although, through the divine element in us, we may rise to them.

Between the pure mysticism of Plotinus and the fanaticism and superstition of the Neoplatonists of the fourth and fifth centuries, who justified or practised heathen sacrifices, divination, oracles, magic, and theurgy, there might seem to be an impassable gulf. But the great system, the centre of which was the unapproachable One, really contained the germs of the most thorough-going superstition that the world has probably ever seen. The theory of emanations necessarily involved a belief in secret sympathies and affinities, linking together all parts of the universe of being. Man himself, through his various faculties and capacities, is in touch with every link in the chain. If, by an almost superhuman effort, transcending any effort of the reason, he can rise in ecstasy to an immediate vision of the inscrutable One, he can also communicate with, and act upon, the lower powers and forms of existence. And he finds allies in the invisible world in the daemons, who mediate between the world of pure intelligence and the world of sense. Thus the Neoplatonists of the fourth century, having found a place in their system for the ancient gods, found no difficulty in communicating with them by prayer, oracle, or oblation, and even believed themselves capable of wielding the forces of nature. Committed from its origin to the old mythology, Neoplatonism in the last age abandoned the reserve of

---

[1] Aug. *de Civ. Dei*, viii. 14 ; cf. Vacherot, ii. p. 127 ; Zeller, iii. 2, p. 510 ; Friedländer, iii. p. 432.

its youth, adopted the whole pagan system, and, in an inevitable decline, lent even the forces of philosophy to deepen the superstition of the age. There is a certain sadness in thinking that Proclus,[1] the last great member of the school, a man of high intellect and almost saintly life, kept all the feast-days in the Egyptian calendar, and believed himself able to call down rain in a time of drought.

Yet it may be doubted whether, even in the last age of paganism, the purer and more elevating side of Neoplatonic speculation had lost all influence, and been completely obscured. We have seen evidence that there was an enlightened class who, while they refused to abandon the religion of their ancestors, were penetrated with the loftier conceptions of the divine nature, which for a thousand years Greek philosophy had kept before the minds of its disciples. Such men, repelled by the baser element in heathenism, yet bound by loyalty and old associations to the past, might readily accept a system which could reconcile a belief in the meaning and sanctity of ancient legend with a lofty moral tone and a faith in the Infinite Father. Fortunately we have preserved to us, among the débris of the fifth century, a book which shows that there were pagans who still drew from the system of Plotinus a real moral and spiritual support.

The commentary of Macrobius on Cicero's *Dream of Scipio*[2] dates probably from the end of the first quarter of the fifth century. It is a curious mixture of old Roman feeling with the best results of Neoplatonic speculation.[3] It is a devotional treatise, with a certain tinge of mysticism. Yet here and there, in discourses of an ethical or mystical tone, we light upon purely physical or mathematical disquisitions which have a flavour of

---

[1] Zeller, *die Phil. der Gr.* iii. 2, p. 709 ; Bigg, pp. 319-321.

[2] It is best known as having preserved to us the *Somnium*

Scipionis from bk. vi. of Cicero's *Republic.*

[3] On the philosophical and other sources of the work *v.* Jan, *Prol.* xi.

Pythagoreanism. From a contemplation of the heavenly reward awaiting virtue, we suddenly pass to a chapter on point, line, superficies, and solid,[1] and the manifold meaning, in man's life and destiny, of the number seven.[2] The Milky Way is the home of the blessed after death.[3] But it is apparently of equal interest to decide whether, according to Theophrastus, it is the juncture of two hemispheres, or whether Democritus is right in regarding it as a tract so thickly sown with stars that their intervals are obliterated, and they present a uniform luminous surface to the distant gazer. After a statement of the doctrine of emanation,[4] we are launched upon a discussion of the planetary motions and the order of the spheres.[5] The question of the influence of the heavenly bodies on human destiny is mixed up with calculations as to the relative size of the earth and the sun.[6] The moon marks the limit of air and ether, of the divine and the perishable ; and in the next sentence we are reminded that our souls are of celestial origin, and that we are exiles here below.[7]

The book is a singular mixture of physics, morals, metaphysics. There is much which harmonises with the best Christian sentiment, side by side with cold statements of what we should regard as scientific theory, but which the author conceives as a theology.[8] Yet the main purpose is to fortify virtuous purpose by the prospect of the reward after death, and the contemplation of the divine origin and the divine destiny of the human soul. The dimensions of the sun and his orbit, the

[1] Macrob. *Som. Scip.* i. 5, 5.

[2] *Ib.* i. 6, 45, nam primo omnium hoc numero anima mundana generata est sicut Timaeus Platonis edocuit. For the references of Macrobius to this part of the *Timaeus* v. Grote's *Plato*, iii. p. 252 n.

[3] Macrob. *Som. Scip.* i. 15, 1-10.

[4] *Ib.* i. 17, 12.

[5] *Ib.* i. 18.

[6] *Ib.* i. 19, 19.

[7] *Ib.* i. 17 ; cf. i. 21, 34, ita animorum origo caelestis est sed lege temporalis hospitalitatis hic exulat.

[8] *Ib.* i. 14, 5, nunc qualiter nobis animus id est mens cum sideribus communis sit secundum theologos disseramus.

periods of the planetary revolutions, the position of the
earth in the solar system, may seem to us subjects
strangely out of place in a treatise apparently intended
to stimulate devout feeling and virtuous conduct.   We
are conscious of a kind of chill in being asked to consider
the relations of numbers, or the vast spaces between the
heavenly spheres, side by side with lofty theories of our
origin, and earthly discipline, and our future in another
world.   Yet the apparent incongruity may be explained.
To Macrobius and his class the Mundus, with all its
spheres, was divine, the efflux of the inscrutable Essence
which, by successive stages of generation, was the source
of the orbs of the sky, of the soul of man, of the meanest
creature possessed of life.   It needs an effort of sympathy
and imagination to enter into the spirit of any outworn
theology.   To understand that expounded by Macrobius,
you must look up into the depths of the heavens on a
summer night, and try to believe that your particular
spark of soul has travelled down to earth through all the
spheres from its source in the divine ether, and that after
its escape from the earthly prison-house it may return
again to its distant birthplace.

The commentary on the *Dream of Scipio* enables one
to understand how devout minds could even to the last
remain attached to paganism.   It presupposes rather
than expounds the theology of Neoplatonism.   Its chief
motive is rather moral or devotional than speculative.
The One, supreme, unapproachable, ineffable, residing in
the highest heaven, is assumed as the source of mind and
life,[1] penetrating all things, from the star in the highest
ether to the lowest form of animal existence.   The
universe is God's temple, filled with His presence.[2]
The unseen, inconceivable Author created from His

[1] Macrob. *Som. Scip.* i. 17, 12 ;
cf. i. 14, 4.

[2] *Ib.* i. 14, 2. And he adds,
what may remind us of some
phrases of S. Paul, sciatque quisquis in usum templi hujus in-
ducitur ritu sibi vivendum sacer-
dotis.

essence pure mind, in the likeness of Himself. In
contact with matter,[1] mind degenerates and becomes
soul. In the scale of being the moon marks the limit
between the eternal and the perishable, and all below
the moon is mortal and evanescent except the higher
principle in man.[2] Passing from the divine world
through the gate of Cancer,[3] mind descends gradually, in
a fall from its original blessedness, through the seven
spheres, and, in its passage, the divine and universal
element assumes the various faculties which make up
the composite, nature of man. In Saturn it acquires the
reasoning power, in Jupiter the practical and moral, in
Mars the spirited, in Venus the sensual element. But
in the process of descending into the body, the divine
part suffers a sort of intoxication and oblivion of the
world from which it comes,[4] in some cases deeper than
in others. Thus the diffusion of soul among bodily
forms is a kind of death; and the body is only a prison,[5]
or rather a tomb, which cannot be quitted save by a
second death, the death to sin and earthly passion.[6]
The soul must not terminate its imprisonment in the
flesh by any voluntary act, but purify itself, and await
the appointed hour when its release will come. Suicide
is not only rebellion against the Great Master,[7] it is also
an act of passion, and the soul,[8] as Plotinus teaches,
which quits this moral life with the soilure of sin upon
it, falls into an abyss from which it may not rise again.
Moreover, the heavenly reward is proportioned to the

[1] Macrob. *Som. Scip.* i. 14, 4-7.
[2] *Ib.* i. 14, 16.
[3] *Ib.* i. 12, 1 ; cf. Plotin. *Ennead*, iv. 3, 15.
[4] *Ib.* i. 12, 8, unde et comes ebrietatis oblivio illic animis incipit jam latenter obrepere.
[5] *Ib.* i. 10, 9. Cf. the Orphic phrase σῆμα τὸ σῶμα, Pl. *Crat.* 400 c ; *Phaed.* 62 B. Virg. *Aen.* vi. 734.

[6] Macrob. *Som. Scip.* i. 13, 6, mori etiam dicitur cum anima adhuc in corpore constituta corporeas inlecebras philosophia docente contemnit. This, however, is an old thought. Cf. Pl. *Phaed.* 67 D, τὸ μελέτημα τῶν φιλοσόφων λύσις καὶ χωρισμὸς ψυχῆς ἀπὸ σώματος ; Sen. *Ep.* 24, *ad fin.*
[7] *Ib.* i. 13, 8.
[8] *Ib.* i. 13, 9 ; cf. i. 13, 16.

degree of perfection which we attain here below,[1] and therefore the mortal term should not be cut short while our probation is still incomplete, and so long as any improvement may be made. It is true that the soul should always strive to remember the source from which it sprang,[2] and regard the body as a sort of hell.[3] Degraded souls who have neglected their time of probation cling to the mortal element after death,[4] and, instead of ascending again to the divine world, are doomed to be imprisoned in brutish forms, and utterly forget their heavenly origin. The only hope of eternal happiness is virtue.[5] Scipio's dream promised eternal felicity to those who have protected, or saved, or aggrandised the state.[6] But there are higher degrees of virtue than that of the heroic and self-sacrificing citizen. While civic virtue moderates and controls the passions, the cleansing virtues may eradicate them,[7] the saintly and mystic virtues may attain to complete forgetfulness of their allurements, and, in a last victorious effort,[8] we may even rise to entire absorption in the Divine. Thus, though the good man will perform the duties of his earthly lot, he will realise that the earth is but a point in the infinitude of the universe,[9] that it is the sphere of the mortal and the transient, and he will be ready to turn an ear to any echo which recalls the eternal harmonies of the heavens.[10] Hence he will make light of glory,[11] and

---

[1] Macrob. *Som. Scip.* i. 13, 15, cum constet remunerationem animis illic esse tribuendam pro modo perfectionis ad quam in hac vita una quaeque pervenit . . .

[2] *Ib.* i. 9, 3.

[3] *Ib.* i. 10, 17.

[4] Cf. Pl. *Phaed.* 81 D, E; Zeller, iii. 2, 530.

[5] Macrob. *Som. Scip.* i. 8, 3, solae faciunt virtutes beatum.

[6] *Ib.* i. 4, 4.

[7] *Ib.* i. 8, 9, passiones ignorare non vincere ut nesciat irasci, cupiat

nihil. How near this comes to the Christian ascetic ideal of that age.

[8] *Ib.* i. 8, 9. Cf. on the Neoplatonic ecstasy, Zeller, iii. 2, pp. 549, 745.

[9] *Ib.* i. 16, 6, (terra) quae tota puncti locum pro caeli magnitudine vix obtinet.

[10] *Ib.* ii. 3, 7, 11, quia in corpus defert memoriam musicae cujus in caelo fuit conscia. On the music of the spheres cf. *Ennead.* iv. 4, 8, μέλος ἂν ᾄσειαν ἐν φυσικῇ τινι ἁρμονίᾳ.

[11] *Ib.* ii. 10, 2

aim only at the approval of conscience. For of this
small spot in the universe, how small a part does our
race possess! The fame of Rome has not passed beyond
the Ganges or the Caucasus;[1] and the most splendid
fame is but brief. Since all human tradition shows how
short is the duration of any historic period. The
universe may be eternal, but fire and flood, in regular
alternations,[2] prevail and sweep into oblivion man and
all his works, save in a few sheltered homes of immemorial culture, like Egypt, which maintain the continuity
of the race. In this scene of mortality and short-lived
hopes, the only wisdom is to nourish the hope of a life to
come,[3] to do one's duty to the fatherland on earth,[4] while
ever mindful of the true fatherland of souls, which is
"eternal in the heavens."[5]

It may be said that the commentary on the *Dream of
Scipio* represents the mysticism of a small circle of philosophic dreamers, and not a general state of moral feeling.
And certainly the seeker for historical truth should not
exaggerate the influence of ideals which in every age are
the guide of only a minority. It is, however, an even
graver fault to fix one's gaze on the baser side of past
ages, and to ignore whatever there is of hope and promise in the slow and painful development of humanity.
Such is not the habit of a sound and scrupulous historical
spirit. Nor is it the attitude of a truly religious mind.
It shows but little faith in the Father of all souls to
believe that He consigns whole generations of His children
merely to the worship of devils, without any glimpse of
Himself, and to dwell on their blind aberrations of superstition in groping towards the light, and on their frantic

[1] Macrob. *Som. Scip.* ii. 10, 3.
[2] *Ib.* ii. 10, 9, res vero humanae
ex parte maxima saepe occidunt
manente mundo et rursus oriuntur
vel eluvione vicissim vel exustione
redunte.
[3] *Ib.* ii. 12, 1.

[4] *Ib.* ii. 17.
[5] Aug. *de Civ. Dei*, ix. 17, illud
Plotini ubi ait: "Fugiendum est
igitur ad carissimam patriam, et ibi
pater, et ibi omnia." Cf. Macrob,
in *Som. Scip.* i. 9, 3.

efforts to calm the terrors and the longings which are inspired by the ineradicable faith in a world beyond the grave.   Rather should we welcome indications that God never utterly forsakes the creatures of His hands, and that in the decay of ancient heathenism there was a moral and spiritual life, which was to be nourished in an unending future by the divine ideals of Galilee.

BOOK II

SKETCHES OF WESTERN SOCIETY
FROM SYMMACHUS TO SIDONIUS

CHAPTER I

FEW inquiries should be more interesting than the attempt to form a conception of the inner tone and life of society in Western Europe on the eve of its collapse. Was society as corrupt and effete as it has been represented? Were its vices, as Salvianus insisted, the cause of the triumph of the barbarians? The judgment of the enthusiastic ascetic of Marseilles has been reproduced by successive generations of moralists and historians. The accusers have been vehement and pitiless. And hardly a word of direct self-defence and self-exculpation from all that crowd of stately nobles, keen dialecticians, and polished litterateurs, has come down to us. It is easy to frame such wholesale indictments against the silent generations of a long past age. It is not so easy to perform the more useful task of realising how they actually lived, and what answer, could they defend themselves, they might make to their accusers.

It is never safe to trust sweeping censure of the morals of a whole age or people. What a picture of our own time might be drawn by some acrid or enthusiastic moralist of the thirtieth century, who should dress up all the scandals of fashionable life hinted at in society journals, all the tales of ruin on the Turf, all the unsavoury revelations of our police courts and divorce courts, and present them to his readers as a fair sample of the way in which the English people were living in the last years of the reign of Victoria! Yet this is the fashion in which satirists or moralists have treated the first century and the last of the society of the Empire. The satirist of the reign of Domitian has left us pictures of depravity and extravagant self-indulgence which are more revolting than anything in the pages of S. Jerome or Salvianus. If society at large had been half as corrupt as it is represented by Juvenal, it must have speedily perished of mere rottenness. Yet when Juvenal died the Roman world had entered on a period of almost unexampled peace and prosperity, a period of upright and beneficent administration and high public virtue, culminating in the reign of the saintly Marcus Aurelius. An intensity of devotion, hitherto strange to it, was giving a fresh life to Roman paganism. Philosophy was diffusing more spiritual conceptions of God, and a humaner charity in the relations of life. The inscriptions, the letters of the younger Pliny, and even the pages of Tacitus, as severe a moralist as Juvenal, reveal to us another world from that of the satirist, a world of severe and elevated virtue, in which the men and women sustain one another in adherence to high principle, in the pursuit of lofty ideals of public duty, or of literary and philosophical studies.[1] If we shudder at the enormities of Tigellinus and Messalina, we should always remember that the same age produced a Thrasea and a Corbulo, an Arria and a Paulina.

Roman satire was perhaps the strongest and most original department of Roman literature. But its judgments must be taken with a good deal of reserve. It was frank and outspoken about deeds of darkness, over which our more timorous delicacy is inclined to throw a veil. It was sometimes almost puritanical in its moral tone and the fierceness of its censures. The moralist represents the old Roman spirit, and draws his

[1] Duruy, *Hist. Rom.* v. pp. 662 *sqq.* ; Boissier, *Rel. Rom.* ii. p. 195.

ideal from an age of simple habits before Rome was corrupted by the arts of Greece and the luxury of the conquered East.[1]   He is apt to forget that luxury is not a
synonym for vice, and that a softened tone need not imply
effeminacy.   He is still more apt to forget that a whole
class should not be made responsible for the folly and
intemperance of a few.   He strikes at the monsters of
vice, who will always appear so long as wealth and
luxury abound, and he leaves the impression that these
are not abnormal specimens, but types.   He ignores[2] the
mass of quiet good sense, wholesome feeling, and self-
control, which in every age lies in shadow behind glaring
and shameless profligacy.   Above all, the very violence
and bitterness with which the moralist lashes the vices of
his time is a proof that his society is not so hopelessly
corrupt as he depicts it.   He is fighting for an ideal
which cannot be a monopoly of his own.   And when he
laments the degeneracy of his contemporaries from the
purer manners of a remote, and perhaps mythical, past, he
is often only expressing personal contempt for the softer
habits of increasing refinement, or else he is speaking as
the organ of a quickened moral sense among the very
men whom he judges so hardly.

   The modern inquirer needs even greater caution in
accepting contemporaneous judgments of the character of
society in the fourth and fifth centuries than in the first.
In the one case an age of splendid public virtue, of great
material advancement, of higher moral ideals, succeeded an
age which we are asked to believe was a period of selfishness, frivolous extravagance, and frantic and unbridled
debauchery.   The Empire was never so beneficent and
so adored by its remote subjects[3] in many lands as it was
under the sons and grandsons of the men who are repre-

---

[1] Cf. Friedländer, bk. iii. p. 15.
[2] Juv. xiii. 26.
[3] See the inscriptions laboriously

collected on this subject in Fustel
de Coulanges, *La Gaule Rom.* p. 177
sqq.

sented as the vilest of mankind.   It was still proud and
erect ten generations after Juvenal and the objects of his
loathing were in their graves.   But the fifth century
closes the career of Rome in the West.   The most spotless virtue, the most heroic energy, would have availed
nothing against the forces which had undermined the
civilisation of twelve hundred years.   There can be little
doubt that there were in the last pagan generation men
who held a more spiritual creed, and had aspirations for
a higher moral life, than their ancestors who conquered
Carthage and Macedonia.   But they represent a failing
cause; they are the rere-guard of a retreating host,
pressed hard by the victorious energy of the Church,
which, conscious that the future belonged to it, was not
always able to do justice to the *régime* which was passing
away.   It is so easy to attribute failure and calamity to
moral causes; and Christian controversialists often failed
to remember the Master's saying about those on whom
the Tower of Siloam fell.   Moreover, even within their
own ranks, the new spirit of asceticism, which could find
salvation only by fleeing from the world, and which, in
the recoil from vice, set up a standard of superhuman
virtue, was not always charitable in its judgments even
of Christians, who, remaining in the world to bear its
burdens, did not escape its stains.   Thus that old society
had not only to endure its own self-reproachful doubts
and questionings in the face of ruin, but the fierce, intolerant criticism of the younger society, which could often
forget its duty to the earthly commonwealth in the raptures
of a mystic devotion, or in the effort to escape from
temptations which may be as powerful in the wilderness
as in the crowded city.   And the anchoret who thundered
against the vices of his age had been bred in the Roman
schools.   He had been nourished in his youth on Juvenal
and Persius and Tacitus.   If he had not all their
literary skill, he had within him a fiercer hatred and

aversion for the sins and weaknesses of men than even
Juvenal had felt.   They were to him the natural offspring
of the daemons of the old mythology,[1] who had, with
hellish ingenuity, corrupted whatever of natural probity
and goodness there was in the old Roman character.
The Christian controversialist could do justice to the
great, virile qualities of his remote ancestors who
worshipped Jupiter and Venus.[2]   He could hardly believe
in the virtue of contemporaries who refused to accept the
faith of Christ.   The Christian controversialists undoubtedly did a great service to humanity when they
held up to loathing the obscenities of the Floralia and
the theatre, and the cruelties of the arena.[3]   But it
should be remembered that some of the better pagans
looked with little approval on these corrupting displays.[4]
Men will often rise above the level of a bad religion, just
as they constantly fall below the standard of a good one.
The severest censors of the morality of the fifth century
are S. Jerome and Salvianus.   And we shall see in the
sequel that the heaviest condemnation of both falls on
populations nominally Christian, or even on classes who
professed to aspire to a peculiar sanctity of life.   When
we read these things we ask ourselves, Can the religion
of the Cross have left men no better than it found them ?
And if we may reasonably distrust the unmeasured
invective of a Christian writer against his co-religionists,
there are even stronger grounds for hesitating to accept the
judgment of an enemy, in a period of fierce controversy,
on the moral state of heathendom.   In this chapter we shall
see what the accusers, whether heathen or Christian, have

[1] Aug. *de Civ. Dei*, viii. 14, 16, 22,
vii. 33.
[2] *Ib.* ii. 13, i. 15. Cf. S. Jerome's
Ep. 60, § 5, quid memorem Romanos
duces quorum virtutes quasi quibusdam stellis Latinae micant historiae ?
[3] Aug. *de Civ. Dei*, ii. 4, 27 ; Pru-

dent. *c. Sym.* i. 378 ; cf. Tertull. *de
Spectac.* 10, *Apol.* 38.
[4] Sen. *Ep.* 7 and 95 ; Juv. vi. 63 ;
Amm. Marc. xxviii. 4, 29 ; xiv. 6,
26, 7, 3 ; Julian. *Fragm. Ep.* § 304
(Hertlein's ed. ii. 389) ; cf. Friedländer, ii. p. 243.

to allege, and then proceed to lay before the reader the actual facts of social life, which can be gathered from the literary remains of the century, extending from the reign of Gratian to the last years of the Western Empire.

The worst that a severe pagan moralist had to say of the moral character of society at the beginning of our period, may be gathered from Ammianus Marcellinus. He was born at Antioch, entered the army at an early age, and had seen great campaigns both in the East and West. He fought under Julian against the Alemanni, and he served in the expedition against the Persians in which that Emperor met his end. In his later years he settled down at Rome to compose a history extending from the principate of Nero to the death of Valens.[1] Ammianus was an honest, high-minded man of the old school. He adhered to the old religion of Rome, but his real creed was probably a vague monotheism with a more decided tendency to fatalism.[2] He could be fair to Christianity, and he evidently disapproved of Julian's exclusion of Christian teachers from the Schools.[3] Whether he is equally fair to Roman society may be questioned. He has the peculiar virtues of the military character along with its narrowness and hardness. A life of hardship spent on the Rhine and the Euphrates was not calculated to make a man a very indulgent, perhaps hardly even a just critic of the splendid, but luxurious and unwarlike society among which he found himself on his return to Rome. Ammianus has left two elaborate pictures of the society of the capital in his time.[4] What strikes a modern student most about them is that they might have been composed with equal truth in the reign of Nero or Domitian. The Roman noble has changed little in three hundred years. It does not

---

[1] Peter, *Die Geschichtl. Litt. über die Röm. Kaiserzeit*, ii. p. 121.

[2] Amm. Marc. xxiii. 5, 5.

[3] *Ib.* xxi. 16, 18 ; xxv. 4,

[4] *Ib.* iv. 6, 7 ; xxviii. 4.

surprise us to hear that the masters of the world are possessed of vast domains in every province, from the rising to the setting sun.   Although they have no longer the political power of their ancestors, they have the vanity of a pampered caste, and they wish to prolong an inglorious name by gilded statues which commemorate nothing.[1]   They ride through the streets in lofty carriages, adorned with a vulgar splendour of dress, which is not redeemed even by its ingenuity.   In their progresses they are attended or preceded by an army of slaves, clients, and eunuchs.   Their choicest pleasures are in swift horses, hurrying through the streets with the speed of the post on the great roads; or in long and elaborate banquets, at which the size and weight of fish or game are recorded, as in Juvenal's day,[2] as a matter of historical interest. Their libraries are opened as seldom as their funeral vaults, but they rave about music and theatrical perform- ances.   Hydraulic organs,[3] and lyres as large as carriages, minister to a degraded taste in music.   In a time of famine, when all foreigners, including the professors of the liberal arts, were expelled from Rome, three thousand dancing girls with their teachers were allowed to remain. If the great man visited the public baths, he would salute effusively some slave of his vices, whom all decent people would avoid.   His only friendships are those of the gaming table.   If a respectable man from provincial parts ventures to call on the great personage, he is received at first with effusive civility.   If the visit is repeated in all honest confidence, he will find that his very name and existence have been forgotten.   The effeminate noble who takes a journey to visit a distant estate will plume him- self on the effort as if he had performed the marches of an Alexander or a Caesar.   He will order a slave to receive three hundred lashes for bringing him his hot water

---

[1] Cf. Sen. *Ep.* 44 ; Juv. viii. 1-20.
[2] Juv. iv. 129.   [3] Cf. Sueton. *Ner.* c. 41.

late. These men, who have not a particle of religious belief, are the slaves of anile superstition. They will not bathe or breakfast or start on a journey till they have consulted the calendar to find the position of a planet.

The vulgar crowd of the days of Marcellinus is the same in character that it had been for four hundred years. *Duas tantum res anxius optat, Panem et circenses.* But it was even more pampered in the reign of Honorius than in the time of Juvenal. The emperors of the third century had added wine, oil, and pork to the dole of corn.[1] There can be little doubt that this mass of deserters from the ranks of honest industry, maintained in idleness by the State, was a hotbed of vice and corruption. All the social sewers drained into its depths. Magnificent baths, erected by successive emperors[2] from Nero to Diocletian, offered their spacious luxury at all hours of the day to the mongrel crew who bred and festered in the slums of the great capital of the world. The hours that were not spent in taverns and low haunts of debauchery were given to idle gossip about the favourites in the games and races.[3] The energy of the once sovereign people exploded in fierce wrangling as to the chances of rival charioteers on whose success the fate of the commonwealth seemed to depend. Probably the mob were never so innocently excited as when they were backing with hoarse cries their favourites in the race. The obscenities of pantomime, in which tales of abnormal depravity were reproduced to the life,[4] the slaughter and sufferings of the gladiatorial combats, gratified, if they could hardly intensify, the instincts of lust and cruelty in a populace which for centuries had been systematically corrupted by the State.

---

[1] Spart. *Sev.* 23; Lamprid. *Alex. Sev.* 26; Vop. *Aurel.* 48; Sym. *Ep.* x. 35; *C. Th.* xiv. 15, 3, xiv. tit. 17; cf. Marquardt, *Röm. Staatsverwaltung,* ii. p. 132.

[2] Lamprid. *Alex. Sev.* 25; Sym. *Ep.* x. 14; *C. Th.* xiv. 5 (*de Man-*

cipibus Thermarum).

[3] Amm. Marc. xiv. 6, 26; xviii. 4, 29-32.

[4] Suet. *Nero,* c. 12; Juv. vi. 63; Prudent. *Peristeph.* x. 221; Sidon. *Carm.* xxiii. 281; cf. Friedländer, ii. p. 285.

The picture of the Roman aristocrat given by Ammianus Marcellinus is certainly not a pleasant one. Yet it is not so dark as the pictures of upper class life in the days of Lucullus, or in the days of Nero. Nay, in many of its features it is hardly worse than might be drawn of English society in the reigns of George II. and George III. *Mutato nomine de te Fabula narratur.* The faults or vices which excited the disgust of the hardy veteran are those of an old society, rendered vain and effeminate by wealth, and served by an army of slaves, a society which was not sobered by any discipline of labour, nor elevated by public interests. We may also suspect that the description is to some extent coloured by the temperament and habits of the old soldier, whose life had been passed in frontier camps. An Indian veteran, who at the present day should settle in London, after thirty years' hard service, might not be more indulgent to our own luxurious classes. And Ammianus may have been wounded by the haughty indifference of one of the most exclusive castes that the world has ever seen. Worldly society is at no time very appreciative of unostentatious merit or service. And Ammianus probably knew the great world chiefly by the vulgarity and frivolity of its least estimable members. Had he been admitted to the circle of the Symmachi and Albini, he would hardly have accused a class, which regarded devotion to letters as the highest distinction of their order, of never entering their libraries. A darker, if not truer picture of that society in the years when Ammianus was composing his history is given by S. Jerome.

S. Jerome outlived Ammianus Marcellinus probably twenty years; but they must have been at Rome about the same time,—in the middle of the reign of Theodosius. The saint received his education under Donatus, probably in the reign of Julian; and, after visiting Gaul and the deserts of Syria, he returned to the capital at the time when the Church was on the eve of its final victory. He was the secretary and intimate friend of Pope Damasus,[1] and for a time was one of the most influential ecclesiastics of Rome. He saw the inner life of the higher clergy, and of those great aristocratic houses, on which, since the visit of S. Athanasius, the ascetic ideal of the Christian life had cast its spell.[2] Jerome became the director in study and devotion of a remarkable group of women—Paula, Lea, Asella, Marcella, and many others, who were of the very cream of the Roman nobility, but who deliberately cut themselves off from worldly society, and in almost conventual seclusion devoted themselves to prayer and the study of the Scriptures.[3] Some of them were accomplished Greek and Hebrew scholars,[4] and, in their minute and careful study of the sacred books, they often taxed the erudition of the great scholar to reply to their curious questions.[5] We hear but little of their husbands and male relatives. The majority of the Roman Senate, even so late as the reign of Theodosius, was clearly pagan in sentiment,[6] if not in belief. There can be little doubt that the husband was often a cultivated sceptic or pagan, while his wife or sister was a Christian devotee. Moving in such a circle, S. Jerome must have acquired a thorough knowledge of the tone and *morale* of the upper class in that period of religious transition which has been described in the first chapter. His evidence as to the moral condition of his time would be invaluable if we could trust the coolness

---

[1] *Ep.* 123, § 10 ; cf. Collombet's *S. Jer.* i. p. 326.

[2] Hieron. *Ep.* 127, § 5 ; for the influence of S. Athanasius's *Life of Antony*, cf. S. Aug. *Conf.* viii. 6.

[3] Hieron. *Ep.* 127, § 7 ; cf. *Ep.* 24.

[4] *Ib.* 108, §§ 26, 28.

[5] *Ib.* 30, 34.

[6] **The** opposite view is founded on Prud. *c. Sym.* i. 566, and on the words in Ambros. *Ep.* 17, § 9, cum majore jam curia Christianorum numero sit referta. But, if so, why did they not attend and prevent the Senate from petitioning the Emperor? If Zosimus (v. 49) is to be believed, the Senate, even after the defeat of Eugenius, were still obdurate. Cf. Seeck's *Sym.* liv. and, for the opposite view, Rauschen, *Jahrbücher*, p. 119.

and fairness of his judgment as much as his knowledge. He was a tremendous and beneficent force in the cause of truth and purity, and he must always be regarded with reverence alike by the student and by the devout Christian. In his fearless determination to ascertain the precise meaning of the sacred text, he offers a splendid example of rare candour and patient industry. In his still more fearless denunciation of moral evil, even in the classes with whom he was most closely associated, and with the risk of ruin to his own reputation, he did a service to the cause of human progress of which the value can hardly be exaggerated.[1] But S. Jerome is a Roman satirist who is sometimes carried away by the love of startling effect and vivid phrase. He is also the ascetic, tortured by the consciousness of human frailty, and again almost intoxicated with the vision of God.

The views which S. Jerome held as to the ideal of virtue, and especially of sexual virtue, are of the extreme monastic type. To him, as to so many others in that day, the world is so full of allurements, the flesh is so weak and sensual, the devil is so cunning in laying snares for the soul, that the only chance of escape lies in absolute renunciation. The Greek ideal of moral perfection, as a middle state between excess and defect of passion, seems to the ascetic impracticable or unworthy. Avarice can only be conquered by selling all one's possessions and giving to the poor.[2] Luxury in dress and food must be replaced by sackcloth and herbs, and an avoidance of the

---

[1] *Ep.* 112, § 20 ; cf. *Ep.* 104 ; 57, § 7 ; 53, § 7, nec scire dignantur, quid Prophetae, quid Apostoli senserint : sed ad sensum incongrua aptant testimonia : quasi grande sit, et non vitiosissimum docendi genus, depravare sententias, et ad voluntatem suam Scripturam trahere repugnantem. In replying to a charge of favouring the heretical views of Origen, he announces a principle which, in theological controversy, is rarely obeyed : Nec bonis adversariorum, si honestum quid habuerint, detrahendum est, nec amicorum laudanda sunt vitia, *Ep.* 83, § 2. For S. Jerome's defence of his character, *v. Ep.* 45, § 2. For the secret of the bitterness with which he was assailed, *v.* Sulp. Sev. *Dial.* i. 9, § 4, oderunt eum clerici, quia vitam eorum insectatur et crimina.

[2] *Ep.* 108, § 19.

bath.[1]   The pleasures of love, which are treated as
merely sensual, must be utterly rejected as debasing to
the elect soul.   Honourable marriage ranks below the
purity of intact virginity, and the recovered chastity of
widowhood.[2]   Nothing can exceed the extravagance
with which S. Jerome, who was an experienced man of
the world, celebrates the self-devotion of Demetrias to
the virgin state.   Her family, like so many others of the
great Roman houses, had been ruined by the invasion of
Alaric.[3]   Rome had been given up to fire and sword.
The fairest provinces were already overrun by the
Sueves and Goths.   The fame of a world-wide empire
and civilisation, the splendid traditions and the hopes of
senatorial houses of immemorial antiquity, were vanishing
amid an agony of regret, all the more pathetic, because
hardly a voice from it comes down to our ears.   Yet the
devotion of Demetrias to the virgin state, according to
her eulogist, exalts her family to a higher pinnacle than
its long line of consuls and prefects have ever reached ;
it is a consolation for a Rome in ashes ; Italy puts off its
mourning at the news ; the villages in the farthest
provinces are beside themselves with joy.   Some of this
is no doubt mere rhetoric, but it is the rhetoric of a man
whose own passions had been conquered only by flight to
the Syrian desert, by incessant vigils, by fasting and
prayer.[4]   And the whole letter to Eustochium, in which
that well-known passage occurs, suggests other considerations which should be kept in view in reading the
criticisms of ancient moralists on their own times.
Probably every modern reader of that letter is lost in

[1] *Ep.* 107, §§ 9, 10 ; xxiii. § 2.
[2] *Ib.* 130, §§ 3, 5. Her father
is felix morte sua qui non vidit
patriam corruentem ; immo felicior
qui . . . nobilitatem insigniorem
reddidit filiae perpetua castitate ;
cf. 22, § 19. The best passage is
123, § 11, sufficit tibi quod primum

perdidisti virginitatis gradum, et
per tertium venisti ad secundum,
id est, per officium conjugale, ad
viduitatis continentiam.

[3] The letter was written circa
414.

[4] *Ep.* 22, § 7.

astonishment that it could have been possibly addressed
by any man to a young woman belonging to one of the
greatest families at Rome. It handles, without the
slightest restraint or reserve, sins and temptations of the
flesh to which we now hardly allude. It is absolutely
inconceivable that any moralist or preacher of our times,
however earnest or fanatical, should address a woman in
such a style.[1] This is not said with any intention of
depreciating S. Jerome, whose character emerged un-
stained from the fiercest ordeal of malignant calumny in
his own time, and has borne the scrutiny of fifteen
centuries. He would be a daring man who would charge
S. Jerome with pruriency. But we may fairly say that
the writer of the letter to Eustochium is likely to let us
know the very worst of his generation, and that he will
not throw the veil of conventional ignorance over deeds
of darkness, which our more timorous delicacy has been
accustomed, at any rate until lately, to treat as non-
existent. Whether unflinching candour or studied
reserve is the best tone to adopt with regard to moral
evil, is a question which need not be discussed. But
that difference of tone between the ancients and ourselves should never be forgotten in studying the
character of a distant past. By keeping it in mind
we may be saved alike from Pharisaism and from an
ungenerous judgment of times which have made a self-
revelation of which we should be incapable.

When we come to examine what S. Jerome has told
us of the moral condition of his time, we are struck with
the fact that his heaviest censure falls on those who, at
least in name, had separated themselves from the world,
the monks and the secular clergy of Rome. It is true
that he consigns Praetextatus, the votary of Isis and
Mithra, to outer darkness.[2] But Praetextatus is not

---

[1] *Ep.* 22, esp. §§ 7, 13.
[2] *Ib.* 23, 3, ille quem ante

paucos dies dignitatum omnium
culmina praecedebant . . . ad

condemned on moral grounds, but as the enthusiastic champion of the old gods. On the other hand, the pontiff Albinus, a staunch though tolerant pagan, is treated by Jerome with marked respect.[1] His unbelief is even made the subject of gentle raillery. His wife was a Christian. His daughter Laeta, who had succeeded in converting her young husband Toxotius, was a devotee after S. Jerome's heart. S. Jerome speaks of Albinus as " a candidate for the faith," and would have hopes that his little granddaughter's hymns to Christ, as she sits on the old man's knees, might win him from his errors. Another great magnate, Cerealis,[2] a man of the world, of great official distinction, wished to marry one of S. Jerome's ascetic friends. Nothing is said of the religious views of Cerealis, but the very silence on the subject probably shows that they were not very decided. Yet S. Jerome describes him as a man of spotless character. Olybrius, another member of the noble class, was probably a Christian, but like his father Probus, the great prefect, was probably not a very ardent one. Along with his brother Probinus, he was celebrated with all the pomp of pagan mythology by the poet Claudian. His virtues as a son, a husband, and a citizen are not less emphatically extolled in a letter of S. Jerome.[3] The saint professed to regard Rome as the mystic Babylon of the Apocalypse,[4] from which the true followers of Christ should flee to the desert, "blossoming with the flowers of Christ." Yet when we look for details, we find little in S. Jerome to

cujus interitum urbs universa commota est, nunc desolatus et nudus, non in lacteo caeli palatio, ut uxor mentitur infelix, sed in sordentibus tenebris continetur ; cf. *c. Johann. Hierosol.* 8, miserabilis Praetextatus . . . homo sacrilegus, et idolorum cultor. The condemnation of Praetextatus is expressly on the ground of his heathen superstition. The inscriptions (*C.I.L.* 1779), in which he and his wife Aconia

Fabia Paulina commemorate one another's virtues, reveal a religious enthusiasm which explains S. Jerome's bitterness ; cf. Seeck's *Symmachus*, lxxxiii. on the whole career of Vettius Agorius Praetextatus.

[1] Hieron. *Ep.* 107, § 1.
[2] *Ib.* 127, § 2.
[3] *Ib.* 130, § 3 ; cf. Seeck's *Sym.* cv. ; Claud. *Cons. Prob. et Olyb.*
[4] *Ib.* 46, § 11.

lead us to believe that the men of the great families, with whom Paula, Marcella, and Melania associated, fell below the moral standard of their ancestors or even below the level of worldly respectability in our own time.

Christian asceticism, however, like every other great movement which has disturbed the routine of life, had its *raison d'être.* There were serious perils to virtue in the household life of the fourth and fifth century, which S. Jerome has laid bare with an unsparing frankness, though probably also with some exaggeration. Among these the system of domestic slavery was the most fruitful of corruption.[1] In the days of Salvianus, as in the days of Horace, the attractive slave-girl too often was the easy prey of her master's lusts; and amours of this kind were regarded even in Christian families with a tolerance which astonishes modern sentiment.[2] Perhaps even more insidious was the influence of female slaves on their young mistresses. The attendants who surrounded the Roman lady at her elaborate toilet, and decked her out in her silks and jewels, were often not the safest companions for inexperienced innocence. Their class had often a bitter hatred of the Christian faith,[3] and spread the most malignant rumours about its professors. They flattered with the ease and familiarity of privileged favourites. The picture of the greed, lubricity, and spitefulness of this chattering crowd,[4] who surrounded the lady of noble rank, was probably a much-needed revelation of one of the worst cankers at the root of Roman society.

S. Jerome, like Ammianus Marcellinus, was disgusted with the display of wealth, which seems to have become more ostentatious and vulgar, as artistic skill and feeling decayed. But in S. Jerome's pages women are the great

[1] Hieron. *Ep.* 54, §§ 5, 6 ; cf. 107, § 4 ; cf. Wallon, *Hist. de l'Esclav.* ii. pp. 325 *sqq.;* Friedländer, i. p. 328.

[2] Paulinus Pellaeus, *Euch.* 166, contentus domus inlecebris famulantibus uti.

[3] Hieron. *Ep.* 54, § 5.

[4] *Ib.* 117, § 8.

offenders.   Their gaudy turbans and elaborate coiffures,
their costly silks and liberally applied cosmetics, and
blazing wealth of jewels, are described with a scorn which
makes the minute observation of detail somewhat surpris-
ing.[1]   The saint often warns his female disciples against
the danger of appearing among the fashionable and showy
crowd.[2]   The danger to female innocence seemed to him
so great that the only safety for a woman lay in cutting
herself off absolutely from the world.   It is hard to
believe that the reserve and delicacy of so many generations of social culture should have grown so helpless in
the face of evil.   And the warm imagination of S. Jerome
has probably exaggerated the peril.   If we may believe
him, the curled and essenced fop was almost irresistible
in those days.[3]   A touch of his hand and a glance from
his eye seem to have placed young women of rank and
breeding at his mercy.   There is probably better ground
for the disgust with which the appearance of the fashionable matron in the streets is described.[4]   She takes her
airing in a litter surrounded by a great troop of slaves
and eunuchs, and closely attended by some foppish major-
domo or favourite domestic, whose pampered air and easy
familiarity sometimes cast a shade of suspicion on his
mistress's fair fame.   But the great danger was the
banquet.   *Difficile inter epulas servatur pudicitia.*[5]   It is
hard for us now to realise that this should be true of a
polished society with an ancient tradition of dignity.
Yet S. Jerome, in his ardour for the ascetic life as the
only path of salvation for frail humanity, places his ban
on what we should regard as innocent enjoyment of a
hospitable table.   The description of the effects, on the
hot blood of the south, of rich wines and delicate meats

[1] Hieron. *Ep.* 54, § 7 ; 108, § 15 ;
127, § 3.
[2] *Ib.* 130, § 18 ; 54, § 13 ; 107,
§ 7.
[3] *Ib.* 117, § 6, dabit tibi bar-
batulus quilibet manum, susten-
tabit lassam ; et pressis digitis, aut
tentabitur aut tentabit.
[4] *Ib.* 54, § 13.
[5] *Ib.* 117, § 6 ; 107, § 8.

in many courses, with the accompaniments of voluptuous
music and suggestive dancing, may represent the tone of
certain circles of his age.   It would be certainly true of
many in the time of Cicero.   But it is difficult to believe
that the high-minded, stately, and cultivated ladies, so
many of whom are known to us,[1] had been exposed to
the contamination of such grossness in their youth, or
that they could not observe the limit between harmless
natural enjoyment and sensual indulgence.   The truth is
that S. Jerome is not only a monk but an artist in words;
and his horror of evil, his vivid imagination, and his
passion for literary effect occasionally carry him beyond
the region of sober fact.   There was much to amend in
the morals of the Roman world.   But we must not take
the leader of a great moral reformation as a cool and dispassionate observer.

About the time when this letter of S. Jerome was
penned, Macrobius represents the leading members of
the pagan aristocracy, Symmachus, Albinus, Flavianus,
Praetextatus, as spending the days of the Saturnalia
together.   The mornings were given up to learned discussions on antiquarian and literary subjects.   In the
evening they met for lighter and gayer conversation at
dinner; and our attention is expressly drawn to the
elegant moderation of that day in food and drink, and to
the banishment of the dancing girl and the buffoon from
the banquet.[2]   The evidence of Macrobius, who is writing
without any *parti pris*, is worth at least as much as that of
S. Jerome on such a point.   And if such was the tone of
the pagan aristocracy, can we believe that the great
Christian houses would be more lax ?

[1] Paula, Hieron. *Ep.* 108; Serena, Claudian. *Laus Serenae* ; Fabia Aconia Paulina, *C.I.L.* vi. 1779 ; Blaesilla, Hieron. *Ep.* 39 ; Laeta, Zos. v. 39.

[2] Macrob. *Sat.* ii. 1, § 4 ; iii. 13.

Compare with this S. Jerome's *Ep.* 117, § 6.   Although Praetextatus is one of the party in the *Saturnalia*, the scene is laid in some year after his death in 385, as appears from the passage i. 1, § 5.

But if S. Jerome deals hardly with the vices of the worldly classes, he is perhaps even more merciless to those of the professedly strict and religious; and it is to the credit of his candour and sincerity that he lays bare with such an unsparing hand the corruption in Christian society, even in the inner circles of asceticism. In some of his descriptions of ecclesiastical worldliness and corruption the very spirit of Juvenal is upon him.[1] And his consuming zeal for a great cause probably made him less merciful to the failings of his own class than a man of the world would have been. Yet, after all allowances, the picture is not a pleasant one. We feel that we are far away from the simple, unworldly devotion of the freedmen and obscure toilers whose existence was hardly known to the great world before the age of the Antonines,[2] and who lived in the spirit of the Sermon on the Mount and in constant expectation of the coming of their Lord. The triumphant Church, which has brought paganism to its knees, is very different from the Church of the catacombs and the persecutions. The Bishop of Rome has become a great potentate surrounded by worldly pomp, and with a powerful voice in the councils of the State.[3] In the reign of Valentinian (367) the rival factions of Damasus and Ursinus had convulsed the city in their struggles for this splendid prize, and in one day one hundred and thirty-seven corpses were left on the pavement of one of the churches.[4] Ammianus Marcellinus, who describes the conflict, thinks it natural that men should so contend for the chance of being enriched by the offerings of Roman matrons, of riding in elegant apparel through the streets, and giving banquets of more than regal splendour. The pagan Praetextatus used to

---

[1] For the satiric vein in S. Jerome, cf. the sketch of Grunnius, the impotent critic, *Ep.* 125, § 18; and the great lady at S. Peter's Basilica, 22, § 32.

[2] Renan, *M. Aurèle*, p. 447; cf. pp. 55, 56; cf. Friedländer, iii. p. 533.

[3] Zos. v. 41.

[4] Amm. Marc. xxvii. 3, 12.

say jestingly to Pope Damasus, that he might be tempted to become a Christian by the prospect of being Bishop of Rome.[1]

Among all ranks of the clergy corruption prevailed. The evils of seduction and captation became so grave that, in an edict addressed to Pope Damasus,[2] the Emperor Valentinian I. sternly prohibited monks and ecclesiastics from entering the houses of widows or orphan wards, and made illegal both *donatio inter vivos* and testamentary bequests in favour of the Church. It may be doubted whether the law was strictly obeyed. The higher clergy generally seem to have lived in very un-evangelical worldly state and luxury.[3] They often entertained at sumptuous feasts great magistrates and prefects. The clerical epicure, brought up in a hovel and fed on milk and black bread in his boyhood,[4] develops an extraordinary delicacy of taste in his later years. He has the nicest judgment in fish and game, and the provinces are distinguished by their ability to satisfy his palate. Holy Orders become the passport to social distinction and dangerous influence. The doors of great houses opened readily to the elegant priest whose toilet was managed by a skilful valet. The clerical profession, so far from imposing restraint, furnished facilities for intrigue. The priest was admitted to the intimacy of superstitious women of the world, which was pleasant and lucrative, but perilous to virtue.[5] The supple and accomplished ecclesiastic has a great advantage among the crowd of morning callers on the rich young matron, who repays his flattering attentions with a present of whatever his covetous eyes have lighted on.[6] The passion for wealth invaded all ranks of the clergy. Many were

[1] Hieron. *c. Johann. Hierosol.* 8, solebat ludens beato papae Damaso dicere ; facite me Romanae ecclesiae episcopum et ero protinus Christianus.

[2] *C. Th.* xvi. 2, 20.

[3] Hieron. *Ep.* 52, § 11 ; cf. Sulp.

Sev. *Dial.* i. 21, 3.

[4] Hieron. *Ep.* 52, § 6.

[5] *Ib.* 52, § 5.

[6] *Ib.* 22, § 16, clerici ipsi . . . extenta manu, ut benedicere eos putes velle, pretia accipiunt salutandi ; and § 28.

engaged in amassing fortunes in trade.[1] They will perform
the most disgusting and menial offices for some heirless
lady on her deathbed.[2] Even the monk in the Nitrian
desert is infected with the universal contagion,[3] and piles
up a secret hoard which his brethren are sorely troubled
to dispose of at his death. If we believe S. Jerome,
numbers of these clerical and monkish impostors became
far richer than they could have been, if they had
remained in the world.[4] They go about asking for alms
to be distributed to the poor, but secretly enrich themselves; making a parade of their bare feet, black cloaks,
and long unkempt hair, they creep into houses and
" deceive silly women laden with sins." Pretending[5] to
live in the greatest austerity, they spent their nights in
secret feasting and sensuality.

The picture which S. Jerome draws of female society
is so repulsive that we would gladly believe it to be
exaggerated. But if the priesthood with its enormous
influence was so corrupt, it is only too probable that it
debased the sex which is always most under clerical
influence. That clerical concubinage, under the pretence
of the severest sanctity, was common, cannot be doubted
by any one acquainted with the writers of the time. S.
Jerome is perfectly explicit on the subject. Men and
women, vowed to perpetual chastity, lived under the
same roof,[6] brazening out the miserable imposture of

[1] Hieron. *Ep.* 52, § 5 ; 125, § 16,
negotiatorem clericum, et ex inopi
divitem, ex ignobili gloriosum,
quasi quandam pestem fuge.

[2] *Ib.* 52, § 6 ; ipsi apponunt ma-
tulam, obsident lectum, purulen-
tiam stomachi . . . manu propria
suscipiunt. Pavent ad introitum
medici trementibusque labiis an
commodius habeant sciscitantur
. . . simulataque laetitia mens in-
trinsecus avara torquetur.

[3] *Ib.* 22, § 33, centum solidos

quos lino texendo acquisierat dere-
liquit, etc.

[4] *Ib.* 125, § 16, non victum et
vestitum, quod Apostolus praecipit,
sed majora quam saeculi homines
emolumenta sectantes ; *Ep.* 60, § 11,
sint ditiores monachi quam fuerant
saeculares.

[5] *Ib.* 22, § 28, et quasi longa
jejunia, furtivis noctium cibis pro-
trahunt.

[6] *Ib.* 22, § 14, eadem domo, uno
cubiculo, saepe uno tenentur lectulo;
cf. Sulp. Sev. *Dial.* i. 8, 4 ; i, 9, 4.

superhuman purity under impossible conditions.   There
is a curious letter of S. Jerome's to a young lady of
position in Gaul,[1] written at the instance of her brother,
which is a singular illustration of the union of superstition and licence.   She makes a profession of leading a
Christian life, yet she has separated from her mother,
and has installed, as master of her house, a " brother "
who is apparently, and is regarded by the neighbourhood,
as equally master of her house and of her virtue.[2]

On a not much higher level are those virgins of the
Church,[3] whose peculiar dress is their only title to the
name which they disgrace, and who strut about the
streets, nodding and leering.   In many so-called Christian
circles the gay, supple " virgin "[4] who would laugh at
jests of doubtful freedom, and who had a relish for spiteful gossip, was much more popular than the " rough and
rustic " person whose religion was not a fraud.   Many
other sketches of female character have been left us by
the pencil of S. Jerome—the sot who justifies her love of
wine with a profane jest,[5] the great lady puffed up by
the honours of her house, and surrounded by a herd of
sycophants, the great lady who passes through S. Peter's,
attended by a crowd of eunuchs, doling out alms with
equal parsimony and ostentation, and repulsing the
importunate widow with blows.[6]   Such scenes and
characters, like those in the Sixth Satire of Juvenal, one
would gladly believe to be brilliant and imaginative
pictures of an exceptional degradation of character.   If
they represent anything like a general tone, it becomes

[1] Hieron. *Ep.* 117.

[2] *Ib.* 117, § 9.

[3] *Ib.* 117, § 7 ; xxii. 13, hae sunt
quae per publicum notabiliter ince-
dunt ; et furtivis oculorum nuti-
bus adolescentium greges post se
trahunt.

[4] *Ib.* 22, § 24-29, ecce vere
ancilla Christi, dicentes, ecce tota

simplicitas.   Non ut illa horrida,
turpis, rusticana, terribilis, et quae
ideo forsitan maritum non habuit,
quia invenire non potuit.

[5] *Ep.* 22, § 13, ubi se mero in-
gurgitaverint, ebrietati sacrilegium
copulantes : Absit ut ego me a
Christi sanguine abstineam ! Even
worse precedes.

[6] *Ib.* 22, § 32.

easy to understand the exodus from the second Babylon,
and the charm of the hermitage in the desert [1] "from
which are drawn the stones whereof is builded the city
of the Great King." It would seem that the Church, in
conquering the citadel of the Empire, had lost the freshness and purity of its early days. It had vanquished
the external power of heathenism; it had still to subdue
the forces of corruption within its own pale. It is at all
times hard for mediocre character to sincerely embrace a
lofty ideal, and the spectacle of grovelling worldliness
and materialism affecting the tone of an elevated
spirituality is not unknown in later days. But in the
fourth century there was found a remnant ready to
sacrifice everything at the summons of an imperious
faith. The members of the proudest houses sold all that
they had, and turned their backs upon state and luxury, in
order to spend the remainder of life in works of mercy
and prayer. And in reading the letters of S. Jerome we
should never forget that he is of that elect company,
that he regards Roman society in the high light shining
from the Cross, and that the Cross to him is not the
mere symbol of a lightly held creed, but an imperious
power, demanding a surrender of will and earthly passion
as complete as the Great Sacrifice of all. The glory of
that age is the number of those who were capable of
such self-surrender; and an age should be judged by its
ideals, not by the mediocrity of conventional religion
masking worldly self-indulgence. This we have always
with us; the other we have not always.

More than fifty years have passed away. The
cataclysm of barbarism has fallen on the West. Provinces have been ravaged, splendid cities have been
desolated, and the imperial power has been shaken to its

---

[1] *Ep.* 14, § 10, O desertum Christi   illi nascuntur lapides de quibus
floribus vernans, O solitudo in qua   civitas magni regis extruitur.

base. S. Jerome, on the news of the earliest disasters reaching him, exclaimed, "The barbarians are strong through our vices."[1]   And this is the text on which another great preacher calls the Roman world to recognise in their calamities the righteous punishment for their sins. Salvianus, a presbyter of Marseilles, must have seen almost the close of the fifth century.[2]   Born probably at Cologne,[3] and educated in the School of Trèves, he had witnessed in his early youth the horrors of the great invasion which laid the cities of the Rhineland in ashes. From these troubles he sought refuge in the south of Gaul, where he lived in intimacy with some of the great bishops of the time,—S. Eucher and S. Hilarius, and the scholarly and ascetic society which made the Isle of Lérins its home. He is a man of keen sympathies and fiery temperament, full of the ascetic ideals of his time. He feels a burning indignation against the selfishness of the wealthy and official class, and an equally passionate pity for the poor and oppressed, which, had he lived in the nineteenth century, would certainly have made him a Socialist of the extremest type.[4]   The thesis of the treatise entitled *de Gubernatione Dei* is very simple.[5] The unbelieving Epicureanism of the day saw in the calamities of Gaul only a proof of the indifference of the Deity to the fortunes of men.[6]   Salvianus saw in them

[1] *Ep.* 60, § 17, nostris peccatis Barbari fortes sunt: nostris vitiis Romanus superatur exercitus.

[2] Gennad. *de Scrip. Eccl.* c. 67, vivit usque hodie in senectute bona. Gennadius was a contemporary of Pope Gelasius, to whom he sent the work quoted, *v.* c. 100. But for doubts about this section cf. Ebert, p. 447, n. 4.

[3] Salv. *Ep.* 1, adolescens quem ad vos misi Agrippinae captus est et de quo aliquid fortasse amplius dicerem, nisi propinquus meus esset.

[4] See *passim* the four books *ad*

Ecclesiam, against avarice; cf. especially iii. 49, pauper beatitudinem emit mendacitate, dives supplicium facultate.

[5] The work was written after 439, for it mentions (vii. 40) the defeat of Litorius at Toulouse; and probably before 451, for the defeat of Attila by the Romans and Visigoths is not alluded to.

[6] The effect of the calamities in shaking men's faith in Providence may be seen in the poem *de Prov. Div.* (wrongly attributed to Prosper Aq.) vv. 25-85.

the clearest evidence of His providential government, punishing sin by leaving the sinner to the appropriate consequences of his misdeeds. The Roman world has deserved its fate by its injustice and oppression, its cupidity, its lack of hardy public spirit, its foul and universal licentiousness. Prefects and governors [1] have been venal and cruel; the minor officials have been even more so. The curiales, the governing order of the municipalities, have been so many tyrants, laying on and levying taxes of which the heaviest burden falls on those least able to bear them.[2] If, by imperial grace, these exactions are lightened, it is not the poor, but the richest class, who feel the relief.[3] Even those who have devoted themselves to a strict spiritual life are tainted by the universal contagion. They will be guilty of the grossest oppression when they get the chance.[4] If they have wealth they are as ready as the most cynical worldling to hoard their money instead of giving it to Christ's poor, and they will actually pretend that their sacred profession exempts them from the duty of such a sacrifice. They, wearing the dress of an ostentatious asceticism, will plead that Christ has no need of their gifts [5]—Christ, who is the universal Sufferer, whose infinite pity makes Him sharer in all the sufferings of His servants. Christ, exclaims the preacher in a passage of rhetorical power, is the most needy in the universe, because He feels the needs of all.

There can be little doubt that the hardened venality of the financial service, and the greed and rapacity of the

---

[1] *De Gub. Dei*, v. 25, iv. 21, vii. 91.

[2] *Ib.* v. 18, ubi non quot Curiales fuerint tot tyranni sunt?

[3] *Ib.* v. 35; cf. v. 30, decernunt potentes quod solvant pauperes. On the corruption of the curiales, see *C. Th.* xii. 1, 117; Sym. *Ep.* ix. 10; also *C. Th.* xiii. 10, 1, on the shifting of fiscal burdens from potentes by collusion of the Tabularii.

[4] *De Gub. Dei*, v. 51-56, licita non faciunt et illicita committunt; temperant a concubitu, non temperant a rapina.

[5] Salv. *ad Eccles.* iv. 22.

great landowners, were the vices which did most to
undermine the fabric of Roman society. Of this we
shall furnish, in a succeeding chapter, ample proofs from
the Roman Code. But Salvianus, like some of the old
Greek philosophers, regarded the love of pleasure as
inevitably linked with the love of gold. The populations
of the great towns, the men who were continually growing richer and more powerful by the impoverishment of
their neighbours, were all alike sunk in the most abomin-
able sensuality.[1] The theatre and the circus had been
for five centuries the great corruptors of the Roman
world. But in spite of the thunders of the Church, and
the calamities of the times, these schools of cruelty and
lust retained all their old fascination far into the fifth
century.[2] Apollinaris Sidonius, about 460, describes, as
still flourishing at Narbonne,[3] that degraded pantomime,
in which the foulest tales of the old mythology were
represented in speaking gesture. The games of the circus
were held at Arles as late as 461, in honour of Majorian.[4]
It is true that, owing to the growing poverty of the
municipalities, these exhibitions had in many places
ceased to be held ; and a self-complacent optimism took
credit for this as a sign of a higher moral tone.[5] But
Salvianus ruthlessly exposes the pretence. The Roman
character, he maintains, is still unaltered, but it no
longer has the means of gratifying its base tastes.
Wherever, as at Rome or Ravenna, the public amusements can still be kept up, the people will flock, as in
old times, to witness them. The baptismal vow to
renounce " all these works of the devil " is forgotten by
a nominally Christian people. The churches are emptied,
the holy mysteries of the altar are contemptuously
deserted for the feverish excitement of the circus.

---

[1] On the corruption of Aquitaine,
v. *de Gub. Dei*, vii. 16.
[2] *Ib.* vi. 49.
[3] *Carm.* xxiii. 283 *sqq.*

[4] Fauriel, *Hist. de la Gaule Rom.*
i. 394 ; Chaix, *Apollin. Sid.* i.
135.
[5] Salv. *de Gub. Dei.* vi. 49, 50.

Even the apparition of the invaders could not abate the
rage of the populace for its accustomed indulgence. The
Christians of Cirta and Carthage were cheering rival
charioteers, or revelling in the turpitudes of the theatre,
when their walls were surrounded by the Vandals.[1]
Like the plague of Athens,[2] or the plague in the Middle
Ages,[3] the disasters and confusion of the fifth century
made men reckless and prone to frantic excesses. The
leading citizens[4] of Trèves, a city which bore the first
and fiercest onslaught of the invaders, and was four
times, within a few years, given up to fire and sword,
were revelling in a frenzy of drunken debauchery when
the enemy were at their gates. Scenes such as these
Salvianus had seen in his boyhood. They had burnt
themselves into his memory, and the recollection of them
accounts for the almost ferocious energy and persistent
iteration with which he denounces the self-indulgence of
his time.

But although we may believe that overwhelming
disaster may have driven men here and there to drown
their sorrow in wild and vicious excitement, it is difficult
to credit the charge of universal and shameless immorality
which Salvianus makes against the men of his province.
That the slave-system is dangerous to the morals of the
masters is the experience of all ages. But what is
dangerous to some, need not be fatal to all. Yet
Salvianus makes no exception in his impeachment of
the morals of Southern Gaul. Every estate is a scene of
prostitution.[5] Aquitaine is one vast *lupanar*. Conjugal

[1] Salv. *de Gub. Dei*, vi. 69.

[2] Thuc. ii. 53, πρῶτόν τε ἦρξε καὶ
ἐς τἆλλα τῇ πόλει ἐπὶ πλέον ἀνομίας
τὸ νόσημα.

[3] Introd. to Boccaccio's *Decam-
eron*.

[4] Salv. *de Gub. Dei*, vi. 72. Salvianus seems to have witnessed
some of these scenes with his own
eyes (vidi ego ipse, etc.).

[5] *Ib.* vii. 16, quis potentum
ac divitum non in luto libidinis
vixit : paene unum lupanar omnium
vita. The conquest of Spain by
the "imbelles Vandali" is accounted for solely by the immorality of the conquered (vii.
27). The sensuality of Roman
Africa is described in even stronger
language (vii. 70), video quasi

faithfulness is unknown.   Except in the ranks of those
who had taken the vow of renunciation, Salvianus will
not allow the existence of a decent virtue.   It is, of
course, never possible to say how a whole population has
lived ; but this is equally true of the attack as of the
defence of moral character.   We can only form a
hesitating judgment on the scanty evidence which has
come down to us, and on general probability based
on experience of human nature.   The indictment of
Salvianus cannot be reconciled with the contemporary
picture of society which we have in the letters of
Sidonius.   And if Salvianus be accurate, the Church
must have utterly failed in raising the mass of the Gallic
people to a higher life.   There must have been no mean
between the small class who renounced fortune and
family ties at the call of Christ, and the monsters of
cruel rapacity and unbridled lust described by Salvianus.
We know minutely the state of the society of Bordeaux [1]
sixty years before the *de Gubernatione Dei* appeared.   In
the cultivated circle there, there is little trace of ardent
Christian belief.   Yet there is also little trace of shameless vice.   The contemporary society of Symmachus at
Rome was severely respectable, in spite of its pagan
sympathies.   If Aquitanian morals, in the time of
Salvianus, were so thoroughly corrupt, then, in spite of
the spiritual triumphs of S. Martin, in spite of the efforts
of a highly organised church, ruled by many bishops of
saintly character and great popular influence, the tone
of provincial society must have fallen below the level of
Ausonius and his friends, and of those grave and strict
provincial senators who, ten generations before Ausonius,
were regarded by Tacitus [2] as the salt of the Roman

---

scaturientem vitiis civitatem . . .
cunctos vario luxus marcore per-
ditos. And again, vii. 75, quis in
illo numero tam innumero castus
fuit ?

[1] See c. 3 of this book.
[2] *Ann.* iii. 55, simul novi homines
e municipiis et coloniis atque etiam
provinciis in senatum adsumpti
domesticam   parsimoniam   in-

world. Salvianus, like S. Jerome, judged the men of his time by a standard which might bear hardly on the most respectable societies of modern Christendom. Salvianus is essentially a preacher. But the preacher, from his vocation, and in proportion to his enthusiasm for righteousness, cannot be a dispassionate observer. His *raison d'être* is to edify, not to describe or analyse with historical accuracy. He will seldom refer to virtues already won ; he will exaggerate faults which he wishes to eradicate ; he will blacken even his own past to exalt the grace that has saved him ; and he will be equally merciless to the sins of those whom he is striving to raise to a higher life. The society of Salvianus, while nominally Christian, was as little inclined as modern society to carry out in daily practice precepts which interfere with material success. The men who did so then lost caste, and were regarded by the polished and selfish world very much as Horace Walpole [1] would have treated an aristocratic friend who had turned Methodist. On the other hand, the man who has made the great renunciation is apt to treat the worldly class as worse than it really is. Its placid materialism, its bourgeois contempt for all ideal aims, irritate to madness the soul to whom death and the Great Judgment and the life to come are the only realities. The grosser sins of a small minority are regarded as the natural product of that absorption in the things of the perishing world which is the choice or the necessity of the mass of men at all times. But the monsters of depravity in every age are probably as rare as the paragons of saintly virtue. And we need not take too literally the *mot* of Salvianus that "the Roman world was laughing when it died."

tulerunt ; cf. xvi. 5. The opinion which Tacitus held, as to the severity of morals in the provinces, is confirmed by the picture which Ausonius gives of his family circle in the *Parentalia*.

[1] H. Walpole's *Letters*, vol. iii. p. 191 (to J. Chute).

CHAPTER II

In the preceding chapter we have reviewed the adverse judgments of some contemporary moralists on the state of society in the fourth and fifth centuries. But we fortunately possess, in the other literary remains of that age, materials for forming an estimate independent of either Christian or pagan censors. The letters of Q. Aurelius Symmachus,[1] the poems of Ausonius, and the *Saturnalia* of Macrobius reveal to us the life of the cultivated upper class, both in the capital and the provinces, in the years immediately preceding the first shock of the great invasions. The poems and voluminous correspondence of Apollinaris Sidonius form an invaluable storehouse of information as to the tone and habits of Gallo-Roman society, in the years when the last shadowy emperors were appearing and disappearing like puppets in rapid succession at the beck of a German master of the forces, and when a Visigothic government had been organised in Aquitaine. Symmachus and Macrobius, although they witnessed the final triumph of the Church, belonged to the ranks of that conservative paganism which made a last stand in defence of the old system of religion, and nourished their patriotic and

---

[1] Q. Aurel. Symmachus was probably born not long after 340, and died not long after 402 (Seeck, xliv. ; cf. Peter, *Geschichtl. Litt.* i. 31). Apollinaris Sidonius was born about 430 (he was adolescens in the year 449, *Ep.* viii. 6), and was alive "three olympiads" after his consecration as bishop of Auvergne in 472 (*Ib.* ix. 12).

aristocratic pride with the dreams of a past that was gone for ever. Sidonius represents a society which, though obstinately Roman in culture and sentiment, had been nominally Christian for two generations, was living in close contact with the German invaders, and was becoming dimly conscious that the old order was passing away.

Q. Aurelius Symmachus belonged to a family which held a foremost place in the last quarter of the fourth century, but was not equal to some others in wealth and antiquity. His grandfather was consul in the reign of Constantine.[1] His father had been prefect of the city in the reign of Valentinian I., and, after holding all the high offices, still survived in the year 382. The line was prolonged through a succession of distinguished descendants. Symmachi appear in the Fasti as consuls in 446 and 485. A female descendant of the orator was the wife of the great Boethius, and the mother of the two consuls of 522.[2] Q. Aurelius Symmachus, the author of the letters, married a daughter of Memmius Vitrasius Orfitus, who was Urban prefect in the reign of Constantius. He was trained in speaking, as so many young Romans of that age were, by a Gallic professor of rhetoric;[3] and in his early youth he formed a close friendship with the poet Ausonius at the court of Valentinian on the Rhine.[4] His earliest efforts in oratory were panegyrics on that Emperor, and on Gratian, delivered at Trèves during the campaigns against the Alemanni. The oratory of Symmachus was greatly admired by his contemporaries,[5] and he was repeatedly

---

[1] Seeck's *Sym.* xli. For the career of L. Aur. Avianius Symmachus see *C.I.L.* vi. 1698.

[2] Rusticiana, the wife of Boethius, bears the name of her great-great-grandmother, the wife of Q. Aurelius Symmachus; cf. the Stemma of the Symmachi in Seeck, xl.

[3] Sym. *Ep.* ix. 88.

[4] *Ib. Ep.* i. 32; Auson. *Ep.* xvii., dum in comitatu degimus ambo.

[5] He was entrusted with the choice of a professor of rhetoric for Milan; his choice fell on S. Augustine. Aug. *Conf.* v. c. 13, § 23; cf. Macrob. v. 1, 7; Prudent. *c. Sym.* i. 632.

selected to put before the Emperor the views of the
Senate on questions of the day. His speech on the
removal of the Altar of Victory is not unworthy of his
fame, and has acquired additional interest from the
replies of his kinsman Ambrose and the poet Prudentius.

The inscription[1] dedicated by Q. Fab. Memmius
Symmachus to the memory of the great senator recites a
long list of offices which he had held. He had been
governor of several provinces, prefect of the city, pontiff
and consul. He was admittedly the chief of the Senate.
Yet probably no public man ever left behind him a
collection of letters of so little general interest. In an
age of great conflicts and great changes, it is startling
to find Symmachus complaining to his correspondents
of lack of matter.[2] Either the government was very
reticent,[3] or Symmachus and his circle were very
unobservant or careless of public affairs. The Senate
was still treated by the emperors with ceremonious
respect, and possessed many valuable privileges. But
after the great reorganisation by Diocletian, it had ceased
to have any share in the government. Like the consulship, it remained as one of those dignified fictions by
which the Roman disguised the vastness of the change
which separated him from the days of freedom. It was
indeed part of the policy of Stilicho to consult and pay
deference to the Senate, and in the troubled years of
Alaric's invasions that body appeared more than once to
exercise some independent authority. But these were
only the illusions of a moment. Occasionally the
Emperor condescended to send it a despatch, the arrival
of which, to men like Symmachus, was an event of the
first importance. That not a moment might be lost, the
august body would sometimes be summoned before dawn

[1] *C.I.L.* vi. 1699.

[2] *Ep.* iii. 10 ; cf. ii. 35, at olim
parentes etiam patriae negotia,
quae nunc angusta vel nulla sunt,
in familiares paginas conferebant.

[3] On this government monopoly
of news *v.* Peter *Gesch. Litt.* i. 363.

to hear the formal words of some despatch which may
have little deserved such eager haste.[1]   To be chosen to
read it to the assembled nobles was a coveted honour,
and Symmachus, to whom the task often fell, is full of
gratitude at being made the interpreter of the " divine
words." [2]   But all this was purely formal. Rome had
long ceased to be the real seat of government. Not a
single rescript in the time of Symmachus is dated from
Rome.   When Honorius paid his triumphal visit in 403,
the palace of the Caesars at Rome had been practically
deserted for a hundred years.   While couriers were
arriving day and night at Milan or Ravenna, and the
imperial council were deliberating on the latest demands
of Alaric, the Eternal City, the hearth of the Roman
race, the home of its gods, in whose name the whole vast
system was carried on, had almost as little influence on
the course of government as Tibur or Praeneste.   Now
and then a feeling of neglect and desertion breaks out, as
in the appeal of Claudian to the Emperor to return to his
true home on the Palatine.[3]   Occasionally the pride of
the Senate is soothed, as when it was consulted about
the war with Gildo.[4]   Its hopes were roused for a
moment when the barbarian conqueror raised Attalus
to the purple.[5]   But, as a rule, a dull, gray atmosphere
seems to brood over the high society of Rome, and we
cannot help wondering how men like Probus,[6] after
governing provinces larger than any kingdom of modern
Europe, could be content with the frigid dignity and the
emptiness of their lives in the capital.

---

[1] Sym. *Ep.* i. 13, nondum caelo
albente concurritur.

[2] *Ib.* i. 95. He asks Syagrius to
thank the emperors "qui humanae
voci divinas literas crediderunt."

[3] *De Sexto Cons. Honor.* 39, 53.

[4] Sym. *Ep.* iv. 5, of the year
397, consulti igitur in senatu more

majorum, ingenti causae devotis
sententiis satisfecimus.

[5] Zos. vi. 6, 7.

[6] Sex. Petr. Probus had been
procons. of Africa, 357-58 ; praef.
praet. of Italy, Illyria, and Africa,
368-76 ; of Gaul, 380 ; of Italy
again, 383-84, and 387. *C.I.L.* vi.
1752, 1753.

The Senate no doubt was impotent and ill-informed. Yet the calm silence of Symmachus in the face of dangers and calamities, which must have struck the most unobservant, is very puzzling.   It may be the proud reserve of the member of a great race, which will not hint, even in a confidential letter, that the commonwealth is in peril.   It may be also that unshaken faith in the destiny of Rome which, only a few years after her capture by Alaric, inspired the last true poet of Rome to celebrate her beneficence and clemency, and to predict for her an unending sway.[1]   The feeling was shared to some extent even by Christian writers like S. Augustine and Orosius.[2] There is a tendency on all sides to treat the menacing troubles of the time as only a passing cloud, as necessary incidents in an imperial career, not worse than Rome had often surmounted in past ages.   Yet, in spite of these considerations, it is startling to read a letter from Symmachus to his son in the year 402, the year of the great battles of Pollentia and Verona, which makes no allusion to the invaders.[3]   He confines himself to the bare announcement of the fact that, owing to the unsafe state of the roads, he has had to make a long detour in order to reach the Court at Milan.

There are a good many glimpses of the state of Rome during the anxious years of the Gildonic revolt.   But we learn more from Claudian than from Symmachus about the meditated transfer of the African provinces to the Eastern Empire.   Symmachus is concerned chiefly with the dignity of his order and the condition of the capital. It was a proud day when Stilicho had to report the opinion of the Senate on the conduct of Gildo,[4] and when *more majorum* the traitor was voted to be a public enemy.   We have many illustrations of Claudian's com-

---

[1] Rutil. Namat. i. 47-140.
[2] Orosius, ii. 2, 6.
[3] Sym. *Ep.* vii. 13 ; cf. Seeck, lxiii.   The detour was made by Ticinum, which lay on the west, to avoid the enemy coming from the east.
[4] Sym. *Ep.* iv. 5.

plaint,[1] " pascimur arbitrio Mauri." The African corn-ships ceased to reach Ostia with their wonted regularity, and the terror of famine spread among the mob of Rome.[2] The masses were becoming sullen and dangerous. There were all the signs of a coming storm. Numbers of the higher families were flying to the safe seclusion of their country seats, and Symmachus prepared to send away his children from the capital.[3] As the chief author of the condemnation of Gildo, he had himself to withdraw for a while to one of his villas.[4] The distress was temporarily relieved by an *oblatio* of twenty days' supplies made by the Senate.[5] And again Symmachus describes the delight with which, from his villa on the Tiber, he saw the corn fleet from Macedonia arrive.[6] But there are few indications that he realised the grave social and economic dangers which are revealed by the Theodosian Code. He once casually mentions that he is debarred from the enjoyment of his country seat by the prevalence of brigandage.[7] There is a slight touch of feeling in a reference to the gloomy appearance of the country which met his eyes in one of his excursions.[8] Yet one would never gather from the passage that hundreds of thousands of acres in once smiling districts had returned to waste. The letters of Symmachus, if they had told us more of public events,[9] might have been among the most precious documents in historical literature. As it is, their chief value lies in what they rather stintedly reveal of the life and tone of the class to which Symmachus belonged. Here we see it for the last time apparently secure in the possession of enormous wealth, great administrative power, and exquisite social culture, seem-

[1] *De Bell. Gildon.* v. 70.
[2] Sym. *Ep.* vi. 14 ; cf. vi. 18, ii. 6.
[3] *Ib.* vi. 26, 66, 21.
[4] *Ib.* vi. 66.
[5] *Ib.* vi. 12, 26.
[6] *Ib.* iii. 55, 82.
[7] *Ib.* ii. 22, sed nunc intuta est latrociniis suburbanitas.
[8] *Ib.* v. 12.
[9] It should be said that he appears to have appended to some of his letters a separate bulletin, containing the news of the day ; cf. *Ep.* ii. 25.

ingly without a thought of the storm which was about to break.

The senatorial order was essentially a wealthy class. It had come to include nearly all the considerable proprietors in Italy and the provinces.[1]   And, as we shall see in another chapter, the wealth and social power of its members were increasing as what may be called the middle class (the *curiales*) rapidly declined in numbers and pecuniary independence.   Of course there were many degrees of opulence in the ranks of the senators.   That some were comparatively poor is evident from the fact that a certain number were relieved of the full weight of imperial imposts.[2]   But we have express testimony, apart from indirect evidence, that the wealth of others was enormous.[3]   A senatorial income of the highest class, exclusive of what was derived from the estates in kind, sometimes reached the sum of £180,000,[4] and that at a time when the ordinary rate of interest was 12 per cent. More moderate incomes, such as that of Symmachus, amounted to £60,000 a year.   Symmachus had at least three great houses in Rome or the suburbs, and fifteen country seats in various districts of Italy.[5]   He had large estates in Samnium, Apulia, and Mauretania.   The tenure of a great office in the provinces gave a man the chance of acquiring such domains.   Ammianus Marcellinus speaks of the estates of Sex. Petron. Probus as scattered all over the Empire,[6] and he broadly hints that

[1] Zos. ii. 38 ; cf. Duruy, vii. p. 176, and Godefroy's Paratitlon to *C. Th.* vi. tit. ii.

[2] *C. Th.* vi. 2, 4, 8.

[3] Olympiod. *ap. Phot.* § 44 (Müll. *Frag. Hist. Gr.* iv.).

[4] Marq. *Röm. Alt.* ii. p. 55 ; cf. Duruy, v. p. 598, on the fortunes of the earlier Empire.   Pallas, the freedman of Claudius' reign, had 300,000,000 sesterces = £3,200,000, cf. Friedländer, i. p. 192.

[5] For the various seats of Symmachus *v.* Seeck, xlvi. ; some may have come to him by his wife from Orfitus, *ib.* l.

[6] Amm. Marc. xxvii. 11, 1, opum amplitudine cognitus orbi Romano, per quem universum paene patrimonia sparsa possedit, juste an secus non judicioli est nostri.   Pliny (*H. N.* xviii. 35) alleges that half of Roman Africa was owned by six persons.   For a description of such an estate *v.* Boissier, *L'Afr. Rom.* p. 150.

that great noble had not always acquired them by the
fairest means.   The elder Sallustius, when he was
vicarius of Spain about 364,[1] probably acquired the property in that province which his son enjoyed a generation later, in the time of Symmachus.   The wealth of
Paula, who abandoned it all to accompany S. Jerome
to Bethlehem, of S. Paulinus,[2] and many others of the
Roman nobility, is known to us from Christian sources.

The fervour of asceticism may have led S. Jerome to
overdraw his picture of Roman luxury.   But there is one
department of expenditure in which the letters of Symmachus reveal an almost reckless profusion.   The praetorship, which every young senator of the highest class had
to assume,[3] was one of the heaviest burdens on the senatorial class, so heavy that some of them preferred to
resign their order rather than undertake it.   It had, like
the consulship, long ceased to confer any power or
authority.   It remained as a disguised form of taxation
for the pleasures of the mob of the capital.   The younger
Symmachus was still a mere boy in the hands of a tutor,
when he was designated for this expensive honour of
amusing the rabble of Rome.   The games which the
young praetor had to provide cost his father a sum equal
to £90,000 of our money.[4]   So far from complaining of
the expense, his father is eager to seize the opportunity

---

[1] *C.I.L.* vi. 1729. The monument
records the gratitude and admiration of the Spaniards.   It is dated
in the consulship of Jovianus Aug.
and Varronianus (364).   Flav. Sallustius had been cons. ord. in 363,
and praet. praef. 361-3 ; cf. Amm.
Marc. xxi. 8, 1. ; Sym. *Ep.* v. 56.
The herds of horses referred to were
on the Spanish estates, Seeck, clvi. ;
cf. Sym. *Ep.* ix. 12.
[2] The wealth of Paulinus is
alluded to in Aus. *Ep.* xxiv. 115 :

ne sparsam raptamque domum lacerataque
            centum
per dominos veteris Paullini regna fleamus.

His wife Therasia was enormously
wealthy, *v.* Greg. Tur. *de Glor.
Conf.* 107.   On the wealth of Paula
v. Hieron. *Ep.* 108, § 5.

[3] *C. Th.* vi. tit. iv. with the Paratitlon.

[4] Seeck, xlvi.   Probus, shortly
after the death of Honorius, in spite
of the enormous losses caused by the
Gothic invasion, is said to have
expended £54,000 on a similar occasion.   Maximus spent £180,000.
Olympiod. § 44 ; cf. Friedländer,
ii. p. 21.

of gaining popularity with the crowd,[1] and rejects with
scorn any idea of parsimony.   His time and energies are
devoted for several years to the preparations for the
spectacle which is to usher his son into the career of
public life.   Symmachus, in everything a devotee of the
past,[2] was nowhere more conservative than in his belief
in the ancient games.   He had put aside the conventional tone of servility in demanding from the reluctant
Theodosius the performance of what he regarded as an
imperious duty to the commonwealth.[3]   But when the
occasion arrived he was ready to act up to his own principles.   Many of his letters are full of the coming games.
He appeals to his friends in all parts of the world to
assist him.   Lions and crocodiles from Africa, dogs from
Scotland, horses from the famous studs of Spain, are all
sought for, and the most anxious provision is made for
their conveyance from these distant regions.[4]   The gladiatorial shows had not yet been suppressed by Christian
sentiment, and Symmachus was determined to have a
band of Saxons,[5] to crown the success of his games.   He
puts as much seriousness into the business as if it affected
the very existence of the State.[6]   His anxiety is over-
powering.   In spite, however, of all his care and profusion, there were many accidents and disappointments.
Some of the animals arrived half dead from the hardships
of their long journey.   Many of the splendid Spanish
coursers had either perished by the way, or were hopelessly disabled.[7]   The crocodiles would not eat and had
to be killed.   Chariot-drivers and players, expected from
Sicily, were, in spite of all searches along the coast,

[1] Sym. *Ep.* ii. 78. Cf. ix. 126 ;
ii. 78.
[2] For an example of his conservatism *v.* ii. 36, opposing a decision
of the pontifical college to allow the
Vestals to erect a statue to Praetextatus.
[3] *Ib. Rel.* 6, beneficia numinis
vestri populus Romanus expectat

. . . sed ea jam quasi debita repetit
quae aeternitas vestra sponte pro-
misit. Cf. *Rel.* 9.
[4] *Ep.* iv. 58-60, 63 ; ix. 12 ; ii. 76 ;
ii. 77 ; ix. 132.
[5] *Ib.* ii. 46.
[6] *Ib.* iv. 8, 60.
[7] *Ib.* v. 56.

nowhere to be heard of.[1]   The most cruel blow of all was
the loss of the Saxon gladiators, who, declining to make
sport for the rabble of Rome, strangled one another before
the hour of their humiliation in the arena arrived.[2]

This is the most interesting passage in the life of
Symmachus as revealed in his letters. The world he
belongs to was the slave of old tradition and conventionality, and, with all its splendour, must have
suffered from *ennui*. The great man's day, just as in
Pliny's time, was filled by a round of trivial social
observances, which were as engrossing and as obligatory
as serious duties.[3]   The crowd of morning callers and
dependants had to be received as of old. All the
anniversaries in the families of friends had to be duly
remembered and honoured. If a friend obtained from
the Emperor the distinction of one of the old republican
magistracies, it was an imperative social duty to attend
his inauguration.[4]   The service of the Sacred Colleges
was another social obligation,[5] although Symmachus hints
broadly that some of his colleagues in the pontifical
college were inclined to flatter the Court by absenting
themselves;[6] and even Flavianus and Praetextatus, who
were pagans of the pagans, sometimes excused themselves
by absence at their country seats or at some pleasure
resort in Campania.[7]   In nothing were the demands of
etiquette more imperious than in letter-writing. Again
and again Symmachus recalls the rule of "old-fashioned
manners," that the friend who goes from home should be
the first to write.[8]   It matters not whether he has any-

[1] *Ep.* vi. 42.
[2] *Ib.* ii. 46.
[3] Two generations later than
Symmachus, Sidonius, describing
high society at Rome, says, utrum-
que quidem, si fors Laribus egredie-
bantur, artabat clientum praevia
pedisequa circumfusa populositas,
Sid. *Ep.* i. 9, 3.

[4] Sym. *Ep.* i. 101.
[5] *Ib.* i. 47, 48.
[6] *Ib.* i. 51, nunc aris deesse
Romanos genus est ambiendi.
[7] *Ib.* i. 47, 51; ii. 53, mihi
tuum munus injungis: fruere deliciis
copiosis; nos mandata curabimus.
[8] *Ib.* vi. 60.

thing to say.   Indeed, it is hard to see why a great
many of these letters should have been written at all.
They are about as interesting as a visiting card, and seem
to have had no more significance than a polite attention.
The stiffness of etiquette, which was introduced into
official life by Diocletian, and which invaded the legal
style of the imperial rescripts, reigns in the correspondence
of the period, even between near relations.   The conservatism of Symmachus, indeed, revolts against the new-
fangled habit of prefixing titles to a friend's name in a
familiar letter.[1]   Still, his own son is " amabilitas tua," [2]
and his daughter " domina filia."   That there were warm
affections and a kindly unselfish nature behind all this
artificial stiffness in the case of Symmachus we shall see
afterwards.   With him and his caste the habit of social
observance, however complicated and engrossing, had
become a second nature, without always freezing the
springs of natural kindliness.

Yet the cold dignity of the life in those palaces on
the Caelian and Aventine, with its endless calls to
frivolous social duties, and its monotony of busy idleness, must have grown irksome at times.   It was not,
perhaps, altogther the coolness of Praeneste, the gay
abandon of Baiae, or the boar-hunting in the woods of
Laurentum, that tempted the fashionable world away
from the attractions of Rome.   Symmachus loves Rome,
with all its turbulence, even in times of scarcity and
tumult, and he will linger in a suburban villa [3] on the
chance of being summoned to a meeting of the Senate ;
but even he feels the need of repose and emancipation
from the tyranny of society.   At one of his country
houses, he is as happy as such a stately self-contained
man will ever show himself, looking after the making of

___

[1] Sym.*Ep.*iv. 30, itane epistularum
nostrarum simplex usus interiit, ut
paginis tuis lenocinia aevi praesentis
anteferas ? redeamus quin ergo ad
infucatos nominum titulos.
[2] *Ib.* vii. 6, vi. 60, 80 ; cf **Ruric.**
Ep. i. 6, 7, 10, 11, 13.
[3] *Ep.* ii. 57, vii. 21.

his oil and wine, laying down a fresh mosaic, receiving a friend or two, or drinking in the quiet freshness of the Laurentine woods that overhang the sea.[1] There is no trace in his letters that nature has for him [2] any of the romantic charm which it had for Ausonius and Rutilius. He was not much of a sportsman even in his youth. He loved the country for its stillness and repose, for the relief it gave from the monotonous strain of social duty which was doubly oppressive to his kind and conscientious nature. Above all, it gave him leisure for converse with the old favourites of his library.

Among the best men of the pagan or semi-pagan aristocracy of that time the passion for literature or erudition was absorbing. With many of them it took the place of interest in public affairs. The company whom Macrobius brings together in his *Saturnalia* were the leaders of Roman society—Praetextatus, Flavianus, two members of the great house of the Albini, Symmachus himself. They are joined by other guests of lower social rank, but equals in the literary brotherhood, Eustathius, a Greek professor of rhetoric, and Servius, the prince of Roman critics. Praetextatus, the arch-hierophant, initiated in all the cults of Syria and Egypt, is the exponent of priestly lore. Flavianus is the master of that augural art which led him to his doom when he espoused the cause of Eugenius and paganism against the Church. The Albini enlarge on the antiquarian exactness of Virgil.[3] There was no originality in the literary enthusiasm of these men. It was an enthusiasm which spent its force in preserving and appreciating what the ages of creation and inspiration had left behind.[4] Prae-

---

[1] *Ep.* ii. 26 ; iii. 23, nunc hic in otio rusticamur et multimodis autumnitate defruimur; vii. 31 ; vii. 15, 18 ; vi. 44.

[2] *Ib.* v. 78, agri quiete delector . . . saepe oculos pasco culturis ; cf. Plin. *Ep.* i. 9 ; Friedländer, ii.

p. 112 *sqq.*

[3] Macrob. i. 17, 1 ; i. 24, 17-19.

[4] On the tastes and learned labours of this circle cf. Peter, *Gesch. Litt. über die Röm. Kaiserzeit,* i. p. 137 ; Jan, *Prol. ad Macrob.* xxii. *sqq.*

textatus, besides giving much attention to the emendation
of the classics, translated the *Analytics* of Aristotle.[1]
Flavianus was an erudite historian, and composed a
volume of *Annals*[2] dedicated to Theodosius. His translation of the *Life of Apollonius of Tyana* by Philostratus
was in vogue in the time of Sidonius, and fragments of
his *de Dogmatibus Philosophorum* were still read in the
Middle Ages.[3]   Sallustius, another great person of the
circle of Symmachus, is known to have emended the
text of Apuleius.[4]   A great noble in Spain, who had a
famous stud, from which Symmachus drew a contribu-
tion for his son's games, seems to have combined in a
rare fashion a taste for horse-breeding with a taste for
literature, and begs the orator for a copy of his speeches.[5]
Symmachus had many literary friends in Gaul, most of
them mere names to us now.   Among them were three
brothers[6] who had been trained in the great school of
Trèves.   One of them had the honour of receiving the
dedication of Claudian's *Rape of Proserpine.*[7]   Another,
Protadius, affects a great taste for sport, but is really a
litterateur, with an ambition to write the history of his
province.   Symmachus, in his friendly way, helped him
with advice and some materials from his library.[8]   If the
history of Protadius was ever written, it shared the fate
of many another work of that age of which the cruelty
or contempt of time has not left even a trace.   There
was no doubt much vanity and love of mutual admiration under all this literary activity.   But in our own
day the apotheosis of self-advertising mediocrity is not

[1] Sym. *Ep.* i. 53, remissa tempora
. . . libris veterum ruminandis
libenter expendis; cf. *C.I.L.* vi.
1779, *d*, vel quae periti condidere
carmina, vel quae solutis vocibus
sunt edita, meliora reddis quam
legendo sumpseras.   Seeck's *Sym.*
lxxxvii. n. 394.
[2] *C.I.L.* vi. 1783; cf. 1782, his-
torico disertissimo.

[3] Sid. *Ep.* viii. 3; cf. Seeck,
cxv.
[4] Cf. the note to the Laurentian
MS. of Apuleius quoted in Seeck,
clvi.; Hildebrand's *Prol. ad Apul.*
lxi.
[5] Sym. *Ep.* iv. 60, 63, 64.
[6] *Ib.* iv. 18-56.
[7] *De Raptu Proserp.* ii., praef. 50.
[8] Sym. *Ep.* iv. 18.

altogether unheard of.   What literary clique can cast
the first stone ?   And, after all, it is better to be vain of
knowledge and literary facility than of wealth or birth.
The very weakness shows a deference for ideals which
rise above the level of bourgeois self-complacency, or of
the stolid pride of inherited rank.

Symmachus was a good man according to his lights,
but he was not a very strong man.   And one of his
weaknesses was literary affectation.   He evidently took
enormous pains with these letters.   He had, as he confesses, little to say, but he says it in the most elaborate
and ingenious style of which he is capable.   Yet he
apologises more than once for his poverty of talent and
phrase, and he is guilty of the amusing falsehood that
his style is unstudied.[1]   To one of his correspondents
he appeals to keep the letter for his own reading, yet
in the same letter he admits that his secretaries, " per
examinis ignorantiam," are preserving copies of what he
writes.[2]   Perhaps, however, this was not all vanity and
affectation.   It is possible to have a modest conception
of one's native talent, along with the ambition that the
fruits of elaborate care and cultivation should survive.
The true Roman, who reverenced the great memories of
the past, had a passionate, though often a futile, desire
to live in the memory of coming ages.

The literary conversations in which some of the
intimate friends of Symmachus take part in the *Saturnalia* of Macrobius (although the matter is often borrowed
from Gellius and earlier writers) [3] probably give a fairly
correct idea of the literary tone and interests of that
circle.   The subject will be dealt with at length in
another chapter.   For the present it is sufficient to say

---

[1] *Ep.* i. 14 ; iv. 27, sum quidem
pauper loquendi.

[2] *Ib.* v. 85, quare velim tibi ha-
beas quae incogitata proferimus.
Cf. his advice to his son to culti-

vate a certain negligence of style
in his letters, a precept which
Symmachus did not enforce by
example, vii. 9.

[3] Peter, *Gesch. Litt.* i. p. 143.

that the literary criticism in Macrobius is far from contemptible. The minute antiquarianism, indeed, may seem to us sometimes rather trifling. But to a Roman, like Praetextatus, who was still loyal to the faith of his ancestors and to the past, every scrap of the ancient lore of his race was precious. And in the minute and often delicate appreciation, not only of the learning, but of the literary beauties of Virgil, we are compelled to forgive and almost to forget the blindness and perversity of a generation who admired the great masters, and yet wrote in a style which they would have thought utterly grotesque. And it must be confessed that there is much to forgive. Equipped by the study of the great masterpieces and the most elaborate training, they yet came to write a style which is in many cases a mixture of imitation, affectation, and barbarism. Ingenuity took the place of originality, extravagance and exaggeration of real force. Style, in fact, became a mere " jargon of experts." And the initiated were never weary of exchanging the most fulsome flattery. In a letter to his friend Ausonius about his poem on the Moselle, Symmachus, while he gently ridicules the minute description of the fishes of that river, yet has no hesitation in ranking his friend with Virgil.[1] The poet returned the compliment by attributing to the oratory of Symmachus all the force and graces of the oratory of Isocrates, Demosthenes, and Cicero.[2] In the year 378 a Greek rhetorician named Palladius arrived in Rome.[3] The fashionable and cultivated world were carried away by his declamation, " his wealth of invention, his dignity and brilliance of diction." If we are inclined to despise such unreal displays, and such extravagant eulogy, it is well to remember that admiration for mental power, even

---

[1] *Ep.* i. 14, ego hoc tuum carmen libris Maronis adjungo.

[2] Auson. *Ep.* xvii.

[3] Sym. i. 15, ix. 1 ; cf. Seeck, ccii.

when misapplied, is better than a Philistine contempt
for things of the mind.   The aristocratic class in the
last age of the Western Empire had many faults, but
they treated talent and culture as at least the equals
of wealth and rank ; and there has seldom been an
age when talent and culture received higher rewards.
Symmachus recommended the brilliant rhetor to the
notice of Ausonius, who was then Pretorian prefect.
Palladius was readily enrolled in the ranks of the
imperial service, and within three or four years had
risen to the great place of master of the offices.[1]   In
the same year Marinianus, another literary friend of
Symmachus, who was a professor of law, rose to the
dignity of vicar of the Spanish province.[2]   The poet
Ausonius is the most brilliant example in that age of
the recognition of literary eminence by the State.   It
has been said with some truth that the reign of Gratian
was quite as much the reign of Ausonius.   Originally
a humble grammarian in the school of Bordeaux, he was
appointed by Valentinian his son's tutor.   Ausonius
possessed the gifts which were then the most admired—
infinite facility, the power of giving novelty and importance to trifles by ingenious tricks of phrase, the art of
flattering with literary grace.   The young Emperor re-
paid the care and recognised the talents of his teacher
by raising him to the quaestorship,[3] the prefecture of the
Gauls, and in 379 to the illustrious dignity of the consulship as the colleague of Olybrius, a scion of one of the
proudest houses in the Roman aristocracy.   The relatives

[1] *C. Th.* vi. 27, 4 (382).
[2] Sym. *Ep.* iii. 23-29. Marinianus is the governor to whom
Gratian's constitution of 383 is
addressed (*C. Th.* ix. 1, 14). He is
also probably the "vicarius" referred to in Sulp. Sev. *Chron.* ii.
49, 3, as being preferred by the
Priscillianist heretics to Gregory

the prefect. Hence it has been
concluded that Marinianus was a
pagan.

[3] Auson. *Grat. Act. pro Cons.*
ii. 11, te ac patre principibus
quaestura communis et tui tantum
praefectura beneficii, etc ; cf.
Schenkl, Prooem. ix.

and friends of Ausonius shared in his advancement. For two or three years nearly all the great prefectures and governorships were held by members of the poet's family.[1] He has also left marks of his ascendency on the Code. Ausonius, at the height of his power and his renown, was faithful to the system of culture which had moulded him. And the famous rescript of 376,[2] which provides for the payment of fixed stipends to the teachers of grammar and rhetoric, was undoubtedly suggested by the old professor of Bordeaux. There is little in the literary productions of that age which a modern reader can admire, and they are only the wreckage of a great mass of probably even less merit. Yet the literary brotherhood, of which Symmachus and Ausonius were leaders, did a service to humanity by their worship of an ideal which their own productions seldom approach.

If the letters of Symmachus are to be taken as a fair picture of the moral tone of his class, we are bound, with some reservations, to form a far more favourable opinion of the state of Roman society than that which is suggested by S. Jerome or Ammianus Marcellinus. There are, it is true, glimpses in Symmachus of the old Roman cruelty, of contempt for slaves and the common people,[3] of selfishness, and lack of public spirit. The Saxons, whom Symmachus had brought at great expense from the far north for his gladiatorial shows, killed one another or committed suicide before the day of combat in the arena arrived.[4] And the usually kind-hearted Symmachus narrates the tragedy with a few words of bitter contempt. He and his friends fought hard to

---

[1] Seeck's *Sym.* lxxiv. ; Schenkl, x.

[2] *C. Th.* xiii. 3, 11. The law is addressed to Antonius, which Scaliger thought a mistake for Ausonius. Godefroy in his Commentary refutes this conjecture. Antonius was a correspondent of Symmachus, *Ep.* i. 89-93. Cf. Seeck's *Sym.* cix.

[3] Sym. *Ep.* vi. 8, ut est servis familiaris improbitas. But this censure was probably deserved ; cf. Salv. *de Gub. Dei,* iv. § 26, c. 5 ; Hieron. *Ep.* liv.

[4] Sym. *Ib.* ii. 46.

avoid the levy of recruits from their estates at the crisis
of the Gildonic war, and actually succeeded in arranging
for a composition in money.[1]　They also showed what
seems an unworthy timidity in the riots caused by the
failure of the corn supplies from Africa.　They removed
their families to the country, and Symmachus had all
preparations made for sending his own children away.[2]
The same selfish weakness is revealed a few years afterwards in the flight of the wealthy classes, when the
troops of Alaric were closing round the city.[3]　There is
much, too, that is revolting or contemptible in the
conduct of public men revealed in the chronicle of those
fatal years.　The cruelty and greed of Heraclian in his
treatment of the refugees who landed in his province of
Africa would be almost incredible if we had not the
express testimony of S. Jerome.[4]　The party, led by
Olympius, who carried out the Catholic reaction against
the policy of Stilicho, seem to have been at once cruel,
incompetent, faithless, and corrupt.　It is difficult to say
whether blindness or perfidy is more conspicuous in the
dealings of the Roman government with Alaric.　Honorius is probably responsible for some of this baseness
and stupidity.　But the great officials who lent themselves to such a policy, if they did not prompt it, cannot
be acquitted.　The Gothic king was as much superior to
his opponents in sincerity and insight as he was in
material force.

Yet these vices and weaknesses in the official class
should not make us unjust to that society as a whole.
Salvianus says that his generation flattered itself on the
purity of its morals.[5]　The guests in the *Saturnalia* of

---

[1] *Ep.* vi. 64.

[2] *Ib.* vi. 12, 21, 66.

[3] Rutil. Namat. i. 331 :
haec multos lacera suscepit ab urbe
　　fugatos.

[4] Hieron. *Ep.* 130, § 7. Heraclian
was the assassin of Stilicho and the
friend of Olympius ; cf. the splendid
contrast of the charity of Laeta,
widow of Gratian, Zos. v. 39.

[5] Salv. *de Gub. Dei*, vi. § 44.

Macrobius claim that their society is free from many of the grosser forms of luxury and dissipation which prevailed among their ancestors.[1]   The *menu* of the pontiff's banquet, at which Lentulus, Lepidus, Caesar, and the Vestal Virgins were present, is treated as disgraceful in its costly and fantastic variety.[2]   Peacocks' eggs are not now even in the market.[3]   There are no censors and consuls, like Hortensius and Lucullus, who spend a fortune in stocking a fish pond, and who mourn the death of a muraena as if it were a daughter.[4]   The insanity which ransacked land and sea for new dainties is now quite unknown.   So far from buying them, we have forgotten their very names.   You will never see a man now reeling drunk into the forum,[5] surrounded by loose companions, nor a judge on the bench so overcome by wine that he can hardly keep his eyes open.[6]   At whose dinner party will you now ever see the dancing girl introduced?[7]   Still less will persons of decent breeding themselves indulge in that rage for the dance which disgraced even the matrons of noble houses in the times of the Punic wars.   There is the same improvement in the tone about the actor's profession, which even Cicero did not regard as disgraceful.[8]   No one would nowadays associate on friendly terms with a Roscius, as Cicero did.   It is possible that this may be the picture only of a more fastidious and refined circle, and that there were great houses where the festivities were not so innocent as those described in the *Saturnalia*. But the testimony of Macrobius deserves at least to be weighed against the invective of S. Jerome.

The contempt for slaves expressed by S. Jerome and

---

[1] Macrob. *Sat*. iii. 13 ; cf. iii. 17, 12.

[2] *Ib*. iii. 13, 11-13, ipsa vero edulium genera quam dictu turpia ?

[3] *Ib*. iii. 13, 2, ova pavonum . . . quae hodie non dicam vilius sed omnino nec veneunt.

[4] *Ib*. iii. 15, 4.

[5] *Ib*. iii. 16, 14.

[6] *Ib*. iii. 16, 16, vix prae vino sustinet palpebras.

[7] *Ib*. iii. 14, 3-7 ; cf. ii. 1, 7.

[8] *Ib*. iii. 14, 11 ; cf. Friedländer, ii. p. 295.

Salvianus[1] is not shared by the characters of Macrobius.
A certain Euangelus in the *Saturnalia* jeers at the notion
that the gods should have any care for slaves.[2]   He is
taken to task by Praetextatus, the great pagan theologian
of the party.   Slaves, Praetextatus says, are men like
ourselves.   There is nothing in the name of slavery to
excite horror and contempt.   We are all the slaves of
God or Fortune.   The greatest in earthly state, the
highest in wisdom, have had to bear the yoke.   The
slave is really our fellow servant, made of the same
elements, subject to the same chance and change, often
with the spirit of the free man in his breast.[3]   The real
slave is the man who is in bondage to his passions.   No
servitude can be so shameful as that which is self-
imposed.[4]   You should treat your slave as a man, even
as a friend.[5]   It is far better that he should love than
that he should fear you.   And how often have these
despised wretches shown the noblest devotion to their
masters, in spite of all the cruelty and contempt with
which they have been treated ?[6]   A slave has been
known to personate his master who was in hiding, and
to submit to the stroke of the executioner in his place.[7]
The slave-girls of Rome once saved the honour of their
mistresses at the peril of their own, and were commemorated for ever in the *Nonae Caprotinae*.[8]   It is quite true,
of course, that these ideas are not peculiar to the fourth
or the fifth century.   They can be traced back in some
form to Seneca, to Plato, to Euripides.[9]   But they are
expressed with a sincerity and good feeling in Macrobius

---

[1] Hieron. *Ep.* 54, § 5; Salv. *de
Gub. Dei*, iv. 26, praecipitantes
fastigia nobilium matrimoniorum in
cubilia obscena servarum; cf. iv.
§ 14.

[2] Macrob. *Sat.* i. 11, 1, quasi
vero curent divina de servis.

[3] *Ib.* i. 11, 6-8.

[4] *Ib.* i. 11, 8, certe nulla servitus
turpior quam voluntaria.

[5] *Ib.* i. 11, 12.   Cf. Sen. *Ep.*
47, servi sunt? immo humiles
amici.

[6] *Ib.* i. 11, 13, 14.

[7] *Ib.* i. 11, 16.

[8] *Ib.* i. 11, 36-40.

[9] Pl. *Leges*, vi. p. 777; Eurip. *Ion*,
854; *Helen*, 730; cf. Boissier, *Rel.
Rom.* ii. p. 363; Wallon, iii. p. 22.

which leave the impression that they are the convictions
of the best and most thoughtful men of his time.

There is nothing brighter and pleasanter in the Letters
of Symmachus than the tenderness of his family affections. It is true that, with his ingrained conservatism,
he clings to the old Roman idea of the womanly character. The Roman matron from the earliest times had
secured to her by family religion a dignified and respected
position. She was to some extent the equal of her
husband in the management of the household. But the
sentiment of ancient Rome forbade her the lighter graces
and accomplishments. She was expected to be grave,
self-contained, chiefly concerned with household duties,
and the nurture of a sturdy and intrepid race. In the
early years of the Empire the ideal of woman's position
and character underwent a profound change. The
change gave rise to many misunderstandings which were
the food of satire. But her status, both in law and in
fact, really rose. There can be no doubt that the Roman
lady of the better sort, without becoming less virtuous
and respected, became far more accomplished and attractive. With fewer restraints, she had greater charm
and influence. She became, more and more, the equal
and companion of her husband, and her influence on
public affairs became more decided. The wife of the
younger Pliny,[1] to take a typical instance, is the partner
in his studies, she knows his books by heart, she shares
all his thoughts. In the last age of the Western Empire
there is no deterioration in the position and influence of
women. In Christian families they cultivate sacred
learning, and take the lead in works of charity and
mercy. Furiola founded a hospital.[2] Laeta, the widow
of Gratian, fed the starving populace of the Capital

---

[1] Plin. iv. 19. He says of his
wife, Calpurnia, accedit his studium
litterarum, quod ex mei caritate
concepit. Meos libellos habet,
lectitat, ediscit etiam ; cf. Friedländer, i. p. 353.

[2] Hieron. *Ep.* 77, § 6.

during its siege by the forces of Alaric.[1] Serena, the
wife of Stilicho, was an accomplished scholar, and was
regarded both by friends and enemies as a serious force
in politics.[2] Placidia, the mother of Valentinian III.,
after all her vicissitudes as the wife of a Gothic chief,
probably wielded greater influence in her son's councils
than any statesman of the time. On the pagan side,
Praetextatus has left an eternal memorial of an ideal
wedded union, in which the wife gives not only love, but
intellectual support and sympathy to her husband.[3]

The old-fashioned Symmachus would probably have
objected to his female relatives taking a prominent part
in any public movement. He stoutly resisted the proposal of the vestals to raise a monument to his bosom-
friend Praetextatus.[4] He praises his daughter, when she
sends him a present of wool-work, for her likeness to the
Roman matron of the great age, who sat among her
maids, directing them at the spindle or the loom.[5] But
Symmachus, for all that, is the most affectionate of
fathers. He never forgets a birthday.[6] His daughter's
illness gives him the most acute anxiety amid all his
public cares. He sends her advice for the care of
her health.[7] The nursery troubles of his little grand-
daughter occupy a good many of his letters.[8] But his
solicitude and affection for his son are even more marked.
When the boy's first tutor dies, Symmachus takes endless
pains to obtain one of equal merit, if possible a man who
had been trained in the Gallic schools of rhetoric.[9] He

---

[1] Zos. v. 39.
[2] Claudian, *Laus Serenae*, 147,
229; Zos. v. 38, ἐν ὑποψίᾳ ἔλαβε
τὴν Σερήναν ἡ γερουσία οἷα τοὺς βαρβάρους κατὰ τῆς πόλεως ἀγαγοῦσαν.
[3] *C.I.L.* vi. 1779:

Paulina nostri pectoris consortio
fomes pudoris, castitatis vinculum.
amorque purus et fides coelo sata
arcana mentis cui reclusa credidi,
munus deorum, qui maritalem torum
nectunt amicis et pudicis nexibus,

pietate matris, conjugali gratia,
nexu sororis, filiae modestia, etc.

[4] *Ep.* ii. 36.
[5] *Ib.* vi. 67.
[6] *Ib.* vi. 79, 80; i. 11; vi. 48, 49.
[7] *Ib.* vi. 58; cf. vi. 4; v. 33.
[8] *Ib.* vi. 32.
[9] *Ib.* vi. 34. Symmachus had
himself a Gallic tutor; cf. Sym.
Ep. ix. 88.

sets himself to rub up his own Greek in order to help his son in his reading,[1] and he reluctantly declines an invitation to the inaugural ceremony of a friend's consulship, that the boy's studies may not be interrupted.[2] When he is on a mission from the Senate to the Court at Milan,[3] at a time when the Goths were ravaging Cisalpine Gaul, Symmachus never fails on every opportunity to write to his son at Rome.[4] There is a pathetic interest about one of these letters,[5] which was probably written when Symmachus was trying, by a devious route, to reach Milan without encountering the barbarian cavalry.[6] He was in bad health,[7] and engaged on a perilous and anxious mission. The letter contains not a single reference to public or private affairs, but advises the boy to correct a too solemn sententiousness in his epistolary style, by putting into it more life and graceful negligence. The writer died soon afterwards,[8] and almost his last wish for his son was that he might be richly endowed with that literary culture which was the strongest passion of Symmachus.

Symmachus may not be a very interesting character, and his letters are certainly dull reading. Yet their polished brevity and their tone of conventional etiquette are apt to make us unjust to the writer. Wedded to a past which was gone for ever, absorbed in the cold and stately life of a class which was doomed to political impotence, struggling to ignore the significance of a religious revolution which was already triumphant before

[1] *Ep.* iv. 20, repuerascere enim nos jubet pietas. Cf. Sidonius reading Menander with his son (*Ep.* iv. 12), and the advice addressed to his grandson by Ausonius, *Idyl.* iv.
[2] *Ib.* v. 5.
[3] *Ib.* vii. 13 ; cf. v. 94-95.
[4] *Ib.* vii. 10, 14.
[5] *Ib.* vii. 9.
[6] *Ib.* vii. 13.

[7] *Ib.* v. 96. Symmachus was tortured with gout and renal disease (vi. 4, 16 ; vi. 73), renum dolore discrucior.
[8] Seeck's *Sym.* lxxiii. Peter (ii. 31) puts his death about 404. I cannot understand Teuffel's calculations in § 418, n. 3. How could Symmachus have been Corrector Lucaniae in 365 if he was born in 350 ? Cf. Seeck, xliv.

his death, he may appear, to a careless reader, a mere fossil, a shadowy and feeble representative of an effete order. Yet the man's very faithfulness to that order gives him a pathetic interest. And his faithfulness, and that of the school to which he belonged, is the sign of a certain strength and elevation of character. So far as the imperial despotism permitted him, he did his duty to the State. He was the most loyal and helpful friend, always ready with influence or advice, and always mindful to "keep his friendships in repair." His friends were among the leaders of Roman society, Christian or pagan, governors of great provinces, barbarian generals, lawyers, and struggling men of letters. They all regarded him as the chief ornament of the senatorial order, the greatest orator of his time, a paragon of all the virtues.[1] Commanding such universal respect, and surrounded by family affection, Symmachus enjoyed a certain subdued happiness. He was the witness indeed of great changes, which shocked and wounded old conservative and patriotic feeling. But he never lost his placid faith in the destiny of Rome. Although he was a devoted pagan, he would not deny that his Christian friends had found another avenue to "the Great Mystery."[2] And a true charity will not refuse to him the same tolerant hope. He is almost the last Roman of the old school, and, as we bid him farewell, we seem to be standing in the wan, lingering light of a late autumnal sunset.

---

[1] Auson. *Ep.* xvii., quid enim aliud es quam ex omni bonarum artium ingenio collecta perfectio ? Prudent. *c. Sym.* i. 632 ; *C.I.L.* vi. 1699 ; cf. Apoll. Sidon. *Ep.* ii. 10, § 5.

[2] *Rel.* 3, uno itinere non potest perveniri ad tam grande secretum.

CHAPTER III

THE SOCIETY OF AQUITAINE IN THE TIME OF AUSONIUS

IN the next view of Roman society which we have to
present to the reader the scene is changed, but hardly
the time. We pass from the society of Symmachus to
the society of his friend Ausonius of Bordeaux.
Bordeaux was remote from the seat of Empire, but it
had a university, which in the fourth century was one
of the most famous in the Roman world, and it was also
a great centre of commerce. Aquitaine must have
suffered much, like the rest of Gaul, in the invasions and
confusions of the third century.[1] But all traces of them
had vanished, and men had almost forgotten that evil
time. In the poems of Ausonius Aquitaine is a land of
peace and plenty, of vineyards and yellow cornfields, and
palatial country seats. The poet can bestow no higher
praise on the valley of the Moselle than to compare its
charms to the richness and beauty of his native Garonne.[2]
The characteristics of the old Celtic or Iberian stocks in
south-western Gaul were still strongly marked.[3] The
ancient language had been spoken by the grandfathers
of Ausonius and his friends.[4] Yet the Aquitaine of

[1] Vop. *Aurel.* c. 6 ; Vop. *Prob.*
c. 13, cum (barbari) . . . per
omnes Gallias securi vagarentur.
The ruins of Ilerda in Spain (Auson.
Ep. xxv. 58) are thought to be
results of the invasion.
[2] *Idyl.* x. 160.

[3] Auson. *Parent.* iv.
[4] Auson. *Idyl.* ii. 9, sermone impromptus Latio ; cf. Sulp. Sev.
Dial. i. 27, tu vero vel Celtice
aut, si mavis, Gallice loquere ; cf.
Fauriel, i. p. 434 ; F. de Coulanges,
La Gaule Rom. pp. 128 - 130 ;

Ausonius was thoroughly Romanised. Its Latin was
the purest spoken in Gaul. Its school of rhetoric had
great renown, and sometimes furnished a professor to the
schools of Rome and Constantinople.[1] Its most brilliant
professor had won his way to the consulship and the
great prefecture of the West. The most intimate relations were maintained between the academic society
of Bordeaux and the literary nobles of the Capital.
Faith in the stability of the Empire and Roman culture
is perfectly untroubled. There is not a hint of those
dim hordes, already mustering for their advance, who
within twenty years will be established on the banks
of the Garonne.

The poems of Ausonius are of priceless value to one
who wishes to know the tone and manner of provincial
life in the last age of the Western Empire. And the
poet himself, with all his faults, is a very interesting
person. He often wastes his skill on unworthy subjects. He is vain, and will flatter extravagantly the
vanity of others. Paying a cold and conventional
deference to the Christian faith,[2] he is still a literary
pagan, incapable of understanding any one who yields to
the higher mystic and spiritual impulses.[3] The charm
of society and of literature satisfies all his longings.
But he has many virtues. Beginning life as a humble
teacher, he rose to the highest place which any subject
of the Empire could attain. Yet he remained true to
his profession and proud of it. There is no such gallery
of academic portraits in literature as he has left us. The
honours of the great world never for a moment shook his
supreme attachment to letters. And he is also most

Jullian, *Ausone*, p. 9. Fauriel and
de Coulanges differ as to the interpretation of the passage in Sulp.
Sev.; cf. Apoll. Sid. *Ep.* iii. 3,
sermonis Celtici squamam depositura nobilitas.

[1] Auson. *Parent.* iii. 16; *Prof.*

Burdig. i. 3; Jullian, *Ausone*, p. 92.

[2] *Ephemeris, Idyl.* i. 16; cf. his
doubts about personal immortality,
Praef. Prof. Burdig. xxiii. 13;
Parent. xv. 11.

[3] See his letters to S. Paulinus,
especially *Ep.* xxv. 50 *sqq.*

faithful to the ties of blood and old friendship.   He has immortalised a family circle who, but for him, would have never emerged from the dim crowd of provincial coteries, who vanish and leave no trace.   The portraits of his grandfather,[1] the last of the old Aeduan diviners, of his father,[2] the Stoic physician of Bordeaux, of that throng of female relatives, wanting, perhaps, in brightness and grace, but with a strong charm of masculine force, of detachment, and seriousness, may seem worthless to the literary trifler, but are pure gold to the student of the history of society.   The author of the poem on the Moselle will live as almost the only Roman poet who has transferred to verse the subtle and secret charm which nature has to modern eyes.[3]   He deserves quite as much to live as the painter of an obscure phase of social life, which in every age is condemned to obscurity by its very virtues.

The *Parentalia*[4] of Ausonius have perhaps an even greater interest than his poems on the Professors of Bordeaux.   Ausonius, like his friend Symmachus, has the virtue of loyalty to old associations.   No one who has ever loved him, helped him, or shared his fortunes is forgotten.   The years of power and splendour at the court of Gratian left him unspoilt and unchanged. Clever, versatile, and ambitious as he was of the honours of the great world, yet when the prize was won, Ausonius gladly returned to the scene where he had taught grammar to raw boys,[5] and to the society of his family and academic friends.   Like others of his house, he lived to a great age.[6]   His wife had died in the early years of

---

[1] *Parent.* iv.

[2] *Idyl.* ii. ; *Parent.* i.

[3] Mr. Mackail has shown his usual sure literary sense in his judgment of this poem, *Lat. Lit.* p. 266.

[4] Composed after his consulship in 379 (iv. 32), and when his wife

had been dead "nine Olympiads" (ix. 8) ; cf. Schenkl, Prooem. xvi.

[5] *Idyl.* iv. 66 :

multos lactentibus annis
ipse alui, gremioque fovens et murmura solvens
eripui tenerum blandis nutricibus aevum.

[6] He must have lived at least till A.D. 390.   For the *Ludus*

their union,[1] and most of his relatives had gone before
him.   With old Roman piety, and in a strain far more
pagan than Christian, he has commemorated their virtues,
and saved them from oblivion.   Few of his circle were
more important in their day than the forgotten worthies
who sleep in any of our country churchyards.   But
their portraits enable us to imagine how quiet people
were living in the last years of Theodosius.

The grandfather of the poet, by his mother's side,
was a member of one of the noblest Aeduan houses in
the territory of Lyons.   In the confusion of the reign of
Tetricus he had to go into distant exile and poverty.
He was an adept in astrology and other superstitious
arts of his heathen ancestors, and among his papers
was discovered the horoscope of his grandson, predicting
the famous consulship of 379.[2]   For his father the poet
had a profound reverence.[3]   Born to modest fortune,
which gave him a place in the municipal councils of
Bazas and Bordeaux, he practised as a physician for the
greater part of his life, till, on his son's advancement, he
was suddenly raised to the prefecture of the Illyrian
province.   He was probably a philosophic pagan, a Stoic
of the type of M. Aurelius, whom he resembles in many
traits.   Yet he had many virtues which we are accustomed
to regard as peculiarly Christian.   He attained the highest
medical skill possible in those days, and gave his advice
without fee or reward to the poor and afflicted.   Careless
of money, yet frugal without meanness, he neither added
to nor impaired his moderate fortune.   Like the sages
whom he followed, he found the true wealth in regulation
of the desires, but he added to this ideal a warmth of charity,
and a certain serenity and sweetness, which softened his

Septem Sapientium is dedicated to
Drepanius Pacatus, procos. of
Africa in that year, *C. Th.* ix. 2,
4. His father lived to about ninety
years, *Parent.* i. 4 ; *Idyl.* ii. 61 ;

cf. Schenkl's *Ausonius*, Prooem.
vii.
[1] *Parent.* ix. 8.
[2] *Ib.* iv. 17-22.
[3] *Ib.* i. ; *Idyl.* ii.

Stoicism. Holding aloof from scenes of strife and rivalry, and the treacherous friendships of the great, closing his ears to all spiteful rumour, leading a life of dignified contentment and quiet beneficence, he seems an almost flawless character, one of those saintly souls who reach a rare moral elevation without support or impulse from religious faith.

The women of the family were one and all of a masculine and almost puritanical type, reminding one, by a certain quietude and grave purity, of what we have read of New England women two or three generations ago. In their untiring industry and anxious care of the household, they realise the old Roman ideal of woman's office. The poet's grandmother, the wife of the old astrologer, although venerated for her spotless character, had left memories of stern rebuke among her descendants.[1] His mother was a model housewife with a mingled sweetness and gravity.[2] One of his aunts stands out from all the women of the circle. Ausonius remembered her love and kindness to him as a boy. But she had conceived a hatred of the ordinary female life[3] of her time, rejected with scorn all thoughts of marriage, and devoted herself to the study of medicine. His sister, left early a widow, combined the same masculine strength with the peculiar virtues of her own sex. Of all the circle, she is the only one who is described as a religious devotee.[4] Ausonius lost his wife early, and the verses dedicated to her memory are the expression of deep and enduring affection, and a life-long regret.[5] The memory

---

[1] *Parent.* v. 10 :
blanda austeris imbuit imperiis.

[2] *Ib.* ii. 6.

[3] *Ib.* vi. 7-11 :
foeminei sexus odium tibi semper.

[4] *Ib.* xii. 7 :
unaque cura
nosse Deum.

She was the mother of Magnus

Arborius, Praef. Urb. 379, 380 ; *C. Th.* vi. 35, 9 ; Sulp. Sev. *Dial.* ii. 10 ; cf. Rauschen, *Jahrbücher*, pp. 44, 64 ; Schenkl, Prooem. xiv.

[5] *Parent.* ix. 10-16 :
haec graviora facit vulnera longa dies.
.   .   .   .   .
volnus alit, quod muta domus silet et
torus alget,
quod mala non cuiquam, non bona
participo.

of pure love and sympathy, the long years which, as they
pass over the silent house, make solitude and the pain
of loss only deeper, have seldom been pictured with
greater and more real affection.   When we read these
sketches, which bear all the marks of minute faithfulness
and sincerity, we can understand the feeling of Tacitus
about the gravity and severity of provincial character.[1]
These people seem to have had little of definite
Christianity.   None of them certainly were carried
away by the ascetic spirit which withdrew their friend
Paulinus from the world.   But they are industrious and
high-minded; they take life almost too seriously; they
have a certain distinction of hereditary virtue.

Ausonius himself, although he has a genuine admiration for the virtues of his family, and really possesses
many of them,[2] was also the most brilliant child of that
Gallic renaissance of the fourth century which extended
from Constantine to Theodosius.   It was a kind of "Indian
summer," a long pause of tranquillity between two periods
of convulsion.   But it was an age of illusions.   The
Empire, which seemed to have regathered its strength,
was mined by incurable disease.   There was a great
energy of academic life, but Roman culture had worked
itself out and was living on its past accumulations.   The
terror of the barbarians who threatened the frontier of
the Rhine seemed for a time to be laid.   Yet the campaigns of Julian and Valentinian, although victorious,
had revealed the unexhausted strength of the enemy.

[1] *Ann.* iii. 55 : xvi. 5.
[2] The personal character of Ausonius appears to have been without reproach.   But he sometimes shows
a lamentable pruriency, as in the
"Cento nuptialis" *Idyl.* xiii.   Ausonius lays the blame on Valentinian
who ordered this miserable desecration of "vates sacer."   He may
well say, piget Virgiliani carminis
dignitatem tam joculari dehones-
tasse materia.   Yet the morality

of Valentinian seems to have been
as irreproachable (Amm. Marc. xxx.
9, 2) as Ausonius asserts that his
own was : lasciva est nobis pagina,
vita proba.   Cf. H. Nettleship,
Lectures and Essays, 2nd series, p.
39.   Referring to the coarseness of
Latin satire, Mr. Nettleship says,
"I should be disposed to refer this
fact not to the moral obliquity of
these writers, but to the conventional traditions of their art."

Ausonius, however, in the remote tranquillity of Aquitaine, had no thoughts of these ominous contrasts. His early years were passed in the class-rooms of some of the professors to whom his pen has given an immortality of which they never dreamed. His uncle, Arborius, a professor at Toulouse, whose brilliant rhetorical accomplishments were rewarded by a high place in the capital of the East, roused his ambition and predicted for him a splendid future.[1] But this ambition had for more than thirty years to be satisfied with the limited opportunities of a provincial university, and perhaps a seat in the Municipal Council. It is needless to imagine, as some have done, that the brilliant professor chafed at the restraints and dulness of his humble sphere. Ausonius had the sanity and strength cf a stubborn race. He had also early caught that passion for Graeco-Roman culture which in receptive spirits had all the force of religion. The worship of the Boeotian Muses was in men of his type a dangerous rival to the worship of Christ.[2] Ausonius was a teacher of grammar at twenty-five ; he was only a teacher of rhetoric at fifty-five.[3] Yet it may be doubted whether he regarded the long interval as a period of monotonous and inglorious toil. Ausonius was not bourgeois in his tastes and ideals. In the poem addressed to his namesake and grandson,[4] although he shows a natural pride in the prefecture and consulship which he has won, he would have the boy face all the troubles of school life, and love his Homer and Menander, his Horace and Virgil as his grandfather had loved them. The lives of some of his professors were humble and obscure. But he retained a high opinion of the dignity of the teacher, and he looks back with pride on the

[1] *Parent.* iii. 16 ; cf. Schenkl, Prooem. viii.

[2] *Ep.* xxv. *ad Paulinum*, v. 73.

[3] See Schenkl's Prooem. viii. ix.

for the dates in the career of Ausonius. He was probably appointed tutor to Gratian between 363 and 368.

[4] *Idyl.* iv. 46.

hundreds of pupils to whom he had handed on the sacred
fire.   It should also be remembered that Ausonius, like
some of his professors, lived on equal terms with the
local aristocracy.[1]   His wife, Attusia Lucana Sabina, was
the daughter of one of the magnates of Aquitaine, of an
old senatorial stock.[2]   His father, the Stoic physician,
must have had weight and dignity in a society so sound
and healthy as we believe that of Bordeaux to have
been in his day.   Even surrounded by the most extravagant pretensions of new wealth,[3] Ausonius would
not have been a mere cipher.   And in the Bordeaux of
Ausonius wealth was not new; birth was respected more
than wealth; and literary eminence perhaps more than
either.

The life of Ausonius in his green old age, when he
had returned from the Imperial Court, to spend his remaining years among his friends, is very much the kind
of life which we shall find the nobles of Aquitaine and
Auvergne leading nearly a century after his death.   It
has been often repeated that Roman society was to the
last essentially urban in its tastes and character, and that
the love of the country came in with the German invaders.
Nothing could be farther from the truth.[4]   Down to the
great invasions of the third century the Gauls were
passionately fond of city life, in which they seemed to
find the finest essence of Roman civilisation.   But in the
fourth century there are obvious signs of a change of
feeling.   In the age of the Antonines the towns were
open, spreading capriciously with ample spaces, liberally
embellished with theatres, temples, triumphal arches, all
the buildings which could satisfy taste, or minister to

---

[1] Cf. the way in which Paulinus
of Nola speaks of him in his *Poems*,
xi. 8, x. 96. Paulinus was one of
the greatest nobles of his province.

[2] *Parent.* ix. 5:
nobiles a proavis et origine clara senatus.

[3] Yet the *nouveaux riches* were
not unknown then; cf. Auson,
Epigr. xxvi.:
quidam superbus opibus et fastu tumens,
    tantumque verbis nobilis, etc.

[4] F. de Coulanges, *La Gaule Rom.*
pp. 207, 209.

convenience or luxury.[1]   In the reign of Gratian and
Valentinian many of them had become fortresses, with
lofty walls built of blocks which had been often quarried
out of the ruins of the theatres and basilicas of an earlier
age.   The space within the walls is cramped, the streets
are narrow and dark.   Everything is sacrificed to the
necessity for military strength.

Ausonius must have spent many years in Bordeaux
when he was toiling as a professor.   But, when he was
emancipated and had attained distinction and wealth, he
could barely endure the life of the town during a short
visit.[2]   He is disgusted with the crowds and noises and
sordid life of its narrow streets, and longs for the spacious
freedom of the country where you can do what you please
undisturbed.   This love for tranquillity and ease, for the
fresh beauty of rural scenery and the abundance of a great
estate, breathes through his poems.   There can be little
doubt that the " life of the chateau " towards the end of
the fourth century has thrown the brilliant city life of the
ancient world into the shade.   The young noble may pass a
few years at Lyons or Bordeaux to attend the lectures of the
professors.   In later years he may visit the neighbouring
city to take part in a festival of the Church,[3] or to attend
a meeting of the Curia.   But his heart is in the country,
and there the best part of his life is spent.

As the life of the towns becomes more squalid and
sombre, the life of the upper class on their rural estates
becomes more attractive.   There are indeed shadows on
the landscape of Ausonius.   Brigands are heard of now
and then,[4] and years of scarcity are not unknown.[5]   Yet

[1] C. Jullian, *Ausone et Bordeaux*,
p. 115.

[2] *Idyl.* iii. 30 ; *Ep.* x. 18 *sqq.*
The same feeling comes out again
and again in the letters of Symmachus ; *Ep.* i. 3, v. 78, agri quiete
delector, vi. 66, vii. 31.

[3] *Ep.* viii. 9.

instantis revocant quia nos sollennia
    Paschae.
cf. x. 16 ;
nos etenim primis sanctum post Pascha
    diebus
avemus agrum visere.

[4] *Ib.* iv. 23.

[5] *Ib.* xxii. 21, 42; *Idyl.* iii. 27.

in spite of an outburst of pessimism which seems to be a reminiscence of Sophocles,[1] the life of Aquitaine in the poet's days was apparently bright and happy, with no foreboding of the storm which was to burst upon it before a generation had passed away. Skilful culture had developed the natural wealth and charm of a favoured region. Stately country seats, on which the accumulating wealth of generations had been expended in satisfying luxurious or artistic taste, rose everywhere along the banks of the Garonne. The cold of winter was the great plague of country life. But these houses had apartments arranged to suit the varying temperature of the seasons. They were furnished with luxurious baths and well-stocked libraries. Their granaries were stored with ample supplies against a stinted harvest.[2] The richer senators had several such estates. The names and sites of two or three belonging to Ausonius have been ascertained by antiquarian care.[3] The great man of course had his anxieties. His vineyard and corn-land and meadow, which were the sources of his wealth, could not be left entirely to the management of the procurator.[4] We hear now and then of a bad year when supplies had to be brought up from near and far,[5] and when the difficulties of transport were severely felt. But the note of Ausonius is gaiety and contentment. He seems to have suffered little from the ennui of provincial life, after all the excitement and splendour of his years of office. The tedium of one estate could be escaped or relieved by passing on to another, or by receiving friends and visiting in return. Travelling by river or road in Aquitaine in those days was probably easier and quicker than it was for the

---

[1] *Idyl.* xv. 48; cf. Soph. *O. C.* 1225, μὴ φῦναι τὸν ἅπαντα νικᾷ λόγον κ.τ.λ.

[2] *Idyl.* iii. 27:
conduntur fructus geminum mihi semper in annum.

[3] Lucaniacus, *Ep.* xxii. 13; Pauliacus, *Ep.* v. 16.

[4] *Ep.* xxii. gives a lively picture of one of these bailiffs.

[5] Auson. *Ep.* xxii.

English squire in the last century.[1]   Couriers passed to
and fro, carrying friendly letters, trifling presents, and as
trifling poetry.   Here and there the teaching of S. Martin
had begun to detach an accomplished and wealthy aristocrat from the worldly life of his order.   But for the most
part the order remained, in spite of its Christian conformity, essentially worldly or pagan in tone and habits,
enjoying wealth and the sense of irresponsible ease and
freedom which wealth can give,[2] and expending its energy
in rural sports or business, in a round of social engagements, or in studying and imitating the great classics
which were the strongest link with the past.   Society in
Aquitaine is very much the same as it was two generations afterwards, when Sidonius visited his friends at
Bordeaux.

Ausonius and his circle of course represent the more
refined and cultivated section of that society.   Just as in
the times of Sidonius, there were some who fell short of
the highest standard of their order.   There is, for instance, an eccentric character named Theon, to whom the
poet addressed some of his epistles.   Theon had an
estate among the sands of Médoc, looking out on the
Atlantic.[3]   His establishment was rather mean, and he
carried on a despicable trade with the peasants of his
district.[4]   His cattle were sometimes carried off by
brigands; but, like the lowland farmer in the days of
Rob Roy, Theon had little taste for extreme measures,
and came to an amicable composition with the freebooters,
on which Ausonius rallies him.[5]   Yet he is a daring
sportsman, and will follow the wild boar with a reckless
ardour, which sometimes brings him and his friends into
danger of life or limb.[6]   At first one cannot help wondering what sympathy there could be between this eccentric

---

[1] Auson. *Ep.* x. 12, citus veni
remo aut rota; cf. *ib.* viii. 5; cf.
Friedländer, ii. p. 8.
[2] *Parent.* viii. 8; *Ep.* iv. 30.

[3] *Ep.* iv. 3.
[4] *Ib.* iv. 16.
[5] *Ib.* iv. 24.
[6] *Ib.* iv. 30.

and rather boorish character and the polished literary
man and courtier.   The link between them was a taste
for poetry, although Theon seems to have been a sorry
verse-writer, and somewhat of a plagiarist.[1]   His conversation may have been better than his verses.   At any
rate, Ausonius reproaches him with not having paid him
a visit for three months,[2] and promises to forgive him a
debt if he will only visit Lucaniacus.

The society of Bordeaux, in the old age of Ausonius, is
known to us from another source than his poems.   In the
year of the poet's consulship, his son Hesperius, who had
been vicar of Macedonia, proconsul of Africa, and Pretorian prefect of Italy, returned to his native place.   The son
of Hesperius,[3] Paulinus Pellaeus, as he is called from the
place of his birth, has left us a curious autobiographical
poem written in his old age, which has a great value both
as a picture of the life of a young noble of the time, and
of the first appearance of the Visigoths in Gaul.   Paulinus was trained in the usual way.   He had Greek and
Latin tutors, with whom he read the great authors.[4]   His
youth was passed in a circle which combined the highest
official experience with the highest literary culture.   Yet
no one would recognise in Paulinus the grandson of the
tutor of Gratian, or the son of the prefect of Italy.   We
cannot help feeling, as we read the *Eucharisticos*, that,
although Paulinus may be a better Christian than
Ausonius, in other respects the race of the poet has
degenerated fast.   Paulinus may have known Greek well,
from the accident of his birth in an eastern province, but
his limping hexameters, and pointless, colourless style,
would have ruffled even the placid good-nature of his

[1] *Ep.* iv. 10.

[2] *Ib.* v. 5 *sqq.*

[3] The precise relationship of
Paulinus to the poet is a matter of
dispute.   Seeck (lxxviii.) maintains
that he was son of Thalassius and a
daughter of Ausonius.   Brandes
(*Prol.* p. 267) holds that the father
of Paulinus was Hesperius, the
poet's son.   Cf. Ebert, *Allgem.
Gesch. der Lit. des Mittelalters*, i. p.
409 ; Schenkl, Prooem. xiv.

[4] *Euchar.* v. 72, 117.

grandfather, if he had lived to read his verses.   The gloss
of humane culture has worn off, and there is revealed a
rather sordid and materialised character, the product of
leisure without higher interests, and wealth without a
sense of public duty.   The descendant of Ausonius and
Hesperius has hardly a word to say about literature and
politics.

Yet, as the revelation of the interior of a great house
in the last quarter of the fourth century, the *Eucharisticos*
has no mean value.   It is perfectly frank and artless.
Paulinus recalls with gratitude the anxious care of his
parents to protect his youthful innocence,[1] but confesses
that, although he avoided scandalous amours, he yielded
to the temptations which a system of household slavery
always offers.   His early studies were interrupted by ill-
health,[2] and, by his doctor's orders, he devoted himself to
field sports, which his father, who had given them up,
resumed, in order to bear him company.   Henceforth his
whole taste was for fine horses with splendid trappings,
tall grooms, swift hawks and hounds, and the most
foppish and fashionable dress.[3]   His tennis balls had to
be sent for to Rome.[4]   Some of his amusements were
not quite so innocent,[5] and in his twentieth year his
parents arranged for him a marriage with the daughter of
a noble house,[6] whose estates had been impoverished by
neglect.   Paulinus resigned his freedom not without
regret.   He industriously devoted himself to reform the
management of his wife's property,[7] roused up the
laggards, renewed the exhausted vines, improved the
culture of the fields, and paid off the fiscal debts.   For
the next ten years he led a life of luxurious repose.   He
plumes himself on being unambitious and fond of ease
and quietness.   He is completely satisfied with the

[1] *Euchar.* v. 154, 166.
[2] *Ib.* v. 125.
[3] *Ib.* v. 143.
[4] *Ib.* v. 146.
[5] *Ib.* v. 166.
[6] *Ib.* v. 180.
[7] *Ib.* v. 194.

enjoyment of his great house, with its ample and elegant
rooms adapted to the varying seasons, his crowds of
young and handsome slaves, his artistic plate and furni-
ture, his crowded stables and stately carriages.[1]   He was,
as he describes himself, a "sectator deliciarum,"[2] and
nothing more.   This self-centred contentment with the
material pleasures of life, this rather vacant existence,
gliding away in ease and luxury, and a round of trivial
social engagements, not the frantic debauchery described
by Salvianus, is the real reproach against the character
of the upper class of that age.   The luxurious repose of
Paulinus and his kind was soon rudely disturbed by the
apparition of the Goths of Ataulphus.

The society of Ausonius seem to be calmly confident
of the permanence of their ideals of culture, and hardly
conscious of the great movement which was setting
towards the life of prayer and renunciation.   Ausonius
is indeed disturbed by the retirement of S. Paulinus,[3] his
favourite pupil, from the world of refinement and social
distinction; but his feeling seems to be purely personal,[4]
that his friend, so richly endowed, with the promise of
such a brilliant life before him, should forget his traditions and his worldly hopes, and bury his gifts in the
cloister.   The work of S. Martin was done when these
letters were written.   Yet S. Martin is never mentioned.
Probably Ausonius had as little conception of the range
and force of the movement as the great senator of Nero's
court had of the world-wide revolution which was to be
the result of the preaching of S. Paul.

Yet the impulse to asceticism, originally propagated
from the Eastern deserts, and stimulated by the preaching and magnetic influence of S. Martin in Gaul, had
gained extraordinary momentum in the last years of
Ausonius.   The   tales   of   wonder   and   miracle   which

---

[1] *Euchar.* v. 205 *sqq.*
[2] *Ib.* v. 216.

[3] Auson. *Ep.* xxiv.-xxv.
[4] *Ib.* xxv. 50.

rapidly clustered round the name of the great preacher
are the surest proof of the power with which his mission
affected the popular imagination.   His *Life*, by Sulpicius
Severus, within two or three years was widely read in
Gaul, Italy, Illyria, and had found its way even to the
solitaries in the deserts of Egypt and Cyrene.[1]   S. Paulinus, who introduced the book to Roman readers,[2] was
one of the first-fruits of the great religious awakening.
He gave up his wealth and consular rank, and the charms
of his great estate on the Garonne, and, after some years
of retreat in Spain, finally settled at Nola.[3]   His example
of renunciation created a profound sensation all over the
West.[4]   It was followed by many of his order.   And
from one of these, Sulpicius Severus, an advocate, and
man of fortune, we have the fullest record of the movement.   He was a dear friend of S. Paulinus, with whom
from his retreat in Gaul he constantly corresponded.
But Paulinus, from some cause, could never succeed in
drawing Sulpicius to the monastery of Nola.[5]

Sulpicius makes no concealment of the forces which
were arrayed against the ascetic movement.   The sceptical
or indifferent scoffed at the miracles of S. Martin.   The
polished man of the world, according to his temperament,
mourned or ridiculed the blind fanaticism which could
desert the ranks of culture and easy-going self-indulgence
for the solitude and austerity of the hermitage.[6]   Even

---

[1] S. Paulin. Nol. *Ep.* xi. 11 ;
Sulp. Sev. *Dial.* i. c. 23, ii. 17 ; cf.
Migne, *Patrol. Lat.* lxi. ; *Prol.* c.
xxx.

[2] Sulp. Sev. *Dial.* i. c. 23, § 4.

[3] S. Paulinus met S. Martin once
at Vienne (*Ep.* 18, § 9).   S. Martin
cured him of some affection of the
eyes (Sulp. Sev. *vit. S. Mart.* c. 19,
3).   For the circumstances of his
conversion cf. *Prol.* cc. iv. v. in
Migne, t. lxi.   As to the precise
time of his stay at Barcelona, and
the relation of his Poems x. xi. to

Auson. *Ep.* 23, 24, 25, cf. Schenkl,
Prooem. xi. *sqq.* ; Rauschen, *Jahrbücher*, Exc. xxiii. ; Ebert, i. p.
297.

[4] Aug. *Ep.* 31, § 5 ; Hieron. *Ep.*
118, § 5 ; Sulp. Sev. *Dial.* iii. c. 17,
§ 3 ; Ambros. *Ep.* 58.

[5] On Sulp. Sev. and his relations
with S. Paulinus, cf. Gennad. *de
Scrip. Eccl.* c. xix. ; Paulin, *Ep.*
xxiv. § 1 ; xi. 6 ; v. §§ 5, 13 ; i. §§ 10,
11.

[6] Sulp. Sev. *Dial.* ii. c. 13, § 7 ;
iii. c. 5, § 4 ; S. Paulin. *Ep.* xi. § 3.

the bishops and secular clergy, who tried to ignore the
great saint and missionary, looked with ill-disguised suspicion on an enthusiasm which had no respect for ecclesiastical routine.[1]   But nothing could check the eager
passion for a spirituality unattainable in the world of
culture and conventionality.   Towards the end of the
fourth century, great religious houses, for common studies
and devotion, began to be founded in Southern Gaul, and
the famous monasteries of S. Victor and Lérins date from
the early years of the fifth century.   Numbers buried
themselves in secluded hermitages among the woods and
rocks, and reproduced in Gaul the austerity and the
marvels of the anchoret life of the Thebaid.

The East had sent the first call to the life of renunciation, and it was from the East that a second powerful
impulse came.   When S. Jerome in 386 retired to the
monasteries of Bethlehem, he became famous over all the
Roman world.   His great personality stood out as prominent and as attractive as even that of S. Augustine.   He
added to the monastic life fresh lustre by his vivid intellectual force, and his contagious enthusiasm for the study
of Holy Writ.   His letters on questions of casuistry or
biblical interpretation flew to the remotest parts of the
Empire.   The charm which his descriptions threw around
the Holy Places drew numbers of pilgrims, even from the
British Isles, to visit the scene of the Nativity,[2] where
the greatest doctor of the Church was with vast labour
striving to make clear to himself and to posterity the real
meaning of the sacred text.   Before the end of the fourth
century, the resources of the monastery at Bethlehem
could hardly cope with the numbers who thronged thither
from the farthest West.   And each pilgrim on his return,

[1] Sulp. Sev. *Dial.* i. c. 24, § 3,
inter clericos dissidentes, inter episcopos saevientes ; c. 26, § 3, soli
illum clerici, soli nesciunt sacerdotes ; cf. *vit. S. Mart.* c. 27.

[2] Hieron. *Ep.* 66, § 14 ; 46, § 10,
divisus ab orbe nostro Britannus
. . . quaerit locum fama sibi tantum
et Scripturarum relatione cognitum ;
cf. 58, § 4.

by the tales of what he had seen and heard, roused the
ardour of others to make the same journey. We have
the description of such a scene in the *Dialogues* of
Sulpicius Severus. In a hermitage in Southern Gaul,[1] a
monk named Postumianus gives an animated account of
his pilgrimage to the East to eager bystanders. He had
crossed the sea in five days to Carthage,[2] and spent a
week among the sands of Cyrene with a hermit who had
erected in the waste a tiny chapel roofed with boughs.[3]
In Egypt he found a conflict on the orthodoxy of Origen
raging between the bishops and the monks,[4] and the
sympathies of Postumianus seem to be with the suspected
father. A journey of sixteen stages brought him to the
cell of Jerome at Bethlehem.[5] Postumianus has the
greatest admiration for the prodigious learning and industry of the saint, but the brother to whom he is telling
his adventures has a grudge against Jerome for his attacks
on the monastic character. S. Jerome's writings had
already a wide circulation in Gaul, and his pictures of
monkish avarice, vanity, gluttony, not to speak of graver
faults, have offended all the more deeply because they
seem to be true.[6] Postumianus on his return visited
Egypt, the land where the ascetic ideal was highest, and
where solitary perfection had worked its greatest wonders.
The Nile was lined with monastic retreats;[7] as many as
3000 monks were gathered in one community. There
the natural waywardness of the human will was crushed
in a terrible novitiate, in which unquestioning faith was
often rewarded by miracle. One novice had passed

---

[1] Sulp. Sev. *Dial.* i. c. 1.
[2] *Ib.* i. c. 3.
[3] *Ib.* i. c. 5.
[4] *Ib.* i. c. 6. Sulpicius himself
was hardly orthodox. His sympathies in his old age were Pelagian; cf. Gennad. *de Scrip. Eccl.*
xix., hic in senectute sua a Pela-
gianis deceptus.

[5] *Ib.* i. c. 8.
[6] *Ib.* i. c. 8, 9; ii. 7, 8. Cf. S.
Jerome's tale of the monk who had
hoarded money; *Ep.* 22, § 33; cf.
Ep. 125, § 16; 52, § 3.
[7] Sulp. Sev. *Dial.* i. c. 10, 17, ad
Nilum flumen regressus, cujus ripas
frequentibus monasteriis consertas
utraque ex parte lustravi.

through a furnace unhurt.[1]   Another had been ordered
for three years to bear the water of the Nile two miles
distant, to irrigate a dead stick till it broke into leaf.[2]
Others had tamed the beasts of the wilderness till they
acquired the feelings and sympathies of man, including
even remorse for sin ![3]   Tales like these, falling on ears
eager for marvels of the power of sanctity, drew many
another wanderer from Gaul to the mysterious East.

These pilgrimages, however, served a more useful purpose than that of satisfying a love of marvels.   The
traveller to or from the holy places was often charged
with letters of inquiry or instruction on questions of
Christian conduct and belief.   S. Jerome had many
correspondents in Gaul who communicated with him in
this way, and some of his most interesting letters were
written in reply to them.   In the early years of the fifth
century a young priest named Apodemius was setting out
to visit the Holy Places, and a Gallic lady named
Hedibia [4] seized the opportunity of sending S. Jerome a
list of questions on theological or practical difficulties.
Hedibia belonged to the same family as Euchrotia and
Procula,[5] who imperilled their fair fame by allowing
themselves to be carried away by the arts or the
enthusiasm of the sectary Priscillian.   She was of an
ancient Druidic house, which had been connected by
hereditary ties with the temple of Belen at Bayeux.[6]
The Celtic god was discovered by the accommodating
theology of Rome to be the counterpart of the Phoebus
Apollo of Greek legend, and the double name Apollo-
Belenus figures on many inscriptions of the imperial
times.   The names Phoebicius, Delphidius, and Patera,
borne by male members of the house, have a hieratic
meaning or association.   When the Druid supe.stitions

[1] Sulp. Sev. *Dial.* i. c. 18, § 4.   [4] Hieron. *Ep.* 120.
[2] *Ib.* i. c. 19, § 3.   [5] Sulp. Sev. *Chron.* ii. 48, § 3.
[3] *Ib.* i. c. 14, § 5.   [6] Auson. *Prof. Burdig.* iv. 9.

were dying away, the family devoted itself to the arts of poetry and eloquence connected with the name of their divine patron.   One member rose to eminence as a teacher of rhetoric at Rome in the reign of Constantine.[1] Two others had a provincial reputation about the same time in the school of Bordeaux.   Another, in the following generation, named Delphidius, after a troubled career in the reigns of Constantius and Julian, ended his life in the same university, and has a place among the Professors of Ausonius.   Hedibia had the mental energy of her race, without any of that tendency to a merely emotional religion which wrecked the peace and tarnished the character of her Priscillianist relatives.   The bent of her mind was evidently towards a careful and honest exegesis of the Bible.   She begins with the practical inquiry, How can perfection be attained, and how should a widow left childless devote herself to God ?   But the majority of Hedibia's questions relate to apparent discrepancies in the Gospels, especially in the narratives of the Resurrection, and to difficulties in the interpretation of some passages in S. Paul's Epistles.

Apodemius was also the bearer of a letter of the same kind from a lady named Algasia,[2] who seems to have lived in the diocese of Cahors.[3]   Algasia asks, Why did John the Baptist send his disciples to ask " Art thou He which should come ? " when he had previously said of Jesus " Behold the Lamb of God " ?   What is the meaning of the text " If any will come after me, let him deny himself " ?   Who is the steward of unrighteousness commended by the Lord ?   But in her list of difficulties there is one which has a pathetic human interest, because

---

[1] Hieron, *Ep.* 120, praef. ; Auson. *Prof.* iv. v. ; cf. Thierry's *S. Jerome*, 412.

[2] *Ib.* 121.

[3] *Ib.* 121, habes istic sanctum virum Alethium Presbyterum qui . . . posset solvere quae requiris. He is probably the Alethius, bishop of Cahors, addressed by S. Paulin. Nol. *Ep.* xxxiii. ; *v.* Greg. Tur. *Hist. Franc.* ii. 13.

it seems to refer to the rumours, growing more and more distinct in the year in which the letter was written, of barbarian movements in the north.   The writer asks S. Jerome for an interpretation of the ominous saying reported by S. Matthew, " Woe to them that are with child and to them that give suck in those days "; and " Pray that your flight be not in the winter, nor on the Sabbath."   S. Jerome of course interprets the words as referring to the coming of Antichrist [1] and the cruelties of persecution.   But Algasia's appeal seems to thrill with the shuddering anxiety of a mother who had heard the tidings that the Sueves and Vandals had passed the Rhine.[2]

[1] *Ep.* 121, c. iv.
[2] According to Prosp. *Chron.* the Vandals crossed the Rhine in the last days of 406. On the date of the letter to Algasia *v.* Praef. in Migne, t. lxxxvi.

CHAPTER IV

THE SOCIETY OF APOLLINARIS SIDONIUS

FOR more than a generation after the period described in the *Eucharisticos* the condition and tone of Roman society in the West lies in obscurity. But when we reach the middle of the fifth century we suddenly emerge into daylight again, under the guidance of Apollinaris Sidonius. There is no relic of that age so precious to the historian of society as the works of the bishop and grand seigneur of Auvergne. He does for the social history of the second half of the fifth century what Symmachus and Ausonius do for the closing years of the fourth.

Caius Sollius Apollinaris Sidonius was probably born at Lyons in the year 431, and belonged to one of the most influential and distinguished families in Gaul.[1] His ancestors for generations had held the highest offices in the imperial hierarchy.[2] His grandfather, distinguished both as a jurist and a soldier, had been prefect of the Gauls under the usurper Constantine.[3] His father held

---

[1] For his proper name see *Carm.* ix. 1 ; Fertig. i. p. 5 n. For his birthplace, Chaix. *S. Sid. Apoll.* i. p. 10; Sid. iv. 25 (caput civitati nostrae per sacerdotium); *Carm.* xiii. 23. See also Germain's *Apoll. Sid.* Exc. 1. For the date of his birth, *v. Ep.* viii. 6, in which he was *adolescens* in the consulship of Asturius (449 Idat. *Chron.*). The

meaning of *adolescens* for that age may be inferred from Jordanes, *Get.* 55, Theodoricus jam adolescentiae annos contingens . . . octavum decimum peragens annum. See Fertig, i. p. 6.

[2] *Ep.* i. 3, cui pater, socer, avus, proavus praefecturis urbanis, praetorianisque, etc., micuerunt.

[3] *Ib.* v. 9 ; iii. 12.

the same office under Valentinian III.[1] His mother
belonged to the family of Avitus,[2] and Papianilla his wife
was a daughter of that great noble who was one of the
last emperors of the West. Sidonius was educated at
the school of Lyons,[3] which still in his time retained
some of its old celebrity. During his years of academic
life, he formed a lifelong friendship with many young
men of the leading families of the province.[4] The
elevation of his father-in-law Avitus to the imperial
throne, in 455, introduced Sidonius at an early age to
the society of the capital. His *Panegyrics* on that
emperor, and on Majorian and Anthemius, gave him a
great reputation as a poet and a man of letters, and for
the last he was specially rewarded with the prefecture of
the city. Five years afterwards, he was chosen bishop
of Auvergne, at the time when it was making a last
stand against the Visigoths. He lived probably about
fifteen years longer,[5] and passed away amid the passionate
grief of his flock, to whom he had been a friend and
protector in all their troubles.

The letters of Sidonius were published at intervals,
towards the close of his life. They are in all 147,
divided into nine books, according to ancient models;[6]
but there were many more which he could not recover.[7]
Sidonius intended his letters to be read by posterity,[8]

[1] *Ep.* viii. 6; v. 9; in the consulship of Asturius, 449.

[2] *Ib.* iii. 1.

[3] *Carm.* ix. 310. Hoenius was
his teacher in rhetoric and poetry,
Eusebius in philosophy, *Ep.* iv. 1.

[4] Avitus the younger, *Ep.* iii. 1;
Probus, *Carm.* xxiv. 90; Faustinus,
Ep. iv. 4. See Chaix. *Sid. Apoll.*
i. p. 23; Fertig, i. p. 7.

[5] The date of his death is doubtful. In *Ep.* ix. 12 he says that he
had been bishop for "three olympiads," which would show that he
was living in 482 (or 484). The

other authority is Gennadius, *de
Scrip. Eccl.* xcii.: floruit ea tem-
pestate qua Leo et Zeno Romanis
imperabant. But this does not
give any certain clue to the year of
his death. See Germ. *Sid. Apoll.*
Exc. ii.

[6] *Ep.* ix. 1. Pliny left ten books,
but the tenth is addressed exclusively to Trajan. Symmachus left
nine books of private letters; another contains Relationes to the
Emperors.

[7] *Ib.* vii. 18.

[8] *Ib.* viii. 2.

and he retouched and elaborated his style,[1] especially in the earlier letters,[2] with a view to publication. It is hardly conceivable that, in their present form, many of them should have been addressed to private friends. They were probably given to the world between 477 and 483.

In the three generations between the consulship of Ausonius and the episcopate of Apollinaris Sidonius, we shall find that the upper class of Gallo-Roman society has changed but little in its ideals and aspirations, or even, in spite of great public calamities, in its external fortune. Yet in that interval events of great historic moment had occurred. The fabric of the Western Empire had been shaken to its base. Ausonius had seen the Alemanni hurled across the Rhine by Valentinian,[3] and chased into the recesses of their forests. In the poems of his tranquil old age the names of the barbarians are hardly ever mentioned. Before the birth of Sidonius they had swept from the Rhine to the Pillars of Hercules. In his early youth Visigoth and Roman had met on many a field in Aquitaine,[4] and as allies they had rolled back the hordes of Attila on the plains of Châlons. In his later manhood, the Western provinces were practically lost to the Empire. The Franks had occupied the lower Rhine. The Visigoths were masters of nearly all Western Gaul south of the Loire. The Burgundians were securely seated on the upper Rhine and the Rhone. Roman dominion in Spain had been reduced by the Sueve and Vandal inroads to a mere corner in the north-east of that great province. The Vandals in North Africa had almost crushed the Roman administration and the Catholic faith, had captured Rome itself, and commanded the Mediterranean with their fleets. The

---

[1] *Ep.* i. 1. He also urged his friends to do the same. Cf. viii. 16; viii. 1.

[2] *Ib.* vii. 18.

[3] Auson. *Idyl.* x. Mosella; v. 422; cf. Amm. Marc. xxvii. 10.

[4] Prosp. *Chron.* a. 436, 439, 451

bishop of Auvergne lived to see his diocese, almost the
last patch of territory in Gaul left under imperial sway,
ceded to the Visigoths, and the last emperor of the West
replaced by a German king of Italy.   The Theodosian
Code reveals the progress of an internal decay which was
even more serious than the onslaughts of the invaders.
Every branch of the imperial service was becoming disorganised.   Corruption was everywhere rampant, and
authority was paralysed.   The weight of taxation was
growing heavier, while the municipal taxpayer was
becoming impoverished, and seeking any refuge from a
system which oppressed the poor and was defied by the
rich.   Yet, in spite of these great changes and this
collapse of authority, the similarity between the world of
Ausonius and that of Sidonius is very remarkable.   Even
in their material condition, the Gallic aristocracy seem to
have suffered little from the general disorganisation.
Within a period of thirty years Narbonne had been at
least twice besieged by the Goths.[1]   Yet in the letters of
Sidonius there is no sign that the tranquil and luxurious
lives of his friends there have been disturbed.   The
villa of Consentius, in the neighbourhood of the town,
still raised its elegant and lofty pile among vines and
olives,[2] with equal charms for the student and the lover
of nature.   Its master enjoyed his old wealth and luxury,
and dispensed hospitality to troops of guests.   Even in
districts occupied by the Germans, the wealth and status
of the upper classes appear to be unimpaired.   Namatius,
a Gallo-Roman, who was one of the admirals of Euric,
with the special charge of warding off the Saxon pirates
from the coast of Aquitaine, when he is not on duty,
leads the placid life of the country gentleman,[3] occupied

[1] In 436 and 462.   Prosp. *Chron.*
and Idat.; cf. Sidon. *Carm.* xxiii. 60:
    sed per semirutas superbus arces
    ostendens veteris decus duelli,
    quassatos geris ictibus molares,
    laudandis pretiosior ruinis.

[2] Sid. *Carm.* xxiii. 37; *Ep.* viii.
4, ad hoc agris aquisque, vinetis
atque olivetis, vestibulo campo calle
amoenissimus.

[3] *Ep.* viii. 6.

with building, hunting, and literature.   In the territory of the Burgundians the fortunes of the upper class seem to have been as little altered.   Bishop Patiens and Ecdicius, the brother-in-law of Sidonius, must have drawn a great part of their revenues from that district.   Yet we shall see Ecdicius able to provide subsistence for 4000 starving people in a season of famine.[1]   And the good bishop, who was a man of private fortune, in a period of similar distress,[2] organised, at his own expense, a system of wholesale relief, not only for the population along the Rhone and the Saône, but also for places far beyond the limits of his diocese.   There is no sign that the great Roman proprietor, so far as the material conditions of his life were concerned, was worse off under the German chief than under the imperial prefect.

That the lower and middle classes suffered cruelly is tolerably certain, but on their condition and feelings Sidonius has little to tell us in his letters.   As a bishop, he courageously stood by his people in the hour of danger, defended their rights, and was full of pity for their sufferings.   His princely charity was long a tradition in Gaul.[3]   But as the great noble, composing elaborate letters to his friends, which he intended for the eyes of posterity, he is almost entirely occupied with the daily life, the peculiar tastes and ambitions of his own order.   Only here and there do we meet with a slight reference to the burden of the taxpayer, the flight of a colonus, the obscure hardships of the petty trader.[4]   All the suffering and reverses of fortune in the classes beneath him, which must have resulted from a great economic revolution, from the oppression of the treasury official, or from the invasions, seem to have had but

---

[1] Greg. Tur. *Hist. Franc.* ii. 24.
[2] Sid. *Ep.* vi. 12, post Gothicam depopulationem, post segetes incendio absumptas, peculiari sumptu inopiae communi . . . gratuita frumenta misisti, etc. ; cf. Chaix, *Apoll. Sidon.* i. p. 319.
[3] Greg. Tur. ii. c. 22.
[4] Sid. *Ep.* ii. 1 ; v. 19 ; vi. 4 ; vi. 8.

little interest for one in whose eyes the men who were descended from prefects and consuls, and who had read Homer and Menander, Virgil and Pliny, together at Lyons or Bordeaux, were the only interesting part of the Roman world.[1]   This class, separated from the masses by pride of birth and privilege and riches, was even more cut off from them by its monopoly of culture. An aristocrat, however long his pedigree, however broad his acres, would have hardly found himself at home in the circle of Sidonius if he could not turn off pretty *vers de société*, or letters fashioned in that euphuistic style which centuries of rhetorical discipline had elaborated.   The members of that class were bound to one another by the tradition of ancestral friendships, by common interests and pursuits, but not least by academic companionship,[2] and the pursuit of that ideal of culture which more and more came to be regarded as the truest title to the name of Roman, the real stamp of rank.   How often does Sidonius remind a friend of the days when they had threaded the mazes of Aristotelian dialectic,[3] or mastered the technique of Latin rhetoric under the same professor at Lyons.   For the stability of the material fortunes of his order he betrays no anxiety. If he has a dim consciousness of decadence, it is of a literary decadence,[4] a failure of industry in the noble and lettered class, a failure in devotion to the ancient models, and in the fastidiousness of the literary sense. The crowd who had no tincture of that lore, who knew not the esoteric language of the initiated, were not perhaps despised by such a perfect gentleman, but they

[1] Symmachus speaks of the Senate as "melior pars generis humani."

[2] Sid. *Ep.* iii. 1 ; v. 9.

[3] *Ib.* iv. 1, tu sub Eusebio nostro inter Aristotelicas categorias artifex dialecticus atticissabas ; cf.

iii. 1.   The best illustration, perhaps, of aristocratic brotherhood is in the letter to Aquilinus, v. 9 ; cf. Chaix. i. 23.

[4] *Ep.* viii. 8 ; ii. 14 ; iv. 17, granditer laetor saltim in inlustri pectore tuo vanescentium litterarum remansisse vestigia ; cf. ii. 10.

were regarded with that blank uninterested gaze which sees in the vulgar only a dim and colourless mass. Sidonius feels a certain disgust even for the best of his German neighbours.[1] They are coarse in their habits, they are ignorant and brutish, and have nothing of that elasticity of mind and delicacy of taste which, even at its worst, the training of the Roman schools imparted. We shall hardly be wrong in supposing that his comparative silence about the lower orders of his own countrymen covers a like repugnance. The ferocious punishment which he dealt out to the boors, who were quite innocently trenching over the soil of his ancestor's grave,[2] displays all the contempt of the mediaeval baron for his serfs.

The letters of Sidonius describe the life and feelings of only a single class of Roman society, but they describe that class with a faithfulness which leaves little to be desired. He professed himself an imitator of Symmachus,[3] but in his delineation of the men with whom he lived, and of the scenery and background of their lives, Sidonius far surpasses Symmachus in minuteness of drawing and in depth of colour. Symmachus cultivates brevity and reserve as a matter of taste and etiquette. He seems almost determined not to be satisfying and interesting. The faults of Sidonius are all on the other side. With perhaps no great powers of reflection, with no abundant stock of ideas, he is yet a minute observer, and has a positive delight in amplifying all the results of observation by means of an enormous, and often barbarous, vocabulary, and by all the arts of a perverted rhetoric, which often puts a strain on language that it will not bear. Let any one read the description of the appearance and habits of Theodoric,[4] of the means by

[1] *Ep.* iv. 1, bestialium rigidarumque nationum corda cornea fibraeque glaciales. Cf. vii. 14, barbaros vitas, quia mali putentur; ego etiamsi boni.

[2] *Ib.* iii. 12.

[3] *Ib.* i. 1, Quinti Symmachi rotunditatem . . . insecuturus.

[4] *Ib.* i. 2.

which the parvenu Paeonius raised himself to the
prefecture before the accession of Majorian,[1] of the
parasite of Lyons,[2] of the delators who surrounded
Chilperic,[3] of Vectius the ascetic country gentleman,[4]
and, while he will find much to offend a sensitive taste,
he will not complain of any want of vividness and colour.
If such a critic should, in other sketches of Roman
society in Gaul, discover a certain sameness and lack of
power to seize the imagination, it would be well for him
to reflect what he himself could have done with similar
materials. The life of a rich, secure, and highly conventional society does not lend itself to descriptions
which enthral the imagination, and satisfy the love of
the various and the picturesque. When the Gallo-
Roman noble had completed his brief career of imperial
"honours," the years of an unruffled and stately life
fleeted away in a colourless and monotonous flow. The
cold, calm dignity of those great houses, with endless
calls to frivolous social duties, and a routine of busy
idleness, must surely have made the nobler spirits sometimes long for the more strenuous and stormy life of
their ancestors. As we turn the pages of Sidonius, we
seem to feel the still, languid oppressiveness of a hot,
vacant noontide in one of those villas in Aquitaine or
Auvergne. The master may be looking after his wine
and oil, or laying a fresh mosaic, or reading Terence or
Menander in some shady grotto; his guests are playing
tennis, or rattling the dice-box, or tracking the antiquarian lore of Virgil to its sources. The scene is one
of tranquil content, or even gaiety. But over all, to our
eyes, broods the shadow which haunts the life that is
nourished only by memories, and to which the future
sends no call and offers no promise.

It may be doubted, however, whether Sidonius

---

[1] *Ep.* i. 11.   [3] *Ib.* v. 7.
[2] *Ib.* iii. 13.   [4] *Ib.* iv. 9.

regarded his society in any such way. He may have
noticed and lamented in his later years a failure of
literary energy,[1] a less delicate sense for what he regarded as purity of Latin style; but for the greater part
of his life the circle of nobles to which he belonged were
enjoying undisturbed the plenty and elegance of their
country seats, and were as devoted as himself to the
literary art. And his circle was very wide. If we
include his letters to bishops and churchmen,[2] it may
almost be said to have embraced the greater part of
Gaul, from Soissons to Marseilles. If we confine our
attention to his secular friends, it certainly covered all
Gaul south of the Loire.[3] The energy with which he
cultivated his friendships or acquaintanceships is truly
admirable. Indeed the best thing about Sidonius is his
genius for friendship. His letters range in all directions,
to Bourges, to Bordeaux, to Marseilles, to Narbonne, to
Lyons, and to many an estate or bishop's house beyond
or within that circle. In the last of his poems,[4] he
sends the volume forth to travel along a winding path to
Narbonne, each stage being marked by some great house
where he, on a similar journey, had spent pleasant days.
The book on its first stage is to brave the criticism of
Domitius, the grammarian of Auvergne. Further on in
its journey it is to visit the seat of Ferreolus, father of
Tonantius Ferreolus, a great prefect of Gaul and ancestral
friend of the poet. It is next to cross the Tarn, and
present itself at Voroangus, the seat of Apollinaris, who
had sat on the same benches with Sidonius at the school
of Lyons. Lingering awhile among the gardens and
grottoes on the Gardon, it passes on, from one friend to
another, till it reaches the stately home of Magnus at

---

[1] *Ep.* v. 10, pauci studia nunc
honorant; cf. viii. 6, ii. 10, iv. 3
ad fin.

[2] Germ., *Apoll. Sid.* p. 136, enu-

merates seventeen bishops with
whom Sidonius corresponded.

[3] The Syagrius of v. 5 lived near
Soissons; cf. Greg. Tur. ii. 18, 27.

[4] *Carm.* xxiv.

Narbonne, whose son was linked to Sidonius alike by ties of marriage and by memories of college life.

It would be a wearisome and fruitless task to carry the reader in detail through the long list of the friends of Sidonius.[1] They are now mere shadows. The circle in Narbonne and its neighbourhood was specially brilliant in the eyes of contemporaries. Sidonius in one of his poems[2] has described this crowd of prefects, consuls, jurisconsults, adepts in every branch of literature, even rivals of the great masters; yet not a name in the long list is known to us from other sources. But although the individual may seem insignificant and uninteresting, the class whom he represents deserves study; and the features of the senatorial class were strongly marked.

In more than one of his letters[3] Sidonius sums up his ideal of the Roman noble, the ideal which he would like his son, as he says, "with the help of Christ," to attain. He should, as an almost religious duty, repay the debt of noble birth by adding to the list of family "honours" some great magistracy in the imperial service. He should, without reducing himself to the level of a bailiff or a money-grubber, attend to the management of his estates.[4] Some of his superfluous wealth may be spent in additions to his country seat, or redecorating his baths and saloons with fresh frescoes and marbles. He will be a keen sportsman,[5] after the manner of his Celtic ancestors. But these pursuits should not absorb all his energy. The noble class, the salt of Roman

---

[1] The task has been piously performed by the Abbé Chaix, t. i. l. 5.

[2] *Carm.* xxiii. 435 ; cf. *Ep.* viii. 4 ; Chaix, *Apoll. Sid.* i. p. 241.

[3] *Ep.* v. 16. He writes to tell Papianilla of her brother's elevation to the patriciate. Note the words : qua de re propitio deo Christo ampliatos prosapiae tuae titulos ego festinus gratatoriis apicibus in-

scripsi ; cf. iii. 6, vii. 12, viii. 7, and *Carm.* vii. 158, quos quippe curules et praefecturas constat debere nepoti.

[4] *Ib.* viii. 8.

[5] *Ib.* iii. 3, flumina natatu, venatu nemora fregisti . . . accipiter canis, equus arcus ludo fuere ; cf. *Carm.* vii. 183, where the exploits of Avitus in the chase are idealised.

society, is a great brotherhood, bound together by the traditions of hereditary friendship and a common culture of priceless value. The true descendant of a great race will train his son in the same arts and accomplishments which moulded his ancestors and himself.[1] He will also, by scrupulous attention to correspondence and social duties, keep warm the feelings of friendship and interest in common studies. Sidonius, at any rate towards the end of his life, was a devout and pious churchman. But to the last, the ascetic ideals of men like S. Jerome and S. Paulinus seem never in his mind to have obscured the ideal of the wealthy and studious country gentleman, with a wholesome well-balanced nature, fond of sport and farming, proud of his family, devoted to his friends, and above all penetrated with a sense of the obligation to carry on the tradition of culture. To be false to letters was to be false to family honour and to Rome.

Pride of birth was one of the strongest feelings in the Gallo-Roman aristocrat. Nor was this much abated by the profession of a severe Christianity. On a remarkable occasion Sidonius was asked by the people of Bourges to nominate a bishop. He delivered an address to justify his choice, and in recommending a certain Simplicius for their suffrages, he lays the greatest stress on his high descent.[2] So in the lives of the saints and great churchmen of that age,[3] the biographer never fails to record the fact of their being of senatorial birth. This class, since the time of Constantine, included all the large

[1] *Ep.* iv. 12 gives a pleasant picture of the bishop reading Terence and Menander with his son ; legebamus, pariter laudabamus jocabamurque ; cf. the care of Ausonius for his grandson's education, *Idyl.* iv., and Sym. *Ep.* v. 5.

[2] *Ib.* vii. 9. Sidonius gives the address in full which he delivered on the occasion : Parentes ipsius aut cathedris aut tribunalibus praesederunt . . . Uxor illi de Palladiorum stirpe descendit.

[3] Greg. Tur. *S. Julian*, prosapia quidem illustris ; *vit. Patrum*, c. 7, sanctus Gregorius ex senatoribus primis ; *Hist. Fr.* vi. 39, est enim (Sulpicius) vir valde nobilis, de primis senatoribus Galliarum ; cf. *vit. Patrum*, c. 8, 16, 20.

landed proprietors of the provinces. It had become in fact, though not by force of enactment, chiefly hereditary. But admission to its ranks was from time to time obtained by the favour of the Emperor,[1] or by the tenure of some of the offices in the Palatine service. The rank which the founder of a family had won by official service, his descendants strove to dignify by attaining still higher place in the imperial hierarchy.[2] With the mass of the senatorial class, the ambition of office sprang rather from personal or family vanity than from the desire of real power. The prefect of the Gauls was a great potentate[3] wielding a far greater power than the monarch of the largest modern European State. Yet the consulship, which had for many ages been a purely ornamental dignity, ranked, in virtue of its ancient glories, far above the greatest prefecture; and the son of a prefect thought that he was at once honouring and surpassing his father, by gaining the shadowy dignity of the consulship.[4]

Yet it may be doubted whether the assertion is absolutely true that all capacity for government in the upper class had died out.[5] We know little of the actual influence on government exercised even by the great prefects of the fifth century. But we can form some conception of the range and nature of their duties from the Imperial Code. The prefect of the Gauls had the financial and judicial administration of three great

[1] *C. Th.* vi. 2, 2, si quis senatorium consecutus nostra largitate fastigium vel generis felicitate. Cf. Godefroy's Paratitlon to vi. 2. In vi. 3, 2 and 3, the distinction is sharply drawn between senatorial and curial estates. Cf. F. de Coulanges, *La Gaule Rom.* p. 180; Duruy. vii. p. 176.

[2] *Ep.* i. 3; iii. 6.

[3] It should be remembered that this prefecture included Britain and Spain as well as Gaul proper.

[4] *C. Th.* vi. 6, 1, diversa culmina dignitatum consulatui cedere . . . decernimus; cf. Auson. *Act. Grat.* ad fin.; Sidon. *Ep.* v. 16, § 4, ut sicut nos utramque familiam nostram praefectoriam nancti etiam patriciam reddidimus, ita ipsi quam suscipiunt patriciam faciant consularem; cf. Friedl. i. p. 206.

[5] De Coulanges, *L'Inv. Germ.* p. 220, la classe sénatoriale elle-même manque de l'esprit de gouvernement.

countries in his hands,[1] and the control of a numerous
body of officials.   Although, from the time of Constantine,
the prefect had no military command, he had to provide
for the commissariat of the legions quartered in his
province.   He had also the superintendence of the great
roads and the postal service.   He had to advise subordinate magistrates on questions of difficulty, and to
hear appeals from their decisions.   Above all he exercised
enormous powers over the levying of taxes and the whole
financial service.   It was his duty at once to secure full
and regular collection, and to check venality or oppression.
It was also his business to give due publicity to all edicts
of the Emperor, and in the framing of these edicts there
is no doubt that the suggestions and advice of a governor
had great weight.   The vast machine had to be kept
running, and any defect in its working had to be brought
to the notice of the Emperor.   In the fifth century the
limits of the great prefecture of the West were steadily
retreating from the Atlantic towards the Mediterranean.
Yet the anxieties of its ruler must have increased as the
times grew darker.   In the career of Tonantius Ferreolus,
one of the friends of Sidonius, we have an example of a
public-spirited noble, and a benevolent and vigorous
governor.   Along with Avitus, he bore a foremost part
in organising the united resistance of Goth and Roman to
the Hun invasion in 451.   And he signalised his tenure
of office in 453 by lightening the burden of taxation in
those disastrous years.[2]   The later Roman Code bears
witness to the strenuous efforts of many high-minded
prefects to check the growing disorganisation of society.
    There can be little doubt, however, that in the

----

[1] On the powers of the Pretorian
prefect see Godefroy's ed. of *C .Th.*
vol. vi. pt. ii. ad init. "Notitia
Praefectorum"; cf. Notitia Dig.
ed. Böcking, t. ii. 13, 14, and 166,
where the Formula Praef. Praet.

is given ; Fauriel, *Hist. de la Gaule
Mérid.* i. p. 351.

[2] *Ep.* vii. 12 ; *Carm.* vii. 315 ;
Fauriel, *Hist. de la Gaule Mérid.*
i. p. 227.

interval between Ausonius and Sidonius the love of
country life had increased, and public spirit or ambition
was declining. Many of the highest class were becoming
mere farmers on a large scale, and cared for little else
than their flocks and vineyards. Sidonius, who had an
almost religious faith in his order, and who regarded
himself as the guardian of Latin culture in an age of
decadence, was revolted by this return to the rude and
solitary rusticity of an earlier time. He was also
alarmed by the passion for money-making which often
accompanied such tastes. Several of his letters are
written to recall these degenerate nobles to their true life
and vocation.[1] And one in particular deserves notice
from tne birth and rank of the person to whom it is
addressed.[2] Syagrius belonged to one of those Gallic
families in which high office was practically hereditary.
He was great-grandson of that Syagrius who was consul
in 381, who was a correspondent of Symmachus,[3] and
from whose daughter Tonantius Ferreolus,[4] the greatest
of Gallic nobles, was descended. The Syagrii were connected with the district of Lyons, and their family estate
lay somewhere near Autun, in the neighbourhood of the
Burgundians. The Syagrius of the time of Sidonius had
fallen away from the example of his ancestors, and from
that ideal of aristocratic life which we have attempted to
describe. Trained in all the literary arts of the Gallic
schools, he had stooped to learn the language of the
conquerors, in which he had acquired a facility which

[1] *Ep.* ii. 14 ; vii. 15 ; i. 6.

[2] *Ib.* viii. 8. The estate of
Taionnacus may have been in the
neighbourhood of Soissons. From
v. 5 it appears that Syagrius was a
master of German.

[3] In the Index to Luetjohann's
ed. of *Sidonius*, the Syagrius of v.
5 is said to be father of the
Syagrius in viii. 8. But Migne

and Chaix (i. 178, 189) are probably right in treating the letters
as addressed to the same person,
the son of Egidius. On Flav.
Afranius Syagrius, cos. 381, cf.
Amm. Marc. xxviii. 2, 9 ; Seeck's
Sym. cx. ; Rauschen, *Jahrb.* p. 85 ;
Sid. *Ep.* v. 17, conditorium Syagrii
consulis.

[4] Sid. *Ep.* i. 7, Afranii Syagrii
consulis e filia nepos ; ii. 9 ; vii. 12.

moves the sarcasm of Sidonius.   But he had sunk even
lower than this.   He had forgotten the long line of his
ancestral dignities and his duty to his country, and
buried himself in his rural property, with no ambition
beyond that of growing fine crops and increasing his
income.   Syagrius may have been a degenerate noble,
but it is also possible that he was a shrewd, sensible
man, who saw the hollowness of the so-called ambition
of his class, who rated cheap the "honours" of a power
no longer able to defend its citizens, and who thought
that his energy might be more usefully expended in
cultivating the friendship of his German neighbours, and
in the management of a great estate, with its crowd of
serfs and dependants, than in playing ball and dice,
exchanging repartees, or applauding with grotesque
exaggeration a literary neighbour's feeble imitations of
Statius or Lucan.

It would be unfair, however, to Sidonius to represent
him as indifferent to the commonplace duties of a great
landholder.   Indeed, the *villa* or senatorial estate must
have demanded some attention from any prudent owner.
The villicus or procurator was often a man of servile
origin, and the Theodosian Code leaves the impression
that these agents had to be carefully watched.[1]   Although
the senatorial estates in Gaul were probably never equal
in extent to those vast *latifundia* which were the ruin of
Italian husbandry,[2] yet they were ordinarily of considerable acreage.   Ausonius had a patrimonial estate near
Bazas, which he describes in modest terms as a *villula*
or *herediolum.*[3]   Yet it consisted of more than 1000
acres, of which 200 were arable land, 100 vineyard, 50
meadow, the rest being woodland.   The estates of the
friends of Sidonius were probably of far larger extent
than that of the poet of Bordeaux.   The nearest approach

[1] *C. Th.* ix. 30, 2 ; ii. 30, 2.   [2] Plin. *H.N.* xviii. 35.
[3] Auson. *Idyl.* iii. 10.

to any indication of their size is contained in a letter
describing the domains of Apollinaris and Ferreolus.[1]
They adjoin one another, and the distance between the
two mansions is rather long for a walk, but rather short
for a ride on horseback.   The great noble, both in Gaul
and Italy, often possessed many of these estates in
different districts, or even in different provinces.   The
lands of S. Paulinus, which Ausonius describes as
" realms," were widely scattered, and when, on his
adoption of the ascetic life, they were sold, " they would
pass," according to Ausonius, " into the hands of a
hundred masters." [2]

   It is characteristic of Sidonius that, while he has left
us several pictures of great mansions, he never gives even
a glimpse of the organisation of an estate.   Yet the
population of these domains formed in itself a complete
and almost self-sufficing community.[3]   The great house
had in its immediate neighbourhood villages which were
occupied by dependants of various grades—slaves or
freedmen, coloni and free tenants, some of them ordinary
labourers, others paying for their holdings both in money
and a stipulated amount of labour.   The buildings for
the slaves, the stables, and granaries, the mill, the olive
and wine-presses, with the workshops, must have formed,
on an estate of any magnitude, a little town, demanding
a good deal of management and careful superintendence.
The superfluous income of the rich man could, in those
days, find investment only in loans on mortgage, or in
the purchase of other properties, or in additions to the
residence of the family.[4]   Building was one of the

---

[1] *Ep.* ii. 9, praediorum his jura
contermina,   domicilia   vicina,
quibus interjecta gestatio peditem
lassat neque sufficit equitaturo.

[2] Auson. *Ep.* 24, 115.

[3] F. de Coulanges, *L'Alleu*, pp.
87, 88.

[4] The law discouraged trading in
the senatorial class, *C. Th.* xiii.
1, 5, cum potiorum quisque aut
miscere se negotiationi non debeat,
aut pensitationem (*i.e.* lustralis
collatio) quod honestas postulat
primus agnoscere. Cf. xiii. 1, 8,
in which feneratores are brought
under the lustralis collatio (*v.*

passions of the Roman aristocrat.[1]   The stern, utilitarian
architecture of the fortified town, its noise and squalor,
repelled him.   On his own lands he gave a free rein to
his taste for beauty or luxury.   The sites of these
ancient country houses seem to have been generally
chosen for some natural beauty, on the wooded banks of
a river or a lake dotted with islands, or at the foot of a
sloping hill, with a prospect of forest, meadow, or rich
cultivated plain.   Sidonius, imitating one of his favourite
models, has left us elaborate word-pictures of some of
these great houses, in Auvergne, on the Gardon, at
Narbonne, or in the neighbourhood of Bordeaux.   His
own house, which came to him by his marriage with the
daughter of the Emperor Avitus, is delineated with a
minute care which reveals in every line a passionate love
of the delights of rural life and scenery.[2]   Domitius, a
professor in the neighbouring college of Auvergne, is
invited to leave the hot class-room and the narrow
streets.   Even in umbrageous Auvergne, "the world is
on fire"; the ground is seamed and scarred with gaping
fissures, the mud is hardening in the bed of the river,
whose failing, languid stream hardly drags itself along.
But in the retreat of Avitacum there is the spreading
coolness which the builder's and the gardener's arts can
win from nature even in the dog-days.   The mansion
has a broad frontage both to the north and the south.
A glen, flanked by two lines of hills, opens on the
southern lawn before the vestibule.   At the south-
western corner are the baths close under a woodclad
height, from which the felled timber drops at the very
mouth of the furnaces.   The heated water is carried
along the walls by leaden pipes.   There are all the

Godefroy's note, and Sid. *Ep.* iv.
24).   Cf. *C. Th.* ii. 33, 4, limiting
the rate of interest which senators
could exact.

[1] *Ep.* v. 11.   Building with dis-

cretion is one of the laudable occupations of the noble ; cf. Friedländer, iii. p. 76.

[2] Sid. *Ep.* ii. 2.   Cf. Plin. *Ep.*
ii. 17.

apartments for luxurious bathing, brilliantly lighted, with walls of gleaming whiteness and domed roofs resting on graceful columns, ending in the *piscina*, where, through curiously-sculptured heads of lions, the cold water from the hillside rushes tumultuously. On these walls no tale of wantonness is figured, although you may see some epigram " neither good enough to make you read it again, nor so bad as to disgust you with the reading." Hard by are the ladies' room and the spinning-room of the maids. After these you find yourself in a long colonnade looking out on the lake, which lies on the eastern side, embosomed in woods. Passing through a long gallery on the south you would reach the winter diningroom, with a cheerful blaze in the vaulted chimney. And from that you may enter a smaller saloon, with a broad staircase leading up to a verandah which overhangs the lake, where the guest, as he cools his thirst, may watch the fisherman buoying his nets. Or you may take a siesta in a chamber screened from the southern heats, where the cicala in the hot noontide, or the nightingale on summer evenings, will lull you to sleep, while the sheep-bell and shepherd's pipe sound from the hillside. Sidonius, with all his conventionality, cannot repress a natural delight in this fairyland of woodland, lake, and bosky islet : it is so green and cool, a paradise of idyllic tranquillity. And yet he describes it in a euphuism, probably the most curiously artificial, in which genuine feeling was ever encased. The master of that domain, of which he sees the inmost charm, sits in his verandah above the lake, coining phrases which he intended to excite the admiration of posterity, but which would have moved the ridicule or disgust of the masters he adored.

One of these country seats was very much like another. They all have apartments for summer and winter, baths, galleries, libraries. Sometimes, as in the case of the Burgus of Leontius,[1] they are strongly fortified with all the art of the engineer. It is clear, from the arrangement of these houses, as well as from the general tone of the literary remains of the period, that their owners passed their lives chiefly in the country. But their solitude was broken by constant correspondence, and by frequent visits. Even in the troubled years which followed the accession of Euric,[2] although the roads were not always safe for couriers and travellers,[3] who were liable to be stopped and questioned, communication among the members of the Gallo-Roman aristocracy was never completely interrupted. The great roads, which opened up the country from the first century, could be traversed rapidly by carriages. But the grand seigneur of the time generally preferred to travel on horseback with a numerous suite. Starting in the cool of the morning, he would halt at noon in some shady spot beside a stream where his servants, sent on in advance, had pitched his tent and prepared the midday meal.[4] The inns were probably few, and, according to Sidonius, they were bad;[5] but the aristocratic traveller could easily arrange, as a rule, to break his journey at nightfall at the house of some friend. The imagined route of the bishop's poems from Auvergne to Narbonne,[6] following a wavering line of country seats, probably

---

[1] Sid. *Carm.* xxii. 117:

> . . . non illos machina muros,
> non aries, non alta strues vel proximus agger,
> non quae stridentes torquet catapulta molares,
> sed nec testudo nec vinea nec rota currens
>
> jam positis scalis unquam quassare valebunt

Pontius Paulinus, who had been Pretorian prefect in the reign of Constantine (v. Jullian's *Ausone*, p. 128), was the builder. He was probably the father of S. Paulinus of Nola, who also bore the name of Pontius; cf. Auson. *Ep.* 24, 103; Migne, *Prol.* t. lxi. c. 1, § 3; Chaix,

Apoll. Sid. i. 222; Luetjohann's ed. of *Sidon.* Ind. Pers. *s.v.*

[2] He succeeded Theodoric II. in 466, and lived till 483, or 485. Cf. Fauriel, i. 347; Luetjohann's *Sidon.* p. 418.

[3] *Ep.* iii. 4; ix. 5; v. 12.

[4] Such a day's travelling is described *Ep.* iv. 8. For travelling by river see viii. 12; cf. Auson. *Ep.* viii. 5.

[5] *Ib.* viii. 11, ne si destituor domo negata moerens ad madidas eam tabernas, etc.; cf. Friedl. ii. p. 23.

[6] *Carm.* xxiv.

represents many a tour of visits made by the author.
On one of these excursions Sidonius found himself once
in the neighbourhood of the two great villas of Voroangus
and Prusianum on the banks of the Gardon, near Nîmes.
Their owners, Tonantius Ferreolus and Apollinaris, were
among his dearest friends. The estates adjoined one
another at the distance of a short ride.[1] Apollinaris and
Ferreolus detained their friend for a week, and had an
amicable conflict each day for his company. It was
difficult to decide between the attractions of these two
princely seats. The gardens of Apollinaris were of
almost fabulous beauty, and might have rivalled the
most delicious scenes in the world of legend or romance.[2]
The gardener's skill had trained the foliage into enchant-
ing bowers, where you might dream away the hot hours
of noon. On the other hand, the home of Ferreolus
offered powerful attractions of a higher kind.[3] Its owner,
the descendant of the great Syagrius, and admittedly by
birth and official rank the foremost of Gallic nobles,
combined remarkable political experience with wide
culture. Though now withdrawn from the great world,
he had borne a splendid part in repelling the Hun
invasion. He had earned the reputation of being a
humane and enlightened prefect, and he was chosen to
represent his province at the famous prosecution of the
corrupt governor Arvandus.[4] His library was amply
stocked with all the literature of pagan antiquity, along
with the newer literature of the Church; and he was
not one of those senators, described by Ammianus, who
entered their libraries as seldom as their family vaults.

---

[1] *Ep.* ii. 9 ; Chaix, i. 210 *sqq.*

[2] *Ep.* ii. 9, Aracynthum et
Nysam, celebrata poetarum car-
minibus juga, censeas ; *Carm.* xxiv.
54-74 :

seu ficto potius specu quiescit
collis margine, qua nemus reflexum

nativam dare porticum laborans
non lucum arboribus facit, sed antrum.

[3] *Ep.* i. 7, Tonantius Ferreolus
was Pretorian prefect in 453.

[4] Arvandus was Pretorian prefect
of Gaul in 469 and impeached at
Rome for treacherous communications with Euric. Sid *Ep.* i. 7.

The daily life at Prusianum, as depicted by Sidonius, shows us the charm and also the weakness of aristocratic society in the fifth century.[1] It is very pleasant, but it seems somewhat self-indulgent and frivolous. When Sidonius arrives in the morning, some of the guests are in the tennis-court, others are eagerly engaged in a game of dice, the more sedate are reading Horace or Varro in the library,[2] or discussing the theology of Origen. The *déjeuner* at eleven o'clock was, "after the senatorial fashion," a short but ample meal ; and the guests, as they sat over their wine, were amused by the recitation of lively tales. The hours of the afternoon were spent on horseback or in the bath. The baths of Ferreolus seem to have been then in the builder's hands, and the company extemporised a bath by the side of a rivulet. A trench was dug along the bank and roofed over with hair-cloth stretched on a framework of branches. Heated stones were flung into the hollow, and a jet of cold water turned on the glowing heap; and the bathers, having enjoyed the vapour for a time, braced themselves by a plunge in the cool stream. The evening closed with a luxurious banquet.

In this pleasant life one hears little of the women of the household, and this silence has been interpreted as a sign that they were ignored and had a humble place in the family. Yet it is hardly probable that, in the full light of Christianity, the position of women was lower than it was in the days of the pagan Pliny or of the semi-pagan Ausonius.[3] The references to women in Sidonius are indeed scanty, but they show that the ideal of female virtue and culture was high. In a letter to a friend about to be married,[4] he points out, by a long series of

[1] Cf. the day at the villa of Consentius, Sid. *Carm.* xxii. 487.
[2] On libraries in the country see Sid. *Ep.* v. 15; viii. 11; viii. 4.

[3] Plin. *Ep. Calpurniae,* vi. 26; vii. 5; Auson. *Parent.* xii. 5; cf. F. de Coulanges, *L'Inv. Germ.* p 212.
[4] Sid. *Ep.* ii. 10.

ancient examples, how women may help to sustain the
literary ambition of their husbands.   In the family of
Magnus of Narbonne the ladies were both pious and
accomplished, and Eulalia, a cousin of Sidonius, who was
married to a son of the house, is described as a very
Minerva.[1]   In the library of Prusianum there were
shelves stocked with religious literature which are
intended for the women of the household.[2]   In another
letter Sidonius sends a friend an elegy on the virtues of
a young matron of Lyons,[3] whose early death was a
public event, and mourned with every demonstration of
grief by the whole community.

There is hardly a trace in the works of Sidonius of
that looseness of morals with which Salvianus charges
his contemporaries in that very province to which so
many of the friends of Sidonius belonged.   There is
indeed one letter,[4] the tone of which rather startles us in
a bishop.   It refers to the irregular connection of a
young noble with a slave girl.   The mistress is treated
with loathing and contempt, but the young man is
absolved rather easily on the score of morals, and commended for having thrown the girl over, and so consulted
his reputation and fortune.   His marriage with a lady of
noble birth seems, in the eyes of the bishop, to atone
for his " error."   Such rare glimpses of self-indulgence
in the members of a rich, idle, and luxurious caste, with
hardly any public interests, and surrounded by crowds of
slaves, do not excite much surprise.   But the picture of
abnormal and universal debauchery given by Salvianus
is absolutely unconfirmed by anything in the pages of
Sidonius.

---

[1] *Carm.* xxiv. 95 :

hic saepe Eulaliae meae legeris,
cujus Cecropiae pares Minervae
mores et rigidi senes et ipse
quondam purpureus socer timebant.

[2] *Ep.* ii. 9, sic tamen quod qui
inter matronarum cathedras codices

erant, stilus his religiosus invenie-
batur, etc.

[3] *Ib.* ii. 8.

[4] *Ib.* ix. 6 ; cf. the passage in the
Eucharisticos, where Paulinus speaks
of a similar error of his youth in
the same tone, v. 165.

In the description of the debauched parasite in Sidonius,[1] we have indeed a specimen of physical and moral degradation which excites horror and disgust.   If the bishop ever gave his flock in the cathedral of Auvergne a sermon in the same style, it must have had a powerful effect.   It is composed with the object of warning a young relative of the horrors of the abyss into which his life might plunge, if he neglected the old rules of conduct.   Yet in reading the piece, one cannot help feeling that the literary spirit, the spirit of Juvenal and the school rhetoric, has possessed the writer.   It is in some respects a powerful piece, but the power is that of a master of words and phrases, who exults in his command of them.   There is no light and shade; the whole is black with the smoke of the infernal streams.[2]   There may have been, there probably were, degenerate Romans who, in an age of violent and sudden change, lost all sense of self-respect, all feeling of Roman dignity and Christian duty, and who determined to make the best, in a sensual way, of an age of convulsion, to sell their compatriots, to flatter their new masters, and to purchase gross pleasure with the wages of their treachery.   All this is probable.   Yet we may well doubt whether, even in the most disorganised society, such specimens of utter moral and physical wreck were often seen as the loathsome wretch whom Sidonius has described for edification and warning.   The love   word-painting is too evident; the strain and staring contrast of verbal antithesis are too marked to give one confidence in the fidelity of the portrait.   The body, deformed in every line and feature by vice, bloated with luxury, and enervated by excess, is described with disgusting and exaggerated emphasis as the fit dwelling of a fouler and uglier soul.   The

---

[1] Sid. *Ep*. iii. 13.

[2] *Ep*. iii. 13, lumina gerit . . . lumine carentia quae Stygiae vice paludis volvunt lacrimas per tenebras . . . facies ita pallida veluti per horas umbris maestificata larvalibus.

whispered slander, the gross innuendo, the affectation of
vivacity without wit, of importance without dignity, the
hungry eagerness for a hospitable invitation, combined
with feigned shyness in accepting, the gross and bestial in ·
dulgence, the ravenous throat and the venomous tongue—
all this, with many traits we have suppressed, is a picture
which we may hope had few counterparts in real life.

Such characters rarely meet us in the pages of
Sidonius. His world was probably quite as Christian in
sentiment and conduct as our own. It inherited also, as
a social and literary tradition, a profound veneration for
the virtues of the old Roman character. It was, above
all, a society dominated by pride, respect for class-feeling,
and imperious good taste. If to the pride and fastidiousness of the polished noble you add the restraints of a
collective Christian sentiment, you have a social tone
which is not likely in general to be prone to gross
indulgence. There is no trace of lubricity on the walls
of the mansions, or in the entertainments described in
these letters.[1] Like the guests in the *Saturnalia* of
Macrobius,[2] Sidonius congratulates his generation on being
more decent than their ancestors. No wanton frescoes,
no suggestive dances and songs, would be tolerated. The
friends of Sidonius, Ferreolus, Ecdicius, Consentius,
Lampridius, Apollinaris, and a host of others, seem to be,
on the whole, as regards private virtue, perfectly regular
and unexceptionable in their lives. It is possible that
class feeling or the reticence of good nature or good taste
may have led Sidonius sometimes to cast a veil over the
faults of the dear and pleasant friends of his youth. Yet
one cannot help having the impression that his silence
about evil is due to its absence, at least in any gross
form, among the people with whom he associated.

---

[1] *Ep.* ii. 2, non hic per nudam
pictorum corporum pulchritudinem
turpis prostat historia, quae sicut
ornat artem devenustat artificem.

[2] *Saturn.* ii. 1, 6.

The real canker at the root of that society was not gross vice, but class-pride, want of public spirit, absorption in the vanities of a sterile culture, cultivated selfishness.   It is difficult for a modern man to conceive the bounded view of society taken by people like Symmachus and Sidonius, the cold, stately self-content, the absence of sympathy for the masses lying outside the charmed circle of senatorial rank, the placid faith in the permanence of privilege and wealth, the apparent inability to imagine, even in the presence of tremendous forces of disruption, that society should ever cease to move along the ancient lines.   The bureaucratic system of government stifled all interest in public affairs in the natural governing class.   Masters of vast domains, yet excluded, as an order, from real political power, the great mass of the senatorial class were condemned to a sterile life of fantastic luxury, literary trifling, or sullen reserve.   They had little care for any but their own caste and family, as the representatives of Graeco-Roman culture.[1]   With what was regarded as a laudable ambition to add to the " honours " of the family, and a strenuous devotion to the study and imitation of the great authors, there seemed to the stately noble no reason why the calm ceremonious senatorial life should not go on for ever. The aim of all true Romans was to reproduce in successive generations the forms and ideas of the great past, undisturbed by any hope or ambition of ever excelling it. To such a condition of death-like repose or immobility had the imperial system reduced the most intelligent class in the Roman world.   Faith in Rome had killed all faith in a wider future for humanity.   Society had been elaborately and deliberately stereotyped.   As a rule, whatever a man's energy or ambition, he was doomed to

---

[1] Sidon. *Ep*. viii. 2, nam jam remotis gradibus dignitatum, per quas solebat ultimo a quoque summus quisque discerni, solum erit posthac nobilitatis indicium litteras nosse.

work out his life on the precise lines which his ancestors had followed.   All ideas of improvement were nipped in the bud, blasted by the stifling atmosphere of a despotism which, with whatever good intentions, received no guidance or inspiration from the thoughts or needs of the masses, and spent all its strength in maintaining unchanged the lines of an ancient system, instead of finding openings for fresh development.   The same immobility reigned in the education of the privileged class.   They felt no material need to stimulate invention and practical energy, and their academic training only deepened and intensified the deadening conservatism of unassailable wealth and rank.   Their training was exclusively literary; its sole object was to make masters of phrase, rhetoricians, skilled and successful imitators of the great masters of the literary art.   Mere style, apart from real knowledge or ideas, was its great aim.   It persistently kept before the pupil's gaze the mythological fancies and literary finesse of the great ages.   As the material force of the Empire slowly waned, the loftier spirits clung all the more tenaciously to the literary heritage from the past of Greece and Rome, as to a standard of unapproachable perfection.   There was no curiosity, no love of scientific inquiry, no hope of further advance.   All that was best in the possible achievements of the human spirit lay behind, steeped in the golden haze of a heroic age.   In front stretched a gray, flat prospect of cultivated mediocrity.   It is hardly too much to say that the despotism of the school tradition was as stifling and fatal to progress as the bureaucratic despotism of Diocletian.

In the time of Ausonius we have caught some glimpses of the ascetic and the intellectual side of the Christian life in Gaul, revealing a spiritual movement in striking contrast to the polished worldly society of the senatorial order, in which class-pride had taken the place of high public spirit, and a dilettante culture had frozen the

springs of moral enthusiasm and energy. The majority
of this class, two generations after Ausonius was in his
grave, resembled him rather than S. Paulinus. Yet here
and there in the letters of Sidonius we meet with a man
who remained in the world, yet was not of it, who, without acting literally on the command to forsake all things
for Christ, strove to live in the spirit of the Sermon on
the Mount. The character of one of these hidden saints,[1]
a certain Vectius, might have been drawn by the author
of the *Serious Call*. He was a man of illustrious rank
and great fortune, but he had learnt the secret of " using
the world as not abusing it." He has all the spirit of
an anchoret under the soldier's cloak, and regards his
position as a trust rather than a property.[2] The spirit of
their master had spread among his serfs and clients. They
are as obedient and dutiful as he is gentle and considerate.
He has still all the tastes of the noble of his time ; he
wears the proper dress of his rank ; he has a pride in
horse and falcon and hound, and the stately serenity of
wealth. He maintains a severe but clement dignity.
He joins the hunt, but he does not eat the game. His
hours are often spent in reading the Scriptures and chanting the Psalms. An only daughter, whom he tends with
a mother's tenderness, consoles him in his widowhood.
Sidonius adds that, with all deference to his own order,
if he could find such graces in his friends, he would prefer
the priestly character to the priest. Sidonius, although
he did not withhold his admiration from the monastic
life, and wrote an elegy on Abraham,[3] the Eastern solitary
who settled in Auvergne, was, after all, one of that class
of prelates who, having been trained in worldly society,
believed in a Christianity which kept in touch with the
world, to renovate it and to govern it.

[1] Sid. *Ep.* iv. Cf. Law's *Serious Call*, c. 8.

[2] Sid. *Ep.* iv. 9, putes eum pro- priam domum non possidere, sed potius administrare.

[3] *Ep.* vii. 17.

Apollinaris Sidonius had reached his forty-second year [1] when, by the popular voice, he was called to undertake the episcopal oversight of the diocese of Auvergne.[2] He had been till then the most typical representative of the aristocratic caste, Christian in profession, but pagan in sentiment and training. He had considered it his mission to deepen the pride of rank and the pride of culture. He became suddenly one of the most devoted pastors and spiritual governors, sharing the dangers and miseries of his flock in the Visigothic invasion, imprisoned by Euric for his devotion, passionately lamented by his people after his death. There is no record of the circumstances of this great change.[3] Yet the contrast between the life of the worldly aristocrat and the Christian bishop is very marked. We have seen the pictures of daily life at the great senator's country seat. Far different was the life of the chiefs of the Church.[4] The bishop lived in the chief town of his diocese, with doors always open. In the early morning hours he received all comers, heard complaints, composed differences, performed many of the duties of a civil magistrate.[5] He celebrated Mass, preached and taught the people in church. He had important functions in connection with the municipal council. If his episcopal seat lay near the court of a German prince, the bishop had the task of conciliating the new barbarian power,[6] and of maintaining good relations between it and

---

[1] The year 472 or 471 for the commencement of his episcopate is inferred from a passage in *Ep.* vi. 1, to Lupus of Troyes ; the letter, written evidently soon after the ordination of Sidonius, speaks of Lupus as having completed *novem quinquennia . . . in apostolica sede.* Lupus became bishop in 427. Cf. Luetjohann's ed. of *Sid.* Ind Pers. ; Germain's *Apoll. Sid.* p. 19 n. ; Chaix, i. 439.

[2] *Ep.* v. 3, utpote cui indignissimo tantae professionis pondus impactum

est ; iii. 1 ; vi. 7.

[3] *v.* Fertig, *Apoll. Sid.* Abth. ii.6.

[4] Guizot, *Civ. en France*, i. 102.

[5] F. de Coulanges, *L'Inv. Germ.* 36, 38 ; Fauriel, i. 376 ; cf. *Nov. Maj.* tit. xii. ; *C. Th.* xvi. 10, 19, xv. 8, 2. For multifarious business brought before bishops cf. Sid. *Ep.* vi. 2, 4, 9, 10.

[6] *Ep.* vi. 12, the Burgundian king used to praise the dinners of Bishop Patiens ; cf. Ampère, *Hist. Lit.* ii. 202 on the relations of S. Avitus with the Burgundians.

the Gallo-Roman population.   He had to superintend the cultivation of the lands of his see, and sometimes he even worked on them with his own hands.   The narrow space left by these active occupations would, if he were a scholar and a thinker, be devoted to the theological or philosophical discussions of the time, and he might, in that age of controversy, have to define his position in some treatise on free-will and grace, or on the nature of the soul.[1]   The real leader of the municipal community in the fifth century, alike in temporal and in spiritual things, was often the great Churchman.   The power of the senatorial class, with all their broad lands and culture, did not extend usually beyond the serfs of their estates.

There were two distinct classes of bishops in the Gallic Church of the fifth century, the monastic and the aristocratic, and the special qualities of both were needed by the circumstances of the time.   The monasteries of Southern Gaul were not only devoted to an ascetic religious life, but to learning and theological inquiry. They were the real centres of the intellectual movements of the age ; and the great house of Lérins [2] had a special fame not only for its sanctity but for its dialectic.   Its atmosphere seems to have been favourable to freedom of thought on the great questions which then agitated Western Christendom.   It was the home of a Pelagian or semi-Pelagian school of thought which long repelled the extreme Augustinian views on the relation of Divine grace to human will.   And it gave many eminent prelates to the Gallic church, Faustus [3] of Riez, Lupus [4] of Troyes, Eucherius [5] of Lyons, and Hilary [6] of Arles.

---

[1] Cf. *Ep.* of Faustus of Riez, printed before the *de Statu An.* of Claud. Mamert.

[2] For an account of Lérins and its foundation, cf. Fertig, *Apoll. Sid.* ii. 46, 47 ; Guizot, *Civ. en France,* i. 121, 165 ; Chaix, *Apoll. Sid.* i. 419 ; Fauriel, i. 403.

[3] Krusch. Praef. in *Faustum,* p. liv.; Sidon. *Carm.* xvi.; Gennad. *de Scrip. Eccl.* 85.

[4] Sid. *Carm.* xvi. 111 ; *Ep.* vi.1.

[5] *Carm.* xvi. 115 ; Gennad. *de Scrip. Eccl.* 63.

[6] *Carm.* xvi. 115 ; Gennad. *de Scrip. Eccl.* 69.

But the aristocratic bishop was perhaps even more needed at that time of social and political disorganisation. He was often very imperfectly equipped with theological learning.   But he had other qualifications which the people of a diocese in the path of the invaders might naturally consider more valuable.   He had wealth for sacred or charitable objects, to build or renovate churches,[1] to redeem the captive among the barbarians, to relieve the miseries of the lower classes who were suffering from the disorder and insecurity caused by the invasions.   He had also the authority derived from rank, and the social tact which made him able to defend his flock against the violence of the German chiefs, or the not less dreaded oppression of the Roman officials.   Sometimes a high-minded aristocrat might accept the office from a sense of duty to the population among whom he lived.   Sometimes it was forced upon him by their clamour.[2]   But the correspondence of Sidonius leaves no doubt that the episcopal chair was often an object of ambition and intrigue of the lowest kind.   At an election to the vacant see of Châlon in 470, there were three candidates supported by rival factions.[3]   One was a man of no character, but of ancient lineage.   Another was an Apicius who had bought the support of a party by the skill of his cook.   A third had promised his supporters, in case of his election, their reward out of the estates of the see. Although the election of a bishop in those days was still in theory by the popular voice, the presiding bishops of the province exercised a preponderant influence ; and in this case, to the confusion of the rival partisans, Patiens and his episcopal colleagues braved all clamour, and laid their hands on the Archdeacon John, a modest man, who

---

[1] As Patiens of Lyons did, Sid. *Ep*. ii. 10; cf. Fertig, iii. p. 36, and Perpetuus of Tours, Sid. *Ep*. iv. 18 ; cf. Greg. Tur. ii. 14.   The latter gives the dimensions of the Basilica minutely.

[2] Cf. Sid. *Ep*. iv. 24 ; *Life of S. Ambrose* by Paulinus, c. iii.

[3] Sid. *Ep*. iv. 25.

had no support, except from his own blameless character.
At another election, to the see of Bourges, Sidonius himself
presided.[1] He found a great number of rival candidates,
among whose claims the people were hopelessly divided,
and one of whom had actually used bribery to gain support. At their request he undertook to nominate a
person for the sacred office, and he justified his choice in
a harangue which is a very valuable relic of the times.
Sidonius, putting aside all the popular candidates, gave
his voice for a certain Simplicius, who was not then in
Holy Orders, but a soldier, and a man of great official
rank and wealth, whose character was highly respected,
and who had proved his devotion by munificence in the
cause of the Church.[2] The nominee of Sidonius was
accepted apparently without a murmur.

The aristocratic bishop may not have been a learned
theologian, but he often showed himself the man for the
times, by great qualities of leadership and by princely
generosity. Sidonius himself, as bishop of Auvergne,
more than atoned by his courage and devotion for the
literary vanity and frivolity of his early life. The Gothic
power had closed round his native district, which proudly
maintained a hopeless resistance.[3] Ecdicius, a son of
Avitus, and brother-in-law of the bishop, raised and
equipped an armed force at his own expense, and performed prodigies of valour against the Goths. But the
attacks were renewed again and again. The walls of the city
of Auvergne were crumbling, and famine was threatening
the defenders.[4] While Ecdicius headed the sorties against

---

[1] Sid. *Ep.* vii. 9. Note the words:
neque enim valuissemus aliquid in
commune consulere, nisi judicii sui
faciens plebs lenita jacturam, sacer-
dotali se potius judicio subdidisset.

[2] *Ib.* vii. 9, hic vobis ecclesiam
juvenis miles . . . extruxit.

[3] *Ib.* iii. 3; the character of
Ecdicius is one of the noblest of his

class. He had not only a high military spirit which was rare among
the nobles of the period, but he was
a man of lavish generosity. Like
Bishop Patiens he fed the starving
people of Burgundy at his own expense; *v.* Greg. Tur. ii. 24.

[4] *Ep.* vii. 7, macri jejuniis praeliatores.

the enemy, Sidonius by his high spirit and his eloquence
sustained and animated the courage of his flock. As a
Catholic, no doubt he was fighting to ward off the encroachments of intolerant Arianism.[1] But the indignant
tone in which he upbraids the bishop who finally surrendered the liberties of Auvergne to Euric, reveals the
passionate patriotism of the Celt and the pride of the
Roman noble.[2] His generosity was equal to his courage.
Gregory of Tours had heard a tale of the good bishop
selling his silver plate to relieve the necessities of his
flock.[3] Another bishop, Patiens of Lyons, was famous in
his time throughout all Gaul for his princely liberality.
When the crops in his diocese had been burnt up in the
ravages of the Goths,[4] he sent supplies, at his own cost,
among the famishing population. His waggons, laden
with grain, crowded all the roads, and his barges were
seen everywhere along the Saône and the Rhone.[5] Arles
and Riez, Avignon and Orange, Viviers and Valence, were
supported by his bounty. He was also, like Perpetuus of
Tours, a great church builder and restorer.[6] Sidonius has
celebrated the splendour of marbles and gold which he
lavished on his new basilica at Lyons.[7]

The Gallic bishops of that day were not less distinguished for learning and eloquence than for munificence

[1] For the massacre or expulsion
of Catholic bishops by Euric see Sid.
Ep. vii. 6, regem Gothorum quamquam sit ob virium merita terribilis,
non tam Romanis moenibus quam
legibus Christianis insidiaturum
pavesco ; Greg. Tur. *H. Fr.* ii. 25.

[2] *Ep.* vii. 7, to Graecus, bishop
of Marseilles. This letter shows
Sidonius at his best, both in spirit
and in style ; cf. Fertig, *Sid.* ii. p.
11.

[3] *Hist. Franc.* ii. 22.

[4] Sid. *Ep.* vi. 12 ; cf. Greg. Tur.
Hist. Fr. ii. 24. Fertig (ii. 25)
points out that Gibbon notices the
charity of Ecdicius in this famine,
but makes no mention of the simi-

lar generosity of Patiens the bishop.
Gregory gives a larger place to
Ecdicius.

[5] Sid. *Ep.* vi. 12, vidimus angus-
tas tuis frugibus vias.

[6] *Ib.* ii. 10. On Perpetuus cf. iv.
18.

[7] See also the verses composed by
Sidonius on the new basilica at
Tours, built by Perpetuus, *Ep.* iv.
18 ; and its description, Greg. Tur. ii.
14. It is uncertain to whom Patiens
dedicated his church at Lyons. Cf.
Chaix, *Apoll. Sid.* i. 32 ; Migne's
note to ii. 10. Patiens built churches
in many other places, Sid. *Ep.* vi.
12, omitto per te plurimis locis
basilicarum fundamenta consurgere.

and power of leadership.   The pulpit in the fifth century
was a great force, and the great prelates were generally
great preachers.   Not the least celebrated orator of his
time was S. Remi, the apostle of the Franks, whose style
Sidonius praises in language of ingenious and alliterative
exaggeration, and whose declamations were eagerly read
and transcribed in Auvergne.[1]   The rhetoric of the great
bishop of Rheims is known to us only by the words of
his famous appeal to Clovis at his baptism.[2]   A similar
fate has befallen the writings of Euphronius of Autun,
who had a great reputation for theological learning, and
was the author of a memoir on the prodigies of the
terrible year of Attila's invasion.[3]   No prelate of that age
rendered more various and splendid service than Lupus
of Troyes,[4] in his episcopate extending over half a century.
He rose to be abbot of Lérins in his early manhood.   In
the first years of his episcopate he accompanied S. Ger-
manus on a mission against the Pelagian heresy in
Britain.[5]   It was believed that his sanctity and dignity
had saved Troyes from the fury of Attila.   He was also
a student with a fine library, and Sidonius had a great
respect for his literary judgment.   His eloquence seemed
to his contemporaries to recall the golden age of Gallic
rhetoric.[6]   Faustus of Riez was the greatest and the most
daring thinker among the Churchmen of his time.   Like
Pelagius, he was a native of Britain.[7]   From his early
youth he was devoted to the study of philosophy, nor
did he abandon it when he became a monk of Lérins.
After being head of that community, he succeeded

---

[1] Sid. *Ep.* ix. 7. An Arvernian
on a visit to the north had managed
to bring a copy of S. Remi's *Declamations* back from Rheims, and presented it to his bishop, who read it
aloud to an admiring circle.

[2] Greg. Tur. ii. 31, adora quod
incendisti ; incende quod adorasti.
Gregory notices the rhetoric.

[3] Sid. *Ep.* ix. 2 ; cf. Chaix, *Sid.*

Ap. ii. p. 75 ; Idat. *Chron.* ad a. 451.
[4] Sid. *Ep.* vii. 13 ; viii. 11.
[5] *Acta S. Jul.* quoted in Index
Pers. to Mommsen's ed. of *Sidonius,*
p. 429 ; cf. Prosp. *Chron.* ad a. 429.
[6] Sid. *Ep.* viii. 11, § 2.
[7] *Ib.* ix. 9, legi volumina tua quae
Riochatus . . . Britannis tuis pro
te reportat ; *v.* Krusch. Praef. liv. ;
cf. Gennad. *de Scrip. Eccl.* 85.

Maximus, his predecessor in the abbacy at Lérins, as bishop of Riez. He was a man of the most saintly life, and in his days of fame and power he never relaxed the abstinence and austerity of the monastic discipline.[1] His sermon, at the consecration of the new basilica at Lyons, carried away his audience. Yet he was the great heretic of the day, and the recognised leader of the powerful semi-Pelagian school in Southern Gaul. His work on Free Grace was assailed with ferocious clamour, and was condemned by Pope Gelasius.[2] But his aberrations from the strict line of orthodoxy were even more serious. He maintained, in a work published anonymously,[3] that the soul was a corporeal substance, and that to attribute an immaterial nature to it was to invest it with a quality which belongs only to God. This heresy was indeed not a novelty. It had been expounded by Tertullian;[4] it had found support from S. Jerome[5] and Cassian,[6] and it seemed to S. Augustine to demand a serious and elaborate refutation.[7] The treatise of Faustus drew forth a reply from Mamertus Claudianus, which, in its subtlety and formal elaboration of proof, has the tone and atmosphere of the scholastic theology of the Middle Ages. Claudian's treatise *de Statu Animae* was dedicated to Sidonius, and the honour was acknowledged in a letter[8] which leaves a grave doubt whether the good bishop understood the question at issue. He has a genuine admiration for Mam. Claudianus, although it is expressed in language of absurd extravagance. But there is not a hint in his

---

[1] Sid. *Ep.* ix. 3, cum novae dignitatis obtentu rigorem veteris disciplinae non relaxaveris.

[2] Krusch. Praef. lix. For specimens of his preaching, v. *Sermones ad Monachos*, Migne, t. lviii., esp. ii. and iv.

[3] v. *Ep.* prefixed to Mam. Claudian. *de Statu An.* ; *Ep.* xx. in the collected *Ep.* of Faustus.

[4] Tertull. *de An.* c. 5, 7.

[5] Hieron. *Com. in Libr. Job*, 25.

[6] Cassian, *Collat.* vii. 13, licet enim pronuntiemus nonnullas esse spiritales naturas, ut sunt angeli etc., ipsa quoque anima nostra vel certa aer iste subtilis, tamen incorporeae nullatenus aestimandae sunt.

[7] Nourrisson, *La Philosophie de S. Augustin*, t. i. p. 170.

[8] Sid. *Ep.* iv. 3.

letters that he regarded Faustus with any feeling but that
of the greatest esteem and affection.   It must be said to
the honour of Sidonius, that he chose and loved his
friends for their character, quite apart from their opinions ;
and he seems to have had an impartial regard for both
the combatants in this controversy.

The great value of Sidonius to the historical student
is that he is so broad and tolerant, and that his charity
embraces so many men of various character and ideals.
He has even a good word for the Jews, as men and apart
from their faith.[1]   His own associations would naturally
incline him to admire the prince bishop, with noble
ancestry and a taste for letters.   But he has a profound
reverence for the ascetic fervour of those who withdrew
from the world to the monastic life, or to the greater
loneliness of the hermitage in the forest.   He had visited
Faustus at Lérins,[2] and seen with admiration the spirit
and discipline of that great society.   In one of his poems
he celebrates that Iona of the Mediterranean, as we may
call it, whose arid sands had been the home of Honoratus, Eucher, and Hilary, all great luminaries of the
Church of Gaul in his early youth.[3]   He sends an account
of an episcopal election to Domnulus,[4] who had retired to
one of the monasteries in the Jura.   In another letter
he acknowledges the affectionate sympathy of an abbot
named Chariobaudus,[5] and sends him a cowl to protect
him against the chills of the midnight service.   Close to
his own episcopal town of Auvergne, a solitary from the
East had settled in a hermitage.[6]   He had suffered per-

---

[1] Sid. *Ep.* iii. 4, Gozolas natione
Judaeus, cujus mihi quoque esset
persona cordi, si non esset secta
despectui.   Gozolas carried his
letters ; cf. iv. 5.
[2] *Ib.* ix. 3 ; *v.* Germain's *Sid.
Apoll.* p. 148, n. 5.
[3] *Carm.* xvi. 91.   Honoratus and
Hilary became bishops of Arles, and
Eucher, bishop of Lyons.

[4] *Ep.* iv. 25, nunc ergo Jurensia
si te remittunt jam monasteria, in
quae solitus escendere jam caelesti-
bus supernisque praeludis habitacu-
lis, etc. ; cf. Greg. Tur. *vit. Patrum,*
i.   For the monasteries in the Jura,
cf. Chaix, ii. 218.
[5] *Ep.* vii. 16.
[6] *Ib.* vii. 17 ; Greg. Tur. *Hist.
Fr.* ii. 21, and *vit. Patrum,* iii.

secution in his native country on the Euphrates; thence
he had passed into Egypt, and lived among the hermits
of the Thebaid.   He was a man of superhuman sanctity,
and men believed that he had superhuman powers.   He
could put demons to flight, give sight to the blind, heal
marvellously inveterate disease.   His powerful personality drew others like-minded to him.   A monastery was
built which became the centre of high religious feeling in
Auvergne.   Thither came the bishop for calm and medi-
tation in the tempest of the Gothic invasion.   When
Auvergne had yielded to the Goth, thither came Euric's
governor, the Count Victorius, and on high festivals the
monastery offered its modest hospitality to the great
nobles and officials of the district.[1]   But the good abbot
was at length worn out with care and austerity, and when
he was on his dying bed, Victorius the governor bent
over him weeping, to close his eyes.   His bishop wrote
his elegy, in which, through all the pedantry, we catch
the tones of a real reverence and affection for a saintly
life.

This is not a history of the religious life of the time.
Our main theme is rather the manners and tone of the
caste who thought far more of Virgil and Statius than of
S. John or S. Paul.   Yet it would be a very maimed and
misleading view of the age of Sidonius which confined
itself to the gay country-house life of Avitacum or Prusianum, and ignored the great spiritual movements, the
fearless quest of truth, the world-forgetting piety, which,
when society seemed sinking into the abyss, were the
promise of a new and better time.   In Sidonius the old
and the new order meet.   He thought himself a Roman
of the Romans, the last champion of an immemorial
culture threatened by the rising tide of barbarism.[2]   He

---

[1] Greg. Tur. *vit. Patrum*, iii.
Gregory narrates how, on one of
these occasions, the guests were
miraculously supplied with wine.

[2] Sid. *Ep.* ii. 10, tantum increbuit multitudo desidiosorum, ut,
nisi vel paucissimi quique meram
Latiaris linguae proprietatem de

ended his life as a devoted Christian pastor who still clung to the great traditions of ancient Rome, but had learned to believe in the grander mission of the Christian Church.

trivialium barbarismorum rubigine vindicaveritis, eam brevi abolitam defleamus interitamque ; sic omnes nobilium sermonum purpurae per incuriam vulgi decolorabuntur.

BOOK III

THE FAILURE OF ADMINISTRATION, AND THE RUIN OF THE MIDDLE CLASS, AS REVEALED BY THE THEODOSIAN CODE

CHAPTER I

WE have hitherto been occupied with the condition of
Roman society in the West as it is revealed to us in its
literary remains. But Symmachus, Ausonius, Sidonius
and their class throw little light on the condition of
other classes than their own, or on the deep-seated and
inveterate diseases which for generations had been undermining the strength of the imperial system. The general
tendency of modern inquiry has been to discover in the
fall of that august and magnificent organisation, not a
cataclysm, precipitated by the impact of barbarous forces,
but a process slowly prepared and evolved by internal
and economic causes. It is probable that the barbarian
invasions of the fifth century were not more formidable
than those of the third, which were triumphantly repelled by the Illyrian Caesars, or than those of the
fourth, which were rolled back by the genius of Julian
and the ferocious energy of Valentinian. The question
why the invasions of the fifth century succeeded, while
the earlier failed, is best answered by an appeal to the
Imperial Code. In the voluminous enactments issued
from Constantine to Majorian, the student has before
him a melancholy diagnosis of the maladies which, by a
slow and inevitable process of decay, were exhausting
the strength of Roman society. He will see municipal
liberty and self-government dying out, the upper class

cut off from the masses by sharp distinctions of wealth
and privilege, yet forbidden to bear arms,[1] and deprived
of all practical interest in public affairs.   He will find
that not only has an Oriental monarchy taken the place
of the principate of Augustus, but that an almost
Oriental system of caste has made every social grade
and every occupation practically hereditary, from the
senator to the waterman on the Tiber, or the sentinel at
a frontier post; and that human nature is having its
revenge in wholesale flight from a cruel servitude and
the chaos of administration.   It will be seen that in a
society in which poverty is almost branded with infamy,[2]
poverty is steadily increasing and wealth becoming more
insolent and aggressive; that the disinherited, in the face
of an omnipotent government, are carrying brigandage
even up to the gates of Rome; that parents are selling
their children into slavery; that public buildings are
falling into decay; that the service on the great post
roads is becoming disorganised.   At a time when every
frontier was threatened, it will be found that the frontier
posts are being abandoned, that there is wholesale desertion from the ranks of the army; while in the failure of
free recruits, the slaves have to be called to arms.   But
the unscientific and inefficient financial system will
chiefly attract the notice of the historical inquirer.   The
collection of imposts in kind opened the door to every
species of corruption.   Still more fatal to pure administration was the system which left to the municipal class
the assessment and collection of the revenue in their
district.   That doomed order are at once branded as the
worst oppressors, and invested with the melancholy glory
of being the martyrs of a ruinous system of finance.[3]

[1] Aurel. Vict. de Caes. c. 33, Gallienus : primus ipse, metu sacordiae
suae, ne imperium ad optimos
nobilium transferretur, senatum
militia vetuit, etiam adire exer-
citum : C. Th. xv. 15, 1.
[2] See M. Duruy's Memoire on
Honestiores and Humiliores in the
later Empire, in Hist. Rom. vi. 643.
[3] Salv. de Gub. Dei, v. 18 ; cf.

Their lingering fate, recorded in 192 edicts,[1] a tragedy prolonged through more than five generations, is one of the most curious examples of obstinate and purblind legislation, contending hopelessly with inexorable laws of society and human nature. In that contest the middle or bourgeois class was almost extinguished, Roman financial administration was paralysed, and at its close the real victors and survivors were the great landholders, surrounded by their serfs and dependants. A volume might be written on the corruption and cruel oppression of the officials of the treasury, servile to the great, tyrannical to the poor, and calmly defying all the menaces of the emperor in their unchecked career of rapacity. The last and deepest impression which the inquirer will carry with him, as he rises from a study of the Theodosian Code, is that fraud and greed are everywhere triumphant, that the rich are growing richer and more powerful, while the poor are becoming poorer and more helpless, and that the imperial government, inspired with the best intentions, has lost all control of the vast machine.

Yet amid all the perverse errors of legislation and the hopeless corruption of the financial service, the candid reader of the Code cannot help feeling that the central authority was keenly alive to its duties, and almost overwhelmed by its responsibilities. It is a superficial view of the time which dwells on the weakness of a Honorius, a Valentinian, or an Anthemius. The Emperor was, indeed, in theory omnipotent; but as a matter of fact he had to depend on his officials, both to advise his decisions and to carry them out. He was assisted by a council of experienced men of high official

---

iii. 50. M. F. de Coulanges (*L'Inv. Germ.* p. 58, n. 1) says: On remarquera que Salvien accuse moins les fonctionnaires impériaux que les magistrats municipaux. Yet cf. *de Gub. Dei*, iv. 21, quid est aliud quorundam, quos taceo, praefectura quam praeda ? v. 25, quibus enim aliis rebus Bacaudae facti sunt nisi . . . improbitatibus judicum, etc.

[1] *C. Th.* xii. tit. i.

rank,[1] some of whom had probably governed great
provinces, and who knew the Roman world, if any men
did.   Moreover, it is plain, from the very wording of
many of the rescripts,[2] that they were suggested by the
prefect or governor to whom they are addressed ; and
one can hardly be wrong in believing that in many of
these last efforts of Roman statesmanship, so sympathetic,
so strangely rhetorical, so full at times of honest indignation, we may have the report of a conscientious governor
returned to him in the imperative form of an edict.
The minute and circumstantial description of oppression
and wrong could hardly have come from any one who
had not heard the tale from the sufferers themselves.[3]
Occasionally, though too seldom it is to be feared, such
complaints came directly to the ears of the Emperor.   The
mass of legislation for the relief of the province of Africa
in the reign of Honorius was the result of at least two
deputations commissioned to represent its grievances ;[4]
and so determined was the Emperor to remedy the
abuses complained of, that he appointed two of the most
experienced and illustrious ex-prefects with full powers
to deal with the disorders of the province.[5]

The Roman world had for ages regarded the Emperor
as an earthly Providence ;[6] and to the end such was the

[1] The Council was called consistorium, the members proceres, con-
siliarii, comites consistoriani. C.
Th. xi. 39, 5 ; ix. 14, 3 (Godefroy
t. iii. p. 108.) ; cf. Spartian vit.
Hadrian. c. 18 ; Amm. Marc. xv.
5, 12 ; xxxi. 12, 10 ; C. Th. vi.
12 ; cf. F. de Coulanges, L'Inv.
Germ. p. 13 ; Duruy, vi. 574.

[2] We frequently meet such phrases
as Sublimis Excellentiae tuae
saluberrimam suggestionem secuti ;
cf. Nov. Th. 45, 47.

[3] Cf. several of the Novellae addressed to Albinus, e.g. Nov. Th.
22, and the description of the fraud
and violence of the discussores,
Nov. Valent. 7.

[4] The emperors Gratian and
Valentinian permitted the provinces, after due deliberation, to
send three delegates to represent
their case to the government, C.
Th. xii. 12, 7. The Curiales and
Defensores sometimes tried to prevent the appeal of the provincials,
xi. 8, 3 ; ix. 26, 2, with Godefroy's
note. The deputation from Africa
is mentioned, xii. 1, 166. Cf. xii.
6, 27 ; Sym. Ep. iv. 46, recommending a similar deputation from
Campania, in 395 ; C. Th. xi. 28, 2.

[5] Ib. vii. 4, 33.

[6] See F. de Coulanges, La Gaule
Rom. pp. 177 sqq.

conception of their office which was entertained even by the weakest emperors. Valentinian III. proclaims that it is his business to " provide for the peace and tranquillity of the provinces ";[1] Anthemius says that he is called " to face the storms of overwhelming calamities." [2]   " It is our care," says the Emperor Martian,[3] " to provide for the welfare of the human race." Yet there are in the later edicts many signs of conscious weakness. Their tone is frequently argumentative and rhetorical. There is an absence of the trenchant brevity with which Constantine or the elder Valentinian were wont to declare their will. It is singular to find an edict against Jews, Samaritans, and pagans opening with an argument for the being of a God.[4]   Elsewhere we meet with philosophical reflections on the innate criminal tendencies of human nature,[5] the hopeless selfishness of the rich,[6] or on the functions of government. The Emperor Majorian in one law describes, with great vividness and passionate force, as if for posterity, the crushing weight of taxation and the hopeless position of the farmer.[7]   Many of these edicts betray the style of the school rhetorician, and yet there is in many of them the ring of genuine sympathy for misery, which the imperial author more than half confesses that he is impotent to relieve. It is impossible to read some of these laws in which the Emperor describes " the agitations and anxieties of his serene mind," [8] without a feeling that

---

[1] *Nov. Valent.* tit. viii. *ad init.*
[2] *Leg. Anthem.* tit. i.
[3] *Nov. Mart.* ii., curae nobis est utilitati humani generis providere : nam id die ac nocte prospicimus ut universi qui sub nostro imperio vivunt et armarum praesidio ab hostili impetu muniantur, ac in pace libero otio ac securitate potiantur.
[4] *Nov. Th.* iii. quis enim tam mente captus, etc.

[5] *Nov. Valent.* v., noxiae mentes caeco semper in facinus furore rapiuntur.
[6] *Nov. Th.* xxi., domesticis tantum compendiis obsequentes bonum commune destituunt.
[7] *Nov. Maj.* tit. iv.
[8] *Nov. Th.* and *Valent.* 51, quae ergo his angustiis remedia providenda sunt mens nostrae Serenitatis exaestuat.

he is probably the man most to be pitied in the Empire.

Of all departments of administration, probably none caused the Emperor greater anxiety than that concerned with the food-supplies of the capital. To provide corn, pork, wine, and oil for the populace had for ages been one of the first tasks of the government.[1] How dangerous any failure in this department might be to the peace of the city, and the safety of the upper classes, we can see clearly in the letters of Symmachus.[2] While the Goths were marching through Samnium and Bruttium, or Gildo or Heraclian were stopping the corn-fleets, or the Vandals were occupying the ports of Africa, the government had to provide for the daily subsistence of a great population. An army of public servants incorporated in hereditary guilds, Navicularii, Pistores, Suarii, Pecuarii, were charged with the duty of bringing up supplies and preparing them for consumption.[3] It is evident, from the legislation of Honorius,[4] that the stress on this department was very severe in the early part of his reign, owing to the troubles of the Gildonic revolt in Africa, and again from the famine of 410. But the difficulty reappears more than once in the laws of subsequent years.[5] One of the hardest tasks of the government was to prevent the members of these guilds from deserting or evading their hereditary obligations. It is well known that the tendency of the later Empire

---

[1] Marq. *Röm. Staatsverwaltung*, ii. 133. The chief authorities for the distribution of oil, wine, and flesh-meat are Aug. Hist. *vit. Sep. Sev.* 23, *Alex. Sev.* 22, 26, *Aurelian*, 48, *C. Th.* xiv. 24, 1, with Godefroy's notes; *C. Th.* xiv. 4, 3.

[2] Sym. *Ep.* vi. 18, 26, 12.

[3] Id. *Rel.* 14, noverat (Aeternitas vestra) horum corporum ministerio tantae urbis onera sustineri. Hic lanati pecoris invector est, ille ad

victum populi cogit armentum, hos suillae carnis tenet functio, pars urenda lavacris ligna conportat, etc. Cf. Paratitl. of Godefroy to *C. Th.* xiv. tit. 2 and 4; Wallon, *Hist. de l'Esclavage*, iii. 173.

[4] *C. Th.* xiii. 5, 34, 35; Zos. vi. 11, describes the effect of the closing of the African ports by Heraclian, λιμὸς ἐνέσκηψε τῇ πόλει χαλεπώτερος τοῦ προτέρου.

[5] *Nov. Th.* 39, 40.

was to stereotype society, by compelling men to follow
the occupation of their fathers, and preventing a free
circulation among different callings and grades of life.
The man who brought the grain of Africa to the public
stores at Ostia, the baker who made it into loaves
for distribution, the butchers who brought pigs from
Samnium, Lucania, or Bruttium, the purveyors of wine
and oil, the men who fed the furnaces of the public
baths, were bound to their callings from one generation
to another.[1] It was the principle of rural serfdom
applied to social functions. Every avenue of escape was
closed. A man was bound to his calling not only by his
father's but by his mother's condition.[2] Men were not
permitted to marry out of their guild.[3] If the daughter
of one of the baker caste married a man not belonging to
it, her husband was bound to her father's calling.[4] Not
even a dispensation obtained by some means from the
imperial chancery,[5] not even the power of the Church[6]
could avail to break the chain of servitude. The corporati, it is true, had certain privileges,[7] exemptions, and
allowances, and the heads of some of the guilds might be
raised to the rank of " Count." But their property, like
their persons, was at the mercy of the State.[8] If they
parted with an estate, it remained liable for the service
with which the vendor was charged.

To maintain such a system, and to counteract the
endless attempts at evasion and corruption to which its
galling restraints gave rise, required constant vigilance,

[1] Wallon, iii. p. 174. *C. Th.*
xiii. 5, 35, universos quos navicu-
lariae conditioni obnoxios invenit
antiquitas, praedictae functioni
conveniet famulari.
[2] *C. Th.* xiv. 4, 8, ad munus
pristinum revocentur, tam qui
paterno quam materno genere in-
veniuntur obnoxii.
[3] *Ib.* xiv. 3, 21.
[4] *Ib.* xiv. 3, 14.

[5] *Ib.* xiv. 3, 20, si quo casu, vel
occultis vel ambitiosis hoc precibus
elicuerit, etc. ; cf. l. 21, etiamsi
nostra elicita fuerint aliqua sub-
reptione rescripta; cf. xiv. 3, 4.
[6] *Ib.* xiv. 3, 11; cf. *Nov. Th.* 26.
[7] *Ib.* xiv. 2 ; *v.* Paratitlon.
[8] *Ib.* xiii. 6, 6; cf. l. 9, which
recalls a navicular property to the
function, even when the sale took
place twenty years before.

which was as constantly defeated.   The navicularii seem
to have exceeded the very liberal allowance of time for
their voyage, which was, under special circumstances,
extended to two years.[1]   While the city was on the
verge of famine, or when supplies were urgently needed
for the army in Gaul, the captains often lingered in port
on any pretext,[2] or made circuitous voyages in pursuit of
their own profit.[3]   And the government was obliged to
order greater despatch, and to prohibit the practice of
private trading in which captains engaged, to the disorganisation of the service.   Sometimes the captains
entered their ships under another name, probably that of
some person of influence, in order to escape their responsibilities.[4]   The functionaries, whose duty it was to
expedite transport, were bribed to wink at malversation
or neglect.   Estates liable for the function were withdrawn from it by fraudulent sales.[5]   In the year 450[6]
the guild of navicularii had been so reduced in numbers
by the desertion of its members to other callings that
the Emperor was obliged to order the restoration of all
persons and estates to the function from which they
had been withdrawn.   Another edict of 455 orders the
return to their various guilds of all corporati who have
deserted their proper duties, in order to enter the army
or the church.[7]   A similar command had been issued in
412 to all governors of provinces to compel the return
of all guildsmen of the city of Rome who had migrated
from Italy.[8]   This law, however, refers not to the stealthy
evasion of onerous functions, but to the wholesale flight

[1] *C. Th.* xiii. 5, 26; cf. l. 21.

[2] *Ib.* xiii. 5, 34, a. 410.

[3] *Ib.* xiii. 5, 33.   The penalty was death.

[4] *Ib.* xiii. 7, 2, multi naves suas diversorum (Potentum) nominibus et titulis tuentur.

[5] *Ib.* xiii. 6, 1.

[6] *Nov. Th.* 38.   The navicularii

amnici referred to were the boatmen who conveyed the supplies up the Tiber.

[7] *Ib.* 26.

[8] *C. Th.* xiv. 2, 4; cf. xiv. 7, 2, of the same year, ordering the re-
turn of the nemesiaci, signiferi, cantabrarii, guilds connected with amusements or pagan rites and processions.   See Godefroy's note.

of all ranks, which had taken place during the invasion
of Alaric, and of which we have such vivid accounts from
S. Jerome and Rutilius Namatianus.[1]

The effects of the Gothic invasion of Italy in the
early years of the fifth century have left many deep
traces on the Code. We can almost hear the distant
sound of the advancing hordes in some of the enactments
issued during the years of Stilicho's ascendency. There
are laws relating to every part of the military system,
and every part is revealing weaknesses. During the
period of the later Empire, landed proprietors had to
furnish recruits in proportion to the size of their estates.[2]
These must have been drawn from the class of coloni,
since the strictly servile class was excluded from the
Roman army.[3] The Code in these years shows that
recruits were urgently needed, not even the Emperor's
own estates being exempted from the levy.[4] Yet we
know that, at the time of the Gildonic war, the senators
exerted their whole strength as a body to resist the call
of the Emperor.[5] And the result of their efforts is seen
in the enactments of 397, which gave them the option
of paying twenty-five solidi for each recruit for whom
they were liable.[6] The exclusion of senators from the
army, and the prohibition of ordinary citizens to carry
arms, had produced their inevitable result. The military
spirit had almost died out among Romans. The army
was swelled by corps of barbarian mercenaries, and the

---

[1] Hieron. *Ep.* cxxvii. § 4; cxxx.
§ 4; Rut. Nam. *It.* i. 331; Claudian.
de Bell. Get. 217.

[2] F. de Coul. *L'Inv. Germ.* p.
145; *C. Th.* vii. 13, 7, of the year
375.

[3] *C. Th.* vii. 13, 8. They are
coupled in this exclusion with cau-
ponae, coqui, pistores, and persons
employed in famosae tabernae.

[4] *Ib.* vii. 13, 12, ideoque ne
patrimonium quidem nostrum a
praestatione (*i.e.* tironum) immune

esse patimur.

[5] Sym. *Ep.* vi. 62, legati ordinis
ex usu actis omnibus reverterunt.
Nam et tironum conquievit indictio
et argenti nobis facta gratia est; cf.
Ep. vi. 64.

[6] *C. Th.* vii. 13, 13. In the law
of Valens and Gratian of 375 the
pretium tironis was fixed at thirty-
six solidi. The pretium fixed in
the edict of 410, calling for recruits
from the officiales judicum of Africa,
is thirty; *C. Th.* vii. 13, 20.

highest military commands were held by Germans.
Ever since the third century the military profession had
been declining in the public esteem.[1]   Recruits were
branded on entering the service, as if they were slaves in
an ergastulum.[2]   The aversion to military service appears
to have been growing.   Towards the end of the fourth
century the practice of self-mutilation to escape service
had become so common that it had to be checked by the
most cruel punishments.[3]   In the years between 396
and 412, Honorius issued nine edicts on desertion and
the concealment of deserters.[4]   The crime seems to have
prevailed in all parts of the Empire, but to have been
specially rampant in Gaul and Africa.   The agents of
great proprietors and the smaller farmers were evidently
glad, even in the face of very severe penalties, to shelter
the absconding soldier on their estates for the sake of
his labour.[5]   Honorius does not, like his predecessors
in 382, threaten to burn the offender alive.[6]   But the
increasing emphasis of his laws, together with the organised search which he instituted, indicates the magnitude
and inveteracy of the evil.[7]   Apparently proprietors or
their agents were not deterred even by the danger of
confiscation from disobeying laws so often repeated.   For
in 440, when the growth of the Vandal power in Africa
urgently demanded an increase of the army, Theodosius
and Valentinian III. were compelled to make the offence
of concealing recruits or deserters by agents or coloni
punishable by death.[8]   Along all the frontiers of the

[1] Duruy, vii. p. 203.
[2] Godefroy's Paratitlon to *C. Th.*
vii. t. 2, p. 254.
[3] *C. Th.* vii. 13, 4 and 5.   That
the proprietor from whose estate
the recruit came was sometimes a
party to the crime is implied in the
words, dominus ejus qui non pro-
hibet gravi condemnatione feriatur.
[4] *Ib.* vii. 18, 9-17.   For deserters
in Gaul at an earlier period cf.

Spart. *vit. Pesc. Nig.* c. 3, desertores
qui tunc innumeri Gallias vexabant,
etc.

[5] *C. Th.* vii. 18, 12, actorem con-
scium severo supplicio damnandum
esse censemus.

[6] *Ib.* vii. 18, 6, flammis scelera
puniantur.

[7] *Ib.* vii. 18, 13.

[8] *Nov. Th.* 44.

Empire forts and castles had for centuries been erected, which were garrisoned by troops called *burgarii*,[1] who, like the guilds of the capital, were held in a species of hereditary servitude. Towards the end of the fourth century these frontier sentinels, especially in Gaul and Spain where their services were soon to be urgently needed, began to melt away. It is difficult to discover the influences which led to their dispersion. But in the year 409 an enactment of Theodosius and Honorius discloses in a startling way the denuded state of the frontier.[2]

In ordinary times slaves, along with tavern keepers, cooks, bakers, and persons following certain infamous callings, were excluded from the army.[3] It must have been a dire extremity which forced the Emperor, *contra hostiles impetus*, to call the slaves to arms by the offer of a bounty and the promise of emancipation.[4] In the same year the free provincials everywhere are appealed to, by their pride in liberty and love of country, to take arms.[5] It was the year in which Radagaisus with his Gothic army of 200,000 men swept down from the Alps on Lombardy and Tuscany. Only once before had Rome been driven to put arms in the hands of her slaves, to repel the advance of Hannibal after the battle of Cannae.[6] The urgency of the crisis is also seen in a law of 404, peremptorily requiring all *possessores* to contribute their share to the preparation and transport of

[1] On the fortification of the limes cf. *vit. Hadrian*, c. 12 ; on the defence of the Gallic frontier by Valentinian, Amm. Marc. xxviii. 2, 1 ; on the Limitanei Milites, with lands granted on condition of military service, *vit. Alex. Sev.* c. 58 ; *C. Th.* vii. 15, 1 ; Marq. *Röm. Staatsverwaltung*, ii. 591.

[2] *C. Th.* vii. 15, 1.

[3] *Ib.* vii. 13, 8.

[4] *Ib.* vii. 13, 16. This belongs

to the year 406, as the names of the Coss. Arcadius and Probus show. On the date of the invasion of Radagaisus cf. Godefroy on *C. Th.* vii. 13, 16 ; Gibbon, c. 30 ; Prosp. *Chron.* ; Zos. v. 26.

[5] *C. Th.* vii. 13, 17. They are promised ten solidi *pacatis rebus*. The bounty offered to slaves in l. 16 is two solidi.

[6] Liv. xxii. 57.

supplies for the army, under a penalty of four times the
amount due by them, without any exemption even for
the Emperor's own estates.[1]

At a time when the rapid movement of troops and
government officials was a matter of the first importance,
the great roads and the posting service seem to have
been getting into a bad state.[2] There are more than
ten edicts of Honorius on this subject from 395.[3] In
another passage of the Code the Emperor says that the
ruinous condition, into which the highways of the
Italian prefecture have fallen, demands the exertions
of all classes for their repair,[4] and he withdraws the
immunity from this burden which former laws had
conferred on the officials of "illustrious" rank. The
regulations for the use of the imperial post had received
close attention from Julian and Theodosius.[5] A special
corps of imperial officers called *curiosi* were charged with
the duty of seeing that these rules were not infringed.[6]
But successive edicts show the difficulty of enforcing
them. Honorius had once more to prohibit the abuse of
the service. Even officers of illustrious rank had the
privilege of using the *cursus publicus* withdrawn from
them,[7] unless they were specially summoned by the
Emperor. The magistri militim are warned that without
special leave they will usurp the privilege at their peril.[8]
The prefect of the city who has done so is told not to
repeat his offence.[9] The use of imperial post-horses on

---

[1] *C. Th.* vii. 5, 2, in excoctione
bucellati (soldier's bread), in trans-
latione etiam annonae nullius ex-
cipiatur persona, videlicet ut ne
nostra quidem Domus ab his
habeatur immunis ; a. 404.

[2] Yet Apollinaris Sidonius travelled easily by the public service
in the year 455 : *Ep.* i. 5, publicus
cursus usui fuit utpote sacris apicibus accito.

[3] *C. Th.* viii. 5, 53-65.

[4] *Ib.* xv. 3, 4, propter immensas

vastitates viarum, certatim studia
cunctorum ad reparationem publici
aggeris volumus festinare ; a. 399.

[5] *Ib.* viii. 5, 12-16 ; viii. 5, 46
sqq.

[6] *Ib.* vi. tit. 29.

[7] *Ib.* viii. 5, 54.

[8] *Ib.* viii. 5, 56.

[9] *Ib.* viii. 5, 55. Florentinus
was one of the friends of Symmachus ; *Ep.* iv. 50, 50 ; Seeck,
cxli.

cross roads is prohibited under a heavy fine.[1]   From the words of the law of 401, this was evidently becoming a grievous abuse, and a heavy burden to the provincials, who had to provide additional horses to meet the strain.[2] One can well imagine that, in those troubled years, persons hurrying to remote districts, to look after their private affairs, would by bribes, or by the illegitimate influence of rank, obtain from the officials of the post facilities of travelling which were fatal to the regularity of the government service, and onerous to the provincials. At the same time there are indications that the efficiency of the service was declining.   An edict of 404 implies that there was a failure in the supply of servants and officials on the great roads.[3]   In Gaul and Spain the muleteers were being stealthily withdrawn[4] or liberated by the higher officials from the function to which they were bound.[5]   The animals in the public stables were not being properly fed, owing to the dishonesty of those in charge.[6]   Corruption had crept into every grade of the service, and in one law the heads of the department are ordered to cease from their exactions and conform to the rules of the ancient discipline.[7]   The body of civil servants styled *curiosi*, as we have said, had as their chief function the superintendence of the posting service on the great roads,[8] specially with the object of preventing the abuse of the privilege of *evectio*.   In addition to this, they were expected to visit remote districts, and keep the government informed of any suspicious move-

---

[1] *C. Th.* viii. 5, 59.

[2] *Ib.* viii. 5, 63, quoniam multos perspeximus inlicita praesumptione paraveredos vel parangarias postulare, etc.

[3] *Ib.* viii. 5, 65.   The mancipes cursus publici, by a law of Gratian, could be absent from their station only for thirty days in the year, viii. 5, 36 ; cf. l. 51.   They were servi publici, viii. 5, 58.

[4] *Ib.* viii. 5, 50, 58.

[5] *Ib.* viii. 5, 58, ideoque Judex qui sibi hoc vindicaverit, ut servum publicum liberet, unam lib. auri per homines singulos, officium quoque ejus, si legem supprimendo consenserit, simili poena multetur.

[6] *Ib.* viii. 5, 60.

[7] *Ib.* vi. 29, 9.

[8] *Ib.* vi. 29, 6, in which their functions are defined.

ments among the population.   It is evident that a police
of this kind in times of confusion was open to dangerous
abuse.   As a matter of fact these officers became so venal
and oppressive that they had to be removed at one stroke
from the province of Africa in 414.[1]

The withdrawal of the *curiosi* from Dalmatia and the
adjoining regions in 415 [2] throws an interesting light on
the state of the country and the public service.   During
the stormy years of Alaric's incursions, numbers of
people in the districts through which he passed were
driven from their homes.   Some fled to less disturbed
parts of the province, and put themselves under the protection of the great proprietors, by whom they were
often detained in a species of servitude.[3]   Others took
refuge in the islands which dot the upper part of the
Adriatic.   In the year 410 [4] the Emperor Theodosius,
probably in pursuance of a compact with Honorius,
ordered a strict watch to be kept in all the ports of
Dalmatia, to prevent any person not provided with
letters from the Roman government from entering his
dominions.   This measure was taken expressly on
account of the usurpations of Attalus and Constantine,
and the occupation of the Western provinces by the
barbarians.[5]   To make this embargo effectual, Honorius
distributed *curiosi* along the various points of communication between East and West, and these officers
grossly abused their power by preventing people from
seeking places of greater security, or by extorting bribes
for permission to do so.   The evil became so intolerable
that by an order of 415 the *curiosi* were peremptorily
removed from the districts which were plagued with such
dangerous surveillance.[6]

[1] *C. Th.* vi. 29, 11.
[2] *Ib.* vi. 29, 12. On the importance of Dalmatia at this time
see an excellent note of Godefroy's
on this law.
[3] Cf. *ib.* v. 5, 2.

[4] *Ib.* vii. 16, 2.
[5] *Ib.* vii. 16, 2, hoc enim et tyran-
nici furoris et barbaricae feritatis
occasio persuadet ; *v.* Godefroy.
[6] *Ib.* vi. 29, 12 ; *v.* Godefroy's
note.

Brigandage had long been a menacing evil in the Western world. Even in the middle of the fourth century the country districts of Italy had become so unsafe that throughout seven provinces the use of horses was forbidden,[1] not only to coloni and shepherds, but to proprietors, with specified exceptions, and their agents. At all times the shepherds of Samnium, Picenum, and Apulia were a wild and lawless race,[2] and easily passed into the ranks of the banditti who pillaged the remote sheep-farms or infested the high roads leading to the capital. And the bailiffs of the great estates appear to have been often in league with the brigands, whose spoils they shared, and to whom they gave facilities for concealment. A law of 383 threatens them with " flammae ultrices " for this crime.[3]   In 391 the right of using arms, which by earlier laws was denied to civilians, was granted to all persons against brigands.[4] In a letter of Symmachus about this time,[5] he tells a friend that his usual migration to his country seat in Campania was prevented by the prevalence of brigandage in the neighbourhood of Rome. In an edict of 399 [6] Honorius refuses the right of using horses, so necessary to their occupation, to the shepherds of Valeria and Picenum. The feeling about this temptation of the shepherd's life is curiously illustrated by a law of 409,[7] which warns all curiales, plebeians, and possessores against sending their sons to be nursed among shepherds. The terms of the edict imply that shepherd and brigand had come to be almost synonymous. But the bands of outlaws were recruited in Italy and Gaul from another

[1] *C. Th.* ix. 30, 1 and 2, a. 364. Brigandage existed in Aquitaine in the time of Ausonius (*Ep.* iv. 23). Cf. Sym. ii. 22, sed nunc intuta est latrociniis suburbanitas.

[2] Cf. *ib.* ix. 31, 1, si vero . . . quisquam nutriendos pastoribus (filios suos), societatem latronum videbitur confiteri.

[3] *C. Th.* ix. 29, 2.

[4] *Ib.* ix. 14, 2.

[5] *Ep.* ii. 22.

[6] *C. Th.* ix. 30, 5 ; *v.* Godefroy on this law.

[7] *Ib.* ix. 31, 1.

class, of whom something has already been said. The
country districts seem to have been infested by men who
had deserted from the standards, and who, in hiding from
the officers of the law, betook themselves to plunder for
support. Full power to crush these dangerous criminals
is given to the provincials in a law of 403,[1] which classes
deserters with *latrones;* and the edict of 406[2] orders
the Pretorian prefect to inflict capital punishment on
fugitive soldiers who have betaken themselves to this life
of crime. From some later parts of the Code, which are
supported by other authorities, there can be no doubt
that the barbarian invasions let loose a great mass of
desperadoes on the countries through which the invaders
passed. Poor men who had lost everything were almost
forced to join the gangs of marauders who swept over the
country.[3] To open a way for such persons to return to
an orderly life, the Emperor in 416[4] proclaimed a
general amnesty for all this class of offences, for which he
finds an excuse in the overwhelming calamities of the time.

In general the signs of growing impoverishment
become more and more frequent, and the tone of the
later edicts shows how deeply the Roman statesmen
were impressed by the misery of the lower classes. A
terrible famine, which raged throughout Italy in 450,
had actually driven many of the poor to sell their
children into slavery. An edict, issued on the suggestion of Aetius,[5] cancelled all such contracts, on repay-

---

[1] *C. Th.* vii. 18, 14, cuncti etenim
adversus latrones publicos deser-
toresque militiae jus sibi sciant pro
quiete communi exercendae publicae
ultionis indultum. This law is a
great confession of weakness in the
government, cf. ix. 14, 2.

[2] *Ib.* vii. 18, 15.

[3] Cf. Salv. *de Gub. Dei*, v. § 24,
c. 6; cf. Apoll. Sid. *Ep.* vi. 4,
where a woman has been carried off
by the Vargi. For brigandage in
Gaul in 369 cf. Amm. Marc. xxviii.

2, 10; and Oros. vii. 25, 2. On
the Scamarae in Noricum cf.
Eugipp. *vit. S. Sev.* c. x. 2. The
Bagaudae in Gaul and Spain had
rather a different character and
origin. The authorities are given
in De Coulanges, *L'Inv. Germ.* p.
102, n. 1; cf. Fauriel, i. 186;
Arnold, *Prov. Administration*, p.
163; Idat. *Chron.* ad a. 441, 443,
449.

[4] *C. Th.* xv. 14, 14.

[5] *Nov. Valent.* 11, notum est

ment to the purchaser of the price which the parents had accepted, with an addition of 20 per cent. The plunder of tombs for the sake of the costly marbles they contained seems to have become a common offence.[1] The edict of Valentinian III. on this subject is full of old Roman sentiment about the dead, and strangely resembles in tone that of Julian in which he deals with the same crime.[2] Its enormity, and perhaps its frequency, are indicated by the heavy penalties which were imposed, torture, death, or confiscation, according to the social grade of the criminal. Other indications of failing resources may be seen in the laws relating to public works and buildings.[3] Already in the reign of Constantine, the Emperor complains of the neglect[4] which was allowing them in many places to fall into decay. The authorities are required by Gratian and Theodosius to repair ancient buildings before undertaking the erection of new ones.[5] Honorius forbids the alienation, on any pretext, of municipal funds which have been long allocated to the restoration or decoration of public edifices.[6] In another edict,[7] the repair of ancient buildings, fallen into a ruinous state, is provided for out of the income of the public lands. It would appear that the municipalities found an increasing difficulty in meeting such expenditure. The appropriation by private persons of public spaces and edifices is dealt with in several laws of the same period.[8] The public officials became very lax or corrupt in permitting the demolition of structures which were often interesting from ancient

---

obscenissimam famem per totam Italiam desaevisse coactosque homines filios et parentes vendere, ut discrimen instantis mortis effugerent. Cf. *C. Th.* iii. 3, 1.

[1] *Nov. Valent.* 5, quisquis ex his quaelibet marmora aut saxa sustulerit paenae mox habeatur obnoxius. The clergy were the greatest offenders; cf. Gregorovius, *Hist. of City of Rome*, i. 226.

[2] *C. Th.* ix. 17, 5. There are seven enactments on this subject in the fourth century.

[3] *Ib.* xv. tit. 1.

[4] *Ib.* xv. 1, 2.

[5] *Ib.* l. 21.

[6] *Ib.* l. 48.

[7] *Ib.* l. 32 ; cf. 34, 35.

[8] *Ib.* xv. ll. 40, 41.

associations or artistic beauty. The Emperor Majorian,
in his too brief reign, exerted himself to check this
vandalism and greed. He denounces, with genuine
indignation, the criminal negligence which had long permitted the beauty of the venerable city to be defaced in
order to provide cheap materials for mean private buildings.[1] Any magistrate for the future conniving at an
infringement of this law is to be punished by a fine of
fifty pounds of gold, and any subordinate official similarly
guilty is to be flogged and have both his hands cut off.
Here and there we get a glimpse of the ruin which the
confusion of the time brought suddenly on a once prosperous class. In the reign of Valentinian III., among
the crowds who were driven from their homes in Africa
by the Vandal invasion, there were many men of rank
and education who found their way to Italy, and some of
them applied in their distress for leave to practise as
advocates in the Italian courts. The Emperor granted
their request in a rescript repealing the constitution of
442, which limited the number of those who were
allowed to plead before the provincial magistrates.[2] The
later pages of the Code will often suggest similar pictures
of many an obscure tragedy to the imagination of the
sympathetic student. Famine and invasion took their
usual tale of victims. But their worst ravages are
usually soon obliterated or repaired by the kindly forces
of Nature. The overwhelming tragedy of that age was
the result not of violent and sudden calamities; it was
prepared by the slow, merciless action of social and
economic laws, and deepened by the perverse energy of
government, and the cupidity and cruelty of the rich and
highly-placed. In the following chapter we shall try to
realise its magnitude and to discover its causes.

[1] *Nov. Maj.* 6, antiquarum aedium dissipatur speciosa constructio et ut
parvum aliquid reparetur magna diruuntur.   [2] *Nov. Th.* 50 ; cf. 34.

CHAPTER II

THE DECAY OF THE MIDDLE CLASS AND THE AGGRANDISEMENT OF THE ARISTOCRACY

THE evidence adduced in the previous chapter as to the disorganisation of important branches of the public service, and the spread of poverty and lawlessness, is sufficiently ominous. Such disorders strike the eye at once and impress the imagination. Yet grave as they are, they are not so serious as other and less patent maladies, which had been long eating out the strength of Roman society. In this chapter we shall try to discover the more deep-seated causes which, far more than the violent intrusion of the German invaders, produced the collapse of society which is known as the fall of the Empire of the West. A careful study of the Code will correct many a popular and antiquated misconception of that great event. It will reveal the fact that, long before the invasions of the reign of Honorius, the fabric of Roman society and administration was honeycombed by moral and economic vices, which made the belief in the eternity of Rome a vain delusion. The municipal system, once the great glory of Roman organising power, had in the fourth century fallen almost into ruin. The governing class of the municipalities, called *curiales*, on whom the burdens of the Empire had been accumulated, were diminishing in number, and in the ability to bear an ever-increasing load of obligations. At the same time, the upper class were increasing in wealth and power, partly from natural economic causes, partly from a determined effort to evade their proper share of the imperial imposts, and to absorb and reduce to dependence their unfortunate neighbours.   In this selfish policy they were aided by the tyranny and venality of the officials of the treasury, whose exactions, chicanery, and corrupt favouritism seem to have become more shameless and cruel in proportion to the weakness of their victims and the difficulties of the times.   And while the aristocratic class were becoming more selfish, and the civil service more oppressive and corrupt, the central government was growing feebler.   It saw the evils which were imperilling the stability of society, and making provincial administration a synonym for organised brigandage.   Its enactments abound with full and accurate descriptions of these disorders, and fierce threats of punishment against the criminals.   But the endless repetition of commands, which were constantly disobeyed, was the surest sign of impotence.   The decay of the middle class, the aggrandisement of the aristocracy, and the defiant tyranny and venality of the tax-gatherer—these are the ominous facts to which almost every page of the later Code bears witness.

Any one who wishes to understand the meaning of the great social catastrophe of the fifth century must fix his attention on the condition and distribution of landed property, and on the classes who possessed it.   The fruits of agricultural industry were at all times the great source of Roman wealth; they were pre-eminently so in the period with which we are concerned.   It is curious to notice how small a part of the Theodosian Code is devoted to the subject of trade and commerce, unless we comprehend under that head the laws relating to the many hereditary guilds which, under the surveillance of the State, were engaged in the production and distribu-

tion of commodities.[1] There is indeed a section dealing
with the special tax on traders (collatio lustralis). But
the commercial class (negotiatores) were, in the fifth
century, probably on a much lower social level than the
humblest landed proprietor. The senatorial order were
forbidden to engage in trade.[2] The curiales, who formed
the governing body of the municipalities, although some
of their members may have been traders also,[3] were
essentially a class of landed proprietors, whose position in
the eye of the State was fixed by their acreage.[4] If
fortunes were accumulated in commerce, they have left
few traces in the pages of the Code. Sidonius, in the
second half of the fifth century, gives an account of the
trading venture of a merchant at Narbonne. The man
has, on the credit of his good character, borrowed a little
money from his friends without other security, and is
going to invest it in purchasing some of the cargo of a
vessel which has come into port. It appears from the
description that the pursuit was not very profitable nor
respected.[5] In one of the later edicts we find merchants
retiring from the greater centres of commerce to remote
places, with the object of escaping the special tax on
their calling. It follows either that the impost was very
heavy, or else that the profits of trade were very small.
It has often been pointed out that the wars and social
confusion of the latter part of the third century gave a
shock to commerce from which it never recovered.[6] In

[1] *C. Th.* xiv. tit. 1, 6. Bk. xiii.
tit. i. deals with the special tax
(lustralis collatio) imposed on
traders ; *v.* a good summary in
Marquardt, *Röm. Staatsverwaltung*,
ii. 230.

[2] Cf. *C. Th.* t. 5, p. 11, Ritter's
ed., and xiii. 1, 21.

[3] *Ib.* xiii. 1, 4 ; *v.* Godefroy's note.

[4] *C. Th.* xii. 1, 33, ut quicumque
ultra vigintiquinque jugera privato
dominio possidens, etc., Curiali
consortio vindicetur.

[5] Sid, *Ep.* vi. 8, Apicum oblator
pauperem vitam sola mercandi
actione sustentat. Notice the contempt for this pursuit expressed in
Nov. Th. 51, quos nisi indigna et
pudenda armato nomini negotiatio
aleret vix possent a famis periculo
vindicari.

[6] Duruy, *Hist. Rom.* vi. 378 ; cf. v.
p. 498 for the state of trade in the
Antonine period. For the shock to
commerce in the third century *v.* De
Coulanges, *L'Inv. Germ.* pp. 102, 103.

that disastrous time the vast destruction of wealth, the interruption of free circulation on the great routes, the loss of confidence, and the portentous depreciation in the currency,[1] must have operated with crushing effect on the trading class. Nor was the fifth century a period more favourable to their pursuits. The invasion of Italy by Alaric and Radagaisus, the invasion of Gaul and Spain by the Sueves and Vandals, the inroads of the Huns under Attila, the raids of Saxon pirates on the shores of the Atlantic, and the presence of the fleets of Genseric in the Mediterranean, must have made the trader's life one of great danger and anxiety, and probably curtailed the volume of commerce to an enormous extent. Law, sentiment, the course of events, were hostile to the prosperity of a great commercial class. The wealth both of the middle and of the upper orders was almost entirely in the soil and its fruits, and, in the absence of free industrial development, there was little capital outside the landed class available for the improvement of agriculture, or for the relief of the farmer who had got into difficulties.

Of the three great classes into which Roman society was divided, the plebeian class, composed of traders, free artisans, etc., who possessed no property in land, may, for our present purpose, be left out of consideration. The other two classes must, from their ownership of the land, and from their relations to one another and to the treasury, engage our sole attention. Of the tone and character of the highest order in the social hierarchy we have attempted to give some account in a previous chapter. They have left us literary materials which enable us to form a tolerably clear idea of their spirit and manner of life; but they seldom speak of their material fortunes or of the classes beneath them, and on these subjects our information must be drawn chiefly from the Code.

---

[1] Duruy, vi. 381; cf. Arnold, *Prov. Administration*, p. 173; Marq. ii. 28.

The senatorial class in the provinces had, since the reign of Constantine, grown to enormous dimensions, partly owing to the policy of the emperors,[1] partly from the efforts of a large number to gain an entrance into the official world, by which they secured at once rank and consideration, and exemption from many onerous burdens and obligations.[2] The order had long ceased to have any connection with the exercise of senatorial functions. Hosts of its members had never even set foot in Rome.[3] The title of senator became merely a social badge, implying generally the possession of considerable landed property, or the tenure of some office or dignity, which was often purely honorary and ornamental. The more ambitious and distinguished families valued themselves quite as much on these official distinctions as on their wealth, and their sons were trained to make it a point of honour to carry on the tradition of official service, and to win, if possible, a higher place than their ancestors had held. But the great mass of the senatorial class were merely landowners on a considerable scale, subject to certain imposts peculiar to their order, but, on the other hand, enjoying certain privileges and exemptions. Of these exemptions the most important was that which relieved senators from municipal burdens.[4]

The municipality, in spite of designations which might

---

[1] Zosimus, ii. 38, ἀπεγράψατο δὲ τὰς τῶν λαμπροτάτων οὐσίας, τέλος ἐπιθεὶς ᾧ τινι φόλλιν αὐτὸς ἐπέθηκεν ὄνομα. The peculiar charges of the senator's position were: (1) the follis glebalis, a land-tax; (2) aurum oblatitium, a gift made on certain anniversaries; (3) the expenses of the games on the young senator being nominated to the praetorship; cf. Godefroy's Paratitlon, *C. Th.* vi. tit. 2.

[2] The special privileges of the senator were: (1) exemption from municipal taxes; (2) exemption from torture; (3) trial by a special court of five taken by lot, *C. Th.* ii. 2; (4) exemption from the aurum coronarium, which was an impost on the curiales; (5) exemption from the onus metati; (6) exemption from collatio ad opera publica.

[3] *C. Th.* vi. 4, 3 and 4. Constantius ordered senators to come to Rome on the occasion of their games when they received the office of praetor; *v.* Duruy, vii. 179.

[4] *C. Th.* vi. 3, 2, senatoriae functionis curiaeque sit nulla conjunctio; 1. 3 is even clearer — a curialibus terris senatoria gleba discreta sit.

suggest other conclusions, was not confined to the walls
of a town;[1] it included, besides the town, a wide area of
rural district extending round it, often for many miles.
From the end of the second century the municipal constitution, as it is described in the Digest and many
inscriptions,[2] had undergone serious changes. In the
century following the reign of Constantine, it had fallen
into irreparable decay.[3] The centralisation of government
and the multiplication of imperial functionaries had extinguished the free civic life, which was in an earlier
period the greatest glory of Roman administration. The
popular assemblies lost their right of electing to the
municipal magistracies;[4] the local senate, or curia, was
no longer composed of men who had held these offices,[5]
but of the landholders who possessed more than twenty-
five jugera.[6] At the same time, the curia became less
concerned with the local interests of its municipality, and
more and more burdened with duties to the imperial
government. Their responsibilities, indeed, as the governing body of their community, were heavy enough. They
had the management of its finances,[7] and full liability for
its debts and deficits. They had the charge of the police,
and of all roads, bridges, and public buildings. They had
certain duties in connection with the corn supply and the
relief of the poor. When they rose to the higher local
magistracies, they had to bear heavy, and sometimes
ruinous, expenses for the amusements of the populace,
prescribed by opinion and custom, if not by law.[8] But
far heavier and more crushing than these were their

---

[1] F. de Coulanges, *La Gaule
Rom.* p. 228.

[2] Wallon, *L'Esclav.* iii. 179 ; see
Marquardt, i. 464, on the Inscriptions of Malaga and Salpensa ; cf.
Arnold's *Rom. Provincial Administration*, pp. 225-237.

[3] Marquardt, i. 510.

[4] *Ib.* i. 468, 469.

[5] *Ib.* i. 503.

[6] *C. Th.* xii. 1, 33.

[7] F. de Coulanges, *La Gaule
Rom.* 244, 251 ; Duruy, *Hist. Rom.*
v. 379, n. 1 ; *C. Th.* xv. 1, 33
("De Op. Publ.").

[8] *C. Th.* ; F. de Coulanges, *La
Gaule Rom.* p. 252; Fauriel, i. 372 ;
Wallon, *L'Esclav.* iii. 181.

obligations to the State. It was the practice of the
Roman government to devolve the collection, and even
the apportionment of a tax, on the class who paid it.[1]
When the imperial authorities issued their precept for a
certain impost payable by the landholders of a district in
money or in kind, the members of the local curia had
not only to fix the assessment on the proprietors in proportion to their holdings, but they had, through some of
their members, the even more invidious task of collecting
the amount payable by each.[2] In addition to all this,
and it was a portentous addition in those times, the
curiales were liable personally for the whole amount, and
had to make good any deficiency in the collection. They
had also onerous liabilities for the military commissariat,
and the maintenance of the posting service on the great
roads.[3] In the assessment and collection of the imperial
taxes there was room for injustice, venality, and cruelty.
And there can be little doubt that the curiales sometimes
abused their trust, so that Salvianus[4] could ask " ubi non
quot fuerint Curiales tot tyranni sunt ? " But fraudulent
gains can have done little to alleviate the weight of a
charge which, as time went on, became more and more
crushing. Moreover, the curial class which had to bear
it was chiefly hereditary,[5] as every other class and calling,
from the highest to the lowest,[6] tended to become. Men
with the required minimum of landed property were,

---

[1] *C. Th.* xi. 7, 12 ; cf. Godefroy's
Paratitlon to xi. 1 ("De Annona et
Tributis") ; cf. xiii. 1, 17.

[2] *Ib.* xii. 1, 117. The principales
are threatened with torture for em-
bezzlement, fraudulent assessments,
and excessive exactions ; cf. l. 54.
The curia chose collectors of revenue
from among its members, and was col-
lectively liable for their fraud or negligence. Cf. xii. 6, 9 ; Fauriel, i. 362.

[3] *C. Th.* viii. 5, 26, 64.

[4] *De Gub. Dei*, v. 18.

[5] The class as a whole is described

often in *C. Th.* xii. 1 as originalis,
ex genere Curiali, familia Curiali
orti, sanguine C. obstricti, etc. Cf.
Godefroy's Paratitlon to xii. 1, t.
4, p. 353.

[6] *C. Th.* x. 20, 15, where even
female descent binds the children
to a corporation. The Burgarii,
or guards of the frontier forts, were
practically public slaves, like the
muleteers, etc., of the cursus publicus. Cf. vii. 14, 1 ; vii. 15, 1,
with Godefroy's notes ; Wallon,
L'Esclav. iii. 176.

from time to time, compelled to enter it.[1] But the
plebeian class, composed of the various corporations of
free labourers, artisans, and petty traders, fenced in and
hampered in all directions by imperial legislation, could
not furnish many recruits to fill the gaps in the curia.
The later legislation seems to actually discourage the
merchant from investing his gains in land,[2] and so becoming a member of the municipal corporation. We
have seen reason to believe that trade in the fourth and
fifth centuries was not prosperous, and the ruinous condition of municipal finance might well deter any one who
had been exceptionally fortunate in commerce from making
an investment which entailed such personal risk and such
incalculable obligations.

The emperors were fully aware of the importance of
a class on which had been laid such a weight of responsibility.   No fewer than 192 enactments in the Theodosian
Code, together with some of the Novellae, deal with the
position and duties of the curiales. The curiales are
described by Majorian as the " nervi reipublicae ac viscera
civitatum," [3] although successive emperors from Constantine to Majorian had to lament that these " sinews
of the commonwealth " were daily growing weaker.[4]
Conventional language or policy indeed kept up the
fiction that the position of the curialis was an enviable
and dignified one.   The municipal body is described in
terms which were originally applied to the Senate of the
capital,[5] and which may have had a certain justification
in the days of free municipal life, when a seat in the
local Senate was reserved for citizens who had filled the
higher magistracies by the choice of the burghers.   When

---

[1] C. Th. xii. 1, 33 ; cf. 1. 53.

[2] Ib. xii. 1, 72. According
to Godefroy's commentary the
merchant investing in land became
doubly liable, as *negotiator* and as
curialis.

[3] Nov. Maj. 1.

[4] C. Th. xii. 1, 13, quoniam
Curias desolari cognovimus. This
is a law of Constantine, dated 326.

[5] Nov. Maj. 1, quorum coetum
recte appellavit antiquitas minorem
Senatum.

the curiales were deserting their functions, abandoning their ruined estates, and trying to hide themselves among serfs, they were loftily reminded by the imperial legislator of the stain which they were attaching to their splendid origin.[1] Doubtless the estimate of social rank is relative, and depends greatly on associations, imagination, and the extent of a man's horizon. At one time the member of the curia in a flourishing municipality may have found his ambition satisfied by local distinctions, and thought he had attained an enviable place when he rose to be flamen of his native town,[2] or provided games for his fellow-citizens as aedile or duumvir.[3] But the growth of the imperial despotism since Diocletian altered the whole character of municipal life. It was a very different thing to be a decurio in the second century and in the fourth or the fifth. From Constantine to Honorius the emperors were vainly struggling to stop a movement which had begun long before Constantine, and which threatened the curial body with utter depletion. The "flight of the curiales" was quite as menacing a danger of the later Empire as the inroads of the barbarians. The curiales fled in all directions, and sought a refuge from their perils and ruinous obligations in every calling. Some of the more wealthy and ambitious managed to get themselves enrolled on the lists of the Senate by diplomas (*codicilli*) surreptitiously or corruptly obtained.[4] Numbers procured admission to some office in the vast Palatine service.[5] Others enlisted in the army,[6] or took Holy Orders. Many

---

[1] *C. Th.* xii. 1, 6. It is a curious commentary on these fine phrases to find in *C. Th.* ix. 35, 2, that curiales, not of the highest order, could be punished by *plumbatarum ictus*, i.e. blows of a whip loaded with lead. These punishments were forbidden by Theodosius, xii. 1, 80.

[2] *Ib.* xii. 1, 77.

[3] *Ib.* xii. 1, 169.

[4] *Ib.* xii. 1, 180, 183, neminem obnoxium Curiae ad incongruam sibi fortunam deinceps aspirare, elicitis codicillis clarissimatus, Magnitudo tua permittat.

[5] *Ib.* xii. i. 22, cum Decuriones ad diversas militias confugiant; cf. ll. 31, 38, 11, 13, 147 ; cf. Arnold's *Prov. Administration*, p. 74.

[6] *C. Th.* xii. 1, 50, and many others.

of the humbler sort were willing to exchange their position for the practical servitude of corporations,[1] such as the corn-importers or the armourers. Many more, in sheer despair, took refuge on some great estate in a dependence almost amounting to serfdom,[2] and sank even to the degradation of marriage with a woman of the servile class.

The motives which prompted men to forsake their municipality were very various, and undoubtedly ambition to rise in the world was one frequent cause of the desertion. Although the position of " decurio " is described by the emperors as one of " dignity " and " splendour," it was vastly inferior to that of the senatorial class. The difference between the two orders was much wider than that between a member of Parliament and a member of a provincial town-council in our days. The senatorial class had not only the prestige of wealth; the greater families had also a practical monopoly of the highest prefectures and offices of state.[3] They were often the descendants of men who had held such offices from time immemorial. They became almost as a matter of course governors, Pretorian prefects, and consuls. Their sons were trained to follow them in the same " career of honours," and had often completed their term of public life and governed provinces larger than most modern European kingdoms at an age when a man of ambition in our days is only getting his foot on the ladder.[4] The years of later life were passed in dignified tranquillity, and the enjoyment of that cultivated society, so stately and so exclusive, but so charming, which has

---

[1] *C. Th.* xii. 1, 149 (navicularii), 62 (collegium fabrorum).

[2] *Nov. Maj.* i.

[3] Sidon. *Ep.* v. 9.

[4] Sextus Petr. Probus, born *circ.* 334, became proconsul of Africa in 356, and Pretorian prefect of Italy, Africa and Illyricum in 368 (*aet.*

34) ; *v.* Seeck's *Sym.* cii. Symmachus, born *circ.* 340, held his first office in 365 (Seeck, xliv.). Olybrius and Probinus were consuls when mere youths. Cf. Hieron. *Ep.* 130, 3 ; Claud. in *Cons. Olybr. et Prob.* 63. Sidonius was prefect of Rome in his thirty-eighth year. (Mommsen, Praef. in *Sidon.* xlviii.)

been described in another chapter. It is little wonder that the ambitious bourgeois of the curial class should have struggled at any cost, by intrigue or by bribery, to raise himself and his children even to the outskirts of such a rank, from the rather sordid and limited ambitions and the wearing anxieties of his original position. If he remained in it, his highest hope could only be to reach the duumvirate, and pass into the select class of the principales,[1] after completing the whole round of duties and charges incumbent on his order. But before attaining that not very lofty eminence, he might find his patrimony eaten away by the claims of his own community, and the inexorable and insatiable demands of the imperial treasury. The numerous constitutions dealing with the migration of curiales into the senatorial class are the clearest proof, at once of the force of the tendency, and of the difficulty of restraining it. In the earlier part of the fourth century, the emperors appear not to have opposed insuperable obstacles to such ambition, provided the finances of the municipality concerned did not suffer.[2] But in the beginning of the fifth century, the rapid depletion of the curiae and the complaints which reached him caused the Emperor to assume a sterner tone. The curiales were bluntly warned not to aspire to senatorial rank.[3] The grant of *codicilli clarissimatus*, often obtained, as we have seen, by

---

[1] The principales (also optimates, Sym. *Ep.* x. 41 ; summi municipum proceres, Auson. *Mosell.* 402) were in some places ten in number, elected by the curia, after a regular ascent through all the duties and honours of their order, and bound to remain in the performance of their functions for fifteen years, *C. Th.* xii. 1, 75, 171, 189. They were exempt from cruel punishments, xii. 1, 61. Cf. F. de Coulanges, *L'Inv. Germ.* p. 37.

[2] *C. Th.* xii. 1, 57. A law of Valens (xii. 1, 69) allows curiales who have become senators prematurely (ante expleta munera) to retain the higher position provided they perform curial duties.

[3] *C. Th.* xii. 1, 183, neminem obnoxium Curiae ad incongruam sibi fortunam deinceps aspirare, elicitis codicillis clarissimatus, Magnitudo tua permittat ; cf. l. 180. Still more trenchant is Novella 8 of Theodosius : lege itaque perpetuo valitura decernimus, nullum posthac Curialem sibimet dignitatis senatoriae infulas usurpare.

underhand means, was peremptorily prohibited; and no
one, bound to municipal functions, was henceforth to be
raised to senatorial rank until he had passed through all
the grades of his original order, and performed all the
duties which were laid upon it. Honorius, in a rescript
addressed to the prefect of the Gauls in 409,[1] prohibits
the principales, who formed the highest class of the
curial body, from being released from their functions
until they had completed a term of fifteen years in their
grade. About the same time all persons of curial
descent in the ranks of the army or the Palatine service [2]
were ordered back to their native cities, and any one of
this class is forbidden henceforth to evade his hereditary
obligations by entering either the military or the civil
branch of the government service. It is well to remind
ourselves that, at the time when these laws were promul-
gated, a considerable part of Gaul had been overrun by
the Germans, and we may very well believe that the
duties and burdens of the governing class of the municipalities in those regions were becoming more harassing
and onerous. To be sent back to the prison-house of
curial slavery from some promising career at Rome, and
to see every opening closed to himself and to his sons for
the future, may well have driven many a man of the
doomed order to despair.

In truth, the curial's position had become one of those
forms of hereditary servitude by which the society of the
Lower Empire was reduced almost to a system of castes.
Introduced into the corporation at eighteen years of age,
he could not, by any effort, legally divest himself of his
inherited position until he had gone the whole round of
official duty. The law did not absolutely prohibit a

---

[1] *C. Th.* xii. 1, 171. Dardanus, to whom it is addressed, was Pretorian prefect again in 413.

[2] *Ib.* xii. 1, 147. This law includes all curiales who had entered the army, the Palatine civil service, the bureau of the Pretorian prefect, and all other similar occupations; cf. ll. 38, 40, 44.

curial from rising to another grade in society, but it made his progress so slow and difficult that escape by legal means was possible to very few. Even when a man had surmounted all barriers, and become an imperial functionary or a senator,[1] his children, born before his elevation, were retained in their original rank, and his property remained liable for the municipal charges of his class. If a man attempted to hasten his rise, or his deliverance, by overleaping some of the stages of duty, he was sent back to the original starting-point. The most splendid dignities conferred by the Emperor himself, which would in other cases raise a man to the Senate, would not avail for those of curial origin; they are to remain in the bosom of their native place, "as it were dedicated with sacred fillets and guarding the eternal mystery, which they cannot abandon without impiety."[2] The curial's personal freedom was curtailed on every side. If he travelled abroad, that was an injury to his city; and if he absented himself for five years, his property was confiscated.[3] Even for a limited time, and for a public object, as for example to present himself before the Emperor, he could not go from home without the formal permission of the governor of the province.[4] He was forbidden absolutely to reside in the country.[5] It is almost needless to say that he had no power to dispose of his property as he pleased, since the State regarded his property as security for the full discharge of all his financial obligations. He could not sell his estate without the permission of the governor of the province.[6]

---

[1] *C. Th.* xii. 1, 69.

[2] *Ib.* xii. 1, 122, maneant in sinu patriae et veluti dicati infulis, mysterium perenne custodiant; sit illis piaculum inde discedere.

[3] *Ib.* xii. 1, 143, 144, ne diu in fraudem civitatum municipes evagentur, etc.

[4] *Ib.* xii. 1, 9.

[5] *Ib.* xii. 18, 1 and 2. These laws are addressed to the Egyptian prefect, and they may refer to the monks and hermits; cf. xii. 1, 63, which treats them with great contempt.

[6] *Ib.* xii. 3, 1 and 2; *Nov. Maj.* 1, nunquam sine interpositione decreti Curiales alienent.

He could not enter into any contract or business relation
which might conceivably weaken the hold of the State
upon his possessions.   He was forbidden, for example, to
accept the agency of an estate,[1] or to rent public lands,
or to farm the taxes.[2]   The curial who had no children
could dispose only of one-fourth of his estate by will,
the remainder being taken by the municipal treasury.[3]
The municipality became the sole heir of an intestate
curial.[4]   If his natural heirs were not citizens of the
place,[5] or if his daughter or widow married a stranger,
they had to resign one-fourth of the property to the
curia.   He could not take Holy Orders without leaving
his curial property in the hands of a proper substitute,[6]
or absolutely abandoning it to the service of the community.   We have not by any means exhausted the
melancholy list of the disabilities and hardships which
were heaped upon this wretched class, but enough has
been said to show the causes of its depletion.   Indeed,
the emperors themselves, while they occasionally apply
to it honorific terms, which to us now sound like grim
mockery, had really no illusions as to its hopeless condition.   It is often described in phrases (*nexus, mancipatio*)
which seem to reduce it to a species of slavery.   The
curial in one law is denied the asylum of the church,
along with insolvent debtors and fugitive slaves.[7]   When
he is recalled from some refuge to which he has escaped,
his worst punishment for disobedience to the law is to
be replaced in his original rank.   Nor could the legislator
at one time find a worse fate for certain malefactors than

---

[1] *C. Th.* xii. 1, 92. The curial is
branded with disgrace for engaging
in a servile occupation, and renders
himself liable to banishment.

[2] *Ib.* xii. 1, 97 ; x. 3, 2, curialibus omnibus conducendorum Reipublicae praediorum ac saltuum
inhibeatur facultas.

[3] See note 3 in Wallon, *L'Esclav.*
iii. 186.

[4] *C. Th.* v. 2, 1, "De Bonis De-
curionum."

[5] Cf. Wallon, iii. 186, n. 4.

[6] *C. Th.* xii. 1, 59, qui partes
ecclesiae eligit, aut in propinquum
bona propria conferendo eum pro se
faciat Curialem aut facultatibus
Curiae cedat quam reliquit (cf. ll.
91 and 98).

[7] *Ib.* ix. 45, 3.

to be relegated to the curia.[1]   The curia had in truth
become an *ergastulum,* and all the ingenuity of lawyers,
all the energy of imperial officers, were occupied for
generations in trying to prevent the escape of the slaves
of the curia.[2]   But the cruelty of their position made
them reckless.   Many fled to the solitude and hard fare
of the hermitage.[3]   Others preferred the servitude of one
of the lower corporations of artisans to the service of the
commune;[4] they hid themselves even among smiths and
charcoal-burners.   Still more placed themselves under the
protection of a great proprietor,[5] and were only too glad
to bury themselves among the crowd of his cottiers and
serfs, where their children, by some slave mother, would
at least be delivered by the ignominy of their birth from
their father's hereditary curse.[6]

While the numbers of the curial class were thus
steadily shrinking, in spite of the cruel determination of
the legislator, the burdens on those who remained were
as steadily increasing in severity.   The curiales were
responsible for the collection of taxes on landed property,
and if the assessments in their district were not fully
paid, they had to make good the deficit to the treasury.
Now there is ample evidence that the tax-bearing acreage
in the end of the fourth century and the beginning of
the fifth was rapidly contracting.   In Campania alone,
once the garden of Italy, more than 500,000 jugera had

[1] *C. Th.* xii. 1, 66 and 108. These
laws of Valentinian I. and Theodosius prohibit the consignment to
the curia as a punishment, but the
prohibition proves the existence of
the practice.

[2] *Ib.* ix. 45, 3, vigore et sollertia
judicantum ad pristinam sortem
velut manu injecta revocentur.

[3] *Ib.* xii. 1, 63, quidam ignaviae
sectatores, desertis civitatum
muneribus, captant solitudinem ac
secreta, et specie religionis cum coeti-
bus Monazonton congregantur. The
law mentions Egypt and the East

as the regions to which it applies
(*v.* Godefroy's note, iv. p. 434).

[4] *Ib.* xii. 1, 62, 149, 162 ; cf. xiv.
8, 1.

[5] *Ib.* xii. 1, 76 ; cf. 146, multos
animadvertimus, ut debita praestatione patriam defraudarent, sub
umbra Potentium latitare . . .
Omnes igitur quos tegunt expel-
lant, ne Clementia Nostra ab con-
tumacia dissimulantium in majorem
indignationem exurgat; ll. 155,
162, 179, 189, occultator detur
flammis ultricibus.

[6] *Nov. Maj.* 1 *ad init.*

gone out of cultivation.[1] Symmachus, who was a large
landowner, complains that agriculture was becoming a
very expensive luxury.[2] The later edicts frankly admit
that over large areas the resources of the landed taxpayer
were exhausted. And the admission is not confined to
words. For in 408,[3] in 413, and again in 418, relief
from the land-tax was granted to large districts in Italy,
in one case to as many as seven provinces. A similar
indulgence was shown to the landholders of Africa, in 410,[4]
in 423, and, in consequence of the Vandal invasion, in 451.
In the meantime the expense of government was probably growing. And, owing to the absence of floating
capital, the government could not, as in modern times,
throw part of its burdens on posterity by creating a
public debt.[5] It is likely that the necessities of the
public administration, as the taxable area went on
shrinking, must have caused a more and more exhausting
drain on the resources of those provinces which still
remained solvent. Even in the absence of statistics and
explicit statements on the subject, there is an overwhelming probability in favour of the theory that the
demands of the imperial exchequer on the curial class
were increasing in proportion to the failure of former
sources of revenue.[6] We hear more and more of the

[1] *C. Th.* xi. 28, 2. The lands
had been first inspected by peraequatores, and ancient documents
consulted (*v.* Godefroy's note).
Referred to in Sym. *Ep.* iv. 46; cf.
v. 12, frustra speravi de peregrina-
tione solacium, cum omnium loco-
rum maesta facies nullas aegro
animo praestet indutias.

[2] Sym. *Ep.* i. 5, namque hic usus
in nostram venit aetatem, ut rus,
quod solebat alere, nunc alatur.

[3] *C. Th.* xi. 28, 4, 7, 12. The
relief in 408 was given immediately
after Stilicho's death, and was demanded by the devastations of the
armies of Radagaisus and Alaric.

The senatorial follis glebalis was
included in the remission.

[4] *Ib.* xi. 28, 6, 13, and *Nov.*
Valent. 7 *ad fin.* The remission in
410 "ob Africae devotionem" re-
fers to the resistance of Africa under
Heraclian to the attempts of
Attalus, the Emperor set up by
Alaric; cf. Zos. vi. 7.

[5] The government met cases of
financial emergency by superindic-
tions. Cf. *C. Th.* xi. tit. 16, with
Godefroy's Paratitlon to xi. tit. 6;
cf. Paratitlon to xi. tit. 1, and
Duruy, vii. 167 n.

[6] F. de Coulanges, *L'Inv. Germ.*
p. 51, disputes this; but cf. c. 17

land-inspectors[1] (*peraequatores*) whose function it was to deal with the ownership of waste lands, and the apportionment or remission of the land-tax. They appear to have been infected with the general venality,[2] and their peculiar duties gave them opportunities, or offered temptations, to favour the more powerful proprietors,[3] and to enrich themselves at the same time. Nor should it be forgotten, in forming an estimate of the curial's economic position, that in the fourth or fifth centuries there was a steady and serious appreciation in gold, and that taxes had to be paid in gold, as well as in kind.[4] In the reign of Valentinian I. the ratio of silver to gold was $14\frac{2}{5}$ to 1.[5] In the reign of the younger Theodosius the proportion was 18 to 1.[6] That is, in less than a quarter of a century the value of gold had risen by more than a fifth. This appreciation involved a corresponding increase of taxes payable in gold. And while the demands of the exchequer were increasing, the landowner was probably getting less and less for his agricultural products. And here we touch what was the chief economic cause of the ruin of the curiales. He was, as we have seen, liable personally for any deficit in the taxes payable by his district. The returns were almost

of the *Decline and Fall*, and Apoll. Sid. *Carm.* xiii. 19 addressed to Majorian. For an earlier time see Zos. ii. 38.

[1] On the duties of peraequatores, as defined in the Code, see Godefroy's Paratitlon to xiii. 11 ; cf. *C. Th.* xiii. 11, 14, 15, 16, with Godefroy's note on l. 16. These laws show at once the fairness of the government, and the opportunities for fraud open to the peraequatores.

[2] *C. Th.* xiii. 11, 10. The corrupt peraequatores are heavily fined in xiii. 11, 7.

[3] *Ib.* xiii. 11, 4, ut quid remissum gratia, quid interceptum fuerit fraude, convincant . . .

[4] *Ib.* xi. 21, 3; cf. xiii. 6, 13;

Duruy, vii. 166.

[5] The calculation is based on a comparison of *C. Th.* xiii. 2, 1, with viii. 4, 27. In the former (A.D. 397) 1 libra of silver is equal to 5 solidi of gold ; in the latter 1 libra of silver is equal to 4 solidi. Cf. Godefroy's notes to both laws. He sums up with the remark : adeo indies auri pretium increvit. Cf. Sym. *Rel.* xxix., paulatim auri enormitate crescente. The yield of the gold-mines seems, from the following laws, to have been diminishing: *C. Th.* x. 19, 3 (365), for the encouragement of gold-mining; x. 19, 5, 6, 7, 9 (to keep the aurileguli to their calling). Cf. Marq. ii. 43.

[6] *C. Th.* viii. 4, 27.

certainly diminishing; the government was inexorable.
The mass of the curiales were themselves small landholders who were unable to compete with the owners of
great estates cultivated by the labour of slaves and
coloni.[1] The land was, as a rule, their only source of
income. As the land became less productive, while the
burdens of their position became heavier, the weaker
curialis must either fly from his municipality, as so many
actually did, or else he must obtain temporary relief, on
whatever terms, from the only capitalist to whom he
could apply, the neighbouring large proprietor. This
absorption of the smaller by the greater landowners, and
the growing power of the latter, is by far the most
interesting and important feature in the transition of
society from the despotism of the Lower Empire to the
régime of the feudal lords.

The senatorial estate was a community by itself,
supplying its own wants, and furnishing supplies for the
neighbouring markets or for the government service.
Part of it was cultivated directly for the lord by slaves;
and the building and carpenter work, the spinning and
weaving, were also carried on by slaves. Another part
of the estate was cultivated by a class designated by
many names, and occupying different grades of dependence.[2] Some of them were strictly serfs, *ascripti
glebae*, who, on the sale of an estate, passed to the new
owner. Some were in the position of metayers, paying
their lord a certain proportion of the produce which they
raised. In other cases they were men who had become
indebted to their lord and, being unable to pay their

[1] Cf. Arnold, *Provincial Administration*, p. 161.

[2] *C. Th.* ix. 10, 3. Cf. the Paratitlon of Godefroy to v. 9, "De Fugi-
tivis Colonis"; Wallon, *L'Esclav.*
iii. p. 252; De Coulanges, *L'Inv.
Germ.* pp. 93, 139. To discuss the
vexed question of the origin and
nature of the status of the coloni
is no part of the purpose of this
chapter. For a review of some of
the different theories see Wallon,
L'Esclav. iii., chap. on "Travail
de Campagne." Cf. Arnold, *Provincial Administration*, pp. 161,
162.

debt, had given up their land, remaining on it to cultivate
it on certain terms.[1] Sometimes they were broken men,
who had deserted their farms from various causes,
poverty, oppression of government officials or powerful
neighbours, or the wish to escape the heavy burdens
imposed on the curial class,[2] and who put themselves
under the protection of some great proprietor. There is
no social phenomenon of the time which deserves closer
attention, for many reasons, than the position of these
free settlers on the great estates. It is an indication at
once of the ruin of the middle class, and of the growing
power of the aristocracy. For nearly a hundred years
the Code gives evidence of the determination of the
emperors to check the tendency towards this form of
patronage.[3] Those who sheltered the fugitive curialis are
threatened with punishments of increasing severity, fines,
confiscation, infamy, till the law of Honorius in 415[4]
orders the agent or bailiff who connives at the offence to
be given to the "avenging flames." But all the vigour
of the government could not make head against an
irresistible tendency of the times. In the reign of
Valentinian III. and in the reign of Majorian, the
authorities have to combat the evil once more.[5] The

[1] Salv. *de Gub. Dei*, v. 39-44.
He distinguishes two classes: (1)
defensoribus suis omnem fere sub-
stantiam suam prius quam defend-
antur addicunt; (2) cum agellos
suos perdunt . . . aut deserunt,
fundos majorum expetunt et coloni
divitum fiunt . . . jugo se inquil-
inae abjectionis addicunt.

[2] *C. Th.* xii. 1, 76, 146 ; *Nov.
Maj.* 1. On the origin of this form
of patronage *v.* Wallon, iii. p. 271.

[3] *C. Th.* xi. 24, "De Patrociniis
Vicorum." The subject is included
in this book xi. which deals with
taxation, because patronage was
exercised to defeat the claims of
the treasury; cf. xiii. 1, 21, which
shows that negotiatores used this

influence to evade the lustralis
collatio. By xi. 24, 2, the patronus
is fined 25 pounds of gold for each
case. In 399 the fine is raised to
40. In l. 5 the offender's whole
property is confiscated. On the
evasion of tribute in Gaul by
potentes, *v.* xi. 1, 26.

[4] *Ib.* xii. 1, 179.

[5] *Nov. Valent.* 9, advenae plerumque tenues abjectaeque fortunae
quorundam se obsequiis jungunt.
Nov. Maj. 1 *ad init.*, illud quoque
sibi dedecoris addentes, ut dum uti
volunt patrociniis potentum colon-
arum se ancillarumque conjunctione
polluerint. Farther on the Emperor
says : vendunt defugas Curiales et
obnoxios corporatos cum eos occulta
depredatione concusserint.

edicts of these emperors describe the condition of such dependants in a manner which singularly harmonises with the contemporary picture given by Salvianus. The injustice of governors and the venality of tax-gatherers have driven many to quit their native cities, and, " forgetful of the splendour of their birth" (it is thus the perilous rank of the curialis is described), to place themselves under the protection of some powerful patron. We need not believe, as Salvianus does, that the rich proprietor deliberately set himself to reduce his clients to serfdom; but it is only too probable that such protégés would inevitably sink to the position of coloni.

It was, however, through direct indebtedness to the great proprietors that the smaller generally lost their independence. As we have seen, there was little capital in that age derived from any other source than land. If a farmer got into difficulties from bad seasons, or under the pressure of taxation and municipal burdens, his readiest resource was to borrow from some rich neighbour.[1] There were many ways by which the great man could lay his hands on his debtor's land, and the Code leaves no doubt that the most unblushing oppression and chicanery were often employed to dispossess him.[2] The accumulation of arrears of interest led to forced sales or donations to escape from an intolerable burden. If a small estate were put up for sale, the great man had few competitors, for there was little capital seeking such investment, and the government actually seemed to discourage a merchant from purchasing land by holding him

---

[1] See an example in Sid. *Ep.* iv. 24. The needy debtor is paying interest at a rate which will double the capital lent in ten years; cf. Chaix, *Sidon.* ii. 236. Permission to senators to lend at 6 per cent is given in *C. Th.* ii. 33, 4 (*v.* Godefroy). *C. Th.* ii. 33, 3 allowed senators who were minors to lend money at interest.

[2] *C. Th.* iii. 1, 8 prohibits secret sales by fugitive curiales: venditiones, donationes, transactiones quae per potentiam extortae sunt, praecipimus infirmari; cf. ii. 9, 4, pacta quidem per vim et metum apud omnes satis constat cassata viribus, respuenda.

liable not only for the land-tax, but for the lustralis collatio, for which, as a trader, he was liable before the purchase.[1] The terms of one law of Honorius make it probable that mere terrorism exercised by great nobles or officials, without any legal rights whatever, often compelled the small farmer to part with his land by pretended sale or gift.[2] The secret sale of property by curiales flying from their municipality was also a growing practice. In spite of all the obstacles which the law interposed to prevent the alienation of such estates, there is clear evidence [3] that, from the time of Alaric's invasion, many sales had taken place without the formalities prescribed when a curialis parted with his estate. The law of Valentinian III., which deals with such cases, shows a tenderness and consideration for the difficulties of an unfortunate class, very unlike the spirit of earlier legislation on the subject. It maintains the validity of all such sales,[4] when effected under the pressure of extreme necessity. But a heavy condemnation is passed on men of official rank who have abused their power by violence,[5] or by refusing payment of the purchase money, to inflict injustice on a needy vendor. The culprit is compelled not only to pay the full price, but to reinstate the unwilling vendor in possession. It is clear that the class of small proprietors had little chance of holding their own in such a time as these laws describe to us. The Code frankly admits the overwhelming nature of the burdens which the State imposed on them. Every year they sank deeper into debt, and every year they were less and less

---

[1] *C. Th.* xii. 1, 72 ; cf. xiii. 1, 4.

[2] *Ib.* iii. 1, 8.

[3] *Nov. Valent.* 10, notum est post fatalem hostium ruinam qua Italia laboravit, etc.

[4] *Ib.* 10, iniquum est, tam justis praecedentibus causis, confectae venditioni ob hoc solum, quia decreti interpositio defuit, adimi firmitatem.

[5] *Ib.* 10, quod si emptor officio et administratione perfunctus, etc., venditori solidorum numerum inferat qui tabulis continetur, possessionem nihilominus perditurus, ut ad dominum redeat cui taliter probatur ablata.

able to meet their liabilities.[1] They could borrow only from the very men who were hungering for their land, and who desired their extinction. The means of compassing their ruin lay ready to the hand of a great proprietor, who, if not in office himself, was connected by social freemasonry with the official class, who could prejudice the judge on the bench, or bribe the meaner officers of the law.

It seems clear, then, that the smaller landed proprietors were, from the various causes which we have described, becoming steadily poorer and less numerous. But while this change, fraught with momentous consequences to Roman society, was in progress, another, in the opposite direction, is equally observable. The upper or senatorial class was growing not only in wealth, but in power. Its affluence can be easily estimated from the letters of Symmachus, from the declamation of Salvianus, and from the picture of Gallic society which Apollinaris Sidonius has left us. Its growing power is written on many a page of the Code. In spite of the vast and complicated machinery which had been elaborated by successive emperors for the administration of the provinces, the task of governing them with purity, economy, and fairness to all classes became more and more difficult. The greatest vigilance and energy were exerted by the central authority to secure the independence of the provincial governors,[2] and to repress the tendency to corruption and oppression among the collectors of taxes and the inferior officers of the law.[3] But the very number of edicts

[1] *Nov. Valent.* 10. usuris in majorem cumulum crescentibus.

[2] *C. Th.* i. 8, 1. Honorati are forbidden to sit with judges on the bench ; cf. the whole of tit. 7, "De Officio Rectoris Provinciae."

[3] *Ib.* ix. 26 and 27, esp. 27, 2, hi qui in Republica versati sinisterius sunt, perpetuo sibi omnes dignitates, vel legitimas vel honorarias, sciant

esse praeclusas. Cf. i. 7, 1, cessent jam rapaces officialium manus, cessent, inquam ; nam si moniti non cessaverint praecidentur. Note that this is a law of Constantine, A.D. 331. The guilty official was degraded to plebeian rank, became *intestabilis*, required to restore fourfold the amount of his illicit gains (which could be recovered from his

directed to these ends discloses the impotence of the emperor. Heavy fines, banishment, torture, death, are all ineffectual to check the inevitable corruption of a bureaucratic government, operating over an area probably the widest which has ever been ruled directly from a single centre. The distance of the seat of government was undoubtedly the greatest difficulty, and it was a difficulty fully recognised by the imperial legislator. With all the facilities of the Roman posting service, it was in many cases only after a long interval that the complaints of the aggrieved provincials could reach the government. The sense of remoteness must have inspired corrupt and unprincipled officials with an audacity which they would not have shown if their conduct had been liable to more instant exposure. But beyond a doubt, the most serious obstacle in the way of pure and honest administration was the power of the provincial aristocracy. In the middle of the fourth century the patronage which enabled the smaller proprietors to evade their share of the taxes was severely dealt with by Valens.[1] At the close of the century the threat of still heavier penalties reveals the fact that the mischief is still rampant.[2] The patronage was probably paid for in a fashion which still further increased the influence of the patron. The upper class or *potentes*, as they are called, not only engaged in trade themselves,[3] but secured the exemption of the regular trader from the tax imposed upon his calling. Creditors with usurious or fraudulent claims[4] induced great lords to give their names to the suit,[5] with the object, no doubt often attained, of over-awing or influ-

---

heirs), and prohibited from holding the same office for a second term. (See ix. 27, 1, 3, 4, and ix, 26, 2, with Godefroy's note.)

[1] *C. Th.* xi. 24, 2, abstineant patrociniis agricolae, etc. Cf. Amm. Marc. xxxi. 14 for the character of Valens as an administrator.

[2] *C. Th.* xi. 24, 5, excellentia tua . . . severiorem poenam nos addidisse cognoscat.

[3] *Ib.* xiii. 1, 21; cf. xiii. 1, 5, which discouraged trading among potentes.

[4] *Ib.* ii. 13, 1; cf. xiii. 1, 15.

[5] *Ib.* xi. 1, 21.

encing the judge. It is needless to say that the rich
were equally energetic in their own interests. We learn,
both from Salvianus [1] and from the Code, [2] that the
wealthier class in Gaul contrived to shift their share of
the land-tax on their poorer neighbours. And in a law
of the very next year we find that the practice of delay-
ing payment of taxes [3] had become so general that
Honorius was compelled to impose a fine of fourfold the
amount on the *morator*. But, without any open defiance
of the government, the upper class had many means of
cheating the treasury. If, for example, an inspector came
down to revise the land assessment, [4] and to settle the
liability for waste lands, it was not difficult for a great
proprietor to see that the settlement was in his favour.
If he did not himself appear upon the scene, his agent
could refuse information about the rating, or otherwise
impede the inquiry. And unfortunately the inspectors,
like so many of the officials of this period, were easily
accessible to bribes or other forms of corrupt influence.
The *procuratores* of the great estates, who, as a class, were
very corrupt and unprincipled, doubtless did many things
of which their masters might have disapproved. They
were generally men of low or even servile origin, [5] wielding almost uncontrolled power in the absence of the proprietor. The government repeatedly shows its distrust of
them. [6] In the time of the invasions they gave shelter

[1] *De Gub. Dei*, v. 28, illud indig-
nius ac poenalius, quod omnium
onus non omnes sustinent, immo
quod pauperculos homines tributa
divitum premunt, et infirmiores
ferunt sarcinas fortiorum.

[2] *C. Th.* xi. 1, 26, nullum gratia
relevet ; nullum iniquae partitionis
vexet incommodum sed pari omnes
sorte teneantur.

[3] *Ib.* xi. 1, 27.

[4] *Ib.* xiii. 11, 2, si Peraequatore
misso, aliquis aut Procuratorem
suum retraxerit, aut colonum ad

contumaciam retractationis arma-
verit, etc. Cf. l. 7 on the corruption of peraequatores.

[5] *Ib.* xii. 1, 92. In prohibiting
a curialis to become procurator, the
Emperor uses these words : ille vero
qui immemor libertatis et generis
infamissimam suscipiens vilitatem,
existimationem suam servili obse-
cundatione damnaverit, deporta-
tionis incommodo subjugetur.

[6] E.g. *ib.* i. 7, 7, moderatores
Provinciae curam gerere jubemus
ne quid Potentium Procuratores
perperam illiciteve committant.

to fugitives with the object of retaining them as slaves.[1] They were in league with brigands,[2] and harboured them on the estates of which they had the management. So lawless had they become that the procurators in several provinces were specially forbidden the use of horses,[3] and they were coupled in the prohibition with those wild herdsmen of Samnium and Apulia who so easily passed into the ranks of professional robbers. They are also associated in several edicts with the crime of concealing deserters from the army.[4] In fact the agent of a remote estate must have often involved his master in the meshes of the law. The procurator seems to have sometimes gone so far as to hypothecate an estate without his master's knowledge,[5] and more than one law deals with this practice, in order to protect at once the owner and the *bona fide* mortgagee. The procurator who engaged in such transactions was a man who was probably accumulating a fortune of his own, and this *peculium*,[6] subject to any prior claim of the master, was made liable for the repayment of unauthorised loans. It may be readily believed that such a class as this, often under no control or supervision, would exercise their power more unscrupulously and oppressively than even the most tyrannical aristocrat. The most serious danger, however, to the small landowner from the great lords lay in the facilities which the latter possessed for corrupting the sources of justice. The governor, who had to hear a case between a wealthy man and a poor man, belonged to the senatorial class, in many cases was a member of the aristocracy of the province in which the case arose.[7] The litigant of

---

[1] *C. Th.* v. 5. 2. The actores and procuratores who disobeyed this law were to be sent to the mines.

[2] *Ib.* ix. 29, 2, si vero Actor sive Procurator latronem domino ignorante occultaverit . . . flammis ultricibus concremetur.

[3] *Ib.* ix. 30, 2.

[4] *Ib.* vii. 18, 5 and 12. The offending procurator is to be capitally punished.

[5] *Ib.* ii. 30, 2, "De Pignoribus."

[6] *Ib.* ii. 32, 1.

[7] *E.g.* Dardanus, Pretorian prefect of Gaul, 409, 413, the grandfather of Apoll. Sidonius (*Ep.* iii. 12),

his own rank could easily bring private pressure to bear on him to influence his decisions. Even an upright man like Symmachus had no scruple in writing to his official friends about cases which were to come before them.[1] It is to the credit of the emperors that they took the severest measures to secure judicial purity. The regulation against governors having a second term of office in the same province [2] was intended to check the growth of connections and influences which might prove too strong for the virtue even of a well-meaning ruler. The danger is still more clearly recognised in the rules which forbade the admission of any one, rich or poor, to an interview with a governor after his court had closed at midday,[3] and which enjoined him in his progresses to refuse invitations to "the luxurious quarters" which his wealthy friends were ready to place at his disposal.[4] Very explicitly, in the year 408, Honorius forbids Honorati to sit on the bench with a judge.[5] All causes are to be heard in open court with the fullest publicity.[6]

A volume might be written on the subject of financial corruption in the last century of the Western Empire. When one wanders through the maze of enactments dealing with fiscal oppression, malversation, and evasion, one knows not whether more to pity the weakness of the government, or to wonder at the hardened cupidity and audacity of the classes which were leagued together in plundering both the treasury and the taxpayer. In the early part of the fifth century, the province of Africa, so essential to the very existence of the capital, yet held by so precarious a tenure, appealed by deputation to the

---

Tonantius Ferreolus, etc. These are not mentioned, however, as instances of corrupt administration.

[1] Sym. *Ep.* iv. 68 ; ii. 41 ; ii. 87.
[2] *C. Th.* ix. 26, 4, si quis Proconsularem aut Vicariam potestatem, etc., iterare temptaverit, fisco ejus omne patrimonium sociari

decernimus.
[3] *Ib.* i. 7, 6.
[4] *Ib.* i. 7, 4, non deverticula deliciosa sectetur. Any diversorium lent to a judex in the face of this law is to be confiscated.
[5] *Ib.* i. 8, 1.
[6] *Ib.* i. 7, 2.

Emperor for relief from its miseries.[1] The complaints relate almost entirely to oppression and injustice in the collection of the various branches of the revenue. The upper classes secured immunity from their proper burdens, or succeeded by unfair assessment in shifting them on to the class less able to bear them. The soldiers and officials grossly abused the right of free quarters in moving through the province.[2] The various grades of public servants whose business it was to collect the revenue,[3] or to press for payment,[4] or to keep the revenue accounts,[5] were all guilty of the grossest fraud, in collusion with each other, or of outrageous terrorism and violence. Alike in Africa and Gaul, the great landowners at this time, taking advantage of the evident weakness and difficulties of the government, either evaded or delayed their payments.[6] In many cases their agents, living in remote independence,[7] offered a stolid resistance to the demands of the treasury, and that at a time when the utmost despatch was needed to prepare for the storm which was ready to burst both upon Gaul and Italy, and when the government had on its hands a troublesome war in Africa. Not content with this, they shielded by their patronage weaker men who had perhaps more excuse for falling into arrears.[8] When corn was urgently needed to save the city from famine, or to provision the troops for Gaul, they allowed vessels bound to the trans-

---

[1] *C. Th.* xii. 1, 166 ; xii. 6, 27 ; vii. 4, 33.

[2] *Ib.* vii. 8, 10. For a good summary of the sufferings of Africa at this time from corrupt officials see Godefroy's note to vi. 29, 11, the law which orders the curiosi to be expelled from the province.

[3] Susceptores, *ib.* xii. tit. 6 ; cf. Fauriel, i. 362.

[4] Compulsores, *C. Th.* xi. 1, 34, with Godefroy's note ; cf. Amm. Marc. xxii. 6.

[5] Numerarii, actuarii, *C. Th.* viii. tit. 1. See Godefroy's Paratitlon,

and cf. l. 4, vorax et fraudulentum numerariorum propositum ; l. 6, numerarii qui publicas civitatum rationes versutis fraudibus lacerare didicerunt, subjaceant tortori.

[6] *Ib.* xi. 1, 25, 26, 27. These laws were issued in 398 and 399.

[7] *Sym.* v. 87, ix. 6, Actores absentium, quibus res longinqua committitur, tanquam soluti legibus vivunt.

[8] *C. Th.* xi. 24, 4, qui fraudandorum tributorum causa ad patrocinia solita fraude confugerint ; cf. Salv. *de Gub. Dei*, v. 38.

port service to be entered in their names.[1]   They bribed
the officers of the census to make false entries of property
liable to taxation, and land-inspectors to relieve them of
the burden of unproductive estates.[2]   If they purchased
an estate from a man in difficulties they would often, by
a surreptitious contract,[3] shift the burden of the capitation-
tax, payable on the coloni of the estate, to the shoulders
of the needy vendor.   By influence or bribes[4] they induced the book-keepers (tabularii) to cook their accounts
in favour of themselves or their clients.   It is difficult
to conceive a powerful and wealthy class, many of whose
members must have known the responsibilities of government, and all of whom might have known the overwhelming difficulties of the time, so lost to all sense of
public duty.

If such was the public morality of the senatorial class,
the tone of the lower grades of treasury officials was not
likely to be marked by greater probity or a higher sense
of honour.   It would be difficult, without writing a
treatise on the subject, to give an exact idea of the
various devices by which the army of treasury officials,
through all its many grades, contrived to defraud either
the government or the taxpayer, or both together.   It
would seem that persons of the lowest origin were finding
their way into the ranks of the service by surreptitious
means.[5]   They are plainly accused of looking to plunder

[1] *C. Th.* xiii. 7, 2, multi naves
suas diversorum nominibus et titulis
tuentur ; cf. xiii. 5, 26, 37.

[2] Deserta praedia added by the
inspectors to a productive estate
were exempted from the senatorial
land-tax by vi. 2, 13 ; cf. xiii. 11,
8 and 12.   The process of ἐπιβολή
or adaequatio is explained in Godefroy's notes to these laws.   Cf. xiii.
11, 10, and Godefroy's notes on xiii.
11, 16.

[3] *Ib.* xi. 1, 26 ; cf. Salv. v. c. 7 ;
Marquardt, ii. 231.

[4] *C. Th.* xiii. 10, 1 and 8, quoniam
Tabularii per collusionem potenti-
orum sarcinam ad inferiores trans-
ferunt . . . Tabulariis erit flamma
supplicium ; cf. Sym. *Ep.* ix. 10.

[5] *Ib.* vi. 27, 18, ad scholam
Agentum in rebus passim plurimi
velut ad quoddam asylum convolav-
erunt, quos vita culpabiles et origo
habet ignobiles, et ex servili faece
prorupisse demonstrat ; cf. vi. 27,
4 for rules of admission to the service.

for the means of buying themselves advancement to higher places.[1] Their character is painted in the blackest colours.[2] They are threatened with every mode and degree of penalty, heavy fines or wholesale restitution of illicit gains, degradation to plebeian rank, death by the sword, by torture, by the " avenging flames."[3] They are prohibited from seeking any renewal of their term of office,[4] in language which an honest service would have resented as an intolerable insult. Yet no expedient seems to have been of any avail to check the headlong cupidity of the time. The evil, so far as we can judge from the Code, is as rampant in the reign of Majorian[5] as in the reign of Constantine. The allurements or the protection of the great, the collusion of comrades equally bent on plunder, remoteness from the seat of empire, the dumb patience of the rustic folk who could not defend themselves, and whose natural protectors were often in league with their plunderers—all these things produced a sense of impunity which the distant sound of imperial menaces seems to have hardly disturbed for a moment.

The susceptores, who were often taken from the curial class, had many opportunities for fraud and oppression.[6] Their business was chiefly to receive the tribute paid in kind for the support of the troops and government service.[7] Sometimes they did not give receipts at once,[8] or they gave them in invalid form, without the particulars prescribed by law. Sometimes they used false weights and

[1] *C. Th.* vi. 29, 11, qui ex collecta provincialium praeda ad majores militias festinant. (It need hardly be said that *militia* is applied to Palatine service generally.)
[2] Cf. Amm. Marc. xvi. 5, § 11, rapere non accipere sciunt agentes in rebus. See the terms of opprobrium collected in Godefroy, Paratitlon to *C. Th.* viii. tit. 1.
[3] *C. Th.* ix. 27, 1 ; xiii. 10, 8.
[4] *Ib.* ix. 26, 2.

[5] *Nov. Maj.* 1, compulsor nihil amplius a Curiali noverit exigendum quam quod ipse a possessore susceperit . . . omnis concussionum occasio removeatur ; cf. the law of Constantine in 315, *C. Th.* viii. 10, 1.
[6] *v.* Godefroy's Paratitlon to *C. Th.* xii. 6.
[7] Susceptores specierum, *C. Th.* xii. 6, 9.
[8] *Ib.* xii. 6, 27.

measures,[1] so that the unfortunate farmer had to furnish more than his proper quota. Or, again, they would lend themselves to tactics by which the validity of a receipt was disputed, and the payment levied a second time.[2] The accountants of the army stores (numerarii, actuarii) were also audacious offenders. They are plainly charged with falsifying accounts and drawing larger supplies than the corps were entitled to.[3] The actuarii seem to have been a particularly troublesome class, and are ordered away from the capital by a law of Arcadius in 398.[4] But it was at the hands of the various officials charged with the duty of enforcing payment and collecting arrears that the provincials suffered the worst cruelties. There was apparently no possible means of restraining them. Their insolence is described most vividly and punished most fiercely in some of the latest laws in the Code.[5] By demanding receipts which had been lost,[6] by over-exaction,[7] by fraudulent meddling with the lists of the census,[8] by mere terrorism and brute force, they caused such misery and discontent that the Emperor[9] had more than once, at all costs to the revenue, to order their removal from a whole province. Their exactions and super-exactions had reached such a point in 440[10] that Theodosius and Valentinian issued a rescript which gave the governors of provinces the power of punishing them without any fear of the Counts of the treasury. But the effect on the collection of the revenue, and, not least, the

---

[1] *C. Th.* xi. 8, 3.

[2] *Ib.* xii. 6, 26; cf. xii. 1, 185, semel securitatem de refusione munerum emissam ab alio Proconsule non liceat refricari.

[3] *Ib.* viii. 1, 15. In the reign of Constantine their frauds were so enormous that the Emperor threatens them with torture for their offences.

[4] *Ib.* viii. 1, 14.

[5] *Nov. Valent.* 7; *Maj.* 4; *Mart.* 2 (cf. Amm. Marc. xxx. c. 5).

[6] *C. Th.* xi. 26, 2.

[7] *Ib.* xi. 8, 2.

[8] *Ib.* xiii. 11, 4 and 10.

[9] *Ib.* viii. 10, 4, universa compulsorum genera ex Africanis provinciis constituimus pellenda, 412; vi. 29, 11, curiosos praecepimus removeri, 414. This also relates to Africa; cf. the removal of curiosi from Dalmatia.

[10] *Nov. Th.* 45 (1) and (2).

slur on the "illustrious" officers, whose powers were thus curtailed,[1] or whose gains were diminished, compelled the Emperor two years afterwards to rescind the former law.   It is only too evident that the Emperor's zeal for honest administration met with deadening opposition in the highest as well as the lowest ranks of the service. The "defensores"[2] of cities had, as one of their most important duties, to protect the taxpayers from over-exaction.   Yet one can see, from a law of 409,[3] that the protection was often not to be relied upon.   The defrauded provincial is directed, in the first instance, to appeal to the defensor, the curia, and the magistrates.   If they refuse to accept his appeal, he is, as a last resort, in the presence, and with the cognisance, of the public clerks and minor officials, to post up his complaint in the more public places of the municipality.   There surely never was a more startling confession of impotence made by the heads of a great administrative system.

Perhaps even stronger proof of the inability of the government to control its servants is to be found in the enormities of the discussores,[4] as they are described to us in some of the later constitutions.   These officials, whose business it was to discover, and call up, all arrears of tribute, were appointed on a regular system; and, in ordinary times, men were not very willing to undertake a function so invidious.   For the arrears were probably

---

[1] *Nov. Th.* 45 (2), cum pietas nostra . . . censuerat ut illustres viri sacri ac privati aerarii Comites facultatem condemnandorum Judicum non haberent. In i. 7, 5 the provincial governors are ordered to go about and exert themselves to bring to light frauds of tax-collectors.   But the counts of the largesses in 452, on the pretext that the financial service was interfered with, actually succeeded in terrorising the governors.

[2] The powers of the defensor are defined in the law of 392, *C. Th.* i.

11, 2, plebem tantum vel Decuriones ab omni improborum insolentia et temeritate tueantur. Cf. *C. Th.* xii. 6, 23 ; *Nov. Maj.* 5 ; Marquardt, i. 522 ; De Coulanges, *L'Inv. Germ.* p. 39.   De Coulanges takes a different view of the defensor's office from most authorities. Cf. Godefroy's Paratitlon to *C. Th.* i. 11 ; Fauriel, i. 375.

[3] *C. Th.* xi. 8, 3.

[4] See Paratitlon of Godefroy to *C. Th.* xi. tit. 26, and the notes to *Nov. Valent.* 7.

quite as often due by the great proprietors as by the
small.   But in the last years of the Empire men seem to
have thrust themselves into the office without any regular
authority.[1]   Their object, of course, was mere plunder,
and they had endless opportunities of enriching themselves.   Many proprietors were deeply in debt, not only
to private creditors, but to the treasury.   Estates were
frequently changing hands, and, in the confusion of a
time of invasion and panic, documents would be lost or
purchases would be made without full knowledge of the
liabilities of the vendor.   The discussor, who had obtained his office by intrigue,[2] came down with a powerful
retinue, obtained doubtless in the same way, demanding
old receipts,[3] presenting a mass of cooked accounts,
which no one could check, least of all the simple farmer.
What followed, as described by the Emperor,[4] resembles
the worst scenes in Turkish provincial government, outrage, torture, imprisonment, murder; and all these
enormities were countenanced, and actively supported, by
officers of the palace and the praetorium, with the aid of
the soldiers of the neighbouring garrison.[5]   Who can
wonder that people exposed to such brutality, in the
name of civilised government, should welcome the rude
justice of the Gothic chief ? [6]

Yet it would be unhistorical and unfair to hold the
imperial government responsible for all these horrors.
Almost every page of the Code bears witness to the
indignant energy with which the Emperor and his Council
strove to check the anarchy of the provincial administra-

---

[1] The discussores of the reign of
Honorius were quite as corrupt, *C.
Th.* xi. 26, 2.

[2] *Nov. Valent.* 7, discussores ad
provinciam non electi, sicut com-
perimus, sed ambientes ire dicuntur, etc.

[3] *Ib.* 7, securitates expetunt
annorum serie et vetustate con-
sumptas, quas servare nescit sim-

plicitas et fiducia nihil debentis.

[4] *Ib.* 7, innumerae deinde caedes,
saeva custodia, suspendiorum crude-
litas et universa tormenta, etc.

[5] *Ib.* 7, collega furtorum Pala-
tinus hortatur, instat apparitio
turbulenta, urget immitis executio
militaris.

[6] Salv. *de Gub. Dei,* v. 36, 37,
c. 8.

tion. But, with a high sense of duty and the appearance of omnipotence, the central authority had lost control of the vast system. The government was growing weaker as the power of the aristocracy increased, and, as we have already seen, the power of the aristocracy was being actually exerted to hamper and defeat the imperial administration. The same paralysis is seen in each prefecture and in each province. For generations there had been many governors slow or negligent in executing the will of the Emperor. Repeated edicts and a rising scale of penalties are a sufficient proof of this. But the prefect or the governor himself, however earnest and determined, was liable to be thwarted by his subordinates or by the intrigues of the Potentes. There are few traces in the fifth century of the grosser forms of corruption or oppression among the higher officials, but there are many proofs of their failure to carry out the intentions of the Emperor. This was no doubt sometimes due to want of a high sense of duty, or of energy, or to illegitimate influence brought to bear upon them. But probably the most potent cause was the contumacy of the lower members of the service, who had their own ends to gain in maintaining abuses. It is certainly significant that in so many laws, while the governor is to be fined for disobedience, his staff are laid under far heavier penalties,[1] some of them of a kind which we should describe as savage.

The last edict which deals with the miseries inflicted by the tax-gatherer sums up, as it were, the imperial legislation on this subject for generations, and in its candid pessimism sounds the death-knell of provincial administration in the West. Its author was the last prince of high purpose and capacity who addressed him-

[1] *Nov. Maj.* 6, ut Judex qui hoc fieri statuerit 20 librarum auri illatione feriatur, apparitores vero . . . fustuario supplicio subditos, manuum quoque amissione truncandos.

self to the hopeless task of reforming a vast service which was honeycombed with corruption. The last Roman Emperor of the West from whom, as statesman or soldier, great things were expected,[1] was foiled in his efforts, both in war and statecraft. And he found his own nobles and civil servants as dangerous enemies of the state as the Vandals. Any one who wishes, at first hand, to know the secret of the disease which was undermining the strength of the imperial system in the West, should read the law of Majorian issued in 458.[2] The fortunes of the provincials are still being eaten away by extortionate and repeated exactions. The municipalities are being deserted by the citizens who have to bear their burdens, but who prefer to abandon everything rather than endure the ingenious chicanery or truculent cruelty of the officers of the treasury. While the smaller proprietors are being bled to death, the agents of the great landowner, in the security of a remote estate, placidly ignore the demands of the collector. The provincial governors seem personally not to be distrusted by the Emperor; indeed they are charged with the task of reforming the fiscal system of their districts. But even they are apt to be misled or cajoled by their subordinate officers, who possess a minute knowledge of the localities, and whose audacity is stimulated by the prospect of enormous gains and the experience of long impunity.

The picture of his times left by Majorian is infinitely sad, and yet, as we said at the beginning of this chapter, it is impossible to ignore the high sense of duty, and the almost effusive sympathy for the suffering masses, which mark the last utterances of the imperial jurisprudence. Just as paganism on the eve of its proscription by the State attained for a moment an elevation and purity higher than it ever reached in the ages of its unchallenged supremacy, so the imperial government was probably never

---

[1] Apoll. Sidon. *Carm.* v. 585.   [2] *Nov. Maj.* tit. i.

so anxious to check abuses of administration, or so com-
passionate for the desolate and the suffering, as in the years
when its forces were being paralysed. It is easy for the
cool economist to criticise some of these measures of alle-
viation as more characterised by sympathy than statesmanship. It has been said that the indulgence to debtors
to the imperial treasury, which was so often granted,
merely threw a heavier load on those taxpayers who
were still able to meet their obligations.[1] But in one
of the later constitutions it is expressly stated that, if
the treasury insisted in all cases on its full rights, it
would ruin the taxpayer, without benefiting the State.[2]
Between 395 and 423, Honorius remitted the taxes over
wide districts in ten different edicts.[3] Similar measures
of the most sweeping character are to be found among
the enactments of later reigns.[4] But in most of these
cases, it is not difficult to find a justification for the
remission in the public calamities, or the cruel super-
exactions of the agents of the fisc. Nor did the Emperor
spare the private creditor in emergencies, any more than
his own exchequer. In 443, so desperate had the
condition of Africa become, that the government felt it
necessary to suspend for a time the right of recovery for
private debts.[5]

In a number of minor measures scattered over the
Code the growing spirit of humanity may be observed.
The governors of provinces are called upon to exercise
the utmost vigilance to check the oppression of the poor
by the agents of the great, and to bring to light the mis-

[1] F. de Coulanges, *L'Inv. Germ.*
p. 59.
[2] *Nov. Th.* 51, si a possessore super
alia, quae praestat has expensas,
requirat, ultimas tenuesque ejus
vires compulsio talis extinguet.
[3] *C. Th.* xi. 28, 2 *sqq.*
[4] *Nov. Th.* 22. The Albinus to
whom this was addressed was probably grandson of the Albinus of
the *Saturnalia.* Cf. Seeck, *Sym.*

clxxix. He was a son of Volusianus
who corresponded with S. Augustine,
and succeeded Rutilius Namatianus
as prefect of the city, Rutil. Namat.
i. 466. He was P.P. of Gaul in
440; P.P. of Italy, 443-448; consul,
444; patrician, 446. The Novellae
seem to show him the great statesman of the time, *Nov. Valent.* 1,
2, 4, 5; *Nov. Th.* 22, 23, 35, 50.
[5] *Nov. Th.* 22.

deeds of the tax-gatherer.[1] It is their duty, along with
the bishops, to visit prisons on the Lord's Day, to receive
any complaints from the prisoners as to their treatment,
and to see that they are sufficiently supplied with food.[2]
Stringent enactments require that persons charged with
crime shall be brought up for trial within a year, and that
prisoners shall not be subjected to unnecessary harshness.[3] By a strict term of prescription, the law strove
to restrain that noxious class who made a trade of
assailing titles to property,[4] or the status of persons who
had succeeded in escaping from a servile or dependent
condition. The evidence of the freedman against his
patron was discredited,[5] and also that of the accused
person who, while confessing his own guilt, attempted
to incriminate another. There are three or four other
measures to which we may refer, as illustrative at once
of the misery of the times, and the humanitarian spirit
of the central government. In the terror caused by the
movements of the Goths at the beginning of the fifth
century many persons, particularly in the province of
Illyricum, had fled to districts which offered greater
security. Some had been carried into captivity and
been redeemed. In many cases they had come under
obligations which were sometimes enforced in a hard
and selfish spirit. Where the fugitive owes nothing but
the gift of food and clothing from his host, the Emperor
dismisses the claim for compensation.[6] But where he
has been bought back from the hands of the enemy, his
redemptor, whose motive was sometimes that of acquiring
a useful serf, is ordered to be content with the repayment
of the ransom, or, as an alternative, with five years'
service. In those same calamitous years there was a

[1] *C. Th.* i. 7. 5, 7.
[2] *Ib.* ix. 3, 7.
[3] *Ib.* ix. 36, 1 and 2; cf. ix. 3,
1, *sqq.*
[4] *Nov. Valent.* 8; cf. Godefroy's

elaborate Commentary on *C. Th.*
iv. tit. 14.
[5] *C. Th.* iv. 11, 2; ix. 1, 19;
ix. 6, 4.
[6] *Ib.* v. 5, 2; *v.* Godefroy's Com.

great famine in Italy, and it appears probable that some masters were tempted to limit the number of mouths on their estates by exposing the infants of their female slaves. The exposed child was sometimes found and treated with kindly human feeling; and the legislator interposed to prevent the cruel master from reclaiming to servitude the creature whom he had consigned to death.[1] The flight of serfs from one estate to another was evidently very common. The law of 419 fixes the limit of thirty years, after which the fugitive colonus, who had found another master, and had probably formed family ties, could not be recalled to the servitude from which he had fled.[2] In the case of a female serf, the limit is twenty years. And if, before that term, she has married, in order to prevent the break-up of a home the law enacts that her second master shall provide a *vicaria*, presumably unmarried, who shall satisfy the claim of her former lord.

These are a few examples of the efforts of government to alleviate that mass of misery and social injustice which it was impotent to cure. To a sympathetic mind, there is no more painful reading than the Theodosian Code of the fifth century. The authors of these laws are generally loaded with the double opprobrium of weakness and corruption. *Les malheureux ont toujours tort.* The system of bureaucratic despotism, elaborated finally by Diocletian and Constantine, produced a tragedy in the truest sense, such as history has seldom exhibited; in which, by an inexorable fate, the claims of fancied omnipotence ended in a humiliating paralysis of administration; in which determined effort to remedy social evils only aggravated them till they became unendurable; in which the best intentions of the central power were, generation after generation, mocked and defeated alike by irresistible laws of human nature, and by hopeless perfidy and corruption in the servants of government.

[1] *C. Th.* v. 7, 2. On the famine cf. Zos. vi. 11, Olympiod. § 4, Sozom. ix. 8.   [2] *C. Th.* v. 10.

BOOK IV

THE BARBARIANS AND THE FUTURE
OF THE EMPIRE

CHAPTER I

THE GENERAL CHARACTER OF THE INVASIONS

No part of the inner life of the fifth century should, in the mind of an intelligent student, excite greater curiosity than the attitude of the Romans of the West to the invaders, and their ideas as to the future of Rome. As he reads the meagre chronicles of the times, he can hardly help asking himself, What did these men think about the real meaning of the sack of Rome by Alaric and by Genseric; of the devastation of the provinces; of the settlement of Visigoths, Burgundians, Sueves, and Vandals in regions which, in spite of temporary incursions, had for centuries enjoyed the Roman peace? Was the end indeed come, the end of so much effort, of so many glories, of that great history of civil and military virtue which had given uniform law and culture to the realms of Alexander as well as to the countries bordering on the inland and the western seas? Or, were the calamities of the time, crushing and calamitous as they were to individual citizens, only temporary and limited in their range, such as the Empire had often before suffered, without serious and lasting effects on the general organisation of society? And as to the causes of the calamity, were they the decline of Roman virtue and skill in statecraft, or were they the anger of the old gods of Rome for the desertion of their altars, or the punishments sent by the Christian's God for luxury and

oppression of the weak ?   Finally, what was to be the
relation of the Empire, if it was to continue, to these
strange immigrants into her territory, and how were they
going to behave to the power which had so long kept
them at bay ?

We propose to collect, from the literary remains of
the period, various answers to these questions.   But
before doing so, there are some general considerations as
to the character of the invasions of the barbarians in the
fifth century, and their settlement in the provinces, which
it will be well to bear in mind in the review which
we propose to make.   The modern, who has only the
popular conception of the events of that time, is apt to
think that the Western Empire succumbed to an over-
powering advance of whole tribes and peoples, animated
by hatred of Rome, sweeping away the remains of an
effete civilisation, and replacing it, in a sudden and
cataclysmal change, by a spirit and by institutions of a
perfectly different order.   Yet, if such were a true
account of the fall of the Roman Empire, the tone and
behaviour of many of the Romans of that time would be
inexplicable.   Here and there there are cries of horror
at the havoc and slaughter which were caused by
some violent incursion.   And, undoubtedly, the capture
of the city gave for the moment a terrible shock
to the ancient faith in the strength and stability of
Rome.   But this was only a transitory feeling.   Confidence soon returned.   The cities and regions, which
are said to have been desolated and ravaged, reappear
with apparently few traces of any catastrophe.   The
government betrays no sign of confusion or despair.
Individual observers may have their doubts and questionings about the course of events, but few seem absolutely
dismayed, and some display a confidence and hopefulness
which would be quite astonishing, if the old popular
conception of the barbarian onslaughts were the true one.

A very cursory glance at the history of the Empire reveals the secret of this *insouciance*. The invasions of the fifth century were nothing new, nor was there anything very startling in the settlement of Germans on Roman soil. From the times of Marius not a century had passed without some violent inroad of German hosts. The myriads annihilated on the field of Aquae Sextiae were but the advance guard of a mighty movement, which was always pressing on to the West or South. Julius, Augustus, Tiberius, had all to throw back successive attacks on the frontier of the Rhine. Marcus Aurelius spent eight campaigns in a struggle with a vast confederacy on the Danube.[1] In the third century almost every province, and even Italy itself, was ravaged, and the Goths,[2] a comparatively new horde, who had worked their way from Scandinavia to the Ukraine, swept the Euxine in thousands of vessels,[3] and harried the towns of Asia Minor and Greece. In the reign of Probus, the Germans captured and pillaged sixty towns in Gaul, and overran the whole province.[4] Another formidable irruption took place in the middle of the fourth century. Enormous numbers of Franks, Alemanni, and Saxons passed the Rhine. A great part of Gaul was overrun, and forty towns along the Rhine were sacked.[5] Once more the invaders were driven back with enormous loss.

The invasions of the third and fourth centuries, in respect of the numbers and impetuosity of the assailants, seem to us now to have been almost overwhelming. The Gothic host of the reign of Claudius is said to have

[1] Jul. Capitol. *vit. M. Anton.* c. 22, gentes omnes ab Illyrici limite usque in Galliam conspiraverant.

[2] Treb. Poll. *vit. Gallien.* c. 6, 13 ; *vit. Claud.* c. 6 ; Zos. i. 30, 31. Cf. Pallmann, *die Gesch. der Völkerwand.* i. pp. 49 *sqq.*; Jordan. *Get.* 17.

[3] Zos. i. 42, ναυπηγησάμενοι πλοῖα ἑξακισχίλια καὶ τούτοις ἐμβιβάσαντες δύο καὶ τριάκοντα μυριάδας : *vit. Claud.* c. 6, 8.

[4] Flav. Vop. *Prob.* c. 13, cum per omnes Gallias securi vagarentur.

[5] Zos. iii. 1, 3 ; Amm. Marc. xvi. 12.

numbered 320,000 men. The Germans who spread
over the whole of Gaul in the reign of Probus must
have been even more numerous, if that emperor
slaughtered 400,000 of them, as he is said to have
done.[1] Yet it does not appear that, at crises so appalling, the Romans ever despaired of the safety of the
State. The letter of Probus to the Senate, to which we
have referred, rather expresses an almost exuberant
confidence.[2] The invaders, however numerous, are in-
variably driven back, and in a short time there are few
traces left of their ravages. The truth seems to be that,
however terrible the plundering bands might be to the
unarmed population, yet in a regular battle the Germans
were immensely inferior to the Roman troops. Ammianus,
who had borne a part in many of these engagements, says
that, in spite of the courage of the Germans, their impetuous fury was no match for the steady discipline and
coolness of troops under Roman officers.[3] The result of
this moral superiority, founded on a long tradition, was
that the Roman soldier in the third and fourth centuries
was ready to face almost any odds. In 356 an immense
multitude of the Alemanni inundated Eastern Gaul.[4]
Julian, the future Emperor, who was then a mere youth,
with no previous training in the art of war, was in command of only 13,000 men, of whom few were veteran
troops.[5] Yet in a very short time not an enemy was
left in Gaul, and the victors were carrying the war far
into the heart of Germany.[6] There must undoubtedly

[1] Treb. Poll. *vit. Claud.* c. 8 ;
Flav. Vop. *vit. Prob.* c. 15. But
on the credibility of Vopiscus *v.*
Peter, *Gesch. Litt. über die Röm.
Kaiserzeit*, i. 150 ; and ii. 281 on
the carelessness of historians in
dealing with numbers.

[2] *Vit. Prob.* c. 15, omnes penitus
Galliae liberatae . . . arantur Gal-
licana rura barbaris bubus . . . nos
eorum omnia possidemus.

[3] Amm. Marc. xvi. 12, 47, Alemanni robusti et celsiores, milites
usu nimio dociles ; illi feri et tur-
bidi, hi quieti et cauti.

[4] Zos. iii. 3, πλῆθος ἄπειρον
ἐπεραιώθη βαρβάρων.

[5] Amm. Marc. xvi. 12, 2 ; Zos.
l.c.

[6] Zos. iii. 4, ἄχρι τῶν Ἑρκυνίων
δρυμῶν τοὺς φεύγοντας ὁ Καῖσαρ
ἐπιδιώξας.

have been much loss of life and property in some of these raids.[1] Yet a very few years after the ravages which were checked by Julian, the valley of the Moselle is described to us by Ausonius as a paradise which shows no trace of the hand of the spoiler.[2] Comfortable granges and luxurious villas look down from every height. The vineyards rise in terraces along the banks, and the yellow corn-lands can vie even with the fertility of the poet's native Aquitaine. The population are prosperous and happy. There is even an air of rustic jollity and gaiety over the scene from which all thoughts of past suffering or coming danger seem to be banished.[3]

Of the same character were the great invasions of the opening years of the fifth century. A great army under Radagaisus, which, according to the lowest estimate, numbered 200,000 men, crossed the Alps and penetrated into Etruria.[4] That the government regarded the danger as serious, may be inferred from the edict which called the slaves to arms.[5] Yet Stilicho, with a force of only 30,000 regular troops, and some Hun and Alan auxiliaries,[6] signally defeated that great host, and the prisoners taken were so many that they were sold for a single *aureus* apiece.[7] In the beginning of the year 406 [8] a horde of Alans, Sueves, and Vandals crossed the Rhine, from which the garrisons had been withdrawn to meet the danger in Italy.[9] The invaders caused great consternation, and undoubtedly inflicted much damage and suffering in their passage through Gaul.[10] But the

[1] Zos. iii. 1.
[2] Auson. *Idyl.* x. v. 156. The poem on the Moselle was composed *circ.* 370 ; *v.* Schenkl, Proem. xv.
[3] Auson. *Idyl.* x. v. 165.
[4] Oros. vii. 37, § 13, secundum eos qui parcissime referunt, ducenta milia hominum. Cf. Zos. v. 26 ; Marcell. *Chron.*
[5] *C. Th.* vii. 13, 16.
[6] Zos. v. 26.

[7] Oros. vii. 37, § 16.
[8] Prosp. *Chron.*, Arcadio vi. et Probo Coss. ; Oros. vii. 38 and 40.
[9] Claud. *de Bell. Get.* 421 :
tutumque remotis
excubiis Rhenum solo terrore relinquunt.
[10] *Carm. de Prov. Div.* v. 25, periere tot urbes (v. 34), Vandalicis gladiis sternimur et Geticis . . . ultima pertulimus ; Rutil. Namat. i. 27-30 ; Hieron. *Ep.* 123, § 16.

districts and cities, which they are said to have plundered
and destroyed, within a generation are found to be once
more flourishing and prosperous.[1]

In the fragmentary annals of the fifth century there
is no sign that the generals of the Empire felt any fear
of an overwhelming superiority on the side of the
invaders. In 426 the city of Arles was attacked by
a powerful force of Goths; but they were compelled
by Aetius to retire with heavy loss.[2] Two years later,
the same great general recovered the Rhineland from the
Franks.[3] In 435 he inflicted a crushing defeat on the
Burgundians, and compelled them to sue for peace.[4] In
the following year Litorius, the lieutenant of Aetius, by
a rapid movement, relieved the town of Narbonne, when
it was hard pressed by famine and the Gothic army.
And although Litorius soon afterwards was taken captive
by the hands of the Goths, the annalist expressly says
that it was the result of reckless ambition and superstitious credulity, not of any inferiority of force.[5] The
invasion of Attila in 451 was probably the most
appalling danger, in respect to the numbers of his
motley host, which the Romans had had to face for
ages.[6] Aetius had only a handful of troops under his
command,[7] and although he was able to rally to his
support Visigoths, Franks, Burgundians, and Saxons, yet
the credit of defeating that fierce and crafty power, which
had reduced all central Europe to vassalage, must be
awarded to Roman daring and organisation. In the last
days of the independence of Auvergne and of the Western

[1] This appears to be the case in
Bordeaux, Paulin. Pell. *Euch.* 240 ;
cf. 284. Compare the state of
Rome after the sack by the Vandals,
Apoll. Sid. *Ep.* i. 5.
[2] Prosp. *Chron.* Theodos. xii. and
Valent. Coss.
[3] *Ib.* Felice et Dionysio Coss.
[4] *Ib.* Theod. xv. and Valent. iv.
Coss.

[5] *Ib.* ad. a. 439, ut nisi incon-
sideranter proelians in captivitatem
incidisset, dubitandum foret cui
potius parti victoria ascriberetur.

[6] Apoll. Sid. *Carm.* vii. 320 ; cf.
Prosp. *Chron.* ad a.

[7] Sid. *Carm.* vii. 329, tenue et
rarum sine milite ducens Robur in
auxiliis ; cf. Fauriel, i. p. 226.

Empire, a mere handful of troops under the gallant Ecdicius,[1] and raised by his own resources, kept the Visigothic army for months at bay, and the Roman showed in this final struggle an almost contemptuous recklessness.

The Germans then were not superior to the Romans in military skill and courage. Nor were they animated by any common purpose or hatred of Rome. So far from having any common purpose, they were hopelessly divided among themselves, and are as often found fighting for the Empire as against it. The Franks on the Rhine were champions of Rome when they were overwhelmed by the invaders in 406.[2] Stilichó had Alan and Hun auxiliaries in his great battle with Radagaisus.[3] It was with Hun cavalry that Aetius and Litorius strove to check the advance of the Visigoths in Southern Gaul.[4] It was with the aid of Visigoths, Franks, Saxons, and Burgundians that Aetius defeated the army of Attila on the Catalaunian plains. Again and again the Visigoths of Toulouse lent their forces to support the Roman power in Spain against the Sueves.[5] The Romans of Auvergne, when they were deserted in its weakness by the imperial government, received help and encouragement in their last struggles against Euric from the Burgundians.[6] It is clear from these facts that the Empire was not an object of hatred to the barbarians. Indeed they were often eager to be taken into its service; and many of their chiefs, like Alaric or Ataulphus, had no higher ambition than to be appointed

[1] Sid. *Ep.* iii. 3, taceo deinceps collegisse te privatis viribus publici exercitus speciem, etc.; cf. Greg. Tur. *Hist. Fr.* ii. 24, multitudinem Gotthorum cum decem viris fugasse perscribitur.

[2] Oros. vii. 40, § 3, multaeque cum his aliae (gentes) Francos proterunt. Fauriel, i. 47.

[3] Zos. v. 26.

[4] Prosp. *Chron.* a. 437, 439.

[5] Idat. *Chron.*, mox Hispanias rex Gothorum Theodoricus cum ingenti exercitu, et cum voluntate et ordinatione Aviti Imperatoris ingreditur.

[6] Sid. *Ep.* iii. 4. The help however, was of doubtful value Chaix, *Sid.* ii. 164.

to high military command. On the other hand, there
was a corresponding readiness on the Roman side to
employ barbarian forces in war. From the earliest days
of the Empire these auxiliaries appear on the army lists.
Germans are found in the bodyguard of Augustus.[1]
They fought under Vitellius in the foremost ranks at
the battle of Cremona.[2] Vespasian had special confidence in the loyalty of the Sueves, and had two of their
chiefs in his service.[3] Marcus Aurelius formed some
corps of Germans for his war with their countrymen on
the Danube.[4] In the third century, the tendency
becomes even more marked. Valerian, in a despatch to
Aurelian, describes an army which included troops from
Ituraea, Arabia, and Mesopotamia, and officers bearing
such unmistakable German names as Hariomundus,
Hildomundus, and Haldagates.[5] Claudius II., after the
great defeat which he inflicted on the Goths,[6] enrolled a
large number of them under his standards. Probus
recruited the frontier garrisons with 16,000 from the
wreck of the great host which had devastated Gaul.[7]
The army of Constantine, in the battle of the Milvian
Bridge, was chiefly composed of Germans and Celts and
Britons.[8] Of similar composition was the army with
which Theodosius defeated Eugenius at the Frigidus.[9]

Some of these barbarian troops took service voluntarily
under an express agreement, stating the conditions on
which they served. Others were compelled to join the
standards as the result of defeat in battle.[10] Some of
them received regular pay and rations; others received

[1] Suet. *Octav.* 49.
[2] Tac. *Hist.* i. 61.
[3] *Ib.* iii. 5.
[4] Jul. Capitol. *vit. M. Anton.* c.
21, emit et Germanorum auxilia
contra Germanos.
[5] Flav. Vop. *Aurel.* c. 11.
[6] Zos. i. 46, ὅσοι δὲ διεσώθησαν, ἢ
τάγμασι Ῥωμαίων συνηρίθμησαν κ.τ.λ.
Cf. Treb. Poll. *vit. Claud.* c. 8.

[7] Flav. Vop. *Prob.* c. 14, accepit
praeterea sedecim milia tyronum,
quos omnes per diversas provincias
sparsit, etc.

[8] Zos. ii. 15.

[9] *Ib.* iv. 56.

[10] v. *C. Th.* vii. 13, 16; Godefroy's note on the Foederati and
Dedititii.

grants of land, which were held on condition of military
service, and which passed to their sons on the same condition.[1]   A page of the Notitia contains a list of more
than twenty corps of these military colonists, under the
name Sarmatae Gentiles, who were settled at various
places from Bruttium to the Alps.[2]   Similar German
corps, under the name of Laeti, had lands assigned to
them in almost every part of Gaul.   The Gallo-Roman
population had been long accustomed to the residence of
these bands on their soil.   Batavi are found at Arras ;
Franks at Rennes ; Sueves at Coutances, Mans, Bayeux,
and Auvergne ; Sarmatians at Paris, Poitiers, and
Amiens.[3]   Occasionally the Laeti proved to be dangerous
neighbours.   Thus we learn from Ammianus Marcellinus
that a body of Laeti, in the troubled year 357, attempted
to capture the city of Lyons, and plundered the surrounding country.[4]   Here we have an anticipation in
the fourth century of what happened more frequently in
the fifth, when Burgundians and Visigoths had obtained
a permanent settlement in Gaul.

We shall see, in a subsequent chapter, that the
establishment of the Germans in the south and east of
Gaul disturbed and alarmed the Romans of the province
far less than we should have expected.   In a short time
the intruders were accepted as more or less friendly
neighbours.   Here again the past history of the Empire
will be found to have prepared men's minds for what,
taken by themselves, would have seemed stupendous
changes.   Just as there were countless incursions for

---

[1] *C. Th.* vii. 20, 12, with Godefroy's note ; xiii. 11, 9 ; Amm. Marc.
xx. 8, 13 ; *Paneg. Constant.* c. 21 ;
Zos. ii. 54.

[2] *Notit. Dig.* ed. Böcking, p.
121 (c. xl.).   Cf. the grants of
terrae limitaneae made to veterans
and their sons on military tenure,
Lamprid. *Alex. Sev.* c. 58, § 4 ;

Flav. Vop. *Prob.* c. 14 ; *C. Th.* vii.
15, 1.

[3] *Notit. Dig.* pp. 119, 120 ; cf.
notes, pp. 1044-1080.   On the Gentiles, not to be confounded with
Laeti, *v.* pp. 1080 *sqq.* ; cf. Eum.
Paneg. Const. c. 21 ; Amm. Marc.
xvi. 11, 4 ; Zos. ii. 54 ; F. de
Coulanges, *L'Inv. Germ.* p. 389.

[4] Amm. Marc. xvi. 11, 4.

plunder before the Sueve and Vandal irruption of 406, so there were many cases of barbarians seeking and obtaining a peaceful settlement within the frontier before the Visigoths settled on the Garonne, and the Burgundians on the Upper Rhine and the Rhone.   Augustus, on receiving the submission of the Ubii and Sicambri, assigned them lands on the left bank of the Rhine.[1] Tiberius transported 40,000 Germans into the same region.[2]   The Germans seem to have been seldom unwilling to enter the circle of the pax Romana.   For instance the Batavians, driven from their own country by civil war, crossed the frontier and settled down as subjects of Rome, and for ages the Batavian cavalry had a brilliant reputation in the Roman army.[3]   In the third century Probus is said to have Germanised the provinces.[4]   He gave a settlement in Thrace to 100,000 Bastarnae, who, we are told, proved themselves loyal subjects of the Empire.   A similar experiment, in the case of the Vandals and Gepidae, seems to have been less successful.   A body of Franks, who had obtained from the Emperor a settlement somewhere in the eastern Mediterranean, proved even less worthy of his generosity.[5] They got a fleet together, spread havoc and confusion through the whole of Greece, wrought great slaughter in an attack on Syracuse, and finally, having been repelled from the walls of Carthage, returned to their home.   The Salian Franks, who had been driven from their old seats and had occupied the region between the Scheldt and the Meuse, were, after some hard fighting, recognised as Roman subjects by Julian.[6]   The most striking example of the eagerness of the Germans to be received on Roman territory was the famous petition of the Goths to the

---

[1] Sueton. *Oct.* c. 21.

[2] Ib. *Tib.* c. 9.

[3] Tac. *Hist.* i. 59, iv. 12; *Ann.* ii. 8; Amm. Marc. xvi. 12, 45.

[4] Duruy, *Hist. Rom.* vi. p. 513; Flav. Vop. *Prob.* c. 15 ; Zos. i. 71.

[5] Zos. i. 71.

[6] Amm. Marc. xvii. 8, 3.

Emperor Valens in 376,[1] to be allowed to place the broad waters of the Danube between them and the terrible Huns, who were then advancing from the East.[2] Probably a million of men, women, and children were transported across the swollen river. They came not as conquerors, but as suppliants for food and shelter, under the protection of Rome. No reader of Gibbon needs to be told the tragic tale of what followed that great migration. It was a turning-point in history.

Among the Gothic chiefs who are seen in the pages of Ammianus Marcellinus making a last stand against the Huns was one named Munderich.[3] Some years afterwards this chief is found in the position of duke on the frontiers of Arabia. Munderich is only one of many of his race who rose under the Empire to high military command and office. This was a necessary result of the policy which, from the time of Gallienus, practically excluded the senatorial order from military service. We have seen German officers commanding corps under Valerian in the third century.[4] Magnentius, who rose to be Emperor on the murder of Constans, was of barbarian origin, and had once belonged to a corps of Laeti in Gaul.[5] Arbogastes, who raised Eugenius to the throne, was a Frank,[6] who, by military ability and commanding power,[7] obtained the post of master of the forces under Valentinian. Theodosius cultivated the intimacy of many of these barbarian chiefs,[8] and one of his principal lieutenants, Modares,[9] who rose to be magister militum, was of Scythian descent. Another barbarian officer, who bore a great part in the events of that period, was

[1] Amm. Marc. xxxi. 3.

[2] Zos. iv. 20; Eunap. § 42, p. 31 (Müll. *Frag. Hist.* iv.); Gibbon, c. 26.

[3] Amm. Marc. xxxi. 3, 5.

[4] Flav. Vop. *Aurel.* c. 11.

[5] Zos. ii. 42 ; ii. 54.

[6] *Ib.* iv. 33.

[7] *Ib.* iv. 53.

[8] *Ib.* iv. 56, ἅμα τῷ παραλαβεῖν τὴν βασιλείαν Θεοδόσιος βαρβάρους τινὰς εἰς φιλίαν καὶ ὁμαιχμίαν ἐδέξατο, καὶ ἐλπίσιν αὐτοὺς καὶ δωρεαῖς ἄλλαις τιμήσας, εἶχε δὲ καὶ ἐν θεραπείᾳ πάσῃ καὶ τοὺς ἑκάστης φυλῆς ἡγουμένους καὶ τραπέζης ἠξίου κοινῆς.

[9] Zos. iv. 25.

Richomer.[1] His career, of which we possess full details,
is a good illustration of the great position which men of
his nationality could attain under the later emperors.
Richomer was a Frank of high birth, and first appears as
count of the domestics in the reign of Gratian. He was
sent into Thrace during the troubles with the Goths to
support the Emperor Valens, and shortly afterwards was
raised to the post of magister militum. After a period
of service in the East, during which he formed a close
friendship with Libanius, he was employed by Theodosius
in high command in the campaign against Maximus.
He had great influence in the imperial counsels, and
lived on terms of intimacy with Symmachus and his
circle. Another Frank chief, Bauto,[2] the father of the
Empress Eudoxia, is said to have wielded an almost regal
power under the younger Valentinian, and his elevation
to the consulship in the same year with the Emperor
Arcadius was celebrated in a panegyric by S. Augustine.[3]
We have taken a few of the more striking examples of
the rise of barbarians to commanding positions. Other
names, such as Fravitta, Gainas, Merobaudes, Stilicho,
will occur readily to any person moderately well read in
the history of the Lower Empire. How many more may
have disguised their nationality under Roman names no
one can tell.[4] But German chiefs not only obtained the
great military commands, they also rose to the consulship,
the highest civil honour which the Emperor had to
bestow. Dagelaephus[5] and Merobaudes[6] were colleagues
of Gratian in this great office. In the reign of Theo-

[1] Amm. Marc. xxxi. 7, 4 ; Zos.
iv. 54, 55 ; cf. Seeck's *Sym.* cxxxv. ;
Godefroy's note to *C. Th.* vii. 1,
13 ; Rauschen, *Jahrbücher*, pp. 18,
22, 172.

[2] Zos. iv. 33, 53 ; Ambros. *Ep.*
i. 24. The question of his religion
depends on the use of the singular
participle *inserviens* in Ambros. *Ep.*
i. 57, 3 ; cf. Seeck, *Sym.* cxli. ;

Rauschen, pp. 59, 65, 203.

[3] *Conf.* vi. 6.

[4] Like Julius Florus and Julius
Sacrovir (the latter only partially),
Tac. *Ann.* iii. 40, and Julius (or
Claudius, *Hist.* iv. 13), Civilis, a
Batavian, Tac. *Hist.* i. 59.

[5] Amm. Marc. xxvi. 9, 1, a. 366.

[6] a. 377. Cf. Rauschen, *Jahr-
büch*, pp. 147, 271.

dosius, Merobaudes, Richomer, and Bauto were consuls
in successive years, and at least five more German names
appear in the reigns of the last emperors of the West.
When an office, which the Emperor himself was proud to
hold, was given so freely to men of barbarian origin, it is
plain that the old exclusiveness had disappeared, and
that the Germans had stolen their way into the very
citadel of the Empire long before its distant outworks
were stormed.[1]

Many of these German officers were men of brilliant
talents, fascinating address, and noble bearing. To
military skill they often added the charm of Roman
culture and a social tact which gave them admission even
to the inner circle of the Roman aristocracy. Symmachus
writes to Richomer as to one of his most valued friends.
He extols his many virtues, and has only one grudge
against him, that he cannot help monopolising all
that is best in Roman society.[2] The friendship of Bauto
Symmachus regards as one of his treasures.[3] Men like
these, great soldiers, and polished men of the world, must
naturally have had great social influence. And, indeed,
there are signs that even in smaller things, such as toilet
and dress, Germans, at the beginning of the fifth century,
were setting the fashion. Three edicts of Honorius,
between 397 and 416, forbid the wearing of trousers,
long hair, and fur coats of the barbarian style within the
precincts of the city.[4] The tone of the law of 416 leaves
no doubt that the rage for German fashions was widespread, and that the previous edicts had been disregarded.

In yet another capacity crowds of Germans had been
introduced into Roman territory. Synesius, bishop of
Cyrene, towards the close of the fourth century complains
that every wealthy household is full of Gothic or Scythian

---

[1] Rutil. Namat. ii. 50.
[2] *Ep.* iii. 58, ad te migravit quid-
quid Romae optimum fuit.

[3] *Ib.* iv. 15, 16.
[4] *C. Th.* xiv. 2, 3, 4; cf. Claud.
in *Ruf.* ii. 78; Rutil. Namat. ii. 49.

slaves, serving as stewards, butlers, bakers, and personal
attendants of every grade.   We know also that from the
first century enormous numbers of Germans were planted
as coloni on estates over all the provinces.   Crowds of
Marcomanni were so distributed throughout Italy by
Marcus Aurelius.[1] The great emperors of the third
century took untold numbers of prisoners,[2] and flooded
the country districts with new tillers of the soil.[3]   In the
words of Probus, the barbarians were ploughing and sowing
for Roman masters.[4] The victories of Julian, Gratian,
Theodosius, and Stilicho, all gained within a period of
fifty years, recruited still further the ranks of rural labour.[5]

It appears then that there was nothing new in the
hostile raids or peaceful settlement of the barbarians on
Roman territory in the fifth century.   For more than
five hundred years the Empire had been resisting the
pressure of barbarism, occasionally suffering heavily for a
time, but always in the end triumphant over mere force.
Yet each successive victory had admitted in increasing
numbers the barbarian element into the frontier posts,
the armies, or the fields and households of Rome.   The
highest military commands had for generations been held
by German soldiers of fortune, who served the State
loyally even against their kinsmen.   A Roman, who had
in his youth seen the Alemanni driven across the Rhine,
and thousands of Germans serving under the eagles in
Italy, who had found in Richomer, Bauto, or Stilicho his
most charming and distinguished friends, and had seen
Frank masters of the cavalry sharing the honours of the
consulship with the Emperor, might, even after the scenes
of 410, have smiled at the suggestion that the Empire
was in any serious danger from the Germans.

---

[1] Jul. Capitol. c. 22, accepitque
in deditionem Marcomannos, plurimis in Italiam traductis.

[2] Treb. Poll. *vit. Claud.* c. 8, § 6.

[3] *Ib.* c. 9, § 4, impletae barbaris

servis . . . Romanae provinciae
etc.

[4] Flav. Vop. *Prob.* c. 15.

[5] Oros. vii. 37, 16.

Nor were the invasions of the first decade of the fifth century of such a uniform and sweeping character as to suggest, even to those who witnessed and suffered from them, a single overwhelming movement, animated by one spirit and advancing to one end. The numbers of the invaders do not appear to have approached the mighty hosts who were defeated by Claudius and Probus in the third century.[1] The forces of Ataulphus may have hardly exceeded 20,000 or 30,000 men.[2] The Burgundian invaders of Gaul were reckoned at 80,000.[3] The entire Vandal horde, young and old, slaves and free, only amounted to the same number.[4] The Frank warriors, under Clovis, did not number more than 6000 men.[5] Moreover, as was pointed out long ago by a great authority, the so-called invasions were events essentially partial, local, temporary.[6] We may add that there was a great variety in their purpose and character. Sometimes a band of no great numbers, bent wholly on plunder,[7] will come down on a countryside and carry off the cattle and peasants from the fields, or effect a stealthy entrance into an unguarded town.[8] Sometimes in greater masses, swelling perhaps to tens of thousands, they will sweep across a whole province, capturing cities, and plundering and burning the farms and country houses. Or, again, in the form of a regular army, claiming to be federated soldiers of the Empire, they will quarter themselves on a province, and draw from its revenues the rations and pay which were assigned to the regular soldiers of Rome. Or, once more, they come with the

[1] Treb. Poll. *Claud.* c. 6; Flav. Vop. *Prob.* c. 15, quadringenta milia hostium caesa sunt.
[2] De Coulanges, *L'Inv. Germ.* p. 437.
[3] Oros. vii. 32, § 11; Fauriel, i. 120, thinks this much exaggerated.
[4] Vict. Vitens. i., qui reperti sunt senes, juvenes, parvuli, servi vel domini, octoginta millia numerati.
[5] Cf. Fauriel, ii. 30.
[6] Guizot, *Civ. en France*, i. 237.
[7] Eugipp. *vit. S. Sev.* c. iv.
[8] *Ib.* c. xxiv. qua nocte Heruli insperate protinus inruentes.

express permission and sanction of the Emperor, as permanent settlers on Roman soil,[1] the chief deeming himself, at first, a military official of the Roman government, and, as the Roman administration falls to pieces, taking into his hands also the control of the civil power, collecting the taxes, dealing out justice, appointing officials,[2] combining, in fact, the offices of prefect and master of the military forces. To all these varieties of relation with Rome must be added the widest differences of religious belief among the invaders. Some, like the Franks, the Saxons, or the Huns, on their first appearance, were still pagan.[3] A number of tribes, such as the Vandals, the Burgundians, the Visigoths, or the Rugi, were Arians;[4] and among these there were various degrees of bigotry, some, like the Burgundians,[5] being comparatively tolerant, while others were inspired with a determined hostility to the Catholic faith.[6] There is another, and perhaps more important, difference to be observed. Some of the invading tribes had only recently come into contact with Roman civilisation. They had perhaps received Roman envoys, and they knew well by report the peace and prosperity which the provinces enjoyed under the Roman sway. But they were untouched by its discipline and tone. Others there were whom the culture of the South had already more than

---

[1] Oros. vii. 43, § 3; Prosp. *Chron.* a. 419, Constantius pacem firmat cum Wallia, data ei ad habitandum secunda Aquitania; Idat. *Chron.* a. 419, per Constantium ad Gallias revocati sedes in Aquitanica . . . acceperunt.

[2] Sid. *Ep.* v. 6, where the Burgundian Chilperic is described as magister militum; Greg. Tur. *H. Fr.* ii. 20, Eurichus autem Gotthorum rex Victorium ducem super septem civitates praeposuit. Cf. Sid. *Ep.* vii. 17.

[3] Salv. *de Gub. Dei*, iv. 67, 81.

[4] Eugipp. *vit. S. Sev.* c. iv. *ad fin.*

[5] Oros. vii. 32 (in 418) speaks of the Burgundians as bound to the Romans in the Catholic faith. And Bishop Patiens is said to be in favour with Chilperic and his queen, Sid. *Ep.* vi. 12, § 3. But in the time of Avitus it is clear that members of the royal family were Arian (*v.* Ampère, *Hist. Lit.* ii. 202), and the people were probably divided. Greg. Tur. ii. 32 describes the people as Arian.

[6] Vict. Vitens. i. 5, 17.

half converted into Romans. Their chiefs may have
held high command under the emperors, and been in
friendly intercourse with the leaders of the Roman
nobility. Many of the rank and file had fought under
the eagles, and had acquired to some extent the discipline
and habits of the Roman army. In their moral and
physical characteristics also the tribes or bands, known
under the names of Goths, Alans, Vandals, or Alemanni,
were, according to Roman writers of this period, widely
different. Salvianus[1] tells us that the Vandals were the
weakest and least formidable race; the Goths chaste but
faithless; the Alans were less treacherous, but licentious
and rapacious; the Burgundians were of a mild and
gentle disposition, and inclined to be on friendly terms
with the Romans in the territories which they occupied.
The Saxons, the Franks, and the Heruli retained their
heathen superstitions, offered human sacrifices, and their
raids were marked by acts of fierce and wanton cruelty,
especially towards the Christian clergy and the inmates
of monastic houses.[2] In the picture of Noricum in the
life of S. Severinus, we may observe nearly all these
various types in close juxtaposition and startling contrast,
from the Christian and half-civilised Ostrogoth, cantoned
in Pannonia, in federal relations with the Empire, to the
fierce pagan Herulian. One of these tribes is on the
point of moving on to seek a permanent home on Italian
soil.[3] The Rugi, whose chief has come under the
magnetic spell of a monk of extraordinary saintliness and
heroic energy,[4] are curbed for a time, and seem to abate
somewhat of their old taste for rapine and violence, and
even to offer a fitful protection to the harassed pro-

[1] *De Gub. Dei*, vii. 64 ; cf. iv. 67.

[2] Eugipp. *vit. S. Sev.* c. xxiv.,
Heruli . . . plurimos duxere cap-
tivos, presbyterum patibulo sus-
pendentes ; *Carm. de Prov. Div.*
45 ; Hieron. *Ep.* 123, § 16.

[3] Jordan. *Get.* lvii.; cf. Pallmann,

Gesch. der Völkerwand. ii. 419.

[4] Eugipp. *vit. S. Sev.* c. v., where
Flaccitheus, the Rugian king, con-
sults Severinus about his fears of
the Goths, then in Pannonia ; cf.
Pallmann's scepticism about the
Life, ii. 390.

vincials.[1]   But the province was constantly overrun by
other bands under various names,[2] Alemanni, Heruli,
Thoringi, scouring the country in search of plunder, and
seizing their prey more often by stratagem and surprise
than by open force.   Here one sees, as it were in minia-
ture, and on a confined scene, many of those varieties of
tribal character, and many of those different impulses and
modes of attack, which may be observed in the wider
field of the whole Western world.

It follows from these considerations that the period
of the invasions presents a mass of complex phenomena,
to which no single comprehensive formula will apply.
We may expect also to find a great variety of feeling
and opinion among contemporary observers as to the
character of the invasions, the fate of the Empire, and
its future relations to the barbarian intruders.   The man
who has lost everything in the sack of his town, and
whose relatives have been carried into slavery by the
raiders, will take a very different view of the invasion
from the great noble, the walls of whose castle protect
him from wandering bands, and who lives on good terms
with the neighbouring chief.   The Churchman, in whom
Roman pride and patriotism have been weakened by
enthusiastic devotion to the ascetic ideal, will not enter-
tain the faith in the mission and destiny of imperial
Rome which is an ineradicable instinct of the noble,
saturated with the historic spirit of that great organisation, and still pagan in sentiment, if not in outward
profession.   We shall now make an attempt to ascertain
the feelings of some of those who witnessed the great
calamities and changes of that time.

---

[1] Eugipp. *vit. S. Sev.* xxii. xxxi. Feletheus promises to protect the
Romans against the raids of the Alemanni and Thoringi.
[2] *Ib.* xxiv. iv. ix. xi. xix.

CHAPTER II

ROMAN FEELING ABOUT THE INVASIONS AND THE
FUTURE OF THE EMPIRE

In the early years of the fifth century the rumours of
the movements of Alaric and Radagaisus created the
liveliest alarm in Italy. Even in the noble poem in
which Claudian celebrates the triumph of Stilicho, full
as it is of the poet's faith in Rome, we seem to feel the
thrill of terror which unnerved all but the bravest in
the previous year. The repair of the walls of the city
by Stilicho,[1] commemorated in inscriptions which are
extant, was the signal for an outbreak of superstitious
terror which carries us back to the early days of the
Republic. All the old omens which portended disaster
were reported [2]—dreams, eclipses, causeless conflagra-
tions, showers of stones, a comet shooting from the
eastern heavens to the quarter from which the Gothic
hordes had issued. Such was the terror that doubts
even arose whether Rome had not reached her fated
term. The augural explanation of the twelve vultures
which Romulus had seen at her foundation [3] was recalled,
and the fears of many blinded them to the fact that, of
the twelve centuries prefigured by the birds, the last had
only half run its course.[4] Many of the wealthy class

---

[1] *C.I.L.* vi. 1188-1190. Stilicho's
name is erased from the Inscr.
1190.

[2] Claud. *de Bell. Get.* 227 *sqq.*

[3] Liv. i. 7.
[4] Claud. *de Bell. Get.* 265 :
tunc reputant annos, interceptoque volatu
vulturis, incidunt properatis saecula
metis.

sought places of security, in Corsica, Sardinia, and the islands off the Etruscan coast.[1] Nay, if Claudian may be believed,[2] there were even thoughts of removing the seat of government from Italy to Gaul. Many an edict of these years [3] confirms the testimony of the poet that the Vandal adventurer, who had risen to be captain of the Roman armies, set an example of high courage and steadfastness to the degenerate nobles, who were ready to abandon without a struggle the venerable seat of order and civilisation at the first sign of danger. Yet it would appear that the panic did not last long. The behaviour of all parties in the fruitless negotiations which preceded the final rupture with Alaric and the sack of Rome shows a remarkable confidence either in the strength of the Empire, or in the moderation of the Gothic chief. On the one hand, the government of Ravenna rejected his successive offers of friendship and support.[4] On the other hand, the Roman Senate acquiesced in his tenure of the office of magister militum under Attalus, the Emperor whom by his orders they created.[5] Both the scornful rejection and the easy acceptance of his claims show that, after the first moments of alarm, Alaric was not regarded as a half-savage invader, the foe of the Roman name and of civilisation. He was after all a Christian.[6] He had served as an officer of Theodosius in the campaign against Eugenius.[7] It is true that the marshes of

---

[1] Claud. *de Bell. Get.* 217 :

jam, jam conscendere puppes,
Sardoosque habitare sinus, et inhospita
Cyrni
saxa parant, vitamque freto spumante
tueri.

Rutil. Namat. i. 327. S. Jerome, writing about this time (*Ep.* 128, § 4), says, nulla est regio quae non exules Romanos habeat.

[2] Claud. *de Bell. Get.* 296 and 315 :

migrantisque fugam compescuit aulae.

[3] *C. Th.* vii. 20, 12 ; vii. 13, 18.
[4] Zos. v. 36.
[5] *Ib.* vi. 6, 7, ἡ γερουσία . . . πᾶσιν ἐνέδωκεν οἷς 'Αλάριχος ἐκέλευσεν . . . τὰς δὲ τῶν δυνάμεων στρατηγίας αὐτῷ τε 'Αλαρίχῳ καὶ Οὐάλεντι παρέδωκεν.
[6] Oros. vii. 39, § 1 ; Aug. *de Civ. Dei*, i. vi.
[7] Zos. v. 5 ; Socr. vii. 10, 'Αλάριχος . . . τῷ βασιλεῖ Θεοδοσίῳ εἰς τὸν κατὰ Εὐγενίου τοῦ τυράννου πόλεμον συμμαχήσας, κ.τ.λ.

Ravenna, to which in the first alarm the seat of government had been removed from Milan, was a secure refuge
for Honorius and his court.   And it is also true that the
Senate may have felt it safer to come to terms with the
man who had the supplies of Rome at his mercy.   Still,
on neither side are there the signs of that paralysis of
terror which seized the upper classes on the first news of
the approach of the Goths.

But in 410, when, after the failure of all negotiations,
the city had at last fallen a prey to the army of Alaric,
everything was changed.   Eight hundred years had passed
since Rome had been violated by the Gauls of Brennus.
In spite of all troubles on the frontiers, in spite of the
alarms of the great invasions of the second, third, and
fourth centuries, the sacred centre of government had
never realised the possibility that her own stately security
would ever be disturbed.[1]   Not only had all true sons of
Rome a religious faith in her mission and destiny, but
they had good reason to rely on the awe which she inspired in the barbarous races who ranged around her
frontiers.[2]   There seemed an almost infinite distance
between the plunder of provinces, which was so constantly and so rapidly avenged, and the violation of the
heart and seat of Roman power.   But now the spell was
broken ; the mystery and awe which surrounded the
great city had been pierced and set at nought.   The
moral force, so much more important in government than
the material, had been weakened and desecrated.   The
shock given by this great catastrophe to old Roman confidence and pride must, for the time, have been over-

---

[1] Yet after the victory of Pollentia Claudian utters the prayer,
which sounds like a prophecy :

procul arceat altus

Jupiter, ut delubra Numae, sedemque
Quirini,
barbaries oculis saltem temerare profanis
possit, et arcanum tanti deprendere regni.

[2] Cf. the words put into the
mouth of the old Gothic warrior in
Claud. *de Bell. Get.* 508 :

nec numina sedem

destituunt.   Jactata procul dicuntur in
hostem
fulmina, divinique volant pro moenibus
ignes :
seu coelum, seu Roma tonat.

whelming.   Yet from all that proud aristocracy, men of
letters and affairs, hardly a word has come down to tell
us what they felt in the wreck of material fortune and
patriotic illusions.[1]   We can only conjecture their feelings on the events of the time from the words of S.
Jerome, penned in his cell at Bethlehem in the year 411.
Although he had fled from the world, he was still a
Roman at heart, steeped in her literary culture, and
proud of her great history.   When the rumour of the
fall of Rome reached him, he broke off his Commentary
on Ezekiel;[2] his voice was choked with sobs as he
thought of the capture of the great city "which had
taken captive all the world."   In an earlier letter,
referring to the invasion of the eastern provinces,[3] he
says that his soul shudders to recite the ruin of his time.
For twenty years all the lands from Constantinople to
the Julian Alps are daily drenched with Roman blood.
The provinces are a prey to Alans, Huns, Vandals, and
Marcomanni.   Matrons and virgins devoted to God,[4] the
noble and the priest, are made the sport of these
monsters.   The churches are demolished, the bones of
the martyrs are dug up, horses are stabled at the altars
of Christ.   "The Roman world is sinking into ruin, and
still we hold our heads erect. . . . Happy Nepotianus
who does not see such things, who does not hear of them.
Miserable are we who have to suffer them, or see our
brethren suffering.   And yet we wish to live, and think
that those who have been taken from such a scene are to
be mourned rather than deemed happy in their fate. . . .
It is through our sins that the barbarians are strong ; it

[1] S. Augustine complains in one
of his letters that no one had sent
him a full and authentic account of
the calamities in Italy, probably
referring to Alaric's first siege ; v.
Ep. 99, § 1.

[2] Hieron. *Ep*, 126, 127, haeret vox
et singultus intercipiunt verba dic-

tantis : Capitur urbs quae totum
cepit orbem.

[3] *Ib.* 60 ; 123, § 16.

[4] Cf. *Carm. de Prov. Div.* 45 :
quare templa Dei licuit popularier igni?
   cur violata sacri vasa ministerii?
non honor innuptas devotae virginitatis,
   nec texit viduas religionis amor.

is owing to our vices that the Roman armies are conquered." And in a letter to a Gallic lady, he speaks
with horror of the countless hordes who have swept from
the Rhine to the Pyrenees. Great cities, like Mainz,
Rheims, Nantes have been wiped out; the provinces of
Aquitaine, Lyons, and Narbonne have been desolated;
thousands have been butchered even in the churches;
and famine has completed the work of the sword. There
was perhaps exaggeration in the rumours which found
their way to the distant monastery at Bethlehem. And
the warm imagination and vehement rhetoric of S.
Jerome have probably deepened the colours of the tragic
tales of massacre and sacrilege which reached him. The
interest of his words for us lies in the passionate regret
felt by the true Roman, and the lesson drawn by the
Christian ascetic. The same lesson we shall find taught
with even greater emphasis by another Christian moralist
who had himself witnessed the invasion of Gaul.[1]

S. Jerome's description of the disasters of the time
may seem exaggerated in the light of the sixty or seventy
years which followed. Yet there can be no doubt that
the moral effect of the capture was for the moment overwhelming. Immense numbers of the various corporations,[2] who were bound to certain crafts and functions,
fled from the city. This must have caused a great dis-
location of the social life of the capital. And in the
year 412 an edict of the Emperor orders all governors of
provinces to compel the return of these fugitives to their
proper functions.[3] There was also a second exodus of
many of the upper class, who fled to Africa and the East.
One case of which we possess the details will help us to
realise the fate of these noble exiles. The Demetrias,

---

[1] Salv. *de Gub Dei*, vii. § 108,
sola nos morum nostrorum vitia
vicerunt.

[2] The corporati included the pistores, catabolenses, suarii, pecuarii,

mancipes thermarum; *v.* Godefroy's
Paratitlon, *C. Th.* xiv. 2.

[3] *C. Th.* xiv. 2, 4; cf. xiv. 7, 2,
and *Nov. Th.* 26.

whose ascetic devotion drew forth the extravagant lauda-
tions of S. Jerome, was a member of one of the noblest
and wealthiest houses among the Roman aristocracy.
The Anicii appear in the consular lists for many years.
One of her ancestors was proconsul of Africa in the reign
of Valerian, another was colleague of Aurelian in the
consulship, and a third held the same great office in the
early years of the reign of Constantine.[1] Her grandfather, Sex. Petronius Probus, had filled more important
offices than any man of his time.[2] The father and uncle
of Demetrias, who were the consuls of 395, have been
immortalised in a poem of Claudian. Demetrias and her
grandmother, Faltonia Proba, having ransomed themselves
from the Goths, and having hired a vessel at one of the
Italian ports, effected their escape, amid great hardships,
to Africa.[3] But when they landed there, they had, in
the words of S. Jerome, to encounter a monster more
cruel than any in the legends of the Western seas.
Count Heraclian was then governor of the province,[4] a
man with an insatiable thirst for wine and for gold. He
was the assassin of Stilicho, and the successor of Olympius
in the leadership of the Catholic party. But his religious
principles were compatible with the grossest and most
heartless cruelty to women and to fellow-Christians. He
had mustered a crowd of Syrian slave-dealers in the
African ports, who were ready to purchase the hapless
refugees; and many a Roman lady of noble birth was
consigned by this ruffian to the ignominy of an Eastern
harem. Proba and her grand-daughter were compelled

[1] See Seeck's *Sym.* xci., with the Stemma of the family.

[2] Cf. Aus. *Ep.* xvi. 19, Probo P.P. :

> dico hunc Senati praesulem,
> praefectum eundem et consulem,
> (nam consul aeternum cluet)
> collegam Augusti consulis,
> columen curulis Romulae.

See the epitaph of Probus in *C. I.L.* vi. 1756.

[3] Hieron. *Ep.* 130, § 7, quae de medio mari fumantem viderat patriam, et fragili cymbae salutem suam suorumque commiserat, crudeliora invenit Africae litora.

[4] Zos. v. 37. He was made governor of Africa as his reward for the murder of Stilicho. Cf. Oros. vii. 42, § 10.

to purchase their freedom, or save their honour, by an
enormous ransom.[1]   Others of their class found their way
to S. Jerome's monastery at Bethlehem in a state of the
greatest destitution.   The number of these visitors was so
great that the saint, although his hospitality was boundless,
sometimes found his studious labours sadly disturbed.[2]

In the meantime, the recovery of confidence and
equanimity at Rome itself seems to have been rapid.   It
is probable that the slaughter and material damage
inflicted by Alaric have been exaggerated.   The ancient
authorities give very different accounts of the matter.
According to some, there was wholesale massacre,[3] and
senators were tortured and put to death in large
numbers ;[4] the city was ravaged with fire,[5] and most of
the great works of art were destroyed.[6]   On the other
hand, Orosius,[7] writing only a few years after the sack,
states that, while some buildings were burnt down, Alaric
gave orders to his soldiers to content themselves with
plunder and to abstain from bloodshed.   Jordanes even
asserts that the Goths did not set fire to any buildings,
and that by Alaric's command they confined themselves
to pillage.[8]   The probabilities of the case are all in
favour of the less tragic view of the catastrophe.   The
three days, during which the Goths remained within
the walls, were short enough for the collection of the
enormous spoil which Alaric carried off in his southward
march.   S. Augustine, who took a gloomy enough view
of the event, distinctly says that very few senators were
put to death.[9]   It is probable that fire may have broken

---

[1] Proba returned to Rome, having
recovered some part of her property.
See the inscriptions to her memory
in *C.I.L.* vi. 1754.

[2] Hieron. *Ep.* 71, § 5 ; cf. *Ep.* 147.

[3] Proc. *de Bell. Vand.* i. 2.

[4] Socr. *Hist. Eccl.* vii. 10.

[5] Hieron. *Ep.* 128, urbs inclyta
. . . uno hausta est incendio.

[6] Socr. *Hist. Eccl.* vii. 10, πολλὰ
τῶν θαυμαστῶν ἐκείνων κατέκαυσαν.

[7] Oros. vii. 38.

[8] Jordan, *Get.* c. 30, spoliant tantum, non autem, ut solent gentes,
igne supponunt, etc.

[9] *De Civ. Dei*, iii. c. 29, Gothic
vero tam multis Senatoribus peper-
cerunt ut magis mirum sit quod
aliquos peremerunt.

out here and there, but the only great building which is
positively known to have been burnt down was the
palace of Sallust,[1] of which the ruins were still standing
in the time of Procopius. Even if Alaric had not been
restrained by policy from a wholesale and wanton destruction of great masterpieces of art, his Goths could not
have wrought such havoc in so short a time. But the
most convincing argument is derived from the poem of
Rutilius Namatianus, who, as he bids a reluctant farewell
to the city which he regards with a passionate love and
reverence,[2] sees only the crowded monuments of her
glory, and has his eyes dazzled by the radiance of her
glittering fanes.[3]

The remains of Rutilius are of great value, because he
is almost the only man of the last pagan generation from
whom we can learn something of the feelings of his class
about the future of the Empire in the face of its perils.
He was a pagan of the pagans, imbued, as we have seen,[4]
with a mingled hatred and contempt for the new ascetic
spirit which had peopled the islands of the Tyrrhene Sea
with men " who are as much afraid to enjoy the gifts of
fortune as to face its reverses." [5]   His paternal estates in
Gaul had been ravaged by the invaders.[6] The ruins of
his home, the streams and groves of his desolated lands,
he feels, are calling him to repair the waste. Yet he
betrays no symptom of despair. Three years after the
siege he had held the office of prefect of the city.[7]
He may have actually seen the Goths within the walls.
But there is hardly a hint that any serious event has

---

[1] Proc. *de Bell. Vand.* i. 2.

[2] Rutil. Namat. i. 47.

[3] *Ib.* i. 93:

confunduntque vagos delubra micantia
   visus.

[4] *Ib.* i. 440 ; v. *supra* p. 46.

[5] *Ib.* i. 445 :

quaenam perversi rabies tam stulti
   cerebri,
dum mala formides, nec bona posse pati.

[6] *Ib.* i. 25.

[7] *Ib.* i. 157-160 ; cf.   Seeck's
Sym. clxxx. His father Lachanius
had held several offices, among
others that of consularis Tusciae, *C.
Th.* ii. 4, 5.

occurred.[1] The temples of the gods are still standing in
their dazzling radiance under the serene Italian sky.[2]
The cheers of the spectators in the circus reach his ears
as his ship still lingers in the Tiber.[3] He feels a passionate regret at quitting "this fair queen of the world,"
so mighty, so merciful,[4] so bounteous, whose visible
splendour is only the faint symbol of her worldwide and
godlike sway. Certainly there is here no querulous and
faint-hearted lamentation over a crushing and appalling
disaster. The troubles of the time, referred to in a few
vague phrases, are treated as merely vicissitudes of
fortune, such as Rome has known before, and from which
she has always risen with renewed vitality.[5] The
enemies of Rome have always repented their success.
"Victoris Brenni non distulit Allia poenam." This faith
in the star of Rome, expressed with such genuine
enthusiasm, seems in Rutilius not to be founded on
the consciousness of material strength. It is rather a
religious feeling springing from a clear perception of the
true mission of Rome and the nature of her services to
humanity : "Quod regnas minus est quam quod regnare
mereris."[6] The triumphs of Rome have been triumphs of
law and equal justice for the vanquished. The child of
Mars and Venus,[7] she has united love and tenderness to
warlike might ; and so has she made of the earth with
its divers peoples a single country.[8] Here Orosius and
Rutilius, the Christian and the pagan, join hands.
"Rome," says Orosius [9] in effect, "has stripped exile of its
terrors. Wherever I go, I find my fatherland, I come as
a Roman among Romans." But the pagan noble has a

[1] Rutil. Namat. ii. 50 :
  et captiva prius quam caperetur erat ;
cf. i. 39.
[2] *Ib.* i. 197.
[3] *Ib.* i. 201.
[4] *Ib.* i. 69 :
  mitigat armatas victrix clementia
  vires.

[5] *Ib.* i. 119 *sqq.*
[6] *Ib.* i. 91.
[7] *Ib.* i. 67.
[8] *Ib.* i. 63.
[9] Oros. v. 2, 1, ubique patria,
ubique lex et religio mea est . . .
quia ad Christianos et Romanos
Romanus et Christianus accedo.

greater faith than the Christian priest in the future of
the Roman sway. Rising superior to all the vicissitudes
of fortune, she is to receive the submission of the trem-
bling Goth ;[1] the pacified nations are still to pay her tribute
and pour their wealth into her bosom ; she may, with no
term set to her dominion, extend her laws over the
coming ages,[2] and have no fear of the distaff of the Fates.
Such were the hopes or beliefs of one who may have seen
the Goth in possession of Rome, and who was returning
to find the same Gothic host settled in his native
Aquitaine. What secret misgivings Rutilius may have
had we can never know, or how he fared when he found
himself once more on his ravaged estate. His life, which
is known to us only for a moment, is, like his poem, a
mere fragment, a bit of wreckage, as it were, appearing for
an instant on the waves and then lost to sight for ever.
His is the almost solitary voice which reaches us directly
from that generation of the high aristocracy of Rome,
which, from whatever cause, pride, grief, confidence in
the stability of a great civilisation, or from the cruelty of
time in engulfing all record of its feelings, is now as
silent as if it had never been.

In the very year in which Rutilius Namatianus was
returning from his prefecture to Gaul, Orosius, the young
Spanish disciple of S. Augustine, was composing his
historical answer to the pagan cry that Rome had
perished in the Christian times. This work has been
already referred to in an account of the last open conflict
between Christian and pagan in the West.[3] It was
composed primarily to confute the open accusations of
the heathen remnant, and to quiet the uneasiness of
doubters on the Christian side. Orosius employed a
limited erudition and a boundless licence of assertion
to prove that the pre-Christian ages had been scourged

[1] Rutil. Namat. i. 142.

[2] *Ib.* i. 133 :

porrige victuras Romana in saecula leges,
solaque fatales non vereare colos.

[3] v. *supra*, p. 67.

with every form of calamity in a degree unknown to his contemporaries, and to deepen every shadow in the history of the past. But worthless as his work is for its main purpose, it has a great value for the light which it throws on the possible future attitude of the Church to the barbarians.

A necessary complement of the view which Orosius took of past history was his determined resolve to minimise the convulsions and the sufferings of his own time. He had suffered personally in the Vandal invasion of Spain ;[1] he must have witnessed some of the horrors described in the Chronicle of Idatius.[2] Yet he can speak of the capture of Rome as a single act of brigandage in a world enjoying general tranquillity.[3] The Goths, in their first onset, might be fierce and rapacious, but they were after all fellow-Christians. Their chief had kept inviolate the Christian churches;[4] the soldiers, in the midst of their pillage, had formed a singular procession to escort the sacred vessels to the basilica of S. Peter, singing hymns as they went. They had no hatred of Rome, no wish to overthrow her empire. Rather their great chiefs, Alaric and Ataulphus, had a singular reverence for Rome.[5] Their strongest wish was to be admitted to any settlement which Rome might assign to them,[6] and they were ready, in return for the boon, to protect her and to restore her power. In his native country Orosius had seen the Germans turning from brigandage and slaughter to the cultivation of the fields. They were beginning to live on terms of amity and good-fellowship with their Roman neighbours, many of whom preferred the rule of the barbarians to the crushing exactions of the Roman treasury.[7]

---

[1] Oros. iii. 20, 5. His native region was probably Tarraconensis ; cf. vii. 22, nos quoque in Hispania Tarraconem*nostram*. . . ostendimus.

[2] Idat. *Chron.*, debacchantibus per Hispanias barbaris, etc.

[3] Oros. iii. 20, 9.

[4] *Ib.* vii. 39.

[5] *Ib.* vii. 43.

[6] *Ib.* i. 16, 3, exiguae habitationis sedem non ex sua electione sed ex nostro judicio rogant.

[7] *Ib.* vii. 41, 7, barbari execrati gladios suos ad aratra conversi sunt

Salvianus tells us the same thing. But Salvianus wrote more than a generation after Orosius. And it is creditable to the insight and candour of Orosius that he should so soon and so clearly have perceived the more hopeful side of the barbarian invasions, and the promise of a rapprochement between the Romans and their invaders. He shows far more discernment and detachment from prejudice than the statesmen of Ravenna who rejected the overtures of Alaric, and compassed the death of Stilicho. In Orosius we see the Church already adapting herself to altered conditions, and willing to come to terms with the new forces.

If we ask what Orosius thinks of the condition and future destiny of Rome, we obtain a somewhat uncertain reply. On the one hand, in spite of all her disasters, Rome still retains her imperial sway intact;[1] on the other, the mighty mass of the once omnipotent Roman commonwealth is beginning to feel the decrepitude of age.[2] Rome will have her term, like the empires of the past, like all things human. Her power was founded on force, and won by bloody conquests, which caused far greater misery over vast spaces of the world than any inflicted by the Gothic inroads.[3] And yet her rule has given a period of extraordinary tranquillity, order, and prosperity to the nations whom she conquered.[4] If you have to fly from one province, you can find a home, a country, everywhere—"ubique patria, ubique lex, et religio

residuosque Romanos ut socios modo et amicos fovent ut inveniantur jam inter eos quidam Romani qui malint inter barbaros pauperem libertatem quam inter Romanos tributariam sollicitudinem sustinere. Compare with this *de Gub. Dei.* v. 26, ac sic actum est ut latrociniis judicum strangulati homines et necati inciperent esse quasi barbari, quia non permittebantur esse Romani.

[1] Oros. ii. 3, opibus spoliata non regno, manet adhuc et regnat in-

columis.

[2] *Ib.* ii. 6, 14, illae quondam Romanae reipublicae moles nunc magis imbecillitate propriae senectutis quam alienis concussae viribus contremescunt.

[3] *Ib.* v. 1, 4.

[4] *Ib.* v. 1, 12, inquietudo bellorum qua illi attriti sunt nobis ignota est . . . in otio nos nascimur et senescimus. An extraordinary statement to be made in the second decade of the fifth century !

mea est."[1]   The Roman peace, the Roman culture, Romania, is greater than Rome and will survive her.   And along with this cosmopolitan feeling, there is here and there a curious emergence of provincial patriotism, the faint dawn, as it were, of modern nationality.   More than once, by a sort of patriotic irrelevance, Orosius enlarges on the stubborn resistance which the Spaniards offered to the Roman generals,[2] and the sufferings from famine and slaughter endured by his countrymen during the struggles of two hundred years.   While recognising the peace and happiness which the Roman Empire had given the world since the coming of Christ, he is hardly so ready as S. Augustine to do justice to the manly virtue by which the Empire was won.[3]   His sympathy is rather for the conquered races.   Rome subdued the world to gratify her love of dominion, her lust for gold and luxury.   The blessings which her rule has diffused are due to the Divine will which has guided the course of history.

Between Orosius at the beginning of the century, and Salvianus and Sidonius who wrote towards its close, we have little to tell us how the Romans regarded the course of events.   The great lettered and noble class is absolutely silent.   The sons and grandsons of the generation of Symmachus, the immediate ancestors of the generation of Sidonius, though they witnessed the conquest of Roman Africa by the Vandals, the invasion of Gaul by Attila, the settlement of the Visigoths in Aquitaine, have not left even a fragment to inform us as to their fortunes, their hopes, or their fears.   The only message we have from that generation comes in three

[1] Oros. v. 2, 1.
[2] *Ib.* v. 4, the victories of Viriathus; v. 7, the war with Numantia; v. 19, Sertorius; vii. 34, Trajan and Theodosius of Spanish origin; cf. Mörner, pp. 37, 38; Ebert, *Lit. des. Mittelalters,* p. 344.

[3] *De Civ. Dei,* ii. 2; ii. 29, O indoles Romana laudabilis, O progenies Regulorum, Scaevolarum, Scipionum, Fabriciorum, haec potius concupisce; cf. *Ep.* 138, § 17, rempublicam quam primi Romani constituerunt auxeruntque virtutibus.

poems, composed by Christians and ascetics who had seen
with their own eyes the great invasion of Gaul at the
beginning of the century.   And it is curious to contrast
with the hopeful optimism of Orosius the horror and grief
of these writers at what seems to them to be the death-
agony of the Roman world.

The poems entitled *Ad Uxorem* and *De Providentia
Divina*,[1] which used to be wrongly attributed to S.
Prosper,[2] and the *Commonitorium*,[3] of S. Orientius are, as
it were, the solitary voices which come to us from the
dim mass of the generation who witnessed the Suevic
and Vandal invasions.   In phrases, often almost identi-
cal, they describe the suffering and terror of the time.
The country is smoking like one great funeral pyre.[4]   Its
strongest and fairest cities have been given up to fire and
sword.   Nothing has escaped the violence of the invaders,
castles on apparently inaccessible rocks,[5] the lonely hermitage buried in the woods,[6] churches guarded by the relics
of saints and martyrs[7]—no place, however strong or
remote or sacred, was safe from their attacks.   The aged
priest has been driven into slavery with his flock,[8] the
mother with her child,[9] the master with his servants.
On all sides there is nothing but war, confusion, and the
treachery of fellow-citizens.[10]   Peace seems to have

---

[1] The author of the *De Prov. Div.*
was a native of Southern Gaul and
had seen the invasion of the Vandals and Goths, v. 34.   The poem
was probably composed about 415 ;
v. Ebert, 317, n. 4.

[2] It has a taint of Pelagianism
(v. 233, 240, 585) of which S.
Prosper was a prominent opponent;
v. Migne's ed. col. 615 ; Ebert, i.
319.

[3] The *Commonitorium* was probably composed in the second decade
of the fifth century, Ebert. i. 410;
cf. Ellis, Pref. to his ed. (*Corp.
Scrip. Eccl.*) of the *Commonitorium*,
p. 194.

[4] *Commonit.* ii. 184 :
  uno fumavit Gallia tota rogo.
Carm. de Prov. Div. 17 :
  animum patriae subiit fumantis imago.
[5] *Commonit.* ii. 169; *Carm. de
Prov. Div.* 35.
[6] *Commonit.* ii. 170.
[7] *Carm. de Prov. Div.* 45.
[8] *Ib.* 59.
[9] *Commonit.* ii. 177.
[10] *Ad Uxorem*, 26 :
  undique bella fremunt . . .
  pax abiit terris, ultima quaeque vides
Cf. *Commonit.* ii. 174 :
  multis
  causa fuit mortis civica proditio ;
Hieron. *Ep.* 118, § 2; 123, § 4,
referring to the same events.

quitted the world for ever, and the end of all things is at
hand. It is probable, as has often been pointed out, that
there may be a good deal of exaggeration in these
descriptions, and a good deal of sacred rhetoric with a
religious purpose. Yet we are bound to take account of
the impression made at the time on a certain class of
minds. The trouble is not by them regarded, as Orosius
regarded it, as almost trivial compared with the slaughter
and rapine and pestilence of former ages. It is not local
and temporary. The fabric of the civilised world is
tottering. Men are abandoning hope in its permanence
and seem to feel themselves on the edge of the abyss.
The poem on the Providence of God dwells specially on
the fact that many were losing faith in the government
of the world by a righteous God. The spectacle of
wholesale and indiscriminate ruin,[1] of the virtuous and
the wicked overtaken by the same doom, drove men
back to the conception of an iron fate, or of an epicurean
deity sitting aloof from the world, powerless over its
destiny, coldly pitiless of its woes.[2]   And along with the
atheistic philosophies of the past returned also its pagan
superstitions.   Refusing to believe in a controlling
Providence, men once more began to interrogate the
stars[3] as to the meaning of the sudden arrest of civilisation, or as to their own personal fortunes in the misery
and chaos of the time. Many years afterwards we shall
find that Salvianus has still to contend against the same
spirit of unbelief.

[1] *Carm. de Prov. Div.* 52 :
idem turbo bonos sustulit atque malos.

[2] *Ib.* 715 :
scrutatis igitur stellarum motibus hoc
est
artis opus, totam subvertere relligionem;
dum nullum curare Deum mortalia
suadet, etc.

[3] This was forbidden by a long
series of laws. In the year 409,
Honorius orders the expulsion of
mathematici, *C. Th.* ix. 16, 12.
But they are found in Rome again
in 410, when Attalus consulted
them (Zos. vi. 7). Sidonius repre-
tents the wife of Aetius as consult-
ing the stars, *Carm.* v. 259 ; cf.
Sid. *Ep.* viii. 11. Lampridius of
Bordeaux believed in astrology.
Not without reason S. Aug. *de Civ.
Dei*, viii. 19, attacks this superstition. Cf. Maury's *La Magie*, c. vi.

Orosius wrote to refute the cavils of the last generation of pagans, who found in the misfortunes of the
Empire an argument against the adoption of Christianity
as the national faith. Salvianus, separated from Orosius
by more than a generation, had an equally controversial
purpose ; but his work is aimed at the scepticism of
professed Christians [1] who were disturbed by the calamities, the imminent overthrow, of a society which had
definitely placed itself under the protection of the Cross.
Orosius had to oppose the convictions of men who
thought the world was suffering from the abandonment
of an old faith, under the protection of which it had
prospered. Salvianus had to deal with the doubts of
the votaries of the new faith, under which the world had
suffered what were thought unexampled disasters. The
treatise *De Gubernatione Dei* was probably written before
451 and after 439.[2] It is perhaps fortunate for its controversial purpose that it was composed before the
victory of the Roman arms at Châlons.

In spite of all the faults of Orosius as a historian, it
may well be questioned whether his treatise is not of
greater historical value than that of Salvianus. The
object of Orosius is to show that Rome had suffered even
worse calamities when she worshipped her ancient gods
than she did in Christian times. And he is probably
not wrong at least when he maintains that the invasions
of the reign of Gallienus caused quite as much misery
and terror as the invasions of the reign of Honorius.[3]

[1] See the opening words of the
de Gub. Dei, incuriosus a quibusdam
et quasi neglegens humanorum
actuum deus dicitur utpote nec
bonos custodiens nec coercens malos.

[2] Ebert, i. 459, n. 5. He mentions
the defeat of Litorius in 439 (vii.
40, Prosp. *Chron.* ad a.), and he is
silent about the defeat of Attila in
451. Teuffel says the latter event
was unknown to him. But the

defeat of Attila may have been
ignored by a writer whose thesis is
the superiority of barbarian virtue.
The reference in vi. 67 (obsessa est
urbs) is to Alaric's, not to Genseric's
capture of Rome. Salvianus lived
possibly till 495 (Gennad. *Scrip.
Ill.* 67, vivit usque hodie ; *v.*
Teuffel, § 462 n. 4 ; cf. Ebert, i.
448 n.).

[3] Oros. vii. 22, 7.

Only once or twice does he strike the dominant note of Salvianus, that it was the theatre, the sensual pleasures of the Roman world, which had drawn down the judgments of heaven.[1] The great object of Salvianus is to heighten the horror of the catastrophe that he may make the moral more impressive. He promises (though the promise is unfulfilled) to prove, as S. Augustine held, that the ancient Romans won and enjoyed their rule by a manly, natural virtue.[2] But the Romans of his day have lost their dominion, and suffered in person and estate, because they are sunk in sensual pleasure, because they have exchanged the sober and strenuous energy of their ancestors for a soft, luxurious and frivolous temper, without nerve to cope with danger, without even enough of imagination to realise it.[3] "The Roman world goes laughing to its death." The invasions are the proper penalty for heinous guilt and thorough corruption of character. The invaders may be Arians,[4] they may be heathens, they have their vices; but in spite of blindness to spiritual truth, the result of faulty teaching or early association, in spite of cruelty and treachery, they are morally far superior to the Roman population. Although they have been denied the full light of the Catholic faith, yet they have never sunk to the level of the Christians of Aquitaine, where every estate is a scene of wholesale debauchery.[5] The Vandals may be a weak and cowardly people,[6] yet they have overthrown the

---

[1] Oros. iv. 21, 5, theatra incusanda non tempora.

[2] Salv. *de Gub. Dei*, vii. 2, si deus annuit cum ad eam negotii partem accesserimus, ut de veteribus Romanis aliqua dicantur, evidenter divino munere adprobabimus tam justum tunc erga illos fuisse domini favorem quam nunc erga nos justam severitatem ; cf. Ebert, i. 463.

[3] *De Gub. Dei*, vi. 80, ita cunctos crimina sua presserant, ut nec

metuerent periculum suum ; praenoscebatur captivitas nec formidibatur ; cf. vi. 72.

[4] *Ib.* iv. 61, 62. He divides them into heretics and pagans, the latter including the Saxons, Franks, Gepidae, and Huns ; cf. iv. 81. On the heretic Goths and Vandals cf. v. 14.

[5] *Ib.* vii. 14 *sqq.*

[6] *Ib.* vii. 27, sed ideo ille infirmissimis hostibus cuncta tradidit, ut ostenderet scilicet non vires valere,

stately Roman civilisation of Africa, and, with its power,
they have swept away its abominations of nameless vice.[1]
A righteous God has given them that great heritage, to
punish the enormous corruption of the Christian and
Roman world.   Nor does Salvianus find the contrast less
marked between the Romans and Germans as political
rulers.   The oppression and peculation of the imperial
officials, and the insolent and fraudulent devices of the
upper class to evade their share of the public burdens
and to crush their poorer neighbours, are probably better
grounded accusations than the charge of universal
sensuality.   For as to the fiscal and economic chaos, the
rhetoric of Salvianus is only too amply supported by the
repeated, but apparently disregarded, edicts of a long line
of emperors.   It is here that the priest of Marseilles
throws a searching light on the actual condition of
Roman society, and on the feeling of the oppressed
towards the new barbarian powers.

In the passionate declamation of Salvianus against the
selfish individualism of the privileged class, and his
equally passionate sympathy with the needy and friend-
less, we seem to hear the tones of modern democratic
statesmanship.   Even the curiales, the middling proprietors, whose position seems to a modern inquirer the
most hopeless in the Roman social system, are treated by
Salvianus as cruel oppressors of those beneath them.[2]
All his pity is reserved for the poor peasant, who,
exposed to the fraudulent arts or high-handed oppression
of the tax-gatherer and the rich proprietor, has only two
courses open to him : either he must place himself under
the patronage and protection of some wealthy neighbour,

sed causam, etc.; cf. Oros. vii. 38,
1, Stilico, Vandalorum imbellis,
avarae, perfidae, et dolosae gentis
genere editus.

[1] *De Gub. Dei*, vii. 63 *sqq.*, ita
enim generale in eis malum impuri-
tatis est, ut quicumque ex eis
impudicus esse desierit, Afer non
esse videatur; cf. vii. 84-87.

[2] *Ib.* v. 18, quae enim sunt . . .
urbes ubi non quot curiales fuerint
tot tyranni sunt.

forfeiting probably both the poor remnant of his property and his freedom; or he must leave all behind, and settle in a district under the sway of a Gothic chief.[1]   To many the latter alternative seemed preferable.   There is nothing in the work of Salvianus more remarkable than the frank admission that, in humanity and justice, the Goth far excelled the Roman,[2] and that many Romans of that day preferred the government of the Goth.

We are trying to get a conception of the thoughts of the Romans of the fifth century about the barbarians and the fate of the Empire.   Orosius and Salvianus are the men from whom we can gather most to satisfy our curiosity.   They wrote, it is true, with a controversial or didactic purpose.   They are not calm scientific observers and reasoners; but they are the only writers of that century known to us who faced the problems raised by the German invasions, and who tried to find an answer to the questions which must have forced themselves on thoughtful minds.   When we compare them with one another, it is not difficult to perceive that in the thirty years which separate the two works, men's ideas as to the meaning of the invasions have undergone a change. Orosius makes light of the barbarian conquests, and, though with some reserve, he does not despair of the future of Rome.   He admits that the Germans can be self-restrained in the hour of victory, and that they are willing to come to terms with their Roman neighbours. But he does not dwell, like Salvianus, on the virtues of the conquerors or the vices of those whom they have defeated.   After all, he seems to think, the Roman world is civilised and Christian, and it may tame and absorb its assailants.   He feels profoundly what Rome has done for the world, by the diffusion of peace and law and culture over so many countries, and he thinks the barbarians may submit to the marvellous influence which, since the

---

[1] *De Gub Dei*, v. 37.   [2] *Ib*. v. 15.

coming of Christ, had made of so many peoples one commonwealth. But Salvianus had seen many things which Orosius did not live to see. In the interval between them, the Vandals had shaken Roman civilisation in Africa to its base. The Gothic power had securely established itself in Southern Gaul. The Roman authority in Spain was confined to a corner in the north-east. The Burgundians were steadily advancing from the middle Rhine towards the valleys of the Rhone and Isère.[1] In the meantime the imperial power was growing daily weaker, and its administration more oppressive and corrupt. And the upper class were taking advantage of the paralysis of the government and of the economic chaos to aggrandise themselves, unrestrained by any public spirit or feelings of pity for the distressed. Can we wonder, then, that to the eye of Salvianus the Empire seems almost in its last throes, while the Germans, in their victorious strength, seem to hold the future in their grasp ? Salvianus, as we have seen, has probably exaggerated the sensual excesses of his countrymen, as he has probably idealised the purity of German morality ; but he discerned the real weaknesses of Rome, the crushing taxation, the cruelty of the official class, the selfish rapacity of the rich, which made many Romans welcome the humaner rule of the Gothic chief. In an age of fierce intolerance, it is singular to find a Catholic extolling the superior virtue of men who denied the deity of Christ. He praises not only their chastity, but their justice, their kindliness to one another, even their tolerance towards those who anathematised

---

[1] From the Panegyric on Majorian by Sidonius, *Carm.* v. 575-76,

Lugdunumque tuam, dum praeteris, aspice victor,

written 458 (Mommsen, Praef. li. ; cf. *Carm.* xiii.), it is clear that Lyons was not in Burgundian hands at that time ; but it must have become theirs soon afterwards. The arguments of De Coulanges to prove that there is no continuity between the settlement of 413 (Prosp. *Chron.* ad a.) and later Burgundian history are perhaps more ingenious than convincing (*L'Inv.* pp. 446 *sqq.*).

them as heretics.[1] The invasions were terrible in their
inevitable slaughter and rapine. But they were not
nearly so terrible as the riot of gross vice and shameless
oppression of which they were the deserved punishment.
Salvianus has no faith in the stability of Roman government, or in the future of Roman society. The ancient
Republic, he says,[2] was strong and wealthy because its
citizens despised wealth and luxury, and were ready to
sacrifice everything for the State. But in his own time
the public treasury is empty, while the rich are growing
daily richer and more rapacious. Christianity has failed
to regenerate the Roman world. The future belongs to
the barbarians.

The last authority to whom we shall refer on the
subject of this chapter is Apollinaris Sidonius of
Auvergne. His works have been already used for the
light which they throw on the life of that wealthy and
noble class which Salvianus overwhelms with his
anathemas. We turn to them once more to discover
what were the views and feelings of a great aristocrat,
regarded also as the foremost literary man of his age,
about the new barbarian forces, under whose shadow
his life was passed, and about that imperial power three
of whose last holders he celebrated on their accession.
Yet, in spite of his great advantages as an observer, we
must not promise ourselves too much help from Sidonius
in our present inquiry. He has not the historian's or
statesman's breadth of view. He has not the detachment
of men like Orosius and Salvianus.

Sidonius belongs to a different world from that of
Orosius and Salvianus. He has not their consuming
earnestness and seriousness of purpose. He was a good

---

[1] *De Gub. Dei*, vii. 39, cum . . .
illi etiam in alienis (Catholicis)
Episcopis deum honorarent . . .
[2] *Ib.* i. 10 *sqq.*, nisi forte antiquis
illis priscae virtutis viris, Fabiis,
Fabriciis, Cincinnatis, grave fuisse
existimamus, quod pauperes erant
qui divites esse nolebant, cum
omnia scilicet studia . . . ad com-
munia emolumenta conferrent, etc.

patriot, and in his later years a devoted bishop ; yet he
never ceased to be the grand seigneur, believing in his
own order with implicit faith, sharing to the full all its
love of stateliness and splendour, and its passion for high
place and distinction.   Above all, he is essentially a
literary man, of the stamp which that age of decadence
most admired.   He is a stylist, not a thinker or inquirer.
There is little doubt that he valued his own compositions
not for their substance, but for those characteristics of
style which we now think most worthless or even
repulsive in them, the childish conceits, the meaningless
antitheses, the torture applied to language so as to give
an air of interest and distinction to the trivial commonplace of a colourless and monotonous existence, the
crowding reminiscences of history and mythology applied
to characters and situations remote from any world of
miracle or romance.   Yet, in spite of all its vices, this
minute word-painting has some value to the historian.
It enables him to revive the picture of Gallo-Roman life
in the evening light before darkness finally settles on the
West.   It also gives us a vivid glimpse of the society of
the capital in the years which followed its capture by the
Vandals.   Above all, though Sidonius has no very great
insight into the real meaning of events, he has left us a
series of pictures of the Germans, the minute faithfulness
and realistic truth of which can hardly be exaggerated.

The early life and associations of Sidonius gave him
peculiar advantages for the study of the barbarians.
Eleven years before his birth the Visigoths had obtained
a settlement in Aquitaine.[1]   During his boyhood and
youth they were making constant efforts to extend their
territory to the south and east.   He must have heard
many a tale of the relief of Narbonne, in 436,[2] by

---

[1] Prosp. *Chron.* ad a. 419, Constantius patricius pacem firmat cum
Wallia, data ei ad habitandum secunda Aquitania.

[2] *Ib.* ad a. 419, Isidoro et Senatore
Coss.

Litorius with his cavalry, and of the defeat and captivity of the same gallant, but over-adventurous, soldier in 439 at Toulouse.[1] He probably heard from the lips of Avitus, whose daughter he married, the story of that encounter before a fortress in Auvergne,[2] so like a tale of the Middle Ages, in which Avitus challenged and overthrew in single combat one of the Hun troopers of Litorius, who were ravaging in their passage the lands which they were engaged to defend. Avitus was one of the lieutenants of Aetius who, for thirty years, till he fell by the hands of Valentinian III., was the foremost general of Rome, and the great stay of her power in the province of Gaul. Franks and Burgundians were pressing down from the Rhine, and the Goths, with intervals of peace, were striving to extend their power from the West. Auvergne alone was left in quiet. But her foremost noble, the future Emperor, was in all those years foremost in the struggles and diplomacy of the time. When the Hun invasion of 451 broke on Gaul, Avitus bore a prominent part in securing the help of the Visigoths against the invader. He was a power at the Gothic court,[3] and he helped to give a tincture of Roman culture to the sons of the Gothic chief who fell fighting for Rome on the plains of Châlons.[4] Five years after that great battle he was raised by the united voice of Goths and Romans to the imperial throne. Accustomed from his earliest youth to associate with men who, like Avitus, made it a cardinal principle of their policy to maintain friendly relations with the Goths, Sidonius is justly regarded as a unique authority on the relations of Gallo-Romans and barbarians.

No one can read the many graphic sketches which

[1] Prosp. *Chron.* ad a. 419, Litorius . . . dum aruspicum responsis et daemonum significationibus fidit, pugnam cum Gothis imprudenter conseruit.

[2] Apoll. Sid. *Carm.* vii. 246.

[3] *Ib.* vii. 342 :
et populis Geticis sola est tua gratia limes.

[4] *Ib.* vii. 497 ; Jordan. *Get.* xl. xli.

Sidonius gives of the various peoples then sweeping across
the Roman Empire, without perceiving that the author
had studied them close at hand. Salvianus is incessantly
declaiming about the virtues of the barbarians, but we
could well spare some of the declamation for a little life-
like colouring. Sidonius, on the other hand, is an artist in
words, although his art is very perverse and corrupt;
and he pleases himself with microscopic fidelity of detail
in rendering the minutest physical traits, the dress and
habits of these races towards whom he felt at once
curiosity and fastidious dislike. If he did not witness
the great struggle with the army of Attila in 451, he
had probably often seen the Hun troopers, with whose
aid Aetius and Litorius,[1] in many a battle from the
Rhine to the Garonne, kept the barbarians at bay for
years; and, in the Panegyric on Anthemius,[2] we can
almost hear the rush of that terrible cavalry, with their
flattened noses and cavernous, yet piercing, eyes, lean-
flanked and broad of chest, bestriding their horses as if
horse and man were one. There is not a tribe which
crossed the Rhine or harried the coasts of Gaul in those
years,[3] whose features or equipment is not flashed on us
in some vivid phrase. The Burgundians, who established
themselves in his native Lyons, were on the whole
friendly neighbours. But they had habits which
offended the taste and senses of the Roman gentleman.
They greased their hair with rancid butter,[4] they sustained their gigantic bulk by ravenous feeding on the
most unsavoury messes, and they deafened their guest
with the harshness and loudness of their voices. The
fierce Herulian, unrivalled for speed in running, has his
cheeks tattooed a bluish green, like the colour of the
waves.[5] You see the Gothic elders trooping to the

[1] Prosp. *Chron.* ad a. 425, 435,
436, 437, 439.
[2] Sid. *Carm.* ii. 243.
[3] Cf. *ib.* v. 476 ; vii. 234, 320.
[4] *Ib.* xii. 6.
[5] *Ep.* viii. 9 ; *Carm.* vii. 236.

council in garments of wild beasts' skins, falling scarcely
to the knee.[1] Fiercest and most daring of all is the
Saxon ranging along the Breton coasts in his coracle of
hides, with his blue fearless eyes, ever appearing when
least expected, vanishing as suddenly as he came, for
whom shipwreck has no terrors, to whom the sea is a
familiar companion, who butchers his captives to gratify
his gods.[2] The Frank stands out on the canvas,[3] with
his blue-gray eyes and yellow hair, his clean-shaved face,
and his tight, short tunic. Sidonius had probably seen
with his own eyes that picturesque wedding procession,[4]
in which the princely young Sigismer strode along behind
his horses glittering with jewel-studded trappings, himself
ablaze with scarlet and gold ; and followed by the young
warriors of his staff in their short green tunics, edged
with purple, and armed with lances and battle-axes.
The description of Theodoric II.,[5] his person, his habits,
and his court, is known to most readers of history. It
is from the pen of a man who had sat at Theodoric's
table and played at dice with him. The smallest details
of the king's personal appearance are noted, his bushy
eyebrows, his sweeping eyelashes, the delicate lines of
the nose and lips, the clean-shaved face, the enormous
muscles of back and leg, the combination in the whole
physique of refinement and strength, of the high-bred,
self-contained ruler of men with the hunter and the
warrior. His religious observance is regular, but more
a matter of habit and self-discipline than of devotion.
His day is that of a man who allows not a moment to
idleness. In affairs of state he listens intently, and says
little. He is a keen sportsman, like his ancestors, and
seldom misses his aim. At his table the dishes are
distinguished by delicate cookery rather than by costli-

[1] *Carm.* vii. 455. Cf. Claud. *de Bell. Get.* 481.

[2] Sid. *Carm.* vii. 369 ; *Ep.* viii. 6, § 15.

[3] *Carm.* vii. 236.

[4] *Ep.* iv. 20.

[5] *Ep.* i. 2. Theodoric reigned from 453 to 466.

ness; and his plate not so much by its weight as by elegance of design. At the gaming-table he is eager to win, but he bears his losses with a smile, and he takes his lucky throws in calm silence. He lays aside for the time the dignity of the prince, encourages free and easy intercourse, and fears nothing so much as to be feared.

Yet, in spite of the vividness of these sketches of barbarian life, the student who expects to find in Sidonius clear and definite judgments on the relations of the Western Empire to its new guests or invaders, or forecasts of its future, will, for the most part, be doomed to disappointment. There are indeed in the Panegyrics, as we shall see presently, occasional flashes of political insight. But the letters are singularly barren of information or reflection on the great perils and problems of the time. Men like Sidonius were far more interested in their friendships, their social pleasures, and their literary pursuits, than in public affairs. They have far more ambition to win admiration for their very perverse literary efforts than to satisfy the curiosity of the historical inquirer of a later age. Yet the letter of Sidonius on the court of Theodoric, apparently written only to gratify curiosity, or to exhibit tricks of ingenious and vivid phrase, had in all probability a serious political purpose.

There is little doubt that, in his early manhood, Sidonius had taken part in a movement, the aim of which was to found a strong Gallic party [1] which, with the aid of the Visigoths, should exercise a powerful influence on the Empire, or perhaps restore the quasi-independence of the days of Postumus and Victorinus. [2] The spectacle of the weakness of the central government was humiliating. It could not protect its subjects, whilst its fiscal oppression was every day growing more cruel. We have only a glimpse of the intrigues and secret diplomacy of this party of Gallic independence; but we can

---

[1] Chaix, *Apoll. Sidon.* i. p. 79.   [2] Treb. Poll. *Tyr. Trig.* 6.

discern that Avitus and his family were deeply involved in them. Avitus himself, who with Tonantius Ferreolus had secured the support of the first Theodoric against Attila, was on the most friendly terms with Theodoric II. Sidonius too was received at the Gothic court, and the description of the king's character and habits, to which we have referred, was sent to Agricola, one of the sons of Avitus. The letter was probably not intended merely for Agricola's eyes, who must have heard often from his father the tales of his intercourse with the Gothic royal family. It is not an improbable surmise that Sidonius knew that the letter would be handed about, and that he wished to give a favourable impression of Theodoric to the younger members of the party who were working for the Gallo-Gothic alliance. That alliance bore fruit in the elevation of Avitus to the throne by the united voice of the mixed Roman and Gothic assembly at the castle of Ugernum.[1] And the Panegyric on his father-in-law, which we shall presently review, is at once the history of the movement, and the fullest and clearest exposition which Sidonius has left of his views on the problems of the time.

The hopes of Sidonius and his party were dashed for the moment by the fall of Avitus. Yet we can discover traces of one more effort to set up an imperial representative of the united Roman and Gothic races in opposition to Majorian. The centre of the movement was Lyons, and once more the Gallo-Romans had Gothic, and possibly Burgundian, support. That Sidonius was deeply involved in the resistance to Majorian appears from the Panegyric on that Emperor,[2] in which, as he frankly confesses, the poet made a return for the clemency with which he had been treated by the conqueror. The traces of

---

[1] Apoll. Sidon. *Carm.* vii. 572; cf. Sirmond's ed. p. 135.

[2] *Carm.* v. 574; *Praef.* l. 13:

serviat ergo tibi servati lingua poetae
atque meae vitae laus tua sit pretium;
Ep. i. 11; cf. Chaix, *Apoll. Sid.* i. 104; Fertig, *Sid.* i. 9.

the struggle are faint and few.   But the Chronicles tell
us of a peace concluded between Majorian and Theodoric
after a battle in which the Goths were defeated,[1] and we
learn from Sidonius that Lyons and the surrounding
country suffered heavily by the exhaustion following on
siege and pillage.   The blow was a crushing one, and
the good-nature of the conqueror to the party which had
opposed him made the victory complete.[2]   Henceforth
Sidonius abandoned all dreams of using the Goths in the
interests of Gallo-Roman ambition.   The accession of
Euric, who was at once more rapacious and more intolerant than his predecessor, clouded all hopes of coming
to terms with the invaders, at least in the mind of a man
like Sidonius.   The attempt of the reckless prefect
Arvandus to do so implied a severance of Gaul from the
empire of Anthemius,[3] and a partition of the province
between the Goths and Burgundians.   Sidonius was,
strange to say, the personal friend of Arvandus, and,
although he was prefect of Rome, when Arvandus was
tried for treason, he gave the traitor his official counte-
nance and support.[4]   This is undoubtedly a blot on the
character of Sidonius, and it is hard to account for his
conduct, especially when we remember that Tonantius
Ferreolus, a close friend of Sidonius, was the leading
prosecutor of the culprit.   But the theory that the poet
was involved in the intrigues of Arvandus is justly discredited by those who know most of that obscure period.
The later years of Sidonius were troubled by the repeated
assaults of the Visigoths on the independence of Auvergne.

[1] Idat. *Chron.*, legati . . . veniunt
ad Gallaecios nuntiantes Majorianum et Theudoricum regem firmis-
sima inter se pacis jura sanxisse,
Gothis in quodam certamine super-
atis.

[2] See the description of the banquet given by Majorian at Arles
after the games, to which some of
the leaders in the hostile movement
were invited.   Sid. *Ep.* i. 11 ; cf.
Chaix, i. 137.

[3] Sid. *Ep.* i. 7, § 5, pacem cum
Graeco imperatore (*i.e.* Anthemio)
dissuadens, . . . cum Burgundioni-
bus Gallias dividi debere confir-
mans ; cf. Chaix, i. 300.

[4] Sid. *Ep.* i. 7, § 5 ; cf. Fertig. i. 18.

He was now bishop of the district, and had thrown upon him the double duty of defending both the liberty and the faith of his people.   He suffered personally for his patriotism by imprisonment for a time in the fortress of Livia.   And his last recorded utterance on political subjects [1] is the pathetic and powerful denunciation of the weakness and treachery which abandoned Auvergne to the Visigoths.

Yet in spite of the high official standing of Sidonius, and his experience of the great world, his letters tell us far less about the general course of government and the fortunes of the Empire than we should have expected. This is specially marked in those letters, otherwise very interesting, in which he describes his second visit to Rome in 467.[2]   As soon as it was known in Gaul that Anthemius had been raised to the throne of the West, the leaders determined to send a deputation to lay before the new Emperor the condition of the province, threatened by the quiet advance of the Burgundians, and more openly harassed and assailed by the ambitious and intolerant king of the Visigoths.   The maladministration of the Roman officials had also reached a height which had become almost unendurable.   Sidonius, one of the deputies, received an imperial summons to Rome,[3] a document which enabled him to command the facilities of the posting service on the great roads and rivers on his journey.   We see that that service,[4] in spite of all the disorganisation described in the Code,[5] was still uninterrupted between Lyons and Rome.   There is not a hint in the letter of any trace of the effect of the invasions and troubles of the time.   The writer's mind is occupied with mythological and historical reminiscences, or the

[1] *Ep.* vii. 7.

[2] *Ib.* i. 5, 6, and 7 ; Mommsen, Praef. xlviii ; Chaix, i. 265.

[3] *Ep.* i. 5, . . . publicus cursus usui fuit sacris apicibus accito.

[4] *Ib.* i. 5, ubi sane moram vianti non veredorum paucitas sed amicorum multitudo faciebat.

[5] *C. Th.* viii. 5 *passim ;* v. *supra,* p. 239.

charm of stream and woodland. As he shoots on a swift barge down the Po,[1] he thinks of the sisters of Phaethon dropping tears of amber, or of the Tityrus of Virgil's *Eclogues*. He is charmed with the concert of birds, whose sounds float to him from sedge and brake; but he seems never to have had thought of the legions who, sixty years before, mustered on those river banks under Stilicho to oppose the hordes of barbarism. When he comes to Ravenna, he can describe, with the vividness of wanton antithesis,[2] its bad water and endless canals, its trading monks, its burglars and sleepy magistrates, but there is not a word of Ravenna when it was the seat of empire and the shelter of the Emperor, not a word about the tragic death of the great statesman and warrior, who fell a victim to the blind hatred of the races and faiths which he wished to reconcile, and was lured to his doom from his asylum at the altar of Christ.[3] When Sidonius arrived at Rome, Anthemius was about to assume the consulship, and the marriage of his daughter with Ricimer, the German master of the army, was about to be celebrated. It was only twelve years since the city had been sacked by the Vandals and Berbers. For fourteen days it had been given up to fire and sword.[4] Although the actual damage to public buildings and monuments was hardly such as to justify the reproach immortalised in the word " Vandalism," yet the loss and destruction of movable wealth must have been enormous. Gold and silver plate from the senatorial palaces, ancient statues of incalculable artistic value, the sacred vessels of the Jewish temple, which had been undisturbed since the time of Titus, along with crowds of noble captives, were

[1] *Ep.* i. 5, Ticini cursoriam escendi, etc.
  Ep. i. 8, in qua palude . . . rerum omnium lege perversa muri cadunt aquae stant, turres .fluunt naves sedent, algent balnea domicilia conflagrant, sitiunt vivi natant sepulti, etc. etc.

[3] Zos. v. 34.

[4] Prosp. *Chron.* ad a. 455 ; Jordan. *Get.* c. 45 ; cf. Gregorovius, *Hist. of Rome in Middle Ages*, i. 210.

carried away to Africa. Yet in this letter of Sidonius
there is not a hint of all this recent ruin. The social
system of Rome appears to be unshaken and unchanged.
The scenes of public resort and amusement, the theatres
and markets, the temples and forums, have the air of
ancient peace. The great city is *en fête*. The law-
courts have suspended their sittings,[1] all business is at a
standstill, the whole population seem to be bent on
making holiday. Sidonius is received by an ancient
prefect named Paulus, who, like his guest, cared more for
elaborate verse-making and turns of phrase than for
public affairs.[2] By him he is introduced to the senatorial
world of Rome and its two great leaders, men of consular
rank—Avienus, who had been one of the embassy with
Leo to Attila in 452,[3] and Basilius, to whom, as Pretorian
prefect, several of the rescripts of Majorian were addressed.[4]
The influence of one or other of these great magnates it
was necessary to gain. When we read the description of
the crowds of clients who thronged their morning recep-
tions,[5] we might fancy ourselves back in the days of
Cicero. Sidonius balanced the relative influence of the
two social potentates and their willingness to serve a
protégé, and resolved to devote himself to Basilius. He
and his patron seem to have given little thought to the
serious objects of the Gallic embassy. They are rather
intent on turning the young poet's literary talent to
account on such a unique occasion. Why should not the
ready verse-maker attract the notice of the new imperial
consul by one of those florid and conventional displays of

[1] Sid. *Ep.* i. 5, quippe cum hoc
ipso tempore . . . vix per omnia
theatra, macella, praetoria, fora,
gymnasia Thalassio Fescenninus
explicaretur. . . . atque etiam nunc
e contrario studia sileant, judicia
conticescant, etc.

[2] Sid. *Ep.* i. 9, deus bone, quae
ille positionibus aenigmata sententiis schemata, versibus commata,

digitis mechanemata facit !

[3] Prosp. *Chron.* ad a. 452, suscepit hoc negotium cum viro con-
sulari Avieno . . . beatissimus papa
Leo auxilio Dei fretus. Avienus
was cos. with Valentinian in 450.

[4] *Nov. Maj.* 1, 8 ; *Nov. Severi,* 1.

[5] Sid. *Ep.* i. 9, arctabat clientium
praevia, pedissequa, circumfusa
populositas . . .

literary skill which, in those days, received greater honour than substantial service to the State? Basilius backed up his friend loyally, the Panegyric on Anthemius was recited amid great applause, and " by the help of Christ," [1] a light use of the sacred name from which the future bishop does not shrink, Sidonius obtained the prefecture of the city. When he had gained the object of his ambition, and was installed in his office, he had to face that constant bugbear of the Urban prefect, the failure of supplies for the mob of Rome. Africa, the great granary of the city, was now in the hands of the Vandals, and the Vandals naturally did not facilitate the passage of the corn-ships to Ostia. Sidonius probably exerted himself to avert the danger. But in his account of the crisis he seems more anxious about his own reputation than about the sufferings of a population threatened by famine.[2] He dreads the curses of the theatre on the unsuccessful minister. In all this gossip of high society there is little reference to the straits of Auvergne, not a hint of the dangers and weakness which were bringing the Western Empire to the verge of the abyss.

It is only in the Panegyrics of Sidonius that we find anything like a broad and comprehensive view of the position of the Western Empire, and its relation to the barbarians and to the East. These poems are disfigured by the most extravagant and tasteless adulation, rendered even more ridiculous and offensive by pinchbeck mythological ornament, which was in that age the one resource of the sterile imagination. They mark probably the utmost extreme of indurated conventionality that literary art has ever reached. Yet, here and there, there is the ring of truth and sincerity in their tone. And, in spite

---

[1] Sid. *Ep.* i. 9, igitur cum ad praefecturam, sub ope Christi, styli occasione pervenerim . . . ; cf. a like use of the Divine name on a similarly trivial occasion in v. 16.

[2] *Ib.* i. 10, vereor autem ne famem Populi Romani theatralis caveae fragor insonet et infortunio meo publica deputetur esuries.

of all its exaggeration, the poem on the accession of
Avitus is of great value to the historian.   It shows a
certain insight into the real state of the Roman world,
although the sceptical reader might be inclined to
attribute this rather to the early associations of Sidonius
than to his own powers of reflection.   It discloses at
once a profound sense of weakness in the central power,
and of the respect, and even awe, felt for it by the
Goths.   It is also a revelation of the force of provincial
or national feeling in Gaul.   A few years before its
composition the army of the Huns had penetrated into
the very heart of Gaul, and had been turned back by
the energy of Aetius, with the aid of the Visigothic
power.   The cities of Northern Italy had been ravaged
by the same terrible invaders, and Rome itself had been
threatened.[1]   Within the space of twelve months Aetius,
the bulwark for thirty years of the Roman power, had
fallen by the treachery of Valentinian III.[2]   The
murderer did not enjoy a long impunity, and Maximus,
who succeeded him also met the same violent death
just before the Vandal fleet anchored in the Tiber.
For fourteen days the city had been at the mercy of
the army of Genseric.   It was under the shadow of such
disasters and tragedies that Avitus mounted the throne,
and that his son-in-law and panegyrist had to perform
his difficult task.

The poem reflects the general gloom.   The flight of
the twelve vultures,[3] which for many ages had been
thought by the Roman to fix the limits of imperial sway,

---

[1] Prosp. *Chron.* ad a. 452.
There were thoughts even of the
Emperor abandoning Italy ; cf.
Idat. *Chron.* Hunni qui Italiam
praedabantur, aliquantis etiam civitatibus irruptis, etc. ; and Marcell.
Chron. ad a. 452, Aquileia civitas
ab Attila Hunnorum rege excisa
est.

[2] Marcell. *Chron.* ad a. 455 ; cf.
the reflections of Sidonius on the
death of Maximus after two months
only of imperial power, *Ep.* ii. 13,
§ 3.

[3] Sid. *Carm.* vii. 55 :

quid, rogo, bis seno mihi vulture Tuscus
aruspex
portendit ?

has now a terribly real significance. The many triumphs of Rome, when the world seemed all too small for her victorious energy,[1] cast a lurid light on a frontier ever shrinking towards the centre. The old feud between Carthage and Rome[2] is revived in the Vandal invasion, but with what different issue! Rome is now a captive, and with her the world is captive in the snares of the unwarlike Vandal. But before that humiliation, she, once queen of the world,[3] has become the mere thrall of the Caesars. There is need for some warlike prince of the mould of Trajan,[4] and only Gaul, only Auvergne, the unconquered, with its memories of Gergovia,[5] of resistance to the greatest Caesar, can furnish such a captain. Yet Rome is but subject to the fate of all things lofty;[6] she has endured as much before at the hands of a Porsenna, a Brennus, and a Hannibal; and as she rose victorious over their assaults, so may she, gathering her ancient spirit, and choosing her leader aright, even now prevail over her foes. But the hope is not in the worn-out race of Rome,[7] but in the vigour of Gaul, which is so neglected and despised. Her foremost son,[8] the lieutenant of Aetius, has helped to keep the Huns, the Saxons, the Alemanni at bay for thirty years. He has made the Visigoths willing friends and companions in arms of the Romans,[9] and trained the Gothic princes to admire the

---

[1] Sid. *Carm.* vii. 96 :
cumque prius stricti quererer de cardine
    mundi
nec limes nunc ipsi mihi . . .

[2] *Ib.* vii. 444 :
    in bella iterum quartosque labores
perfida Elisseae crudescunt classica
Byrsae.

[3] *Ib.* vii. 102 :
    sum tota in principe, tota
principis, et fio lacerum de Caesare
regnum.

[4] *Ib.* vii. 116 :
        Trajanum nescio si quis
aequiperet, ni fors iterum tu, Gallia,
                        mittas
qui vincat . .

[5] *Ib.* vii. 150.

[6] *Ib.* vii. 124 :

    sat celsa laborant
semper . . .

[7] *Ib.* vii. 52 and 540 :
        portavimus umbram
imperii, generis contenti ferre vetusti
et vitia ac solitam vestiri murice gentem
more magis quam jure pati.

[8] *Ib.* vii. 232 :

nil sine te gessit, cum plurima tute sine
                        illo.

[9] *Ib.* vii. 511 :
        Romae sum te duce amicus,
    principe te miles . . .

(the words attributed to Theodoric.)

laws and literature of Rome,[1] and has united Goth and
Gallo-Roman in a common effort to save the Empire at
once from its own weakness and from the Vandal.[2] The
skin-clad squadrons, under his leadership, will once more
follow the trumpets of Rome, as they did on the Catalaunian plains.[3] There is doubtless ludicrous exaggeration in the words in which the Gothic king expresses his
wish to wipe out the blot on his ancestor's fame in
having violated the sacred city.[4] Yet Sidonius has, after
all, only put in rhetorical form the admiration for Rome,[5]
and the wish to serve her, expressed by Ataulphus to his
Roman host of Narbonne, according to the tale narrated
by Orosius.[6] In spite of all their ravages, the Goths did
recognise the superiority and suzerainty of Rome. They
had fought for her against Sueve and Vandal in Spain.
They had saved Gaul for her from Attila. Under a
Gallic prince they were ready once more to lend their
swords to rescue her from the ruin which seemed to be
impending. The chronicler is right in saying that
Avitus was raised to the imperial throne by the united
voice of the Goths and the *honorati* of Roman Gaul.[7]
And it is the confession of the weakness of Rome, and
the revelation of this union of feeling between provincial
and barbarian, which gives its historical value to the
Panegyric on Avitus.

The speedy fall of Avitus, who proved so unworthy of
the eulogies of his son-in-law, disappointed the ambitious
or patriotic hopes of Sidonius and the Gallic party.
They made an abortive attempt, with the aid of the

[1] Sid. *Carm.* vii. 497 :
  parvumque ediscere jussit
ad tua verba pater, docili quo prisca
  Maronis
carmine molliret Scythicos mihi pagina
  mores.

[2] *Ib.* vii. 441.
[3] *Ib.* vii. 349 :
  ibant pellitae post classica Romula
  turmae.

[4] *Ib.* vii. 506 :

  sed di si vota secundant
excidii veteris crimen purgare valebit
ultio praesentis . . .

[5] *Ib.* vii. 501.
[6] Oros. vii. 43, § 4.

[7] Idat. *Chron.* ad a. 455, ipso
anno in Galliis Avitus Gallus civis
ab exercitu Gallicano et ab honora-
tis, primum Tolosae, dehinc apud
Arelatum, Augustus appellatus . . .

Goths and Burgundians, to set up another emperor in the person of Marcellinus,[1] a brilliant soldier, who had fought by the side of Aetius,[2] and on his death, like Aegidius in Northern Gaul, established an almost independent principality in Dalmatia. Lyons was the centre of the new Gallic movement, and suffered severely in the struggle which followed the accession of Majorian.[3] That great soldier and far-sighted statesman was diverted for the moment from his supreme task of crushing the Vandal power. He crossed the Alps in 458, defeated the Goths, and inflicted a heavy chastisement on Lyons.[4] Its territory was ravaged, and the community had to bear a heavy fine in the shape of increased tribute, which, however, the clemency of the victor afterwards remitted. Sidonius atoned for his share in these events by a Panegyric on the new Emperor before a great concourse at Lyons, when the district had returned to its wonted tranquillity.

The piece has not the tone of pessimism about the Empire which characterises the Panegyric on Avitus. Rome, the warrior queen of the earth, is seated on her throne, clad in purple robes, but armed as well.[5] On her helmet rises a diadem of towers; her left arm bears a shield blazoned with the legends of her infancy, her right uplifts a lance of ivory that has drunk the blood of men. All her provinces from the remotest East are pouring their peculiar treasures at her feet. Before her Africa flings herself in supplication[6]—Africa, now the prey of a brigand,[7] the son of a slave-girl, whose violence

---

[1] Sid. *Ep.* i. 11, cumque de capessendo diademate conjuratio Marcelliana coqueretur. Cf. Fertig, i. p. 9 ; Chaix. i. p. 104.

[2] Procop. *Bell. Vand.* i. 6.

[3] Sid. *Carm.* v. 575.

[4] This fact proves that in 458 Lyons was not yet occupied by the Burgundians. Cf. F. de Coulanges, *L'Inv. Germ.* p. 450.

[5] Sid. *Carm.* v. 13.

[6] *Ib.* v. 53.

[7] Line 52 :

        famula satus olim
     hic praedo . . .

Cf. Procop. *Bell.Vand.* i, 3, Γιζέριχος δὲ νόθος : Sid. *Carm.* ii. 358 :

        cum serva sit illi
     certa parens.

is only softened by unaccustomed luxury.[1] She mourns
her old fated quarrel with Rome,[2] and begs to be delivered from her oppressor. The energy of Latium is
slumbering, but Rome has always been grandest in
adversity. Her fortune keeps sleepless watch even
without a soldier.[3] Rome has now a warrior whom the
ages summon as fittest for the task. Of a warlike stock,[4]
he has been the rival of Aetius in many a dim combat
on the rivers of the north against the chivalry of the
Franks.[5] He has already swept the Vandals and the
Moors from the shores of Campania,[6] and he is now
preparing on both seas a fleet larger than that which
bore the hosts of Xerxes, or than that which fought at
Actium. And he is gathering to his standards the
warriors' of every tribe from the Baltic to the Euxine.[7]
For him " the harmonious sisters have spun the threads of
gold."[8] And yet amid all the fresh hopes of revived
imperial power there is an undertone of provincial discontent. If Roman Africa calls for relief from Vandal
oppression, Gaul, the country of Majorian, the scene of so
many of his triumphs, has her grievances too. For the
greater part of a century, ever since the accession of
Gratian, she has seen nothing of the masters of the world,
and has been ignored by them.[9] She has borne gladly
the expense of Majorian's great enterprise against the
Vandals, but she is crushed with the weight of the
imperial tribute.[10] The panegyrist seems here, while

[1] Sid. *Carm.* v. 331 :
spoliisque potitus
immensis robur luxu jam perdidit omne
quo valuit, dum pauper erat.
In v. 390 the Vandals remain on
board their galleys while their
Moorish soldiers are ravaging Campania.
[2] *Ib.* v. 85 :
da veniam quod bellum gessimus olim,
. . . fatis cogor tibi bella movere.
[3] *Ib.* v. 84 :
et vigilat vestrum sine milite fatum.

[4] *Ib.* v. 108.
[5] *Ib.* v. 207 ; cf. 291.
[6] *Ib.* v. 385.
[7] *Ib.* v. 442, 473.
[8] *Ib.* v. 369 :
aurea concordes traxerunt fila sorores.
[9] *Ib.* v. 355 :
mea Gallia rerum
ignoratur adhuc dominis ignoraque
servit.
[10] *Ib.* v. 447 :
Gallia continuis quamquam sit lassa
tributis.

paying due honour to the victorious Emperor, and
deprecating his anger, to hint at the causes which had
led the Gallic party at Lyons to set up a rival for the
succession.   Provincial or national feeling is still as
strong as when two years before it raised Avitus to the
throne.

Majorian, the "young Marcellus" of the last years of
the Western Empire, with all his old Roman spirit and
statesmanlike insight, failed in his mission, and was
treacherously slain by Ricimer.   Majorian intended to
wield the full force of the State at once against the
Vandals, and against the oppression and corruption
which were eating out the heart of society.   But this
independence did not suit the ambition of the Sueve
soldier of fortune who now practically ruled the Empire,
and who either killed or dethroned four successive
emperors.[1]   On the fall of Majorian he set up Severus,
the most obscure and shadowy of the Emperors of the
West.[2]   For eighteen months after the fall of Severus
the throne was vacant.   The "unanimity" of the two
empires was broken, and Ricimer was master of the
West.   But the Vandal power was sweeping Roman
commerce from the seas and devastating the whole coast
of the Mediterranean.[3]   The Senate roused itself to send
a deputation to Leo imploring him to give them an
emperor.   Leo recommended Anthemius, a Byzantine
noble of high lineage, who had married Euphemia, the
daughter of Marcian;[4] and Ricimer, from whatever cause,

[1] *Nov. Maj.* 1, addressed to
Basilius.   Note in particular the
restraint on the use of the posting
service, and on the exactions of
compulsores.   Many other modes
of exaction are condemned under
severe penalties; cf. iv.   "De
Indulgentiis Reliquorum."   Cf.
Idat. *Chron.* Majorianum de Galliis
redeuntem, et Romano imperio vel
nomini res necessarias ordinantem,

Rechimer livore percitus et invi-
dorum consilio fultus, fraude inter-
ficit circumventum.

[2] Sid. *Carm.* ii. 317.

[3] *Ib.* ii. 349:

          hinc Vandalus hostis
urget et in nostrum numerosa classe
    quotannis
militat excidium.

[4] *Ib.* ii. 67, 194, 216.

consciousness of power, or, more probably, dismay at the position of affairs, accepted the choice, and the arrangement was to be crowned by his marriage with the daughter of the newly designated Emperor. It was on the occasion of Anthemius entering on the consulship at the opening of 468 that Sidonius, as we have seen, through the influence of Basilius, found himself, for the third time, charged with the task of delivering a panegyric on the new occupant of the throne.[1]

It was a task of peculiar difficulty for several reasons, both public and personal. The accession of a " Greek Emperor," [2] though acquiesced in by the Senate, and hailed with signs of superficial enthusiasm by the people, was yet a great shock to Roman pride. More than half a century before the accession of Anthemius, Claudian, who gave literary utterance to the deepest feelings of the old Roman party,[3] expressed all its hatred and scorn for the rival capital, and its servile and effeminate nobles.[4] It is not in accordance with human nature that the ancient home of the Empire should have become less sensitive and jealous in the years which saw her losing one after another her richest provinces, more and more at the mercy of her barbarian mercenaries, and at last under the heel of a barbarian general. But her leading spirits, whose thoughts Sidonius probably reflects, must have been fully conscious of the straits to which the capital of the West had been reduced. The appeal to Leo to give them a new chief was in itself the most open confession of weakness. Yet to celebrate such an occasion in the presence of the best blood of Rome, without offending Roman pride too deeply, was a trying task, and the panegyrist might well call on Apollo and the Muses

[1] Sid. *Ep.* i. 9.
[2] *Ib.* i. 7, pacem cum Graeco imperatore dissuadens (in the letter quoted from Arvandus to Euric).
[3] See the dedication of a statue to him in the Forum of Trajan, " Senatu petente," *C.I.L.* vi. 1710.
[4] Claud, *in Eutrop.* i. 173, 427. The contempt probably reaches its height in ii. 136, and 326-341.

to aid him in his effort.[1]   He does not disguise the fact
that Italy is no longer what she was.   She has still her
old wealth and plenty, but, in the mythological scenery
of the poem, her limbs are palsied with age,[2] and she has
ceased to wear her arms.   Rome, the city, on the other
hand, is still the martial goddess, with glittering spear
and helmet, and her shield crowded with the tale of
legendary glories.[3]   But she is begged to lay aside her
pride, to recognise the failure of her native princes, and
to seek a more fortunate ruler in the East.   Italian statesmanship, the policy of isolation, has failed.   The Vandal
is insulting with impunity the former mistress of the
world.   The poem of Sidonius does not attempt to hide
the fact that the great city of the West is suffering from the
decay of age, and tottering under the burden of her destiny.[4]
He makes a frank acknowledgment that the resources of the
Western Empire cannot cope with the craft and violence
of the Vandals, who are ravaging the coasts of Italy.[5]

The appeal of Rome to the East for help is not without dignity.   There is the old Roman pride in the recital
of the great captains who subjugated the vast territories
from the Adriatic to the Euphrates.[6]   But there is also
a mournful tone in the confession that this great inheritance has passed for ever from the hands that won it.
Rome has resigned, along with so many provinces, her
old ambition and her pride of empire.   She asks no more
to throw her bridges over the Araxes, or to hear her
trumpets sound at the gates of Bactra and Babylon.[7]
The division of the Empire is an established fact.[8]   But

---

[1] Sid. *Carm.* ii. 307.

[2] *Ib.* ii. 327-329 :

segnior incedit senio . . .
sed tamen ubertas sequitur, etc.

[3] *Ib.* ii. 394.

[4] *Ib*, ii. 451 :

totum hunc tibi cessimus axem.
Et nec sic mereor, nostram ut tueare
senectam ?

[5] *Ib.* ii. 352 :

praeterea invictus Ricimer, quem publica
fata
respiciunt, proprio solus vix Marte repellit
piratam per rura vagum, qui proelia vitans
victorem fugitivus agit.

[6] *Ib.* ii. 451.

[7] *Ib.* ii. 441-448

[8] *Ib.* ii. 65 :

valeat divisio regni
Concordant lancis partes.

the division need not mean discord.   In the presence of
the menacing danger from a hostile Africa, which has
done what Carthage could not do, the jealousies of the East
and West fade away.   Their united counsels may yet
restore the fortunes of the Roman world.

Sidonius had an even more delicate subject to deal
with in the ascendency or tyranny of Ricimer.   The barbarian master of the West had dethroned the poet's
father-in-law and crushed the hopes of Majorian.   He
had kept the imperial throne vacant for many months,
and his policy was to cut off Italy from the Eastern
Empire.   Yet it must be admitted that the poet's skill
was not unequal to the task.   Ricimer's royal birth is
adroitly used to explain why the base-born Vandal king
will not come to terms with him.[1]   Genseric cannot forget that the grandfather of his enemy inflicted a crushing
defeat on the Vandal hordes in Spain.[2]   And Ricimer
has shown himself worthy of his descent from the warlike Goth.   He has beaten the Vandals at Agrigentum.[3]
The terror of his name holds back the Ostrogoth in Pannonia and the Frank on the Rhine.[4]   Yet even his force
and authority cannot cope with the dangers of the time.
He is not armed with the majesty of a Roman emperor,
and in the call for a warrior-prince,[5] who will be his own
general, we can without much difficulty discern a covert
censure on the overweening ambition of the man who
would tolerate on the throne none but a mere creature
and tool of his ambition.

In this attempt to realise the feeling of different
sections of the Roman world in the presence of the

---

[1] Sid. *Carm.* ii. 360 :
> tum livet quod Ricimerem
> in regnum duo regna vocant . . .

The mother of Ricimer was the
daughter of Wallia, king of the
Visigoths.

[2] Idat. *Chron.* Wandali Silingi in
Baetica per Walliam regem omnes

exstincti ; cf. Sid. *Carm.* ii. 362.

[3] Sid. *Carm.* ii. 367.

[4] *Ib.* ii. 377.

[5] *Ib.* ii. 382 :
> modo principe nobis
> est opus armato, veterum qui more paren-
> tum
> non mandet sed bella gerat . . .

invaders, we have had very various answers to our
questions.   The Roman world was wide, the circumstances of its provinces were very different, and there
was an immense variety in the manner in which the
invaders behaved to the Roman population.   The shock
of the first great inroad was tremendous, but, on the
other hand, there were many causes which reduced the
force of its impact.   The moral ascendency of Rome,
both over her subjects and her assailants, was magical.
It inspired confidence in the one even in the hour of the
darkest crisis ; it restrained the impetuous violence of the
others, even when Rome seemed to be at their mercy.
The pagan noble was moved, both by his faith and his
traditional lore, to believe that the gods, who had led
their worshippers to such a beneficent use of a sway won
by heroic effort, would not allow such a career to be
abridged.   The pagan of another order saw in the
calamities of the Empire only the just punishment
for the abandonment of ancestral religion.   On the
Christian side there was no greater unanimity.   Many,
whose faith was not equal to such rude assaults,
abandoned all belief in a controlling Providence.   Others
found in the calamities of the time the righteous and
deserved punishment of a world, nominally Christian, but
really the slave of the grossest vice.   Others again,
comparing the present with the past, tried to convince
themselves that their own sufferings were nothing exceptional in the history of the world, and had a glimmering prospect of a future in which Rome and barbarism,
culture and force, would be reconciled in a new and
better order.

Sidonius, from the circumstances of his career stands
apart from the rest.   He united many sides of that age
of transition.   He was a wealthy noble whose whole
associations and training inspired him with faith in
Rome.   He was also a patriotic Gaul who had aspira-

tions for the political future of his native province. He had associated with emperors, and borne a great part on the stage of public life at Rome, when, in spite of all external troubles, social routine was undisturbed, the machine of government ran smoothly, and the majesty of the great city seemed still proud and erect. On the other hand, if he had not seen the first inroads at the beginning of the century, he had witnessed the invasion of the Huns in 451, the conquest of Africa by the Vandals, and the paralysis of the Roman world, both in the East and West, caused by their command of the sea. From his earliest youth he had also seen the Visigothic kings carrying on a comparatively civilised government at Toulouse or Bordeaux, sometimes attacking Roman cities, but as often fighting in the cause of Rome. He had led a secure and prosperous life for years between the Visigothic and Burgundian territories. He himself, and many of his friends, had been in friendly intercourse with the Germans. The Panegyrics are the productions of his earlier years, before he had a defined ecclesiastical position; the great mass of his Letters belong to the time when he was the chief pastor of Auvergne. In the former we have rather the views of the ambitious courtier who is in touch with the governing class, and reflects their ideas; in the latter we have the thoughts and life of the senator and church dignitary, whose range is rather bounded by the social or ecclesiastical life of his province. We have already seen what the letters of Sidonius tell us of the ordinary life of a provincial senator in the society of his friends and the enjoyment of his estate. In what follows we shall find them not less valuable as a picture of Roman life in a district which, having been little troubled by its Gothic neighbours for half a century, was, after a gallant resistance, compelled to accept their rule in the closing years of Sidonius.

CHAPTER III

RELATIONS OF ROMANS WITH THE INVADERS

In the previous chapter an attempt has been made to collect the views and feelings of persons, representing various localities and differences of circumstance and character, about the condition and future of the Empire in the face of its assailants. We shall in this chapter now try to discover what was the actual condition of a Roman population in invaded territory, and what were their relations to the invaders. On this subject the letters of Sidonius are, as we have said, of great importance. But perhaps even more important and more vivid is the glimpse of a life passed in Aquitaine, during the years when the Goths were about to establish themselves there. The autobiography of Paulinus of Pella was composed about 460,[1] five years after Sidonius had made his reputation at Rome by the Panegyric on Avitus, and about as many years before the death of Theodoric II. But Paulinus and Sidonius belong to different generations. The one saw the first storms of the invasion

---

[1] Paulin. Pell. *Euch.* 12 :

altera ab undecima annorum currente
              meorum
hebdomade sex aestivi flagrantia solis
solstitia et totidem brumae jam frigora
              vidi . . .

On the dates in the life of Paulinus cf. Brandes, *Pref. ad Euch.* (*Poet. Christ. Min.*) pp. 273 - 276 ; cf.

Ebert, p. 408, n. 2. Line 478 of the *Eucharisticos*, with the emendation of *bis* for *his*, tallies with l. 12. The result of the comparison shows that Paulinus received the Eucharist in 421, when he was forty-five years of age, and that his poem was composed in 459, when he was eighty-three.

of 406 ; the other lived to see the Roman power in Gaul finally submerged.

The father of Paulinus, after serving as vicarius of Macedonia and proconsul of Africa,[1] returned to his native Bordeaux in the year 379, his son being then three years of age. In that year the boy's grandfather, Ausonius, was raised to the consulship.[2] Paulinus, in his early youth, must have therefore enjoyed the rarest advantages for becoming either a statesman or a man of letters. His grandfather had retired from public life to enjoy his renown and literary ease among friends and relatives. Ausonius had controlled the affairs of vast provinces, and lived among the men who knew the secrets of the Empire. Whatever we may think of his literary rank, he was at any rate clever, versatile, full of literary knowledge, a thorough man of letters, according to the ideas of his time. His grandson must have constantly heard his talk about literature and politics. Yet, in the poem of Paulinus, there is hardly a trace of appreciation for literature, or of insight into public affairs.[3] You would never conjecture that the writer had lived among men who had held the highest offices, and to whom literature was as their mother's milk. He saw prefects and consuls of his own family returning from their years of office. He saw the army of Ataulphus in possession of Bordeaux, besieging Bazas, and retreating into Spain. He was intimate with some of the German leaders.[4] He lived to see the Gothic power firmly established in Aquitaine, the Vandals masters of Northern Africa, and sweeping the coasts of the Mediterranean with their fleets. He must have heard many a rumour of the failure of revenue, of the collapse of administra-

---

[1] Seeck's *Sym.* lxxviii. ; Ebert, *Lit. des Mittelalters,* i. p. 405.

[2] Paulin. Pell. *Euch.* 48 :
anni
ejusdem Consul, nostra trieteride prima.

[3] He says that his studies were interrupted by ill-health, v. 119.

[4] *Ib.* 346 :
regis dudum mihi cari.

tion, of the flight of free Romans to escape the ever-
growing pressure of the imperial treasury,[1] of the
slaughter in countless battlefields, of the wasting famine
and pestilence which tracked the path of the invaders
across the Pyrenees. And yet there is hardly a word in
Paulinus which shows any political insight, any feeling
for the impending fall of a great imperial system. In
fact, one of the most curious things in the poem is the
indifference of the writer to the progress of great events,
and his acquiescence in the intrusion of the strange
guests who quartered themselves in Bordeaux for a time
in 414.[2] In his earlier days he is absorbed in the
enjoyment of ease and idleness,[3] and a well-ordered
establishment, with troops of servants, elegant banquets,
and artistic plate. In his later years he had become
devout, and regarded the events of his time rather as a
personal discipline and call to the religious life. He
combines in fact, at different periods, two types of
character, which were common in the ranks of the
Roman noble class; on the one hand, the man who
loses all ambition for the distinctions of the great world
in farming, building, hunting, and the soporific pleasures
of the country; on the other, the man who, with a
different kind of self-absorption, forgets the world, the
fortunes of his fellows, and the ties of family love, in the
effort to save his own soul.[4]   His poem was written

---

[1] He alludes, however, to *fiscalia
debita* on his wife's estates, v. 199 ;
cf. 424, Romanumque nefas—which
he says has left him nothing of his
grandfather's estate.

[2] Paulin. Pell. *Euch.* 285.

[3] *Ib.* 200-216 :

        propere mihi fida paravi
otia, privatae post impendenda quieti.
quae et mihi cara nimis semper fuit
    ingenioque
congrua prima meo mediocria desideranti,
proxima deliciis et ob ambitione remota,
    etc.

[4] The most startling kind of
spiritual selfishness is to be found
in the letters of S. Paulinus Nol.,
e.g. *Ep.* xxv. § 7, necessitudines
nostrae carnales, quanto cariores
nobis sunt, tanto nos discruciant
et fatigant ; cf. *ib.*, volo, inquit,
vos sine sollicitudine esse, hoc est,
ut nihil praeter Deum et salutem
nostram cogitemus. Nam uxor et
filii, quamquam et ipsa divinitus
nobis pignora data sint, tamen
gravissima curarum onera sunt.
On this principle Melania is praised

apparently more for his own edification than for the enlightenment of posterity. He can think only of his personal fortunes and his salvation; but this very concentration on himself makes him, for the historical inquirer, specially valuable. Paulinus discloses to us, with almost startling vividness, the effects on the fate of one great house, first of the violent invasions of the Sueves and Vandals in 406, and then of the more peaceful occupation of Bordeaux by the Visigoths eight years afterwards. The first of these events occurred in the thirtieth year of Paulinus,[1] and disturbed his placid, unambitious enjoyment of the estates which had come to him by his marriage. He mentions casually the losses which he suffered by the ravages of the barbarians, but he lays much more stress on the family troubles caused by his father's death about the same time. Evidently the damage from the invasion was not very serious, for, a few years later, at the time of the Gothic occupation, he speaks of himself as enjoying ease and luxury and manifold blessings.[2]

The occupation of Bordeaux by the Visigoths under Ataulphus is known to us only from the *Eucharisticos*, but it is one of the most interesting glimpses of the history of that age. When Ataulphus entered Gaul in 412, carrying the princess Placidia with him in an honoured captivity, it would appear, both from the authorities and the probabilities of the case, that he came as an ally or lieutenant of Honorius.[3] But his

---

for neglecting her child, *Ep.* xxix. § 9, nemini parvulum suum verbo, ut dici solet, alendum, erudiendum, tuendum mandare dignata est.

[1] *Euch.* 232:

transacta aevi post trina decennia nostri . . .
hostibus infusis Romani in viscera regni.

[2] *Ib.* 283, 284.

[3] Jordan. *de Reb. Get.* c. 31.

Honoriumque augustum quamvis opibus exhaustum, tamen jam quasi cognatum grato animo derelinquens, Gallias tendit. Ubi cum advenisset, vicinae gentes perterritae in suis se coeperunt finibus continere ; Oros. vii. 43, 3, satis studiose sectator pacis militare fideliter Honorio imperatori ac pro defendenda Romana republica impendere vires Gothorum praeoptavit.

relations with the imperial government were fluctuating
and precarious.   On the one hand, certain promises had
been made to him of supplies for his troops.[1]   On the
other hand, his requisitions were met by demands for
the restoration of the Emperor's sister, whom Constantius,
the general of Honorius, claimed for his bride.   Sometimes the Gothic king seems to be acting as a faithful
servant of Honorius, and again he is in open hostility
to him.   When he first arrived in Gaul, Ataulphus
proceeded to check the ravages of the Franks and
Burgundians who were pillaging the province.[2]   Then,
when Jovinus was proclaimed Emperor at Mainz by
Goar, the Alan and the Burgundians, it is said that,
at the instigation of the ex-Emperor Attalus, the Goths
supported the movement.[3]   But within a year they
turned their arms against Jovinus, besieged him in
Valentia, and handed him over to Honorius.[4]   Once
more Ataulphus demanded his promised supplies, and
once more the Roman officials, who were quite unable to furnish them, renewed their demand for the
surrender of Placidia.   The Goths, probably to open
communication with the sea, attempted to surprise the
great port of Marseilles;[5] but they were foiled by the
energy of Count Boniface, who seems to have had a
personal encounter with Ataulphus, in which the Gothic
chief was wounded.   By whatever means, the Goths
had established themselves at Narbonne, which was
then a great port and flourishing centre of trade,[6]
although the changes of nature have now cut it off

---

[1] Olympiod. *Fragm.* § 21, ed.
Müller, Ἀδάουλφος ἀπαιτούμενος
Πλακιδίαν, ἀνταπῄτει τὸν ὁρισθέντα
σῖτον.

[2] Jordan. *Get.* c. 31.

[3] Olympiod. *Fragm*, § 17, ὅτι
Ἰοβῖνος ἐν Μουνδιακῷ τῆς ἑτέρας
Γερμανίας κατὰ σπουδὴν Γωὰρ τοῦ
Ἀλανοῦ καὶ Γυνταρίου, ὃς φύλαρχος
ἐχρημάτιζε τῶν Βουργουντιόνων,

τύραννος ἀνεγορεύθη πρὸς ὃν παρα-
γενέσθαι ˝Ατταλος Ἀδάουλφον παρ-
αινεῖ.

[4] *Ib.* § 19.

[5] *Ib.* § 21.

[6] Narbonne was then a great port
of departure for Africa; cf. Sulp.
Sev. *Dial.* i. 3, 1; Auson. *Nob.*
Urb. 13, 18.

from the sea. It was the home of a wealthy and lettered aristocracy,[1] and again and again, in the generation following Ataulphus, it was assailed by the Goths.[2] In Narbonne Ataulphus for a time seems to have quartered himself, and there he won the hand of Placidia, and wedded her solemnly according to old Roman rites. The wedding took place in the house of Ingenius, the foremost citizen of Narbonne.[3] Ataulphus, arrayed in gorgeous Roman dress, presented to his bride fifty youths laden with gold and gems, the spoils of Rome in the sack of 410. Romans and Goths united in rejoicing over the event, and Attalus, the ex-Emperor, bore a leading part in the singing of the epithalamium. In wedding the daughter of Theodosius and the sister of Honorius, the Gothic king was working for political ends, as well as gratifying private affection. His marriage was the symbol of that union of Roman and German in the cause of civilisation which was the dream of his life. And in those days at Narbonne probably took place that famous conversation between Ataulphus and his Roman host,[4] a report of which Orosius had heard in the cell of S. Jerome at Bethlehem. Ataulphus said that he had once in his youth dreamed of overthrowing the power of Rome; but experience had taught him that the Roman rule was the rule of law and order and peace. In maturer years, his great object was to unite the two races, and to support the civilising influence of Rome by the swords of the Goths. But Rome did not quite trust or appreciate her champion. Constantius, who controlled the Gallic policy of Honorius,[5] had been the rival of

[1] Cf. Sid. *Carm.* xxiii. 37.

[2] Prosp, *Chron.* ad a. 436.

[3] The scene is fully described in Olympiod. *Fragm.* § 24.

[4] Oros. vii. 43, 5.

[5] v. *C. Th.* xv. 14, 14. Constantius was of Illyrian origin. He was mag. mil. in 412, consul with Constans in 414, patrician in 416. He held the consulship twice afterwards, and was finally joint emperor in 421. He married Placidia in 417 and became by her father of Valentinian III. See the personal description of him in Olympiod. § 23.

Ataulphus for the hand of Placidia, and he was not likely to grow more accommodating after the wedding at Narbonne. Probably, almost certainly, the dearest wish of Ataulphus was to obtain a recognised position for himself under the Roman government, and a settlement for his troops on the Roman soil in Gaul. If these things were not freely granted him, he must take them by force.

Thus it comes about that in the poem of Paulinus we find Ataulphus in possession of Bordeaux, his soldiers being quartered as "guests" on the Roman inhabitants. But he would not openly break with Rome, though he might quarrel with an emperor. To make his position legitimate, he raised Attalus once more to the purple, as Avitus forty years afterwards was raised by the united voice of the nobles of Gaul and the Goths of Theodoric II. It is at this point that the fortunes of Paulinus become involved in the wanderings of the Goths. His position as a great noble saved him from the intrusion of Goths as compulsory guests.[1] But it also marked him out as a fitting holder of high office under Attalus, the Gothic Emperor.[2] Paulinus, who had no very heroic impulses, and valued ease and tranquillity above anything else, quietly acquiesced in the Gothic rule, disguised by the show of imperial legitimacy, and reluctantly accepted the shadowy office of "count of the private largesses" to a phantom emperor, an office probably as formal as it was brief. He was, as he tells us, only one of many who deemed it politic to accept the Gothic peace,[3] and who found it quite as real and effective as the Roman peace under a Roman prefect of the fifth century, like Arvandus or Seronatus.

Suddenly the Goths prepared to leave Bordeaux. What were the precise influences or motives which led

CH. III *RELATIONS OF ROMANS AND INVADERS* 353

them for a time to abandon their attempted settlement in
Gaul, and to cross the Pyrenees, must for ever remain a
mystery. According to one authority, Constantius compelled them to pass into Spain by interrupting their
communications with the sea.[1] If we believe Jordanes,
the Gothic king was moved by the sufferings of the
Spaniards, and determined to relieve the country from
the ravages of the Vandals.[2] At any rate, he gave the
order for the evacuation of Bordeaux. But the Goths did
not quit the town as peacefully and innocently as they
had entered it. It was given up to fire and pillage.[3]
Paulinus, in spite of his official rank, was stripped of all
his possessions. Indeed, he seems to have suffered all
the more from the very favour which had been previously
shown to him. In other cases the Gothic " guest "
quartered on a family might shield it from rapine. But
Paulinus had no such protector. His only consolation
was that the honour of the female members of his household was severely respected.[4] He fled with his family to
Bazas, where he probably had some property, and where
other and even more startling adventures awaited him.[5]

There is no more curious and instructive episode in
the history of the invasions than the tale of the siege of
Bazas as it is described by Paulinus. The Goths, compelled by the policy or strategy of Constantius to retire
from Southern Gaul, gave the reins to old instincts, and

---

[1] Oros. vii. 43, 1, Gothos a
Narbona expulit atque abire in
Hispaniam coegit interdicto praecipue atque intercluso omni com-
meatu navium et peregrinorum usu
commerciorum. It is noteworthy
that the three towns which Ataulphus occupied or tried to seize, Narbonne, Marseilles, Bordeaux, were
great ports and centres of trade.

[2] Jordan. *de Reb. Get.* c. 31, con-
firmato ergo Gothus regno (*i.e.* the
Roman power) in Gallis Spanorum
casu coepit dolere, etc. Cf. Idat.
Chron. ad a. 409-415. Wallia, on

the death of Ataulphus at Barcelona, waged a fierce war with the
Vandals.

[3] *Euch,* 314.

[4] *Ib.* 323 :

cunctarumque tamen comitum simul et
    famularum,
eventum fuerant nostrum quaecumque
    secutae,
illaeso penitus nullo adtemptante pudore.

[5] *Ib* 332 :

patria majorum et ipsa meorum.

His grandfather, the father of
Ausonius, was a native of Bazas ;
cf. Auson. *Idyl.* ii. 4.

felt themselves entitled to plunder where they were not to be allowed to settle peacefully. Outside the town of Bazas was a mingled host of Goths and Alans. Within, a servile revolt had broken out, supported by some of the free-born youth, who had made a plot to assassinate the leading nobles. Paulinus himself narrowly escaped, and his would-be murderer met his punishment at the hands of another.[1] But Paulinus confesses that his nerves were shaken.[2] He longed to be released, with his household and friends, at once from the perils which beset him within the walls, and from the hardships of a prolonged siege. As count of the largesses to Attalus, he had been on friendly terms with the leaders of the Goths and their auxiliaries. And he particularly remembered that he had an old friend in the chief of the Alans, who was reluctantly supporting the Goths in their assaults on the Roman towns.[3] This chief was probably the Alan Goar who, in the year in which Ataulphus entered Gaul, joined with the Burgundians in raising Jovinus to the imperial purple at Mainz.[4] In doing so, he deemed himself to be acting in the service of Rome, at a time when the rest of his people were, with the Sueves and Vandals, plundering and burning the cities of Gaul, and marching on to a final settlement in Spain.[5] How Goar came to join the Goths we do not know; but when Jovinus and his brother fell, Goar and his Alans may have felt constrained to join the power which seemed likely to have a future in the great province of the West. Paulinus found little difficulty in making his way to the quarters of the Alan king.[6] But Goar declared that he could neither give him protection

[1] *Euch.* 340.

[2] *Ib.* 345 :

sed mihi tam subiti concusso sorte pericli,
quo me intra urbem percelli posse viderem
subrepsit, fateor, nimium trepido novus
    error.

[3] *Ib.* 346, 352 :

quod scirem imperio gentis cogente Goth-
    orum
invitum regem populis incumbere nostris.

[4] Olympiod. § 17, *Fragm.*

[5] Prosp. *Chron.* ad a. 406 ; Oros. vii. 38, § 3. Prosper and Orosius mention Alans along with Vandals in the passage of the Rhine and in the devastation of Gaul and Spain.

[6] *Euch.* 354, ad regem intrepidus nullo obsistente tetendi.

in the besiegers' lines nor a safe conduct back into the town, and that he could only help him by being himself admitted into Bazas.[1] In truth, the Alan chief was eager to escape from his enforced alliance with the Goths and Attalus, their shadowy Emperor. He had served one emperor who had fallen, he was connected with another who seemed likely to have the same fate; and he probably thought it safer to take the side of Honorius. He gave the Romans his son and his wife as hostages,[2] and speedily the crowds upon the walls of Bazas saw themselves fenced in by the waggons and armed warriors of the Alans,[3] who were now ready to defend the place which they had just been helping to capture. The Goths seem to have felt the desertion of their allies as a crushing blow, and they abandoned the siege.[4] They marched away, to reappear shortly in the same regions for a longer stay. But Goar and his Alans, who stand out for a moment in such vivid light in the dim and confused annals of those years, vanish as suddenly, and we hear of them no more.

The fortunes of Paulinus for the remaining forty-five years of his life are not particularly interesting, except as an example of what numbers of his class, in Italy, Gaul, and, above all, in Africa, must have suffered in those times. On the departure of the Goths, he thought at first of betaking himself to his maternal estates in Greece and Epirus, which were very extensive.[5] But he seems to have been prevented from doing so by the timidity of his wife, or by her love for her native Gaul.[6] On the other hand, his property at Bordeaux, which had descended to him from Ausonius, had suffered by the Gothic occupation, and from the unscrupulous conduct of fellow-Romans, among whom he seems to include some of his

---

[1] *Euch.* 358-361.
[2] *Ib.* 379.
[3] *Ib.* 386.
[4] *Ib.* 390.
[5] *Ib.* 410.
[6] *Ib.* 494.

own family.[1]   At any rate he regarded a return to his
old home as impossible.   He was surrounded by a large
number of relatives, exiles like himself, and a crowd of
female slaves, dependant on him.[2]   Yet he would have
given up the struggle, and taken refuge in the cloister, if
the holy men, whom he consulted, had not advised him
to repent of his sins and cultivate a severer life, without
quitting the world.[3]   Having given himself to religious
study, he was for a time carried away by the semi-
Pelagian views which at that time had many adherents
in Southern Gaul.[4]   In his forty-fifth year, at Eastertide,
he definitely returned to the church of his baptism by
receiving the Eucharist.[5]   He was meanwhile sinking
into poverty.   His female relations dropped off one after
another.   His sons left him, one taking Holy Orders,
another returning to Bordeaux, where he succeeded in
recovering some of the family property with a Goth
as neighbour.[6]   For by this time, it must be remembered,
the Goths had returned to settle permanently in Aquitaine.   The fate of this second son is obscurely told.
But he appears to have been for a time in favour with
the Gothic court, and then to have suffered from its displeasure.[7]   As for Paulinus, he spent his old age in
cultivating a small patch of ground in the outskirts of
Marseilles, which was still under imperial rule.[8]   His
fortunes were at a low ebb when, to his surprise, he
received one day from an unknown Goth the purchase
money of a portion of his ancestral estate at Bordeaux,
which the conscientious German would not appropriate
without compensation.[9]

[1] *Euch.* 424.   [2] *Ib.* 459.
[3] *Ib.* 456.   [4] *Ib.* 471.
[5] *Ib.* 475 :
ad tua, Christe Deus, altaria sacra rever-
    sus
    te miserante tua gaudens sacramenta
    recepi
ante hos ter decies super et bis quattuor
    annos . . .

Brandes (p. 275) is right in referring
this to the Eucharist, and not to
Baptism ; cf. Ebert, i. 408.

[6] *Euch.* 498.
[7] *Ib.* 514.
[8] *Ib.* 520.
[9] *Ib.* 575.

It is a startling and pleasant incident in the history of that stormy time, a time apparently so full of violence and injustice, but really, as we believe, less unjust and violent than a superficial glance might lead us to think. There had been sweeping and desolating invasions of Gaul and Spain. But the Visigoths came not as mere lawless plunderers, but as soldiers of the Empire, and finally as permanent settlers, seeking a home after their wanderings, amid the wealth and peace of a Roman province. In moments of irritation or uncertainty, when the great imperial power seemed to be now haughty or faithless, now weak and shrinking, and unworthy of its place, the Goths, forgetting the associations of years and their ancient awe of imperial power, would resume their old fierceness and pride. But we can have little doubt that, when they settled in a Roman province, their strongest desire was to have a share of the peace and prosperity which Rome had given to the world, and to maintain order and justice between man and man. The Gothic or Burgundian chief comes not as an enemy of the Empire; his strongest ambition is to be its appointed champion, and if he receives his commission, he will draw his sword even against his German compatriots. He may, when his advances are slighted, quarrel with an emperor; but he has no quarrel with Rome. It he does not obtain the recognition which he seeks, he never dreams of imperial power for himself; he sets up, by the voice of his army, a rival emperor, as Roman armies had often done before; and with such an emperor in his camp, he tries to maintain his allegiance to Rome in her own despite. This is the clue to the puzzling narrative of the Visigothic movements in the early part of the fifth century. Sometimes the Goths are besieging Roman towns, sometimes they are fighting in Spain against Sueves and Vandals on behalf of Rome. The weakness of the Empire, the faithlessness or folly of imperial functionaries, the pride and capricious passions of his following, the mere necessity of finding subsistence for his wandering tribe—all these influences might often deflect the policy of a German chief from the line which his instinct and ambition would have followed. But in the greater leaders the longing for repose from incessant migrations and tribal blood-feuds, and the reverence for Rome as the great source of peaceful order, fruitful industry, and culture, never died out. And just in proportion to their greatness, they realised the greatness of Rome.

When Apollinaris Sidonius was born, the Visigoths were firmly established in Aquitaine by Roman authority.[1] But his native Lyons was not the residence of Burgundian princes for more than thirty years afterwards,[2] and it was only in the very last years of the Western Empire that Auvergne was abandoned to the Visigoths. For the best part of his life, therefore, Sidonius knew the Germans rather as neighbours than as masters. He saw four successive princes of the Visigoths, and between the reigns of Theodoric I. and of Euric, the relations of the Visigothic power to Rome passed through many phases. Wallia, the founder of the Visigothic power in Gaul, obtained a settlement by a definite agreement with the Empire, although we have no information as to its terms and conditions. The Goths were foederati, in a certain sense subjects, although, within the territory assigned to them, their princes had extensive powers. It was no new relation that was created by the pact with Wallia. And it was sometimes broken and interrupted, as similar ties between Rome and her foederati had often been before.

---

[1] Idat. *Chron.* 419, per Constantium ad Gallias revocati, sedes in Aquitanica a Tolosa usque ad Oceanum acceperunt ; cf. Prosp. *Chron.*, data ei (Walliae) ad habitandum secunda Aquitania.

[2] Lyons was evidently under the direct power of the Emperor when Sidonius delivered the Panegyric on Majorian in 459. *Carm.* v. 576 : Lugdunumque tuam . . . aspice victor. Cf. Chaix, *Apoll. Sid.* i. p. 110.

Sometimes German auxiliaries had been known even to pillage the lands of Roman towns.[1] In 422 the Goths were serving under Castinus, the Roman magister militum, against the Vandals in Spain.[2] Three years later a strong Gothic force was defeated by Aetius in an attempt to capture Arles.[3] Then there is a time of quiet, in which peaceful relations are restored. But once more, in 436, the Goths made an attempt on Narbonne, which was relieved in a daring movement by the cavalry of Litorius.[4] There were several battles between them and the Roman generals in those years, in one of which eight thousand Gothic warriors were left on the field.[5] Then came the defeat of Litorius at Toulouse in 439, followed by a renewal of the former peace.[6] For many years this calm was undisturbed, and in 451 Theodoric loyally and gallantly supported the imperial generals in the great battle of Châlons.[7] The son and immediate successor of Theodoric broke the long peace by another attempt on Arles, which was frustrated by the personal charm and diplomatic skill of Tonantius Ferreolus.[8] The reign of Theodoric II., with which the early manhood of Sidonius coincided, was on the whole friendly to the Empire. Theodoric fought in several campaigns for Rome against the Sueves and the Bagaudae in Spain.[9] He helped the Gallic party to raise Avitus to the throne,[10] and he lent the support of his arms to the party at Lyons which, on the fall of Avitus, strove once more to assert the power of Gaul.[11] Yet we find him in 462 in possession of Nar-

---

[1] Amm. Marc. xvi. 11, 4, laeti barbari ad tempestiva furta sollertes invasere Lugdunum incautam, etc.

[2] Idat. *Chron.*, Castinus Mag. Mil. cum magna manu et auxiliis Gothorum bellum in Baetica Wandalis infert.

[3] Prosp. *Chron.* ad a. 425.

[4] *Ib.* ad a. 436.

[5] Idat. ad a. 438.

[6] Idat. and Prosp.

[7] Prosp. and Sid. *Carm.* vii. 349.

[8] Sid. *Ep.* vii. 12.

[9] Idat. ad a. 456 ; Jordan. *Get.* xliv. ; cf. Fauriel, i. 251.

[10] Sidon. *Carm.* vii. 511 :
Romae sum te duce amicus,
principe te miles.
Cf. Fauriel, i. 244.

[11] Sid. *Ep.* i. 11 ; cf. Fauriel, i. 258 ; Chaix, *Apoll. Sid.* i. 105.

bonne,[1] which had been surrendered to him by the Count Agrippinus, to secure the aid of the Goths in his conflict with Aegidius.

During all these years, the district in which Sidonius lived suffered nothing from any hostilities with the Goths. We have seen, on the contrary, that he belonged to a circle which cultivated friendly relations with the Gothic kings, and the aim of whose policy was to maintain an alliance with them which might influence the fortunes of the Empire or secure the peace and independence of Gaul. Sidonius had been received at the court of Theodoric II., and had formed on the whole a very favourable opinion of his character, which he hastened to communicate to his friends.[2] There was probably a political purpose underlying his friendly picture of Theodoric; but Sidonius evidently feels also a curious interest in that strange scene, stimulating the minute and careful observation which makes his descriptions of the barbarian invaders of Gaul precious to the historian. There is no trace of the disgust which the genial Burgundians sometimes aroused in the mind of the fastidious Roman gentleman. There is no trace of any fear or suspicion of the Gothic power.

Sidonius had family connections with Lyons, and he visited that district shortly after it had been occupied, in some fashion or under some title, by the Burgundians. In the year 456 the Burgundians had served in the army of Theodoric II. against the Sueves in Spain.[3] Seven years afterwards it appears from a letter of Pope Hilary[4] that one of their leaders in that expedition, Gundioc, is installed at Vienne, with the title of

[1] Idat. *Chron.* ad a. 462, Agrippinus Gallus et comes et civis, Aegidio comiti viro insigni inimicus, ut Gothorum mereretur auxilia, Narbonam tradidit Theudorico.

[2] Sid. *Ep.* i. 2.

[3] Jordan. *Get.* c. 44.

[4] Hil. *Ep.* ix. ad Leontium, episcopum Arelat. Gundioc had apparently appealed to Hilary against some episcopal encroachments of Mamertus. The letter is dated in the consulship of Basilius, *i.e.* 463.

magister militum, and also exercising some control over episcopal elections. The Burgundian power was firmly established at Lyons before 474. There is no sign that they gained the territory on the Rhone by a violent conquest. The royal family were connected by marriage with Ricimer. They were in federal relations with the imperial power,[1] and their chief was probably allowed to occupy these new territories as a soldier of the Empire. Just as the corps of Bretons under Riothamus was engaged by Anthemius to guard the frontiers of Berry,[2] so the Burgundians were to be a bulwark on the east against the advance of the Visigoths. At the time of the visit of Sidonius, Chilperic, son of Gundioc, having expelled his brother Gundobald, was governing the region about Lyons and Vienne, with the title of magister militum.[3] Chilperic and his queen seem to have abandoned the Arianism of their family. The king endowed liberally the monks of Lupicinus.[4] The bishop Patiens, by his boundless charity and lofty character, commanded the admiration of the queen. The only danger to Romans seem to have been from the intrigue and calumny of some of their own race, who strove to poison the king's mind.[5] But Sidonius speaks of him with the highest respect as a soldier and a man. There is nothing to show that the provincials are suffering from the effects of violent conquest or oppressive rule. Their worst foes are those of their own household.

But although Sidonius has no serious charge to make against the Burgundians as rulers, his fastidious taste cannot reconcile itself to their society, especially on festive occasions.[6] When a friend wrote to ask him for

---

[1] Jordan. *Get.* xlv. Burgundzonum gentem . . . in eo tempore foederatam.

[2] *Ib.* xlv., quod conperiens Anthemius Brittonum solacia postulavit, etc.

[3] Sid. *Ep.* v. 6. This letter belongs to the year 474, *v.* Momms. Praef. lii.

[4] Greg. Tur. *vit. Patrum*, c. i. 5.

[5] Sid. *Ep.* v. 7.

[6] Sid. *Carm.* xii.

a wedding-song, the poet finds composition amid such
surroundings quite impossible. How could one think of
a decent verse among these hirsute giants of seven feet,
whose German songs you have to applaud in the middle
of coarse festivity which offends every sense ? This is
the worst Sidonius has to say of the Burgundians. They
were a jovial, kindly people, rather fond of good fare,
unrefined in their habits, but anxious to be on good terms,
with the Romans,[1] and even willing to give them material
help against the attacks of the Goths, although occasionally, like more modern allies, they were not always
to be trusted.

Down to the accession of Euric to the chieftainship
of the Visigoths in 466, the Romans of the circle of
Sidonius had suffered but little from the presence of
the Germans in Gaul. But, with the appearance of
Euric on the scene, there was an ominous change. This
was partly due to the growing weakness of the Empire,
which could no longer make its power respected, as
Aetius and Boniface had done in the earlier days of the
Gothic settlement in Gaul. It was also the result of
the oppression and treachery of Roman governors. A
prefect like Arvandus not only plundered the people of
his province, and shocked and insulted them by his
excesses and caprice, but he encouraged the Gothic king
to make an open rupture with Rome.[2] A governor like
Seronatus, a monster and enigma of opposite vices,[3] at
once ridiculous from his weaknesses, and dreaded for his
cruelty and greed, drove numbers to the woods to escape
his clutches, and he actually established the Gothic law
in place of the Theodosian Code in his province.[4] But

---

[1] See the very favourable character of this people given by Orosius,
vii. 32, § 13. For the fairness with
which they treated the Romans in
their territory see *Leg. Burgund.*
(*Mon. Germ. Hist.*) cap. xxxi. liv.

[2] Sid. *Ep.* i. 7.

[3] *Ib.* ii. 1.

[4] *Ib.* ii. 1, leges Theodosianas
calcans Theodoricianasque pro-
ponens. Written in Euric's reign,
the word Theodoricianas being used
probably for paronomasia.

in addition to these causes must be reckoned the personal temperament of Euric. Although he may have conscientiously believed that it was his mission to fill the void which was being left by the collapse of the Roman administration, there is no doubt that he was by nature despotic, ambitious, and, above all fiercely bigoted and intolerant. He had a sincere hatred of the Catholic faith, a hatred so intense that, to use the words of Sidonius,[1] he seemed not so much the ruler of a people as the head of a sect.

Jordanes relates that Euric, perceiving the frequent changes of Roman emperors, determined to make himself master of the Gauls in his own right.[2] The historian of the Goths seems by the words *suo jure* to mark a new departure in policy. And the history of Euric's reign confirms the statement. He began by a campaign in Spain, which left the Empire hardly a corner of that great province. He next turned his arms against the Breton troops under Riothamus, who guarded Berry for the Empire.[3] The Bretons were defeated, and fled into the territory of the Burgundians. Auvergne remained the solitary district left under the direct sway of Rome. Its people, as Sidonius proudly recalls,[4] claimed to be kinsmen of the Romans, and had again and again fought stubbornly for their independence. Placed between the Burgundians and the Visigoths, they might now seem to be in desperate straits. Yet it would appear that their leaders felt no overmastering fear of the Visigothic power, and that they had even dreams of founding an independent state in the heart of Gaul, which, if the Empire

[1] Sid. *Ep.* vii. 6, ut ambigas ampliusne suae gentis an suae sectae teneat principatum.

[2] Jordan. *Get.* c. 45.

[3] *Ib.* c. 44, 45. This event is probably referred to by Greg. Tur. ii. 18, Britanni de Biturica a Gothis expulsi sunt. There is a letter of Sidon. to Riothamus, iii. 9, in which he complains that the Bretons have carried off a poor farmer's slave.

[4] Sid. *Ep.* vii. 7, audebant se quondam fratres Latio dicere ; cf. Fertig, ii. 11.

could no longer protect it, might protect itself. After all, the Germans were not very numerous.[1] The Visigoths who occupied Aquitaine under Wallia, after all their losses from battle and disease, could not have been more than 30,000 strong. That they were not invincible had been proved again and again by the armies of Aetius. And they did not in the end make an easy capture of Auvergne.

The order of events in the conflict with Euric is difficult to determine. Sidonius persuaded a relative, of great hereditary influence with the Goths,[2] to attempt by diplomatic means to check their advance towards the Rhone. But the effort, if it was made, was fruitless. The Gothic army closed round Auvergne. Ecdicius seems to have been absent at the commencement of the siege, being probably occupied in trying to gain the support of the Burgundians, with whose princes he was on intimate terms.[3] Suddenly he was seen by the watchers on the half-ruined walls approaching with a small troop of cavalry.[4] He charged and routed the enemy with great slaughter, and was welcomed by the Arvernians with extravagant demonstrations of joy. Although he was nominally magister militum, he had no imperial troops at his command, and, at his own expense, he raised a small force,[5] with which he punished

---

[1] Fauriel, *Hist. de la Gaule Méridionale*, i. 114; cf. F. de Coulanges, *L'Inv. Germ.* 438. Oros. vii. 32, 11, puts the Burgundians at 80,000 in the fourth century. But this is probably exaggerated, and gives no clue to their numbers in the fifth, after so many vicissitudes; cf. De Coulanges, p. 444. The losses of the Visigoths may be estimated from such passages as Oros. vii. 43, 11. But any calculations on such a subject are rendered very untrustworthy by the fact that important tribes were being constantly swelled (1) by fragments of other small wandering bands,

(2) by fugitive slaves, (3) by free Romans flying from over-taxation, etc.; cf. Salv. *de Gub. Dei*, v. § 36. Cf. Paulin. Pell. *Euch.* on a revolt of slaves at Bazas, v. 334.

[2] Sid. *Ep.* iii. 1 *ad fin.*, vestra tamen auctoritas pro dignitate sententiae sic partem utramque moderabitur, etc. Avitus, to whom the letter was written, was connected through his mother with Sidonius.

[3] *Ib.* iii. 3.

[4] *Ib.* iii. 3.

[5] *Ib.* iii. 3, taceo deinceps collegisse te privatis viribus publici exercitus speciem.

the enemy's devastations in repeated sorties. In one of these engagements the Goths lost so many men that they determined, when they retreated, to decapitate the slain, so that the extent of their loss might remain uncertain.[1] Then in a fit of repentance at leaving so many of their comrades unburied, they returned and consumed their remains in the flames of some burning houses.

The energy of the famishing garrison was stimulated by the great personal influence of the bishop, who, while Ecdicius was harassing the besiegers, used all the aids of religion to keep up the courage of his flock. Yet it seemed a hopeless struggle. Dissensions broke out among the inhabitants;[2] some were ready to surrender, some actually left the town, probably to join the Goths. Sidonius summoned to his aid Constantius, an aged priest of Lyons, who combined the influence of high birth with a singular piety and purity of character. The old man undertook the long journey, involving great hardships and danger, in midwinter.[3] His presence seems to have had a great effect in silencing cabals and divisions, and in restoring a calmer courage. Sidonius had also some hope from the arrival from Rome of the quaestor, Licinianus.[4] But, beyond bringing the title of patrician to Ecdicius, it does not appear that the mission of Licinianus had any effect.[5]

Licinianus probably had to report demands from the Gothic king, the concession of which would have involved, not only the surrender of Auvergne, but of the last remaining strip of Roman territory surrounding the seat of

---

[1] Sid. *Ep*. iii. 3.

[2] *Ib*. iii. 2, cum inveneris civitatem non minus civica simultate quam barbarica incursione evacuatam.

[3] *Ib*. iii. 2. He is the Constantius to whom Sid. dedicated

the Letters, *Ep*. i. 1; vii. 18; viii. 16.

[4] *Ib*. iii. 7.

[5] *Ib*. v. 16. Written at such a time, this letter is a curious illustration of the inordinate value set upon such distinctions by the senatorial class.

the prefecture at Arles.[1]   But the bishop of Auvergne, still offered a bold front to the dangers which threatened to submerge his diocese.   He had heard of the wonders which the Rogations, established by Mamertus Claudianus of Vienne,[2] had worked on a population maddened with superstitious terrors, and he determined to introduce the solemn rites among his people.   With processions and prayer he strove to fortify their spirits for a final struggle; while at the same time he summoned Ecdicius from Lyons once more to head the resistance.   Meanwhile fresh negotiations were going on between Euric and the Emperor.   The attitude of the Goths was so threatening that it was determined at a council held at Milan to send Epiphanius, bishop of Pavia, to treat with the Gothic king.[3]   The tale of the bishop's journey to Toulouse is told with suspicious rhetoric by Ennodius.   Euric professed himself disarmed by the words of the holy man, and promised to be at peace with the Empire.   But apparently he said nothing of the conditions of the peace. As the result of this embassy, the negotiations were placed in the hands of four bishops, including Graecus of Marseilles and Faustus of Riez.   Euric was a persecutor of the Church as well as an enemy of the imperial authority in Gaul.   We can only infer what were the influences which led the bishops to agree to the cession of the valiant Auvergne.   But the bitterly reproachful letter, addressed by Sidonius to his brother bishop of Marseilles, leaves little doubt that personal and ecclesiastical interests had a certain influence in the arrangement which finally handed over Auvergne to the Goths.[4]   Churchman as he was, Sidonius in this letter shows that he was still quite as much the proud Arvernian noble, the proud Roman

[1] Chaix, *Apoll. Sid.* ii. 164-173; cf. Fertig, ii. 14.

[2] Sid. *Ep.* v. 14; cf. vii. 1.

[3] Ennod. *vit. S. Epiphani,* pp. 351 *sqq.* (*Corp. Scrip. Eccl. Vindob.*).

[4] Sid. *Ep.* vii. 7, parum in commune consulitis; et cum in concilium convenitis, non tam curae est publicis mederi periculis quam privatis studere fortunis.

senator, holding fast to the memories of his Celtic ancestors and to the privilege of Roman citizenship. In the passionate earnestness of this protest, and its tone of lofty public spirit, one forgets the literary vanity and frivolous ambition which were the only faults of Sidonius.

Patriotism was perhaps an even stronger feeling in Sidonius than devotion to the Church. But his efforts to save Auvergne from Euric were stimulated by dread for the future of Catholicism in his diocese, if it fell under the power of an Arian ruler. Ever since his accession, the Gothic king had shown a pitiless temper to the orthodox faith. Some bishops and priests had been actually put to death ;[1] others had been driven into exile. Sidonius enumerates nine sees in Aquitaine or Novempopulana which were kept without a chief pastor.[2] The sacraments ceased to be regularly administered, and the churches everywhere fell into ruinous decay. The doors dropped from their hinges, the entrance was grown up with briars, and cattle browsed round the very altar.[3] Even in the towns, meetings of the Christian people for worship became less and less frequent. The bishop was deeply concerned for the effects on faith and discipline of this violent interruption of the channels of the Divine grace. Yet he uttered no harsh or uncharitable word about the persecuting king whom he seems to regard as a sincere bigot.

Of the terms and conditions of the treaty by which, with the assent of the four bishops, Auvergne was resigned to the Goths, we know nothing definitely. It is possible that the episcopal negotiators, while abandoning the rights

---

[1] Greg. Tur. *Hist, Fr.* ii. 25, sacerdotes vero, alios dabat exsilio, alios gladio trucidabat ; Fertig, ii. 18. For similar persecution in Africa cf. Vict Vitens. i. 5, 17 ; ii. 7 ; esp. the edict of Huneric, iv. 2, ut nullam ordinandi haberent licentiam sive episcopos, sive presbyteros.

[2] Sid. *Ep.* vii. 6.

[3] *Ib.* vii. 6, videas armenta . . . etiam herbosa viridantium altarium latera depasci.

of the Empire, may have secured concessions to the Church. It may be that Euric's fanaticism was not altogether uncontrolled by policy, and that after all he set the peaceful government of a province before its conversion to his own faith. At any rate his subsequent organisation of Auvergne was the work of a statesman and not of a sectary. Leo, his Catholic minister of state, probably had a potent voice in this settlement. A Catholic Gallo-Roman, Count Victorius, was appointed governor, who, if his morals are impeached by Gregory of Tours,[1] seems to have been on friendly terms with Sidonius, and the bishop has given a much more favourable account of his character than we receive from the historian of the Franks. But the resistance of Auvergne headed by its bishop had been obstinate, and might be revived. Some of the leaders, and among them the chivalrous Ecdicius,[2] had to fly beyond the reach of Euric's arm. His treatment of Sidonius was not so harsh as we might have expected. The bishop indeed was relegated for a time to a fortress named Livia,[3] near the Spanish frontier; but his worst hardship was having to listen to the rough accent of his Gothic guards and the drunken squabbles of two old Gothic crones who disturbed his rest.[4] His correspondence was not stopped, although, from some phrases, we can see that it was watched, and that political references had to be very guarded. One of his correspondents was Euric's secretary of state, the accomplished Leo, at whose request Sidonius occupied his leisure in translating, or transcribing, the

---

[1] Greg. Tur. *Hist. Fr.* ii. 20 ; cf. Sid. *Ep.* vii. 17, giving a description of the reverence with which Victorius attended the death-bed of the monk Abraham. On the extent of his jurisdiction Sirmond points out that in Gregory's time, Dux, the title he gives to Victorius, was governor of several towns, Comes of one, Sirm. *Sid.* p. 79.

[2] Jordan. *Get.* xlv., Ecdicius diu certans cum Vesegothis neo valens antestare, relicta patria . . . ad tutiora se loca collegit.

[3] Sid. *Ep.* viii. 3. Livia was probably somewhere between Narbonne and Carcassonne ; *v.* note in Migne, and the Ind. Loc. in Momms. ed. ; Sirm. p. 82.

[4] *Ep.* viii. 3.

Life of Apollonius of Tyana by Philostratus,[1] and who used his influence to mitigate and shorten the bishop's captivity.[2] In a well-known letter, which may possibly have come under the eyes of Euric, Sidonius flatters, in his most elaborate style, the literary skill of his friend Leo, and the far-reaching power of the king, the terror of whose name overawes the Franks on the Rhine and the Vandals beyond the sea. Leo had probably little difficulty in obtaining the release of the bishop, who soon afterwards betook himself to Bordeaux.

The causes of his residence at Bordeaux are left rather obscure. It is conjectured that it was a sort of exile, a mild extension of his imprisonment at Livia.[3] Sidonius had been the soul of the Arvernian resistance to Euric. His influence, both as a bishop and a great noble, was formidable, and he had close relations with the Burgundians, who had lent their support to Auvergne during the siege. We can hardly wonder if Euric thought it prudent to keep Sidonius away from his diocese for a while. But Sidonius had also probably reasons of his own for being at Bordeaux.[4] It would appear from a letter written at this time that he was trying to recover an estate, which came to him by his marriage with the daughter of Avitus.[5] His friend is a lucky Tityrus who has recovered his lands, and can now tune his lyre among his planes and myrtles. Probably during the bishop's confinement at Livia some one had taken advantage of the confusion of the times to appropriate the charming

---

[1] *Ep.* viii. 3 ; *v.* Sirmond's note, which makes it probable that Sidonius sent Leo a carefully transcribed copy of the original work ; cf. *Ep.* v. 15, where he sends Ruric a carefully emended copy of the Heptateuch. Sym. *Ep.* ix. 13 ; cf. Fertig, ii. 22.

[2] *Ib.* viii. 3, cujus incommodi finem post opem Christi tibi debeo.

[3] Mommsen, *Praef. in Sid.* xlviii.

[4] See Fertig, ii. 23.

[5] *Ep.* viii. 9, necdum enim quicquam de hereditate socruali vel in usum tertiae sub pretio medietatis obtinui. On the appropriation of conquered lands by the Germans see Fauriel, *Hist. de la Gaule Mér.* i. 142 ; Chaix, *Apoll. Sid.* ii. p. 205 ; F. de Coulanges, *L'Inv. Germ.* 538 ; cf. *Leg. Burgund.* cap. liv.

woods and meadows of Avitacum. Whatever the true account may be, his stay at Bordeaux was somewhat prolonged.

While he was at Bordeaux, he used his literary facility to propitiate the Gothic court. A complimentary inscription for a present which a friend of Sidonius was making to Queen Ragnahilda,[1] in those days when women were beginning to exercise the influence which culminated in the chivalrous cult of their sex, may have had its intended effect. But a poem addressed to Lampridius,[2] one of the crowd of facile versifiers, whose conventional art then obtained such a strange vogue, probably did more than weightier compositions to relieve the stress on Auvergne, and to restore Sidonius to his flock. The letter in which the poem is forwarded to the prosperous courtier has a tone of depression and melancholy, as if this pompous and overcharged flattery of Euric had been wrung from Sidonius by the necessities and distresses of his position. He is an exile from his beloved Auvergne, hanging on the outskirts of the Gothic court, unable to obtain the restitution of his estate. But the poem is also evidently intended for the ear or eye of the Gothic king. Sidonius has only once within the space of two months had a sight of the monarch who is occupied with worldwide cares. The complaint of the neglected suitor is relieved by the grossest flattery of the new barbarian power to which all the peoples of the world, from the wild Saxon pirate to the princes of Susa, are bending submissively and bringing their tribute.[3] Burgundian and Ostrogoth recognise his supremacy. And even the Roman, hard pressed by the Scythian hordes, entreats the potentate of the Garonne to succour the weakness of the Tiber. So low had sunk

---

[1] *Ep.* iv. 8. The verses were composed to be inscribed on the edges of a cup which Evadius wished to present to the queen of Euric. Evadius is by some thought to have been the successor of Victorius in the governorship of Auvergne ; cf. Chaix, *Apoll. Sid.* ii. 290.

[2] *Ep.* viii. 9.

[3] *Ib.* viii. 9.

the pride of the great noble, who in his earlier days celebrated before the élite of Rome the triumph of imperial prestige and diplomacy over Gothic force ; so low had fallen the faith of Romans in the future of Rome.

The Panegyric on the power of Euric, however, had its reward. The bishop was restored to his diocese, and his later years are not marked by any incident connected with our present subject.[1] They belong to ecclesiastical history. Sidonius submitted to the inevitable triumph of Visigothic power, and devoted himself henceforth to the duties of his see and to a diligent correspondence with his ecclesiastical brethren. It is probable that he was also engaged during these last years in collecting and polishing his letters for the eyes of posterity.[2] He has secured the immortality he longed for, but it is for merits very different from those on which he hoped to rest his fame.[3] His works will live for ever as a precious monument of an obscure period, in spite of the tricks and affectations of a style elaborated with an extraordinary perversity of art. Yet, notwithstanding the pathetic failure of his efforts to charm as a master of style, the devotion of the man to a literary ideal, however false and distorted, is one of his most admirable traits. His faith in letters in a time of decadence covers a multitude of literary sins. To the class whom Sidonius represents, culture became more precious as the external grandeur of the Empire waned and faded ; we may also say that it became more precious as it showed signs of its decay. That it was decaying Sidonius clearly saw.[4] He praises a friend for being one of the few in whom still lingered the traces of a vanishing literary sense. The mass even

---

[1] For the pathetic story of his death cf. Greg. Tur. *Hist. Fr.* ii. 23.

[2] Germain's *Apoll. Sid.* pp. 73 *sqq.* ; cf. Mommsen's Praef. l.

[3] *Ep.* i. 1.

[4] *Ib.* iv. 17, sermonis pompa

Romani, si qua adhuc uspiam est, Belgicis olim sive Rhenanis abolita terris in te resedit. There is a letter of Auspicius to Arbogastes in which the latter is styled Comes Trevirorum.

of the educated were too sluggish to maintain the strenuous pursuit of literary purity which was the great pride of the schools of Gaul.[1]   They have not the energy to resist the incursions of barbarous and vulgar idiom. Yet there never was a time when the higher class were more bound, if only as a duty to their order, to hold fast to their literary heritage.   For, as the career of political ambition was closed, the only brand of nobility left was that of literary distinction.[2]   The military and the civil power alike were passing into the hands of barbarians. Sidonius may have had a real admiration for the character and bearing of Theodoric II.; he may have been overawed by the vivid energy and commanding power of Euric; but, apart from their military and political success, the Germans were, to the lettered bishop, the representatives of mere brute force,[3] ignorant, cramped, and uncultivated, with none of the polish and elasticity of intellect, which only generations of social and academic discipline can give.   They were the spreading darkness before which the borders of the light were slowly receding.

The feelings of Sidonius for the Germans were probably those of most of his class, and they found a vent in pungent satire,[4] which did not spare even the court of the Burgundian king.   Many of the great nobles probably held aloof from all intercourse with the Germans, and secluded themselves in the solitude of

---

[1] *Ep.* ii. 10, tantum increbuit multitudo desidiosorum ut nisi vel paucissimi quique meram linguae Latiaris proprietatem de trivialium barbarismorum robigine vindica-veritis, eam brevi abolitam defleamus interemptamque.

[2] *Ib.* viii. 2, nam jam remotis gradibus dignitatum, per quas sole-bat ultimo a quoque summus quisque discerni, solum erit posthac nobili-tatis indicium litteras nosse.

[3] *Ib.* iv. 1, bestialium rigidar-umque nationum corda cornea fibraeque glaciales.

[4] *Ib.* v. 8, tu tamen nihilo segnius operam saltem facetis satirarum coloribus intrepidus impende, nam tua scripta nostrorum vitiis pro-ficientibus tyrannopolitarum locu-pletabuntur.   Sirmond, p. 57, refers the words to a satire of Secundinus on the Burgundian princes.

their great estates, where they maintained among their numerous following a sort of independence, and were probably not often troubled, so long as they quietly accepted the new *régime*. There were others who fortified themselves in strong castles,[1] built in lonely valleys, or on unassailable sites among the mountains, where the feudal life of the middle age, in its main features, had already begun.[2] One at least of these strongholds, in Haute Provence, has been identified.[3] It is situated in a deep and lonely glen fenced in by precipitous rocks, among which can still be seen the traces of the engineer's art. The place was fortified, as an inscription tells, by Dardanus, prefect of the Gauls, between 409 and 413, the years when the army of the Visigoths was seeking a home in Southern Gaul. It is probable, too, that many of the villae in the more open country about this time were strengthened with towers and fortifications which provided security without interfering with the amenity and comfort of the country seat. There is such a fortress described in one of the poems of Sidonius,[4] the Burgus of Leontius, at the confluence of the Dordogne with the Garonne. The house had the charms and conveniences of the ordinary country house, the vestibules and colonnades, the summer and winter apartments. But over all rose a lofty keep, with soaring towers, and of a fabric so solid that no engine known to ancient warfare could shake or undermine it.[5] Yet it is probable that the Gallo-Roman

---

[1] *Ep.* v. 14 *ad init.*

[2] F. de Coulanges, *L'Inv. Germ.* pp. 199, 540 ; *L'Alleu*, p. 93.

[3] See the inscription in *C.I.L.* xii. 1524 ; cf. Fauriel, i. 560. Dardanus was P.P. in 409 ; cf. *C. Th.* xii. 1, 171. He induced Ataulphus to desert Jovinus, and slew that usurper with his own hand. He was a friend of SS. Jerome and Augustine ; cf. Olympiod. § 19 ; Aug. *Ep.* 187; Hieron. *Ep.* 129.

Sidon. *Ep.* v. 9 blackens the character of Dardanus. But this opinion may be accounted for by the fact that Auvergne had supported Jovinus, and that some of its magnates had been put to death for their share in the movement. Greg. Tur. ii. 9.

[4] *Carm.* xxii.

[5] *Ib.* xxii. 120 :

    non illos machina muros
  non aries . . .
    quassare valebunt.

nobles had little to fear from any open assault of German forces in regular war.   The real danger was from irregular bands or from gangs of brigands, which were as often recruited from the wreck of Roman society as from the invaders.   But all the evidence goes to show that the great Roman families suffered little in the invasions either from violence or from confiscation.[1]   Salvianus, writing at least a generation after the occupation of Aquitaine by the Visigoths, describes the life of the nobles as wealthy and luxurious even to excess.[2]   We have found in Sidonius the picture of a society, tranquil and opulent, which has suffered nothing, and which fears nothing.   The chroniclers of the following age, such as Gregory of Tours, in many a genealogy, leave the clear impression that in the middle of the sixth century many of the old senatorial families were in secure possession of the lands and rank of their ancestors.

But, while probably the majority of the Gallo-Romans secluded themselves from contact with the new masters of their province, there were evidently a considerable number who, from necessity or policy, were willing to place their services at the disposal of the conquerors, some in honourable employment as high officials, others in less reputable ways.   Both at Lyons and Bordeaux, the assistance of the skilled administrator or diplomatist who could bring tact and knowledge of traditional methods to the tasks of government, or who could conduct skilfully the voluminous correspondence with Roman and barbarian powers, was in much request.   Latin was, of course, the language of the civilised world.   The dialects of the German tribes were many and various, and provided no available and predominant medium of communication.   The Visigothic princes are said to have

---

[1] F. de Coulanges, *L'Inv. Germ.* p. 540.
[2] Salv. *ad Eccles.* iii. § 87; *de Gub. Dei*, vii. § 12, in omnibus quippe Galliis, sicut divitiis primi fuere, sic vitiis; cf. § 50.

acquired from Roman courtiers a taste for Virgil.[1] But they must have needed the assistance of lawyers, learned in Roman jurisprudence, and secretaries trained in the use of the approved and elaborate idiom in which the Romans of that day expressed themselves. Euric is said, on the doubtful authority of Ennodius, to have needed an interpreter in his interview with Epiphanius.[2] It is hard to believe that so able and energetic a prince, face to face with the problem of governing a Roman population, should not have learned enough Latin to carry on an ordinary conversation. But, with all the ramifications of his power and influence, he could not dispense with men who were able both to advise him on matters of policy and express his views in diplomatic language. Just as Rome had for generations employed barbarian chiefs in her armies, so the barbarian kings had to employ the knowledge and technical skill of Roman lawyers and rhetors in their chanceries. There is no more striking figure among this class than that of Leo, the minister of Euric, during the last years of the independence of Auvergne. He was one of the cultivated upper class of Narbonne, and descended from the great orator Fronto.[3] His reputation, both as a jurist and a literary man, stood very high.[4] Leo appears to have combined the fervour of a true Catholic with the old-fashioned Roman virtues. His influence with Euric was powerful, and to it we may probably attribute the restoration of Sidonius to his diocese, and the tolerant administration of Auvergne under a Catholic and Roman governor. It is certainly a curious fact that a sincere Catholic like Leo should have shared the counsels and influenced the policy of a bigoted Arian like Euric.

---

[1] Sid. *Carm.* vii. 496.

[2] Ennod. *vit. S. Epiphani*, p. 354 (ed. Vindob.), taliter tamen fertur ad interpretem rex locutus.

[3] Sid. *Ep.* viii. 3, suspende peror-

andi illud celeberrimum flumen quod in tuum pectus per succiduas aetates ab atavo Frontone trans-funditur.

[4] Sid. *Carm.* xxiii. 446.

Another Gallo-Roman of this time, Syagrius, belonging to a consular family at Lyons, was secretary to the Burgundian king.[1] He was occupied, according to Sidonius, in translating Latin despatches into German, and Sidonius, with much exaggeration, describes how the polished scholar, nourished on Cicero and Virgil, had so mastered the German idiom that the barbarians dreaded to perpetrate a barbarism in his presence.[2]

The ascendency of such men was due to their knowledge of affairs, their legal learning, or their literary skill. But, if we may judge by the case of S. Avitus, some of them did not shrink from fortifying their influence by a flattery and address not always creditable to the courtier's principles. S. Avitus, a Roman of high rank, was bishop of Vienne in the reign of Gundobald, and wrote some despatches, still extant, on his behalf to the Eastern emperor. The Burgundian prince was an Arian,[3] but Avitus affects to believe that he is a sound Catholic at heart, and styles him the protector of the Catholic faith. Gundobald had compassed the death of his two brothers, Chilperic and Gundemar, and that of Chilperic's queen;[4] yet the bishop does not hesitate to say that Gundobald had shed pious tears for their fate, and congratulates him on the good fortune which had reduced the number of the royal family and yet preserved to the world all that sufficed for the Empire. The probability that the object of S. Avitus was to make a powerful convert will hardly be allowed to excuse such a flagrant disregard of truth and decency.

[1] Sid. *Ep.* v. 5. This Syagrius was great-grandson of the Flavius Afranius Syagrius who was consul in 381, and who was a friend of Symmachus and Ausonius (Seeck's *Sym.* cix.). His tomb near Lyons was still shown in the middle of the fifth century (Sid. *Ep.* v. 17). The family was probably of Gallic stock. Their estates may have been near Soissons (cf. Greg. Tur. *Hist. Fr.* ii. 18). Sirmond, *Sid.* p. 54.

[2] *Ep.* v. 5, quod te praesente formidet linguae suae facere barbarus barbarismum.

[3] Greg. Tur. *Hist. Fr.* ii. 32.

[4] Avit. *Ep.* v. ; cf. Ampère, *Hist. Lit.* ii. 203.

But arts like these seem innocent when we turn to another class of Romans who flourished at the German courts by means of the most shameless treachery and corruption. They are described in a letter to a man, whose brother Apollinaris had been secretly accused to King Chilperic of striving by his intrigues to secure the accession of Vaison to the new Emperor, Julius Nepos.[1] Apollinaris was thus threatened with ruin by one of those wretches of his own race, who saw the chance of gain in the general unrest and insecurity. This tribe of delators are depicted by Sidonius with a grotesque elaboration of antithesis, which might create a suspicion of his truthfulness if it were not for the tone of genuine contempt, the "saeva indignatio," which runs through the whole description. Versed in the intricacies of the law, they use their knowledge to pervert the course of justice by every species of chicanery, calumny, and corruption. They are ready to attack every right and sell every concession. Every class in the community is made to feel that it is at the mercy of their spite or their cupidity. Mere vulgar adventurers, they are "intoxicated by their new wealth" and filled with envy of the noble order whose birth and breeding overshadow them. It is very characteristic of the class and period to which Sidonius belongs that the delator's ignorance of social usage and his errors in dress are lashed with almost as great severity as his crimes; and it is a welcome gleam of sunshine in this scene of vulgar rapacity to learn that Sidonius' friend, Apollinaris, was saved from his peril by the kindly and womanly arts of the pious queen of Chilperic.[2]

---

[1] Sid. *Ep.* v. 6 and 7, namque confirmat magistro militum Chilperico, relatu venenato quorumpiam sceleratorum fuisse secreto insusurratum tuo praecipue machinatu oppidum Vasionense partibus novi principis applicari. Sirmond, p. 55, says "novus princeps" is a Roman emperor, but, in the rapid succession of emperors, it is not clear who is referred to. In Luetjohann's edition of *Apoll. Sid.* (p. 423) the reference is said to be to Julius Nepos, who succeeded Glycerius, the nominee of Gundobald.

[2] *Ep.* v. 7, temperat Lucumonem nostrum Tanaquil sua. She had a

The German governments, which succeeded to the Roman administration, undoubtedly were as anxious as their predecessors to prevent plunder and violence in their territories.[1] But in the period of transition which we are describing, boundaries were fluctuating and uncertain, social bonds were relaxed, and authority was weakened. There are indications that the roads were not always safe, and that couriers might have their despatch bags examined.[2] Some of the letters of Sidonius are written with an obvious reserve, as if they might come under the eyes of persons who would use the contents to the prejudice of the writer. In one written in Burgundian territory, Chilperic and his queen are veiled under the names of Lucumo and Tanaquil.[3] At another time of some anxiety, the bishop employed a friendly Jew to convey a letter to Narbonne.[4] We are accustomed to think of the German kings as wielding an overwhelming power over a crushed and conquered population. But the Roman population far outnumbered the invaders, and the Roman nobility were wealthy, powerful, and, above all, bound together by the closest ties of tradition and culture. That the Germans inspired fear is certain; but it is equally certain that they were very sensitive to the good or evil opinions held about them by their Roman neighbours, and especially to the opinion of an exclusive and fastidious caste.

Sidonius, unfortunately, does not tell as much as we could wish of the fortunes of the " dim silent masses " who suffer most in great social convulsions. Yet, with the somewhat bounded vision of the Roman aristocrat

great reverence for Bishop Patiens, *Ep.* vi. 12 omitto te tali semper agere temperamento, sic semper humanum, sic abstemium judicari, ut constet indesinenter regem (Chilpericum) praesentem prandia tua, reginam laudare jejunia. For her tragic end *v.* Greg. Tur. *Hist. Fr.* ii. 28.

[1] *Leg Burgund.* (*Mon. Germ. Hist.*) cap. ix. xi. xxv. xxvii. xlvii.
[2] Sid. *Ep.* ix. 5, apices nostri incipient commeare, quoniam cessant esse suspecti ; cf. v. 3, iii. 4.
[3] *Ib.* v. 7.
[4] *Ib.* iii. 4. Gozalas natione Judaeus . . . defert literas meas quos granditer anxius exaravi.

of the Lower Empire, Sidonius in his later years displays
a genuine Christian sympathy with suffering, which he
strove to alleviate by charity and episcopal influence.[1]
The agony of grief and desolation into which his orphaned
flock were thrown by the death of their bishop seems
still to throb in the pages of Gregory of Tours; [2] and he
has left here and there sketches which reveal, as if by a
sudden flash, the vicissitudes of fortune to which the
humbler class in those days had to submit.

The country districts suffered more from brigands
than even from German bands on the warpath or from
German spies. We have seen that in the last century
of the Western Empire brigandage was one of the most
menacing evils of the times. The ranks of the robber
class were swelled or supported by the agents and
shepherds on lonely estates, by deserters from the army,
by bankrupt farmers and broken men, who, flying from a
society which had crushed and defrauded them, rose up
fiercely against it, and gratified the instincts at once of
greed and of revenge.[3] The great noble in his strong
house, surrounded by troops of clients and serfs, could
protect himself against the attacks of these desperadoes;
but the sufferings of the meaner sort may be inferred
from a single incident recorded in a letter of Sidonius.
A poor woman of the lower class had been carried off by
the robber bands known in Gaul by the name of Vargi.[4]
She had been taken to Troyes and thence to other places.
Her relatives for a long time followed her traces in vain.
At last they tracked her to Auvergne, where she had

---

[1] See the tale in Gregory of
Tours about his giving his plate
in charity, nesciente uxore, *Hist.
Fr.* ii. 22.

[2] Greg. Tur. *Hist. Fr.* ii. 23,
cumque illuc (*i.e.* in ecclesiam)
illatus esset, conveniebat ad eum
multitudo virorum ac mulierum,
simulque etiam et infantium plan-
gentium atque dicentium : Cur nos

deseris, pastor bone, vel cui nos
quasi orphanos derelinquis?

[3] Salv. *de Gub. Dei*, v. §§ 24, 25,
on the Bagaudae ; cf. Eugipp. *vit.
S. Severin.* c. x., latrones . . . quos
vulgusscameras appellabat ; Fauriel,
i. 57 ; Zos. vi. 2 ; Sirmond, ed.
Apoll. Sid. p. 65.

[4] Sid. *Ep.* vi. 4 ; cf. ed. Apoll.
Sid. in *Mon. Germ. Hist.* p. 447.

been sold in the public market, a certain Prudens of Troyes having involved himself in the transaction by signing the contract. She passed fortunately into the hands of an agent of Sidonius, and her friends appealed to the bishop for redress. He found that blood had been shed in effecting her capture, and that her relatives were determined to have satisfaction from the offenders at all costs. And he writes to Lupus of Troyes to secure the help of his great authority in arranging an amicable settlement of what threatened to be a dangerous feud. In another letter we have the tale of a man in deacon's orders, who, with his family, "had fled from the whirl-wind of the Gothic ravages," and had settled on some church lands of the diocese of Auxerre.[1] The squatter had sown the ground hastily for the next harvest, and Sidonius pleads with the episcopal owner that the refugee may be excused by his poverty from paying the rent for which he was liable. Another incident of obscure misfortune shows that the Romans had often as much to fear from their allies as from their enemies. Anthemius had engaged a corps of 12,000 Bretons, who were quartered under a chief Riothamus on the Loire, to check the advance of the Visigoths to the north.[2] The Bretons were defeated by Euric at Déols, and fled into the territory of the Burgundians, then on friendly terms with the Romans.[3] But they were dangerous neighbours for the people of Auvergne, and supplemented by raids the precarious pay of the Empire. In one of these they

[1] Sid. *Ep.* vi. 10, hic cum familia sua depraedationis Gothicae tur-binem vitans in territorium tuum delatus est.

[2] Jordan. *Get.* c. xlv. The name of the chief is variously spelled, Riotimus, Riothimus, Riutimud, Rotimus, but there is little doubt he is the same as the Riothamus of Sid. *Ep.* iii. 9.

[3] Greg. Tur. *Hist. Fr.* ii. c. 18,

Britanni de Biturica a Gotthis expulsi sunt, multis apud Dolensem vicum peremptis. As to whether this corps were insular Britons or Armorican, *v.* Fauriel, i. 302 ; Jordan. *Get.* c. xlv. says they came to Berry by sea : quorum rex Riotimus cum duodecim milia (v.l. milibus) veniens in Beturigas civitate (v.l. civitatem) Oceano e navibus egresso susceptus est.

carried off the slaves of a poor farmer, who appealed to his bishop for redress.[1] Sidonius wrote to the Breton chief explaining the man's grievance, but he seems to have had some doubt about the reception which his humble client would meet with among these lawless warriors.

Alike in Gaul and in Spain, the horrors of pestilence and famine haunted the track of the invaders.[2] In the invasion of Auvergne the Visigoths burnt the standing grain.[3] The country people whose crops were destroyed were often far from markets and depots of supplies, and must have been reduced to terrible straits for food. This was the condition in the later years of Sidonius, both of his own diocese and of a wide stretch of country along the Rhone. Two men, who in spite of their rank in their own age would otherwise be hardly known to us, have had their names perpetuated for merciful munificence in their efforts to relieve the miseries of a famishing population. One is Ecdicius,[4] the son of Avitus, and the chivalrous defender of Auvergne in its last struggles with the Visigothic power; the other is Patiens,[5] the saintly and princely bishop of Lyons, whose sanctity cast a spell on the fierce temper of the Burgundian kings.

Yet the student of Sidonius will find the notices of violence and widespread calamity faint and infrequent. There is nothing in the fortunes of Gaul in his days to match the social chaos and penury and suffering of Noricum, which were relieved for a time by the heroic efforts of S. Severinus.[6] There is a wide interval between

[1] Sid. *Ep.* iii. 9.
[2] Idat. *Chron.* ad a. 409, fames dira grassatur, adeo ut humanae carnes ab humano genere vi famis fuerint devoratae, etc. ; Sid. *Ep.* vii. 7, macri jejuniis praeliatores . . . avulsas muralibus rimis herbas in cibum traximus.
[3] Sid. *Ep.* vi. 12, post segetes incendio absumptas peculiari sumptu,

inopiae communi per desolatas Gallias gratuita frumenta misisti.

[4] Greg. Turg. *Hist. Fr.* ii. c. 24.
[5] Sid. *Ep.* vi. 12.
[6] For the distress and disorganisation in Noricum cf. Eugipp. *vit. S. Severin.* c. iii. iv. x.; for the measures of relief taken by Severinus cf. c. xvii.

the first wild cries of terror or actual suffering which
rose as the Sueves and Vandals swept over Gaul, and
the more or less willing acquiescence in the rule of
the Burgundians and Visigoths.   In the early years
of Euric's reign, while the fate of Auvergne was still
undecided, there must undoubtedly have been much
suffering, especially among the lower classes of the
Gallo-Roman population, and there must have been a
general sense of insecurity and an interruption of intercourse and business.   Yet the impression left by the
letters of Sidonius is that men of his class suffered more
in their hopes and sentiments than in their material
fortune.   Their abandonment by the Empire, their final
severance from the great imperial system, caused a shock
of grief and indignation which finds voice in that
passionate letter which sounds like the epitaph on
Arvernian freedom.   They seemed to be losing their
heritage in the long tradition of Roman culture.   It is
not fear of the Germans, nor even fastidious dislike for
their rude and unpolished ways, that wrung from the
Roman noble his indignant lament for the betrayal of
Arvernian liberties and citizenship by brother churchmen
in conclave with the ministers of the Visigothic king.
He could force himself to accept the rude hospitality of
the Gothic or Burgundian court; he had proved that he
did not fear to face the Germans in battle; but the
illusions of his youth about the great centre of order
and culture were vanishing, and he watched with anxious
foreboding the darkness which was descending on the
West.

BOOK V

CHARACTERISTICS OF ROMAN EDUCATION AND CULTURE IN THE FIFTH CENTURY

CHAPTER I

CHARACTERISTICS OF CULTURE IN THE FOURTH AND FIFTH
CENTURIES

THE purpose of this chapter, as indeed of this book as a
whole, is to describe the tone of that society which,
even when nominally Christian, drew its intellectual
life from pagan literature. We shall have to do with
the culture of conventionality and tradition, slowly but
surely fading from lack of fresh impulse and inspiration,
not with the newer and purely Christian culture, which
strove to employ the forms of ancient literature in the
service of the dogma and spiritual ideals which were
destined to mould the future of the West.

It was not, indeed, without long hesitation that the
Church brought itself to assimilate what was best, and
best fitted to her purpose, in the literary tradition of
paganism. And in this long process of accommodation
the West was slower and more reluctant than the East.[1]
While S. Clement of Alexandria was ready to admit that
for the Greek world philosophy "was a schoolmaster to
bring it to Christ," Tertullian denounced the teaching of
the literature of mythology, and strove to deepen the gulf
between Athens and Jerusalem, between the pagan
academy and the Church.[2] Nor was the suspicion of

[1] Ozanam, *Civ. au Vme Siècle,*
i. 374.
[2] Tertull. *de Praescrip. Haeret.*
c. vii., ipsae denique haereses a

philosophia subornantur . . .
miserum Aristotelem qui illis
dialecticam instituit, artificem
struendi et destruendi. . . . Quid

pagan literature entertained by the great doctors of the
West without good grounds. In the fourth century
Hellenism was almost synonymous with hatred of the
Christian faith, and the reaction of Julian was a combined effort of the schools and temples to arrest the
advance of a movement which threatened both alike.
It is true that the order in which Julian ironically
banished Christians from academic life shows that many
of them must have been engaged in it.[1]   And many
of the Christian fathers and controversialists were
originally teachers of rhetoric.[2]   Yet in the long truce
between the two religions which ended with Gratian, the
dread of the allurements which lurked under a pagan
education was amply confirmed by wholesale apostacy
which, even in the reign of Theodosius, had to be restrained by the terrors of the law.[3]   In those very years
Licentius, a dear friend of S. Augustine, and one of his
companions in the retreat of Cassiciacum, was irresistibly
drawn back into the world of pagan seductions by the
subtle charm of literature.[4]

Yet, in spite of all these dangers and suspicions, the
Church of the west, with that practical, statesmanlike
prudence which seldom deserted it, began, in the fourth
century, to come to terms with pagan culture, as it
accommodated itself even in some degree to pagan superstition.   The attitude of S. Paul to the educated world

ergo.   Athenis et Hierosolymis ?
Quid academiae et ecclesiae. Nostra
institutio de porticu Solomonis est.
But Tertullian is not consistent,
for he admits that much may be
gained from the ancient discipline ;
cf. Boissier, *La Fin du Pag.* i. 235.

[1] The edict itself is not extant.
But cf. Julian's *Ep.* 42, δίδωμι δὲ
αἵρεσιν μὴ διδάσκειν ἃ μὴ νομίζουσι
σπουδαῖα : Amm. Marc. xxii. 10,
7 ; Oros. vii. 30, § 3 : Aug. *de Civ.
Dei*, xviii. c. 52.

[2] S. Cyprian (Hieron. *de Vir. Ill.*
67) ; Arnobius (Hieron. *Chron.* ad

a. 329) ; Lactantius (*ib.* ad a. 319 ;
he was tutor of Crispus) ; S. Augustine (*Conf.* iv. 7, 12). Cf. Greg.
Tur. *Hist. Fr.* ii. 31, on the rhetorical training of S. Remi ; Gennad.
de Scrip. Eccl. c. 60.

[3] *C. Th.* xvi. tit. 7.

[4] Aug. *Ep.* 26 ; Paulin. Nol. *Ep.*
8. S. Paulinus tries the charm of
verse to secure the restoration of
Licentius. Cf. Rauschen, *Jahrbücher*, p. 248. The father of
Licentius was Romanianus, referred
to in Aug. *Conf.* vi. c. 14.

was no longer possible. It was no longer true "that not many wise are called." Although probably a majority of the Senate were either pagan or neutral even at the end of the century, many of the noblest and most cultivated had from the time of Constantine become Christian. And above all two men, S. Jerome and S. Augustine, born about the middle of the century, and destined to influence more than any others the future of the Western Church, were penetrated with the spirit of the ancient schools. And their attitude to the pagan culture determined finally the attitude of the Church.

In both S. Jerome and S. Augustine the opposite tendencies represented by Tertullian and by Lactantius can be clearly seen. S. Jerome was the most brilliant pupil of the Roman schools under Donatus. He was essentially a savant. When he fled to the deserts of Chalcis he took his books with him.[1] The famous dream in which he was summoned before the throne of Christ, and condemned as still a mere Ciceronian, in spite of his promise to forsake the profane studies of his youth, left him really impenitent and unchanged.[2] It is true that, in a letter to Pope Damasus, he denounces "the songs of poets, the wisdom of the world," the pomp of rhetorical phrase, "as mere food of daemons."[3] Yet not many years afterwards, in a letter which is a glorification of learning, he boldly defends his constant reference to profane authors by S. Paul's quotations from Aratus and Menander.[4] He would have the Christian maiden from her earliest years trained in the best Greek and Latin literature.[5] He himself taught the great authors to the boys of Bethlehem. S. Augustine, although he had not the erudition of S. Jerome, had an equal admiration for

[1] Hieron. *Ep.* v. § 2.
[2] *Ib.* xxii. § 30, ad Eustochium.
[3] *Ib.* xxi. § 13.
[4] *Ib.* lxx. § 2.
[5] *Ib.* cvii. § 9, discat Graecorum versuum numerum. Sequatur statim Latina eruditio.

what was best in the thought and expression of the great ages. The tale of Dido could move him to tears.[1] In combating the theodicy of Varro, he never fails to speak with admiration of his enormous learning and industry.[2] His reverence for Plato is only second to his reverence for Holy Writ,[3] and he would almost have forgiven the pagans if they had erected a temple to him.[4] The old rhetorical training, which left its mark on everything he wrote himself, he valued as a splendid discipline for the man who had to move or persuade his fellows. It is true, the ancient apostles and prophets are models of the highest eloquence or dialectic.[5] They obey all the rules of art unconsciously. But those not so close to the source of inspiration cannot dispense with that training in literary technique which had been elaborated by the skill and experience of eight hundred years. Whatever is good in the ancient tradition should be jealously preserved, " profani si quid bene dixerunt non aspernandum." In leaving the scene of their heathen bondage, Christians may with a good conscience, like the Hebrews, despoil the Egyptians of their more precious treasures. In the treatise *De Ordine*, S. Augustine has sketched a system of education, in outline resembling that of the seven liberal arts, but inspired by a lofty ideal unknown to Martianus Capella.[6]

In spite of the peril from pagan literary associations, the "spoiling of the Egyptians" had begun before S. Augustine was born. It was seen that the various forms of literary expression which the ancient world had forged

---

[1] *Conf.* i. c. 13, flebam Didonem extinctam ferroque extrema secutam.

[2] *De Civ. Dei*, vi. c. 2, qui tam multa legit ut aliquid ei scribere vacuisse miremur . . . vir tantus ingenio tantusque doctrina, etc.

[3] *Ib.* viii. c. 8.

[4] *Ib.* ii. c. 7, quanto justius tali-bus (*i.e.* philosophis) divini honores decernerentur ! Quanto melius in Platonis templo libri ejus legerentur, quam, in templis daemonum Galli abscinderentur, etc.

[5] *De Doctr. Christ.* iv. 7 ; cf. Hieron. *Ep.* xxx. § 1.

[6] Augustine, *De Ordine*, ii. cc. 8-16.

with infinite pains and delicate art, in epic or lyric verse, in oratory or historic narrative, might be made vehicles of Biblical history, of Christian truth and doctrine, of fresh views of the succession of empire and the providential government of the world.   Juvencus, a Spanish ecclesiastic of the reign of Constantine, narrated the gospel history in not altogether faultless hexameters.[1] Proba, in a cento of Virgilian verse, related the story of the Creation, the Fall, and the life of the Redeemer.[2] The elder Apollinaris,[3] about the middle of the fourth century, composed an epic of Old Testament history, Christian tragedies in the style of Euripides, and Christian odes in the style of Pindar.   His son turned the Gospels into dialogues after the manner of Plato.   The forms of lyric verse were applied with a skill not unworthy of the great age to the praise of the Christian martyrs by Prudentius.   Orosius and Sulpicius Severus recast the history of the world in the light of a divinely guided evolution. Such works as these, and many a sacred oration moulded by the rules of rhetoric, are a powerful testimony to the stubborn vitality of the ancient tradition.   But while they wear the conventional garb of the pagan past, they are animated by a spirit which is at deadly feud with it. They belong to the mediaeval or the modern world. Great as the merits of some of them may be, radiant as they are with the promise of the dawn, yet for the purpose of this work we must turn our gaze rather to the literary class, which, even within the Christian pale, still clung to the culture which dreamt only of the past.

The aim of this chapter being rather to describe and account for the tone of a class than to appraise particular

---

[1] Juvenc. *Evang.* iv. 806; Hieron. *de Vir. Ill.* c. 84, floruit sub Constantino principe.   Cf. *Ep.* 70, § 5.

[2] Teuffel, ii. 430, n. 15.   Schenkl's *Prooem ad Prob.*, *Corp. Scrip. Eccl.* t. xvi.

[3] For an account of the Apol-linares v. Socr. *Hist. Eccl.* iii. c. 16. He gives a good statement of the attitude of liberal Christianity to ancient literature.   Note τὸ γὰρ καλὸν ἔνθα ἂν ᾖ, ἴδιον τῆς ἀληθείας ἐστίν.   Boissier, *La Fin du Pag.* i. 239.

works of literature, we are hardly concerned with the
vexed question whether the fifth century belongs to the
history of Latin literature at all. Certainly the literary
devotees of that despised period would have indignantly
reclaimed against any attempt to sever them from the
society of their literary ancestors. And, indeed, any
attempt to draw a hard and fast line between classical
and mediaeval seems to be rather futile and arbitrary.
If, with the grammarian, you close the line of classical
writers with Suetonius, the brilliant Claudian, who, so far
as style goes, might have been a contemporary of Statius,
is isolated from his peers. If, on the other hand, you fix
the limit at 405,[1] the date of Claudian's last poem, you
admit within the classical pale the bald and scrappy
gossip of the Augustan History and the elaborate inanities
of Symmachus; while comparatively correct and important writers, like Rutilius Namatianus, Orosius, and
Prosper, are shut out. To fix the limit at 476 would be
to make the disappearance of a shadowy emperor the
sudden term of a great national literature, which did not
spend its force for many centuries after the age of inspiration. It is a more profitable task to try to realise, in an
age of decadence, the powerful and unchanging character
of Graeco-Roman culture, which, amid all failure of
originality, and all contending currents of provincial
temperament and invading barbarism, never relaxed its
hold on the educated class.

It may be admitted that the culture of the fifth century
is not a fascinating study. The idolatry of mere literary
form combined with poverty of ideas, the enthusiastic
worship of great models without a breath of the spirit
which gave them their enduring charm, immense literary
ambition without the power to create a single work of
real artistic excellence—this is not a subject which promises much interest; and the literary remains of the

[1] Mackail, *Lat. Lit.* pp. 277, 278.

fifth century are generally dismissed to oblivion in a few contemptuous phrases.   Yet the Epigoni deserve a little notice for the sake of the ancestry of which they were so proud, and the culture which they tried to save.   They may even claim some attention for their own sake. History shows few examples of an aristocracy more devoted to letters than to war or sport or politics.   And with all their vanity and literary affectation, the great nobles of the fifth century preserve a certain distinction in their loyalty to things of the mind.

It would be difficult to exaggerate the force and permanence of the literary influence exercised by the Roman schools of the West.   Style might degenerate from the great standards, but the standards were never forgotten ; and the passion for style of some sort was as strong under Theodoric as it was in the reign of Trajan.   Magnus Felix Ennodius was born just three years before the dethronement of the last Emperor of the West,[1] and, after a chequered career, became bishop of Pavia.   His boyhood was spent in Gaul, in the years when the last traces of Roman administration in that province were disappearing.[2]   His student life at Milan coincided with the great struggle between Odoacer and Theodoric, in which Italy was flooded by a fresh host of invaders.   Yet, born and reared as he was amid such political confusion,[3] Ennodius is as complete and artificial a product of the rhetorical discipline as Ausonius or Symmachus.   His style, indeed, is as awkward and obscure as it is conventional and elaborate.   But the man is penetrated with the old school traditions.   Even in addresses on sacred subjects, he is incapable of speaking in a simple, straightforward style ;[4] and his letters teem with the most incon-

---

[1] Ennod. *Eucharist.* p. 399 (ed. Hertel. Vindob.), tempore quo Italiam optatissimus Theoderici regis resuscitavit ingressus . . . ego annorum ferme sedecim, etc.

[2] Ebert, i. 433.
[3] See the description in Ennod. *Eucharist.* pp. 398, 399.
[4] Ennod. *Dictio* 5, "Incipientis Episcopi."

gruous pagan allusions.[1]   He has thought it worth while
to preserve for the eyes of posterity a long series of
declamations on conventional and unreal themes, such as
the professor of rhetoric for many ages had been accustomed to set his pupils.   They are of precisely the same
kind as that which occupied the Roman youth in the
days of Juvenal and Pliny : the words of Dido when she
saw Aeneas departing, or of Menelaus at the sight of
burning Troy; an invective against one who demanded
the hand of a vestal as a reward for his achievements, or
against a father who claimed to be supported by his son
whom he had refused to redeem from captivity.   Symmachus and Ennodius are separated by more than three
generations.   In those hundred years, so full of great
social changes and disasters, the whole framework of the
Empire and of society in the West had been dislocated.
The Church and the barbarians had triumphed.   And yet
the Christian bishop of 500 is as much wedded to the
literary tradition of the past as the pagan noble of 400.

This persistence of academic tradition was to some
extent due to the sterility and failure of original power
which characterises Roman literature after the first
century of the Empire.   The period of the Silver Age
was distinguished by a brilliant effort of talent and literary
ambition.   But it was after all a short-lived effort, and
the barrenness of the three following centuries is one of
the most striking facts in the history of literature.   In
spite of long periods of prosperity and good government,
the higher intellect of Rome seems to have been overtaken by a paralysis, and incapable of making any further
advance.[2]   During all that time no scientific discovery,
no fresh native movement in Roman literature, was made.
The force seems to have been wanting to conceive and

---

[1] For a brief account of these
most unreadable *Epistles* v. Ampère,
Hist. Lit. ii. 214.

[2] Teuffel, *Rom. Lit.* ii. §§ 267,

340 ;   Nettleship, *Lectures and
Essays*, 2nd series, p. 115; Mackail,
Rom. Lit. pp. 187, 202.

carry to completion any considerable and enduring work.
Tacitus had no worthy successor in history.   Statius
has no rival in poetic art till the meteor-like appearance
of Claudian.   The influence of the great Greek masterpieces to inspire fresh effort in Roman literature seems
to have been spent with the Augustan age.   But Hellenism in another form reasserted itself in the reign of
Hadrian, and perhaps not less vigorously in the reign of
Julian.   In both these movements, however, the dominant
influence was the new sophist, the itinerant lecturer.
Erudition without critical judgment, finesse of style
without purity of taste, took the place of originality and
enthusiasm for ideas.   Moreover, the growing centralisation
and bureaucratic character of the imperial government
extinguished the last flickerings of interest in political
life, which had been failing even before the advent of the
Empire.   Civilisation became every day more stereotyped
and materialised.   The hardiest spirits, even to the very
end of the Western Empire, could barely conceive any
change in the established order.   And the academic
system partook of the universal stagnation.   Indeed there
are many reasons why in every age the academic system
should, of all parts of the social organism, be the most
unchanging.   Nothing is harder to reform or to inspire
with fresh aims than an ancient scheme of education.
The teachers are conservative from habit and sentiment.
They know no other system than that in which they have
been trained, and, from one generation to another, they continue to transmit the tradition which they have inherited.
The brilliant and successful pupil is apt to idealise the
studies of his youth, and to refer to their influence the
mental keenness and polish which may have come to him
from society and contact with the world.   Ausonius in
his later life saw much of courts and camps.   He was
one of the inner circle who surrounded the throne of
Gratian ; he was raised to the prefecture and the consul-

ship.   Although he had been for thirty years a professor,
he was for all that a versatile and ambitious man of the
world.   Yet in his old age his thoughts turned back to
his early studies and companions, and he has left us the
portraits of nearly thirty of the professors of Bordeaux,
traced with the curious minuteness of a wistful affection.
Most of them lived and died obscure, and would never
have been heard of but for his verses.   Yet he sees
them all, even down to the *primus magister*, who was too
fond of wine,[1] and who was hardly equal to his humble
task, surrounded by a kind of reflected glory.   The duty
of saving their names from oblivion is to Ausonius one
of piety and gratitude to the hands which unlocked to
him and his friends the treasure-house of the Golden Age.[2]

It must also be remembered, in seeking to account for
the persistence of the Graeco-Roman training, that that
system had the passionate support of the pagan sentiment
which blazed forth in the fourth century, and which,
under Christian forms, lingered on among a large class
far into the fifth.   Libanius the last great sophist, used to
say that religion (*i.e.* paganism) and culture were close
friends.[3]   And he claimed that rhetoric had restored
Julian to the worship of the gods.   Nor can there be any
doubt that that Emperor's attempted revival of the old
religion was inspired by the schools.   To Julian Hellenism meant not only the literary tradition of Greece, but
the old mythology interpreted or reanimated by the
philosophy of Alexandria.   Hellenism was necessarily in
its origin and essential qualities the foe of Christianity,
and hence Julian treated the interpretation of Homer or

---

[1] *Prof. Burdig.* xxi. 7 :

creditus olim fervere mero ;

ix. 2 :

et te quem cathedram temere usurpasse
  loquuntur
nomen Grammatici nec meruisse putant.

[2] Compare his own appeal, as his
old tutor, to S. Paulinus, *Ep.* xxiii.
23 :

ego sum tuus altor, et ille
praeceptor primus, primus largitor hono-
  rum,
primus in Aonidûm qui te collegia duxi.

[3] Liban. iii. 43, quoted by Capes,
Univ. Life in Ancient Athens, p. 121.

Plato by a Christian teacher as a kind of contamination or profanity,[1] very much as a good Catholic might think of the celebration of the Holy Mysteries by a Protestant minister. It may be doubted whether the Christian teachers who returned to their classrooms after the failure of Julian's reaction were less enthusiastic admirers and interpreters of the classics than the avowed pagans.[2] Many of them were Christians only in name, hovering in the uncertain twilight which an easy-going monotheism or pantheism cast over the frontiers of the opposing creeds. To such men the pursuit of literature was the highest end, and, as such, incompatible with the consuming passion for a new spiritual life. They did not, indeed, believe in the old divinities, but mythical names and conceptions were so deeply worked into the texture of the great master-pieces which they expounded, that style or literary finish seemed inconceivable without a pagan colouring. And the love of letters, in the old-fashioned way, was to them the finest flower of Roman civilisation, and of that social order which seemed to the privileged class so incapable of any amendment or advance. That, and not any ideal of renunciation, was the true and highest aim of the heirs of Graeco-Roman culture. To be false to the Muses, after having been initiated into their mysteries, was a species of treachery and unfilial ingratitude, even when the renunciation was sanctified by the name of Christ.[3] It was making choice of barbarism in place of Romania ; it was disowning one's spiritual ancestors, and separating oneself, to imitate the words of the humanist of a later day, from the great company of "brethren beloved in Homer, Virgil, and Plato." One such desertion has a peculiar interest, and even a certain pathos.

---

[1] Jul. *Eq.* 42, ἄτοπον μὲν οἶμαι τοὺς ἐξηγουμένους τὰ τούτων ἀτιμάζειν τοὺς ὑπ' αὐτῶν τιμηθέντας θεούς.

[2] *C. Th.* xiii. 3. 6. This law of Valentinian, A.D. 364, practically repealed Julian's by making "vita et facundia" the only qualifications for teaching.

[3] Auson. *Ep.* xxiv. 118 ; xxv. 60.

The conversion of Paulinus, the greatest Aquitanian noble of his time, created an immense sensation both among the worldly class and in the ranks of serious Christians.[1]   His position made him a conspicuous figure, and his desertion of the ideals of his caste was felt to be an event of grave import.   We are fortunate in having preserved to us some letters which passed between Paulinus and his old professor, Ausonius, and which record with a singular delicacy of feeling the rupture of an old friendship, and the widening of the chasm between pagan culture and Christian ideals.

Paulinus belonged to one of the richest and noblest families in the Roman world.[2]   He had broad estates in Aquitaine, and his marriage with Therasia brought him an accession of wealth.   Trained by Ausonius at the school of Bordeaux, he had an immense reputation for the kind of literary ability which was prized by that age.[3] Before his thirtieth year he had held the consulship and the governorship of a province.[4]   In all respects he was a typical Roman noble of the time, and seemed bound to his order by ties which nothing could sever.   The circumstances of his conversion are rather obscure.   But his temperament, as well as the influence of his wife,[5]

---

[1] Ambros. *Ep.* 30. For the obloquy incurred by S. Paulinus see his *Ep. to Sulp. Severus*, 1, § 2, si nos interdum profana vel stulta quorundam saecularium verba circumlatrent ; cf. Sulp. Sev. *vit. S. Mart.* c. 25.

[2] He may have been the son of the Pontius Paulinus who owned the Burgus celebrated by Sidonius (*Carm.* 22) ; cf. Ambros. *Ep.* 30, splendore generis in partibus Aquitaniae nulli secundum. His estate, Hebromagus, is mentioned by Auson. *Ep.* xxii. and xxiv. 126. Greg. Tur. *de Glor. Conf.* 107, ex nobili stirpe ortus Tarasiam similem sibi sortitus est conjugem, habens divitias multas. Cf. Rauschen, *Jahrbücher*, p. 352.

[3] Auson. *Ep.* xix. and xx. ; cf. Hieron. *Ep.* 53, § 3. Paulinus, however, like S. Augustine, was not a good Greek scholar, Paulin. *Ep.* 46, § 2, nam quomodo profectum capere potero sermonis ignoti.

[4] See Prol. c. 3 in Migne's ed. *S. Paulin. Nol. ;* Auson. *Ep.* xx. 3, and xxiii. 34. On the date of his consulship, which does not appear in the Fasti, cf. Rauschen, *Jahrbücher der Christ. Kirche*, p. 24, n. 7. Can he be the Paulinus, governor of Epirus, in *C. Th.* xvi. 2, 22 ? Cf. Prol. in Migne, t. lxi. c. 3.

[5] Auson. *Ep.* xxiii. 31, Tanaquil tua nesciat istud. Cf. Greg. Tur. *de Glor. Conf.* 107.

probably gave him an early inclination to a mystical and
ascetic Christianity.   There is also a tradition that he
came under the influence of S. Martin, who miraculously
cured his eyes of some malady.[1]   Suddenly he disappeared
from the society of Bordeaux, and buried himself in a
town of North-Eastern Spain.   The news came with a
shock to his friends, and especially to his dearest friend,
Ausonius.   The poet, whose great virtue was a perfect
faithfulness to old ties, had a fatherly tenderness for
Paulinus.   He had watched his growing skill in the arts
of style, and hailed his early efforts in authorship with
perhaps extravagant praise.[2]   He was scarcely able at
first to believe that one so trained, so gifted, so bound to
Roman society by rank and culture and friendship, could
exchange its charming freemasonry and urbanity for the
loneliness and hard austerity of the monkish life.[3]   He
wrote to Paulinus some letters in which he used all his
art to recall him to the splendid world he had forsaken,
by appeals to affection, to the love of glory and stately
fortune, above all to the pleasures of lettered society.[4]
The pained feeling of desertion was intensified by a
silence of three years, during which Paulinus had made
his renunciation of wealth and worldly estate final and
complete.   Yet the old semi-pagan man of the world is
not betrayed into any bitterness against a fanaticism
which must have been to him as repulsive as it was
unintelligible.   And, on the other hand, the cultivated
recluse, who was about to devote his culture to the
glorification of S. Felix of Nola, is full of tenderness
and gratitude to his old master.[5]   But we feel, and they

[1] Sulp. Sev. *vit. S. Martini*, c.
19 ; cf. c. 25, praestantissimumque
nobis praesentium temporum illustris viri Paulini exemplum in-
gerebat.

[2] Auson. *Ep.* xix. Paulinus had
composed a poetical epitome of
Suetonius, *de Regibus*.

[3] *Ib.* xxv. 61 :

patriosque istic sepelibis honores?

[4] *Ib.* xxiii. 33.   Is there anything in the letters of Ausonius to
justify the expression "bittere
Vorwürfe" in Rauschen, *Jahrb.* p.
428 ?

[5] Paulin. Nol. *Carm.* xi. 8 :
cura mihi semper fuit, et manet, officiis te
omnibus excolere, affectu observare fideli

felt, that they were sundered by an impassable gulf. Ausonius prays to the Muses of Boeotia to give back his friend to the poetry of Rome.[1] The Muses, indeed, to Ausonius were no more than the consecrated literary symbol for the inspiration of the great ages. Yet he could not conceive the force of the faith which could move a scholar and a poet to forget his Horace and Statius in preparing for the terrors of the judgment to come. The lines in which Paulinus, after long silence, announced that he was dead to the world, and that the irrevocable choice had been made, are a monument of the irresistible force of the ascetic movement, and make one feel that the admiration of Ausonius for his pupil of old days was not all undeserved:[2] "Why bid the Muses, whom I have disowned, return to claim my devotion?[3] Hearts vowed to Christ have no welcome for the goddesses of song, they are barred to Apollo. Time was when, not with equal force, but with equal ardour, I could join with thee in summoning the deaf Phoebus from his cave at Delphi. . . . Now another force, a mightier God, subdues my soul.[4] He forbids me give up my time to the vanities of leisure or business, and the literature of fable, that I may obey his laws and see his light, which is darkened by the cunning skill of the sophist, and the figments of the poet who fills the soul with vanity and falsehood, and only trains the tongue . . Against His coming, my heart quakes and trembles to its inmost fibres,[5] my soul has terrible foreboding of the future, lest, bound fast by weak, fleshly cares, and loaded with the weight of worldly things, when, through the opened heaven, the awful trumpet sounds, I may not be able to lift myself on light pinions to meet the coming of the Lord. . . . This is my fear, my torment, that the last day may overtake me

[1] Auson. *Ep.* xxv. 73 :

Latiis vatem revocate Camoenis.

[2] Paulin. *Carm.* x. 304-324.

[3] *Ib.* x. 22:

negant Camoenis, nec patent Apollini
dicata Christo pectora.

[4] *Ib.* x. 30. [5] *Ib.* x. 304.

slumbering in thick darkness, and wasting my moments on empty cares. What shall I do, if, while my languid eyes are slow to open, the Christ should reveal himself in flashing splendour from His palace in the skies; and if, dazzled by the sudden radiance of the Lord, coming in the opened heavens, as the glory bursts upon me, I have to seek a mournful refuge in the darkness of night?" The solemn farewell which the monk of Nola bade to the studies of his youth and the great world reveals alike the force of the new ascetic ideal, and the enthralling influence of pagan culture.

The most powerful influence in perpetuating the literary tradition was the system of the Roman schools, supported by imperial authority. Roman education under the Republic was free and unregulated by the State. In the flourishing period of the Empire, the State undertook the control and the support of the higher education, without curtailing the liberty of private teachers. Under the later Empire it extended its interference with the discretion of local authorities in the appointment and remuneration of professors, until, in the year 425,[1] an edict of Theodosius and Valentinian asserted the sole authority of the government in education, and made penal the opening of schools by unauthorised persons. Already, in the time of the first Caesar, the old Roman system of private domestic education was going out of fashion, and Rome possessed twenty schools of a public character. The professors of the liberal arts,[2] who were then for the most part Greeks, received full civic rights. Vespasian paid an annual stipend of 100,000 sesterces to the teachers of rhetoric,[3]

---

[1] *C. Th.* xiv. 9, 3.

[2] Sueton. *Jul. Caes.* c. 42, liberalium artium doctores, quo libentius et ipsi urbem incolerent et ceteri appeterent, civitate donavit.

[3] Sueton. *Vesp.* 18, primus e fisco Latinis Graecisque rhetoribus annua centena constituit; cf. Boissier, *La Fin du Pag.* i. 194. It is highly improbable, as M. Boissier points out, that a salary of £800 would be given to any but a metropolitan professor; cf. Friedländer, i. p. 223.

but this liberal provision was almost certainly confined to the teachers of the capital. Succeeding emperors, Hadrian,[1] the Antonines,[2] and Alexander Severus,[3] continued the same policy in the provinces, in some instances endowing the professorships, which they created, out of the imperial funds, but in the majority of cases making them a charge on the municipality. Alexander Severus, a prince who had a strong taste for school rhetoric and poetry,[4] founded bursaries for poor scholars, and erected class-rooms.[5] The Emperor Constantine was not less earnest in his care for the academic system. The edicts of 321, 326, and 333 [6] reaffirm all former enactments as to the position of public teachers; they also confer on them entire exemption from a large number of onerous functions and liabilities, both imperial and municipal. They relieve professors from military service, from the compulsory reception of public guests, whether soldiers or civilians, from the heavy responsibilities of the curia; while teachers are, notwithstanding, left free to accept curial magistracies and honours. Their persons are made in a fashion sacrosanct, and any insult or outrage offered to them is heavily punished. At the same time these privileges and exemptions are extended to their wives and children. And the Emperor's motive for dealing so liberally with the teaching profession is explicitly stated in the words, " quo facilius liberalibus studiis multos instituant." These provisions are worthy of the son of Constantius Chlorus, who, in the last years of the third century, placed the rhetorician Eumenius at the head of

[1] Ael. Spart. *Hadrian*, 16, omnes professores et honoravit et divites fecit ; cf. c. 14.

[2] Jul. Capitol. *Ant. Pius*, c. 11, rhetoribus et philosophis per omnes provincias et honores et salaria detulit.

[3] Lamprid. *Alex. Sev.* c. 44.

[4] *Ib.* c. 35, aut orationes recitantes aut facta veterum canentes libenter audivit ; cf. c. 30, lectioni Graecae operam majorem dabat.

[5] *Ib.* c. 44, rhetoribus . . . salaria instituit, et auditoria decrevit et discipulos cum annonis pauperum filios modo ingenuos dari jussit.

[6] *C. Th.* xiii. 3, 1, 2 and 3. Professores are coupled in these laws with Medici.

the revived school of Autun, with a salary of 600,000 sesterces.[1] The law of Julian, issued in 362,[2] for the first time asserts the right of the Emperor to revise the appointments to professorships made by the local authorities. In a few cases, such as that of Eumenius, the Emperor had made the appointment himself; in a few others he had empowered a trusted person,[3] or a board,[4] to make the selection. But, in the great majority of cases, the chairs had been filled by the local curia,[5] with, perhaps, the assistance of the neighbouring magnates. Julian, while he required candidates in the first instance to submit their character and claims to the scrutiny of these authorities, expressly reserved to himself the final sanction of any appointment which they might make. His avowed reason for doing so is to give greater weight to their decision,[6] but there can be no doubt that his real motive was to prevent the election of Christians to these posts; for, although the municipal bodies might be bad or niggardly paymasters, there is no reason to believe that, as a rule, they were less competent to make proper appointments to academic chairs than the imperial advisers at Rome. Among the members of the local curia there would generally be, not only a certain number who had received an academic training, but also professors or ex-professors, who, though by the law of Constantine[7] not liable for the charges of the curia, were freely admitted to its ranks. Ausonius and some of his

---

[1] Eumen. *Or. pro Scholis instaurandis*, c. 11, salarium me liberalissimi principes ex hujus rei publicae (*i.e.* Autun) viribus in sexcenis millibus nummum accipere jusserunt.

[2] *C. Th.* xiii. 3, 5.

[3] Herodes Atticus was so empowered by M. Aurelius, Philostr. *vit. Soph.* ii. 2, 2 (quoted by Boissier, *La Fin du Pag.* i. 199).

[4] Lucian, *Eun.* 8, ἐν τούτοις ἦν τοῖς δικασταῖς ἡ διατριβή καὶ τὸ κεφαλαῖον ἤδη τοῦ σκέμματος τοῦτο ἐτύγχανεν ὄν, εἰ δοκιμαστέος εὐνοῦχος ἐπὶ φιλοσοφίαν παρελθὼν καὶ νέων προστασίαν ἐγχειρισθῆναι ἀξιῶν.

[5]. For the evidence on this point v. Godefroy on *C. Th.* xiii. 3, 5.

[6] *C. Th.* xiii. 3, 5, hoc enim decretum (Curialium) ad me tractandum referetur ut altiore quodam honore nostro judicio studiis Civitatum accedat.

[7] *Ib.* xiii. 3, 1.

professional friends probably sat in the curia of Bordeaux. And they were, to say the least, as competent to select a professor as the men who surrounded the Emperor in the Consistorium.

The proper remuneration of the teaching staff probably exercised the vigilance of the emperors to a much greater degree than the mode of its appointment. From the beginning of the fourth century, and probably earlier, the financial pressure on the curiales was becoming more and more severe. Education is generally the first department in which the ordinary man will begin to retrench. We might safely believe, even if we had not the express testimony of Libanius,[1] that an impoverished municipality would cut down the salaries of its professors, or pay them very irregularly. The famous law of Gratian, issued in 376, is perhaps the most striking illustration of the anxiety of the emperors for the worthy maintenance of academic studies. The edict was issued just two years before Ausonius, who had been the Emperor's tutor, was raised to the prefecture of the Gauls, and three years before his consulship. It is reasonable to suppose that the old professor of Bordeaux, who was so loyal to his colleagues and his profession, had suggested to the Emperor the expediency of improving their position. It may be inferred from the Code that the payments to professors from the municipal funds had become less liberal and less regular. Gratian, while he leaves the great towns free to elect their teachers, strictly prescribes the stipends which the various grades of professors shall receive.[2] The rhetors are to have a salary of 24 *annonae ;* [3] the grammarians, both Greek and Latin, are to be paid half

---

[1] Boissier, *La Fin Du Pag.* i. 197 ; Sym. *Ep.* i. 79, v. 35, which show that professors' incomes were precarious at the end of the fourth century.

[2] *C. Th.* xiii. 3, 11, ut singulis urbibus quae Metropoleis nuncu- pantur nobilium Professorum electio celebretur. Metropoleis must be interpreted with Godefroy : non illae quae primae omnium erant, verum omnes frequentissimae.

[3] For similar allowances by annona (*i.e.* diarium unius hominis)

the salary of the rhetors.   But in Trèves, which was the
great seat of Roman power at the time, a higher scale of
salaries is fixed.   The teacher of rhetoric is to have 30
annonae, the Latin grammarian 20, and the Greek grammarian, "if a competent person can be found," has to be
content with the salary appointed for other localities.

The poems of Ausonius furnish indications of a
greater difference in the incomes of professors than any
established by this edict.   Some of the grammarians of
Bordeaux were evidently living in obscure poverty.[1]
On the other hand, several professors of rhetoric enjoyed
comparative wealth,[2] kept a good table, and lived on
equal terms with the local aristocracy.   In that day the
exemption from taxes and public burdens which they
enjoyed was of great pecuniary value.   In addition to
their regular stipends, they had also the fees paid by
their pupils.   There can be no doubt that the classes of
some professors were large, although how large we can
hardly pretend to say definitely.[3]   Ausonius speaks of
the one or two thousand who were trained by Minervius
for the bar and for senatorial rank.[4]   A liberal education
was not only a social necessity, a badge of rank; it was
also, for the ambitious youth, the surest passport to a
place in the imperial service.   The profession of arms
and the pursuits of commerce were alike practically
closed to Romans of the upper and middle ranks.
The heir to a great estate was required, by the opinion

cf. Amm. Marc. xxii. 4, 9.   When
Julian once asked his gorgeously
dressed barber, quid haberet ex
arte compendii, vicenas diurnas
respondit (tonsor) annonas, etc.
Lamprid. *Alex. Sev.* c. 42.

[1] Auson. *Prof. Burd.* vii. 10.

litteris tantum titulum adsecutus,
quantus exili satis est cathedrae, etc.

Cf. viii. 6, x. 40.

[2] *Ib.* xvi. 9 :

nobilis et dotata uxor, domus et schola,
    cultae
principum amicitiae contigerunt juveni.
xviii. 8.
xix. 5 :
            opulensque senectus—

[3] The attempt is made in Julian's
Ausone et Bordeaux, p. 72.

[4] *Prof. Burd.* i. 9 :

mille foro dedit haec juvenes, bis mille
    Senatus
adjecit numero, purpureisque togis.

of his class, to qualify himself for his position by
acquiring that culture which had distinguished his
ancestors for generations, and which marked off the
Roman noble from the barbarian chief; the youth of
humbler fortune might hope by means of his education
to find a place in that great army of functionaries
who surrounded the Emperor and the great provincial
governors.[1]   A popular and successful teacher had therefore probably large classes, and his ordinary fees were
swelled by presents from some of his wealthier pupils.[2]
A rhetor was often a rich man, living in the best society,
and married to an heiress of some wealthy family.[3]

The aim of the imperial legislation, expressed in
several edicts, was to leave the professor of the liberal
arts free and unimpeded in his studies.[4]   But the profession of letters in the Lower Empire was also one
of increasing worldly honour and consideration.[5]   The
senatorial class, as we have seen, prided themselves on
their culture quite as much as on their birth and
opulence.   And they held in corresponding estimation
the class whose business it was to maintain the literary
tradition.   Symmachus, at the beginning of the century,
and Sidonius towards its close, were aristocrats to their
finger-tips, valuing even to excess hereditary rank.

---

[1] Cf. Seeck's *Sym.* cxli. for the
career of Minervius, Florentinus,
and Protadius, three young Gauls
from Trèves.   Mallius Theodorus
was of humble origin, and began
his public career as magister epistularum under Gratian (Seeck,
cxlix.).   Neoterius, who became
prefect and consul, began his
career as notarius in the service of
Valentinian (Amm. Marc. xxv. 5,
14).   Men of high birth also entered
the service.   Sex. Petronius Maximus was tribune of the Sacred
Consistory and notarius in his
nineteenth year.   See the inscription to him set up by the emperors

in 421 (*C.I.L.* vi. 1749).
[2] Herodes Atticus made a present
to his teacher of 15 talents ; but
this, of course, was exceptional.
Capes, *Univ. Life in Ancient Athens*,
p. 60.
[3] Citharius a Greek grammarian
of Bordeaux,

> conjugium nactus cito nobilis et locu-
>   pletis, etc.

Prof. Burd. xiii. 9.   Cf. xxiii. 5.
[4] *C. Th.* xiii. 3, 3, 4, and 18.
[5] See the four laws of Theodosius
and Honorius between 414 and 428,
C. Th. xiii. 3, 16-19, which confirm
and enforce the laws of Constantine,
xiii. 3, 1, 2, 3.

Both of them were absorbed in the interests of their
order, the *melior pars generis humani,* as they regarded it.
Yet both Symmachus and Sidonius admitted freely to
their inner circle men who owed their position solely to
literary skill and dexterity of the kind then admired.
They lived on terms of fraternal intimacy with men
whose days were spent in the drudgery of the class-room.
In one of his letters[1] Sidonius describes the charms of
Avitacum to a grammarian of the school of Auvergne, in
order to tempt him to spend the dogdays in its shades.
Symmachus took the greatest interest in the worldly
advancement of his literary friends,[2] and regarded the
liberal endowment of academic studies as a "mark of a
flourishing commonwealth." He hailed especially the
elevation of Ausonius and his family to high rank and
office as a worthy recognition of the dignity of letters.[3]
And, indeed, mere academic merit has seldom in history
led to such power and worldly distinction. For several
years it may be said with truth that the government of
the West was in the hands of the family of Ausonius,
who held all the great prefectures.[4] The poet himself
added to the prefecture of the Gauls the ancient honours
of the consulship. His commanding influence can be
traced in not a few of the imperial constitutions. It has,
indeed, been plausibly suggested that the ex-professor's
administrative capacity was not equal to his poetic art,[5]
and that during his prefecture the government of Gaul
was combined with that of Italy in the hands of his son

[1] Sidon. *Ep.* ii. 2.
[2] Sym. *Ep.* i. 79, Priscianus
frater meus cum primis philosophorum litteratura et honestate
censendus senatu auctore salarii
emolumenta consequitur.

[3] *Ib.* i. 20.

[4] The authorities will be found
in Seeck's *Sym.* lxxix. lxxx. ; omnes
summi per Occidentem magistratus

unius familiae quasi patrimonium
erat.
[5] Seeck's *Sym.* lxxx., sed poeta
noster grammaticus quam administrator melior fuisse videtur. . . .
Itaque nova ratio excogitata est qua
nomen praefecti Ausonio remaneret,
totum autem magistratus onus
Hesperio incumberet, et Galliae
cum Italia conjunctae sunt, etc.
Rauschen, p. 28.

Hesperius. It is certainly noteworthy that the edicts
relating to the Western provinces are, during Ausonius'
year of office, with one exception, addressed to his son.[1]
If this be so, it merely shows how determined the
Emperor was, even at the cost of some disturbance of the
official routine, to permit his old tutor to enjoy the
highest honours which the Empire had to bestow.

It is not a mere empty boast, prompted by national
vanity, that the tradition of Graeco-Roman culture, in
the last century of the Western Empire, was maintained
most vigorously in Gaul. So far as secular literature
was concerned, Italy, Spain, and Africa had spent their
force. The schools of Gaul in the fifth century, although
literary studies were showing unmistakable signs of
decadence, were still generally prosperous; and it is from
them chiefly that we must draw our conceptions of the
character of Roman culture in the last years of the
Empire of the West. There was something in the Celtic
nature which seemed to respond with peculiar energy
to the stimulus of the rhetorical training.[2] The eloquence
of the Gauls was celebrated before the Roman occupation. In the ancient Greek colony of Marseilles the
training of the Hellenic schools had been early established,[3] and Marseilles was at one time a favourite resort
of students from Italy, and, according to Strabo, threw
even Athens into the shade. In the reign of Tiberius,

[1] C. Th. viii. 5, 35, de numero
veredorum quae uno die ex uno loco
moveri possunt.

[2] Juv. i. 44 ; xv. 111, Gallia cau-
sidicos docuit facunda Britannos.
M. Antonius Gnipho, a Gallic
rhetor, was tutor of J. Caesar and
Cicero; M. Ant. Gnipho, ingenuus
in Gallia natus . . . Docuit primum
in Divi Julii domo, pueri adhuc . . .
(Suet. de Ill. Gram. c. vii.); Domi-
tius Afer, famous in the reigns of
Caligula, Claudius, and Nero (Tac.
Ann. xiv. 19), was from Nîmes
(Hieron. Chron. ad a. 46 A.D.,

Domitius Afer Nemausensis clarus
orator habetur). Caligula established oratorical contests at Lyons
(Suet. Calig. c. xx.)

[3] Strabo, iv. 5 (181), πάντες γὰρ
οἱ χαρίεντες πρὸς τὸ λέγειν τρέπονται
καὶ φιλοσοφεῖν ὥσθ' ἡ πόλις μικρὸν
μὲν πρότερον τοῖς βαρβάροις ἀνεῖτο
παιδευτήριον . . . ἐν δὲ τῷ παρόντι
καὶ τοὺς γνωριμωτάτους Ῥωμαίων
πέπεικεν ἀντὶ τῆς εἰς Ἀθήνας ἀποδη-
μίας ἐκεῖσε φοιτᾶν φιλομαθεῖς ὄντας.
Cf. Tac. Ann. iv. 44, where Massilia
is mentioned as the retreat of a
studious exile.

the school of Autun, established soon after the Roman
conquest, was thronged with the youth of the noblest
families.[1]   Marseilles lost somewhat of its former
academic renown, but the schools of the east and centre
of Gaul appear to have maintained a vigorous existence
even through the troubles of the third century, and the
fame of the florid Gallic eloquence reached its height in
the Panegyrists.[2]   Yet it was only in the fourth century
that the Roman language and literature were completely
naturalised on Gallic soil.   Traces of the ancient dialects
still lingered even among the educated class.   The father
of Ausonius, who was of an old Gallic stock, spoke Latin
badly.[3]   A member of the same family, Paulinus of
Pella, tells us that he was much more at home in Greek
than in Latin.[4]   In the beginning of the fifth century
Sulpicius Severus represents a Gallic monk as apologising
for the barbarism of his rustic idiom.[5]   But the literary
renaissance of the fourth century completed the Roman-
isation of the great province of the West, and made it
the last stronghold of Roman culture.   In this movement
the more ancient schools of the South-East failed to
maintain their old prestige.   The school of Marseilles is

---

[1] Tac. *Ann*. iii. 43, Augustod-
unum Sacrovir occupaverat et
nobilissimam Galliarum subolem,
liberalibus studiis ibi operatam, etc.

[2] Hieron. *Ep*. xxxvii. 3, sermo
compositus et Gallicano cothurno
fluens.   It is worth noting that
this letter is a criticism of a work
by Rheticius, bishop of Autun, on
the Song of Songs, of the value of
which S. Jerome has evidently a
poor opinion.

[3] Auson. *Idyl*. ii. 9 :

sermone impromptus Latio, verum Attica
    lingua
suffecit culti vocibus eloquii.

[4] *Euch*. 75 :

protinus ad libros etiam transire Maronis
vix bene comperto jubeor sermone Latino.

But it should be said that Paulinus

was born in a Greek-speaking province.

[5] Sulp. Sev. *Dial*. i. 27, vereor
ne offendat vestras nimium urbanas
aures sermo rusticior.   It is absurd,
however, as De Coulanges (*La Gaule
Rom*. p. 128) points out, to infer,
from the following words, *Celtice
aut si mavis Gallice loquere*, that
the monk Gallus, who apologises
for his *rusticior sermo*, spoke one of
the old dialects of Gaul (cf. Fauriel,
i. 434).   The passage in Sidon. *Ep*.
iii. 3, tuaeque personae quondam
debitum quod sermonis Celtici
squaman depositura nobilitas nunc
oratorio stylo . . . imbuebatur,
need not mean that the nobles
actually spoke Celtic in the youth
of Ecdicius, i.e. *circ*. 430.

little heard of in the fourth century. Autun, after its momentary revival under Eumenius, also sank into obscurity. The really prosperous and vigorous seats of academic life in this period were Trèves on the north-eastern frontier, and the schools of Aquitaine in the West. Trèves for some years was the seat of empire and the favourite residence of the emperors,[1] and Gratian, as we have seen, tried to attract to its schools the foremost talent by specially high stipends. But the attempt was, from the circumstances of the time, foredoomed to failure. Trèves was essentially a great military position, confronting the menacing tide of barbarian invasion. Within little more than a generation from the date of the law which was to endow it with an academic primacy, Trèves was four times given up to fire and sword by the Germans.[2] Magnificent ruins still remain to attest the favour and magnificence of the Caesars. But the school of Trèves vanished without leaving a trace. It was in rich and fertile Aquitaine, far removed from the more sudden and desolating inroads of the Germans, that academic life was destined to linger longest, and to show the most enduring vitality. There were, indeed, still a number of academic centres elsewhere, at Lyons,[3] Arles,[4] Auvergne, Vienne,[5] which still maintained a certain activity in the fifth century, under teachers of some mark. But " Palladian " Toulouse,[6] Narbonne, and, above all, Bordeaux, had by far the greatest reputation.

[1] See the number of constitutions dated from Treviri between 368 and 378 in the Chronologia of the *C. Th.* t. i. Cf. Auson. *Ordo Nob. Urb.* iv. :
pacis ut in mediae gremio secura, quiescit, imperii vires quod alit, quod vestit et armat.

[2] Salv. *de Gub. Dei*, vi. 39, 75, expugnata est quater urbs Gallorum opulentissima.

[3] Lyons had still a reputation when Sidonius and his friends attended the lectures of Eusebius there, *Ep.* iv. 1. Cf. viii. 6; Chaix, *Apollin. Sid.* i. 202.

[4] Arles, as the seat of the prefecture, took the place of Trèves in the fifth century, and legal studies flourished there. See the letters to the jurist Petronius, Sid. *Ep.* ii. 5, v. 1.

[5] Chaix, *Apollin. Sid.* i. 207.

[6] Sid. *Carm.* vii. 436; xxiii. Cf. Auson. *Parent.* iii. 11.

The city on the Garonne in the days of Ausonius was recognised as the foremost school of rhetoric in the Roman world, and its fame attracted even Italian scholars. Symmachus, the leader of the Senate, and the most accomplished man of letters in Italy, acknowledged the debt which he owed to the rhetorical training of Aquitaine.[1] Minervius, of the time of Ausonius, had a brilliant career at Rome and Constantinople.[2] Narbonne, Poitiers, and Toulouse filled their chairs with brilliant teachers from Bordeaux. On the other hand, Bordeaux seldom needed to import her professors. Of the twenty-five who are commemorated by Ausonius, only five were of alien origin.[3]

Even the most famous universities of the Empire seem, from a modern point of view, to have been only moderately equipped. A few of the greater cities, such as Rome or Constantinople, had professors of the four faculties, as we may call them, of grammar, rhetoric, philosophy, and jurisprudence.[4] But probably only the first two of these departments were represented on the staff of most provincial schools. Even a school so famous as Bordeaux seems to have had no professor of philosophy or jurisprudence.[5] The great legal universities were Rome, Constantinople, and Berytus: yet we cannot suppose that young men preparing for the bar of the prefectorian courts in Gaul had to go for their training to these distant schools. It is clear that legal studies

[1] Sym. *Ep.* ix. 88, Gallicanae facundiae haustus requiro ; non quod his septem montibus eloquentia Latiaris excessit, sed quia praecepta rhetoricae pectori meo seneq olim Garumnae alumnus immulsit est mihi cum scholis vestris per doctorem justa ccgnatio. Cf. i. 9.

[2] Auson. *Prof. Burd.* i. 4 ; Hieron. *Chron.* ad a. 358, Minervius Burdigalensis rhetor, Romae florentissime docet. So Arborius was called

from Toulouse to Constantinople (Auson. *Parent.* iii. 16).

[3] Jullian's *Ausone*, p. 69.

[4] *C. Th.* vi. 21, 1. This law confers the title of Comes primi ordinis on three grammarians, two sophists, and one jurist by name. Teachers in general who have discharged their duties for twenty years with efficiency are to be raised to the same rank.

[5] Ausonius, *Prof. Burd.*, speaks only of grammatici and rhetores.

were vigorously carried on at Arles, Narbonne, and in Southern Gaul generally.[1] Sidonius eulogises, with his wonted intemperance of language, the legal learning of some of his friends.[2] One of them, the accomplished Leo, who came to fill the difficult post of secretary to Euric,[3] is described as a jurist worthy to rank with the greatest of antiquity. In philosophy there was probably little real training in those days except at Athens; but even at Athens philosophy had sadly degenerated, and "the golden chain of the Platonic succession" was within a few years to be broken by the edict of Justinian. S. Jerome says that in his time philosophical study had ceased to form a part of a liberal education.[4] And there are few traces of a genuine interest in philosophy to be found in the purely literary remains of the fifth century. It is true that Sidonius has several friends who are devoted to Plato,[5] and from one passage in his letters we might even infer the existence of a Platonic school in Southern Gaul. He reminds Probus, a member of an accomplished family at Narbonne, of their common Aristotelian studies in the class-room of Eusebius at Lyons.[6] Another friend united in a very singular way a devotion to the tenets of Plotinus with an ardent love of farming.[7] For the wedding of another young Platonist Sidonius wrote an epithalamium,[8] which is probably the most curious composition that was ever produced for such an occasion. In keeping with the sober tastes of the bridegroom, Minerva, instead of Venus, is the leading figure in the scene. She repairs to the land of Erechtheus, where in a gorgeous

---

[1] Fauriel, i. 407.

[2] Sidon. *Carm.* xxiii. 446, 465; cf. *Ep.* ii. 5, v. 1.

[3] Sid. *Ep.* iv. 22, cotidie namque per potentissimi consilia regis totius sollicitus orbis pariter negotia et jura, foedera et bella . . . cognoscis.

[4] *Ep. Gal.* lib. iii. c. 5, quotusquisque nunc Aristotelem legit?

Quanti Platonis vel libros novere, vel nomen? Vix in angulis otiosi eos senes recolunt.

[5] *Ep.* iv. 11.

[6] *Ib.* iv. 1, sic jam tu sub Eusebio nostro inter Aristotelicas categorias artifex dialecticus atticissabas.

[7] *Ib.* i. 6; iii. 6.

[8] *Carm.* xv.

temple are seated all the sages and philosophers of Greece, only Epicurus, in the interests of sound morality, being excluded.   They are all characterised in some way, but with either a banality or a grotesqueness which almost excludes the possibility of any thorough or serious conception of their systems.   If the philosophic bridegroom was the accomplished Platonist he is represented to have been, he must have shuddered at the lines which sum up his great master's teaching.   The climax of absurd bad taste is reached when, under the very eyes of the virgin goddess, Lais is depicted in the act of clipping the rough beard of a cynic philosopher with perfumed scissors![1] In the eulogy on the Emperor Anthemius, among his many qualifications for the throne there is an enumeration of the philosophers he had studied.[2]   It is a mere string of names, with here and there some purely anecdotic and external trait, added for literary effect.   The philosophic study of that age probably concerned itself, chiefly as Anthemius is said to have done, with learning

> quidquid laudavit Scythicis Anacharsis in arvis,
> quidquid Pythagoras, Democritus, Heraclitusque
> deflevit, risit, tacuit ; quodcunque Platonis
> ingenium, quod in arce fuit, docet ordine terno, etc.

One cannot help thinking, in reading such lines, that, in the circle of Sidonius, Greek philosophy was only a hunting-ground for lively or picturesque allusion, and not a subject of genuine scientific interest.   It is probably not uncharitable to believe that most of these men had only vague and scrappy notions of Thales and Pythagoras, Socrates and Plato, caught up from the lectures of the grammarian on some school classic.

[1] A reminiscence of tales of the amorous propensities of Diogenes such as are found in Lucian, *Hist. Ver.* ii. 18 ; Athen. xiii. 54 (588),   ἧς καὶ Ἀρίστιππος ἦρα, καὶ Δημοσθένης ὁ ῥήτωρ, Διογένης τε ὁ κύων.

[2] Sid.*Carm.* ii. 156.

The impression as to the conventional and superficial character of philosophic study in the secular schools of the fifth century will be confirmed by reference to the handbook of the liberal arts compiled by Martianus Capella, a rhetor of Africa.[1] This book had an extraordinary popularity in the Middle Ages.[2] It formed the basis of academic training for centuries. In the eleventh century it was translated into German. It is found in the catalogue of the great monastic libraries, and was commented on by great schoolmen. It is difficult to conceive the state of culture when this mixture of dry traditional school learning and tasteless and extravagant mythological ornament, applied to the most incongruous material, with an absolutely bizarre effect, could have been applauded as a sweetener of the toils of learning. Its fanciful setting might seem to a modern reader a deliberate attempt to burlesque the delicate handling of myth by the author of the *Phaedrus* and the *Republic*. Yet there is no doubt that Capella was a serious and practical teacher, and his book represents thoroughly both the spirit and the system of the academic discipline of his age. The first two books are given up entirely to fable, in prose and verse. Mercury, the god of eloquence, is to espouse Philology. The destined bride must be elevated to the divine estate of her lover,[3] but she is first compelled to discharge, in somewhat disgusting fashion, her load of erudition,[4] in the shape of parchment rolls, blackened and mouldy with age, or covered with hiero-

---

[1] The date of Martianus Capella is uncertain, some placing him at the end of the fifth century, others in the middle of the third (*v.* Eyssenhardt's Praef. c. 1). The only thing at all certain seems to be that he must have written before the Vandal invasion of Africa (Eyssenh. pp. vii. viii.).

[2] Ozanam, i. 355 ; Ebert, *Lit. des Mittelalters*, i. 483. Greg. Tur. *H.*

Fr. x. *ad fin*, refers to Capella as the regular handbook in the liberal arts in his age. For the great number of MSS. *v.* Eyssenhardt's Praef. xx. *sqq.*

[3] Mart. Cap. i. 40, ipsamque nupturam deo convenire non posse nisi si per senatus consultum mortalis esse desineret.

[4] *Ib.* ii. 135, 136.

glyphic symbols and figures of geometry.   She is borne,
amid the songs of the Muses [1] through the starry spheres
and along the Milky Way, to the palace of the king of
heaven.[2]   There, before an august council of gods and
godlike sages, at the request of the bride's mother, her
dowry is fixed; the marriage contract and the lex Papia
Poppaea are formally recited.   The Seven Sister Arts are
assigned as her attendants.   One of these is Dialectic,
but she represents something very different from the
sublime science which Plato meant by that name.[3]   The
book on Dialectic is really a treatise on formal logic, in
which we meet once more all the old plagues of our
youth, Accidens and Proprium,[4] Aequivocum and Univo-
cum, Substantia Prima and Substantia Secunda.   There
is hardly a reference to the great vivifying thoughts of
Greek philosophy.   And when we survey the ranks of
the celestial Senate, although the names of illustrious
philosophers are there, we feel that they are only brought
in to swell a pageant marshalled by mere school rhetoric.
Homer,[5] Virgil, and Orpheus sound the lute beside Archimedes and Plato, who are turning spheres of gold.
Thales is moist, Heraclitus is aglow, Democritus is involved in a cloud of atoms.   While Pythagoras is thread-
ing the labyrinth of certain celestial numbers, Aristotle is
in anxious quest of Entelechia among the heights of
heaven.   The strain is only relieved by Epicurus coming
upon the scene with a pile of roses and violets.   In such
feeble reminiscence and tasteless frivolity do the glories
of the Lyceum and the Academy reach an ignominious
close.

   We are dealing in this chapter with secular and semi-
pagan culture which lived on the ancient tradition.   But
it is well to remind ourselves that within the pale of the

---

[1] Mart. Cap. ii. 117.
[2] *Ib.* ii. 208.
[3] Pl. *Rep.* vii. pp. 532, 535.

[4] Mart. Cap. iv. 355, 365, 347.
[5] *Ib.* ii. 212.

Church there has seldom been a freer and more vigorous intellectual life than there was in the fifth century. We have already referred to the great semi-Pelagian school which had its home and centre in the religious house of Lérins, and which numbered among its adherents some of the greatest and saintliest of the Gallic ecclesiastics of that age. But there was another controversy going on at the same time, which, though conducted by churchmen and inspired by theological motives, followed the lines, and to some extent the spirit, of the ancient philosophy. Faustus of Riez, a former abbot of Lérins,[1] had revived the theory held by some of the early fathers, that the nature of the soul is corporeal.[2] We are not concerned here with the arguments used to maintain this thesis; but it was a theory which lent a support to orthodox views of future punishment, and it appears to have been widely accepted and freely discussed. Mamertus Claudianus,[3] the accomplished and able priest of Vienne, composed an elaborate treatise in answer to the views of Faustus. He starts from certain theological premises; but his method of proof is essentially of the antique pattern. And in his second book he supports his argument by copious references to the Greek and Roman philosophers.[4] In these the ecclesiastical attitude to philosophy stands in marked contrast to the merely traditional and academic. Sidonius refers to but one dialogue of Plato by name, the *Phaedo*,[5] and then only to the Latin translation of it by Apuleius. Claudianus seems

[1] Gennad. *de Scrip. Eccl.* 85. The letter is usually printed along with Mam. Claudianus, *de Statu Animae*. Cf. Engelbrecht's ed. *Corp. Scrip. Eccl. Lat.*

[2] *E.g.* Tertull. *de Anima*, c. 5, 7, dolet apud inferos anima cujusdam, et punitur in flamma, et cruciatur in lingua . . . per quod punitur . . . hoc est corpus. Cf. Überweg, *Hist. Phil.* i. 305, "The soul has the same form as the body, and is delicate,

luminous, and aeriform in substance. If it were not material, it could not be acted upon by the body, nor would it be capable of suffering."

[3] Gennad. 83. His character is delineated by Apoll. Sid. *Ep.* iv. 11.

[4] In the *de Statu Animae* reference is made in detail to Thales, Pythagoras, Epicurus, Philolaus of Tarentum, Archytas, Hippo of Metapontum, Zeno, Plato, Porphyry, etc.

[5] *Ep.* ii. 9 ; *Carm.* ii. 178.

to know his Plato, and gives copious translations from the dialogues.[1] The treatise has faults of methods and science; but it is a serious attempt, by an acute and well equipped man, to deal with a difficult subject in a philosophic spirit. It was dedicated to the bishop of Auvergne in the most complimentary terms, and the bishop of course acknowledged the honour done to him. He employs every adjective in his vocabulary, and every name in his memory of literature, to describe the almost irreconcilable excellences of the style of Claudianus; but he never once approaches the subject of the book.[2] There is not a hint to show that he had grappled with the problem of Claudianus' treatise, or that he had formed any opinion as to the author's success, except as a mere manipulator of phrase.

It appears, then, that in the secular academic discipline of the fifth century nothing deserving the name of serious philosophic inquiry found a place. Nor was there anything of real science, unless we dignify by that name the strange jumble of inaccurate geography, mystical mathematics, and traditional astronomy, which is to be found in the mediaeval handbook of Capella. It was on the two kindred studies of grammar and rhetoric that the energy of university teaching expended itself, as it had done for centuries. The energy was great; the method was thorough and elaborated by ages of critical experience. The effect on the pupil's mind and character was probably more profound than any system of education has ever produced. Whether it was entirely salutary is another question. But no one can properly appreciate the literary, and even the moral, tone of that age, without a comprehension of the spirit in which the professors of

---

[1] E.g. *de Statu An.* ii. 7.

[2] Fertig, *C. S. Apoll. Sid. und seine Zeit*, iii. p. 11, suggests that Sidonius did not wish to declare himself against Faustus, who was a personal friend. But I doubt whether Sidonius had any taste or capacity for serious philosophic thought.

rhetoric and grammar performed their task, and the limits within which they moved.

Even in provincial colleges there were at all times both Greek and Latin grammarians among the professors.[1] The schools of the West never forgot the source from which their tradition was derived, and the revival of letters in the West in the fourth century was also a revival of Hellenism. Eumenius, the famous professor of Autun, who was a forerunner of the movement in Gaul, was of Attic descent,[2] and Greek studies for a time occupied a prominent place. Boys seem to have begun Greek early. The father of Ausonius knew it well, although he was a poor Latin scholar.[3] The same is true of Paulinus of Pella, who was made to read Homer and Plato in his fifth year.[4] Ausonius would have his grandson begin his literary studies with Homer and Menander.[5] Far on in the fifth century, some of the friends of Sidonius appear to have continued their Greek studies in mature life. Lampridius declaimed with equal facility in Greek and Latin.[6] There was a passion for Greek poetry in the cultivated circle of Narbonne,[7] and Sidonius does not scruple to compare their verses with those of the great classics. Yet, in spite of all this, we are compelled, from various indications, to conclude that in the fifth century the study of Greek in the West was declining. It is well known that S. Augustine, with all his learning, was an in-

---

[1] *C. Th.* xiii. 3, 11 (at Trèves); cf. vi. 21, 1 (Constantinople). Auson. *Prof. Burd.* viii. xiii. xxi.; Paulin. Pell. *Euch.* 117.

[2] Eum. *pro Restaurandis Scholis,* c. 17, quamvis enim ante ingressum pueritiae meae intermissa fuerit eorum exercendis studiis frequentatio, tamen illic avum quondam meum docuisse audio, hominem Athenis ortum, Romae diu celebrem.

[3] Auson. *Idyl.* ii. 10.

[4] *Euch.* 72:

nec sero exacto primi mox tempore lustri
dogmata Socratis et bellica plasmata Homeri
erroresque legens cognoscere cogor Ulixis.

[5] *Idyl.* iv. 45. Sidonius reads Menander with his son, *Ep.* iv. 12.

[6] Sid. *Ep.* ix. 13:

declamans gemini pondere sub stili coram discipulis Burdigalensibus.

[7] Sid. *Carm.* xxiii. 100 *sqq.*

different Greek scholar.[1] Ausonius did not apply himself
to the study in his youth, and laments his negligence.[2]
The Latin grammarians held a higher position and
received higher pay than the Greek.[3] In the famous
edict of 376 for the establishment of chairs in Gaul,
provision is made for one Greek grammarian at Trèves;
but the Emperor seems to have some doubt whether a
competent professor can be found.

The lectures of the grammarian were for many ages
conducted on the system of reading, interpreting, and
commenting on the standard works of antiquity.[4] In
the earlier stages, the teaching was not above that of a
low form in one of our grammar schools.[5] In its more
ambitious efforts it would, in a very unmethodical, and
perhaps superficial way, correspond in some degree to the
liberal studies of our universities. Among the grammarians of Bordeaux, there were men of slender parts
and learning.[6] But, taken in its highest range, the profession demanded a wide, if not a very profound knowledge of many subjects, not at all akin to one another.
Great stress was laid on good reading, with proper
attention to accent and expression.[7] As we might
expect, the grammarian very much preferred the poets to

[1] Aug. *Conf.* i. c. 13, quid autem
erat causae, cur Graecas litteras
oderam, quibus puerulus imbuebar,
ne nunc quidem mihi satis ex-
ploratum est. Teuffel, ii. 447.

[2] *Prof. Burd.* viii. 14 :

   neque disciplinis
   appulit Graecis puerilis aevi
      noxius error.

[3] *C. Th.* xiii. 3, 11, viginti
Grammatico Latino, Graeco etiam,
si qui dignus reperiri potuerit,
duodecim praebeantur annonae.

[4] In *C. Th.* vi. 21, 1, the qualifications of the good professor are
enumerated : blameless character,
skill in teaching, fluency, delicacy
in interpretation, and copiousness
of disquisition ; cf. *Juv.* vii. 229-
240.

[5] Auson. *Prof. Burd.* xxi. 5 :
   elementorum prima docebas
      signa novorum.

[6] *Ib.* ix. 2 :
nomen Grammatici nec meruisse putant;
cf. x. 45.

[7] Quintil. *Inst. Or.* i. c. 8, su-
perest lectio ; in qua puer ut sciat,
ubi suspendere spiritum debeat,
quo loco versum distinguere, ubi
claudatur sensus, unde incipiat,
. . . demonstrari nisi in opere ipso
non potest. Cf. Auson. *Idyl.* iv.
47, "Ad Nepotem " ;

   tu flexu et acumine vocis
innumeros numeros doctis accentibus
      effer,
affectusque impone legens, etc.
Idyl. v. 3, 4 ; cf. Aug. *De Ord.*
ii. 14.

the prose writers as a field for exposition, and great
attention was given to prosody and metre with a view to
imitation. After grammatical analysis came attempts at
literary appreciation. Difficult passages were discussed
and paraphrased, and the pupil's attention was drawn
to striking metaphors or delicacy of artistic expression.
But when all this was done, the grammarian's task was
not finished. He had then to attack the subject matter,
and to make the text the occasion for communicating a
multifarious mass of information. This was the field of
the higher learning of the age; and a grammarian of the
first rank required a certain mastery of many branches of
knowledge—etymology, history, jurisprudence, pontifical
lore, geometry, music, astronomy. The notes of Servius
on Virgil, or the *Saturnalia* of Macrobius, or the third
book of Capella, probably give a fairly accurate notion of
the lectures of the grammarians. At one time the pupil's
attention will be called to the physical formation of the
letter sounds or to differences of archaic usage;[1] at
another to the etymology of Aprilis or Janus, Idus or
Artemis, consul or classis.[2] Or the text may call for an
interpretation of the myths of Saturn,[3] or the epithets
Lycius or Pythius given to Apollo. Or the erudition of
Virgil will be illustrated by a disquisition on pontifical
law as to the washing of sheep on *dies festi*,[4] or on the
epithets which he applies to the Penates, or on his knowledge of the ritual of the Apolline worship at Delos.
And in some of these discussions it is interesting to
notice that the Greek grammarian has but a slight
esteem for the competence of his Latin colleague to track
the subtle allusions of a curious learning.[5]

[1] Mart. Cap. iii. 261, *e.g.* D
appulsu linguae circa superiores
dentes innascitur, P labris spiritu
erumpit, R spiritum lingua cris-
pante conraditur, etc. Cf. Quintil.
Inst. Or. i. 4, 9; i. 7, 4.
[2] Macrob. *Sat.* i. 12, 12; i. 8,

6; i. 15, 6; i. 15, 20; cf. Quintil.
Inst. Or. i. 6, 33.
[3] Macrob. *Sat.* i. 17, 50, 36.
[4] *Ib.* iii. 6, 2; iii. 4, 10; iii. 3, 11.
[5] *Ib.* v. 19, 31, quem litteratores
vestri nec obscurum putant . . .
quasi Graecae lectionis expertes.

The minute antiquarianism of such books as the *Saturnalia* may seem often to degenerate into trifling. The etymologies current in the Roman schools are of course hopelessly arbitrary and unscientific.[1] Yet the literary judgment and taste are not by any means so feeble as the general character of that age might lead one to expect. The teacher who confined himself to mere superficial explanation of the text, without any attempt at a deeper appreciation of his author, was regarded as a sorry master of his craft.[2] A very interesting part of the *Saturnalia* is that which is devoted to an exhaustive criticism of Virgil. And this probably shows us the grammarian of the fourth century at his best. Of course he inherited much from many generations of forgotten critics, like the Oxford lecturer on Plato and Aristotle in our own day. But it is pleasant to see that these dilettanti, who were accustomed to award every dull poetaster among their friends a place among the immortals, profoundly admired Virgil, and can give reasons for their admiration. They can see both his unapproachable beauties and his defects. They know their Homer well, and they see all the debt that Virgil owes to Homer. Here and there Eustathius, who leads in this exposition, notices that the later has improved upon the older poet.[3] But it is admitted also that Homer has a "bright speed" and sureness, which Virgil never approached.[4] And, with all his rapid power, Homer often gives graphic details which Virgil slurs over or omits.[5] In one passage of the *Aeneid* it is pointed out that only "a lifeless corpse" remains in the Latin imitation.[6] It is also noted that Virgil has copied even the faults of his model, and that where he has not Homer's guidance he is sometimes weak. But, on the

---

[1] *E.g.* i. 17, 7 ; i. 9, 9.

[2] *Ib.* i. 24, 12.

[3] Macrob. *Sat.* v. 11, 1-5.

[4] *Ib.* v. 13, 2.

[5] *Ib.* v. 13, 17, 18.

[6] Virg. *Aen.* xi. 751, 756; Macrob. *Sat.* v. 13, 28-30.

other hand, ample justice is done to Virgil's peculiar
power and charm.   His range of learning is illustrated
with great minuteness; especially his command of
sacerdotal lore [1] calls forth the admiration of men who
have made it the study of their lives.   There are
reminiscences of the schools, but also some true criticism,
in the eulogy of the poet's rhetorical skill, which is so
various and yet so apparently obedient to the rules of
traditional art.[2]   The critic in Macrobius shows that
Virgil is as much orator as poet, and that his dramatic
sympathy has exhausted every variety of oratorical
style.[3]   His strange pathos,[4] which is stirred by the
weakness of age or infancy, by the memory of a distant
home in the warrior's death-agony, the sacredness of
ancestral altars, the imagined feeling of dumb or inanimate
things, the sentiment that consecrates stream and grove, is
traced to its many sources with a sincerity which makes
us forgive the touches of pedantry.   The great poet is
" an organ of many stops."   He has all the variety of
Nature, his great teacher.[5]   And though he appropriates
freely, he always makes good his title to the loan by an
added felicity, which often more than atones for the
original theft.[6]

In the schools of the fourth and fifth centuries Virgil,
among Latin poets, holds the foremost place.   There is
hardly any author to whom S. Augustine so frequently
refers in the *City of God*.   He has a boundless admiration for the " noblest of all poets," [7] whose charm has
sunk so deep in the minds of Roman youth that nothing
can efface its influence.   Tully and Maro are the most

---

[1] Macrob. *Sat.* iii. 9, 16, videturne
vobis probatum sine divini et
humani juris scientia non posse
profunditatem Maronis intellegi ?
The previous part of bk. iii. contains many proofs of this.

[2] *Ib.* v. 1, 1.

[3] *Ib.* v. 1, 7.

[4] *Ib.* v. 3.

[5] *Ib.* v. 1, 18.

[6] *Ib.* v. 3, 16, hic opportune in
opus suum quae prior vates dixerat
transferendo fecit ut sua esse
credantur.

[7] *De Civ. Dei,* i. c. 3.

dangerous rivals of the Hebrew Scriptures in the studies of S. Jerome.[1] Virgil is one of the literary idols of Ausonius. To Apollinaris Sidonius he is the prince of poets, worthy of a place beside Homer.[2] The poets who came next in popularity were Horace and Terence. The imitations and reminiscences of the former in Sidonius are only less numerous than those of Virgil.[3] Terence was a favourite author in Auvergne in the fifth century;[4] Sidonius makes frequent reference to him, and read the *Hecyra* with his son. Among the older Latin poets, Lucretius and Catullus seem to have been least studied and imitated.[5] The copiousness, elegance, and skilful technique of Statius made him a special favourite with Ausonius, Claudian, and Sidonius,[6] and many phrases and turns of expression in the descriptive poems of the bishop can be traced to the Silvae and the Thebais. Not less marked is the influence of Claudian in shaping the Panegyrics of Sidonius.[7] But the imitator has little of the genuine power, the dignity, and chiselled classical purity of his model. Among Latin prose writers the influence of Cicero, which in the fourth century was very marked on writers like Lactantius, seems to have been feeble in the fifth. The younger Pliny was one of the most approved models in prose.[8] Symmachus studied his style closely. Sidonius professes to follow in the

---

[1] *Com. ad Gal.* lib. iii. c. 5, nostis enim et ipsae quod plus quam quindecim anni sunt, ex quo in manus meas numquam Tullius, numquam Maro, numquam gentilium litterarum quilibet auctor ascendit.

[2] Sid. *Ep.* v. 13 :

princeps poetarum Publius Mantuanus ;

cf. v. 17. Geisler, *de Apoll. Sidon. Studiis*, has collected all the passages in which Sidonius has quoted or imitated Virgil, pp. 5-9.

[3] Geisler, pp. 11-19.

[4] Sid. *Ep.* ii. 2, iv. 12 ; cf. Fertig, i. 6 ; Geisler, p. 41.

[5] Geisler, pp. 42, 43 ; cf. Index Auctorum in Schenkl's ed. of Ausonius.

[6] The influence of Statius on Sidonius is profusely illustrated by Bitschofsky, *de C. Sollii Apoll. Sid. Stud. Statianis.*

[7] Geisler, p. 28 ; cf. Fertig, iii. 15.

[8] Macrob. *Sat.* v. 1, 7. For the favourite authors of Symmachus see Seeck's *Sym.* xlv.

footsteps of Symmachus and Pliny.[1]   Pliny's cultivation
of epistolary style accounts for his prominence in an age
when that species of composition was so much admired
as it was in the fifth century ; but there is a vein of
affectation in Pliny which probably caught the taste of one
of the most conventional writers who ever lived.   Down
to the close of the Western Empire, as in the time of the
Antonines, Sallust was perhaps the most generally admired writer of prose, and the greatest favourite in the
class-room.[2]   His terse brevity, his archaisms and philosophical reflections, above all his rhetorical tone and
colouring, recommended him to writers who were always
seeking for striking effects in style.

The opposition between the purely literary and the
antiquarian and historical interest in the study of the
classics seems to have been as marked in that age as it
has been since the Renaissance.[3]   Beside the idolaters of
form and phrase, there were students devoted to the
worm-eaten volumes which few ever opened.   Some of
these black-letter scholars figure in the portraits of the
Bordeaux school.   One of them, a young assistant professor,[4] had a passion for these untrodden ways of obscure
research in pontifical science, and the origins of Roman
institutions.   Another was said to be master of all the

---

[1] *Ep.* i. 1, 1 ; cf. iv. 22 :

> ego Plinio ut discipulus assurgo ;

iv. 3. For the extent and character
of Pliny's influence on Sidonius, cf.
Geisler, pp. 55 *sqq.* ; Fertig, iii. p.
21.

[2] Apoll. Sid. *Carm.* ii. 190, qua
Crispus brevitate placet ; xxiii.
152 ; Macrob. *Sat.* v. 1, 7, breve in
quo Sallustius regnat.   For his
influence on Sulpicius Severus
v. Bernays quoted in Teuffel, *Lat.
Lit.* ii. p. 449 ; cf. Ebert. i. 330 ;
and the defence of Sallust against

his detractors in Aul. Gell. iv. 15.
S. Augustine refers to him very
frequently, but chiefly for his moral
reflections ; *de Civ. Dei*, vii. 3 ; ix.
9 ; ii. 18 ; iii. 10.   Cf. Cook's
Catiline, xxxi. *sqq.*

[3] See Mark Pattison's *Casaubon*,
on the contrast between the Italian
and the French humanists, pp. 508-
510 ; cf. Jebb's *Bentley*, p. 220.

[4] Auson. *Prof. Burd.* xxii. :

> ignoratis
> assidue in libris, nec nisi operta legens,
> exesas tineis, Opicasque evolvere char-
> tas
> major, quam promtis cura tibi in studiis
> etc.

lore in the six hundred volumes of Varro.[1] If we may judge by the use made of Varro by Macrobius and Martianus Capella,[2] that great savant was the source from which most of the grammarian's learning, required for class-room purposes, was drawn.

Some of the great minds in the later times of the Republic and under the Early Empire had floating before them the vision of a liberal propaedeutic,[3] which should embrace a thorough study of history, jurisprudence, philosophy, all the sciences which are required to form the perfect orator. Such a course of study would have corresponded to our conception of a liberal education, aiming rather at the thorough discipline of the mind than at a narrow, special training,[4] limited by that crass and purblind utilitarianism, which, in our own day, threatens to obscure the fundamental ideas of education. The Grammar of the Roman schools might conceivably have been enlarged and developed into such a bracing discipline, based on real knowledge, and inspired by an ideal of progess ; but unfortunately it was in practice inseparably associated with the reading and interpretation of a certain number of authors, who had been canonised by the judgment of time. Knowledge was not pursued or imparted for its own sake, but as a means of illustrating the sacred texts. The pupil's gaze was perpetually turned backwards to the masterpieces of ancient wisdom, to

---

[1] Auson. *Prof. Burd.* xx. 10 :

> omnis doctrinae ratio tibi cognita,
>   quantam
> condit sexcentis Varro voluminibus.

For a similar taste in the time of Sidonius cf. *Ep.* viii. 16, unde enim nobis illud loquendi tetricum genus ac perantiquuum ? Unde illa saliaria vel Sibyllina vel Sabinis abusque Curibus accita, quae magistris plerumque reticentibus, promptius fetialis aliquis aut flamen aut veternosus legalium quaestionum aenigmatista patefecerit. Cf. Quintil.

Inst. Or. i. 6, 41.

[2] See Eyssenhardt's *Praef. ad Mart. Capella*, c. 3.

[3] Cic. *de Or.* i. 6, ii. 30 ; Tac. *Dial. de Or.* 30.

[4] Subacto mihi ingenio opus est, ut agro non semel arato, sed novato et iterato . . . Subactio autem est usus, auditio, lectio, litterae ; Cic. *de Or.* ii. 30. Cf. Quintil. *Inst Or.* i. 10, 7, quae (artes) etiam cum se non ostendunt in dicendo nec proferunt, vim tamen occultam suggerunt et tacitae quoque sentiuntur.

whose divine excellence all the treasures of erudition and
science were offered as a sacrificial tribute.   The teacher
might indulge occasionally in divagations and irrelevant
disquisitions, but he was really chained to the author
whom it was his business to interpret.   It can hardly be
wondered at that the function of the grammarian, besides
having a sterilising effect on the teacher's mind, sank in
repute, and became a mere drill preparatory to the
brilliant exercises of the rhetorical school.[1]   It is true
indeed that teachers of rhetoric had often served an
apprenticeship as grammarians; but the rise was regarded
as a great improvement in their position, and that not
merely in income, but in social rank.   On the day on
which Ausonius introduced his imperial pupil to the
study of rhetoric, he received the honour of a Count of
the Empire.[2]   Probably far more thorough knowledge was
needed to make a good grammarian than to make a popular
rhetorician.   Nor can it be said that less ability is
required to interpret properly a chorus of Aeschylus, or to
track the delicate allusions of Virgil, than to dress up the
pompous banalities which are the stock-in-trade of the
popular speaker of all ages.   It is only the Philistine
who will depreciate the sympathetic tact which is
necessary to elucidate the often mysterious utterances of
an original genius, belonging to an age removed from our
own by time and countless associations.   Yet, in actual
fact, that profession or study will always be better paid,
and held in higher honour, which acts directly on men,
and produces results which the mass of men can feel and
see for themselves.   The poor grammarian of Bordeaux
may have often been the more gifted and learned man,

[1] There are several sneers at
grammatici in Macrobius; cf. *Sat.*
v. 22, 12. But Suet. *de Ill. Gram.*
iv. says: veteres grammatici et
rhetoricam docebant. And in Quintilian's time the grammarian was
encroaching on the province of the
rhetor; cf. *Inst. Or.* ii. 1, 5.

[2] Auson. *Grat. Act.* 2, 11, tot
gradus nomine comitis propter tua
incrementa congesti.

but it was the rhetor who was summoned to the Court
and made prefect of a province.

It is difficult for an age nurtured on exact history
and science, and vividly interested in public affairs, to
understand the almost hysterical excitement which the
itinerant professor of rhetoric could excite in the second
or in the fourth century.   If he was a man of reputation
in his art, people rushed to hear him declaim, as they
will do in our times to hear a great singer, or actor, or
popular preacher.[1]   Provincial governors, on a progress
through their district, would relieve the tedium of
official duties by commanding a display of word-fence
or declamation by such a master as Proaeresius, reward
him with the most ecstatic applause, and conduct him
home in state after the performance.   A man like
Libanius associated on equal terms with the highest
civic dignitaries.   In the last years of the fourth century,
at a time of great events and momentous changes,
Symmachus, when writing to Ausonius,[2] finds the only
interesting subject at hand to be a rhetorical display
which a rhetorician named Palladius had just given at
a fashionable gathering; and words almost fail to express
the admiration of that ordinarily calm and dignified
senator for the performance.   It is singular that a man,
who could himself speak with great effect on a serious
occasion in the Senate, or before the Emperor, should
be so carried away by an unreal exhibition of school
rhetoric.   But the fact remains that this power of using
words for mere pleasurable effect, on the most trivial or
the most extravagantly absurd themes, was for many
ages, in both West and East, esteemed the highest proof
of talent and cultivation.[3]   The student of rhetoric in

[1] Eunap. *Proaeres.* 145, 146,
Boissonade's ed.

[2] Sym. *Ep.* i. 15, quoniam deerant
digna memoratu . . . tempestive

Palladii nostri declamatio **auxit**
paginam meam.
[3] For a defence of this taste see
Capes, *Univ. Life in Ancient Athens*,
pp. 87, 88.

the fifth century could say with even more truth than Seneca, " Non vitae sed scholae discimus." [1]

The term rhetoric, as applied to the higher course of instruction in the Roman schools, is, for our period at least, perhaps rather misleading to a modern reader. The rhetorical training of free Rome had been a necessity of public life, when the power of speech in law courts or popular assemblies was a great political engine. And in the work of Martianus Capella, which was to be the text-book of the Middle Ages, rhetoric is still treated as if the student were a contemporary of Cicero.[2] All through the five centuries of the Empire, during which oratory had almost ceased to have any practical power, the Roman schools maintained the tradition which had been founded by Corax and Tisias,[3] and which had produced such triumphs of practical oratory at Rome in Cicero and Hortensius. The old theories of the proper divisions of a discourse, of the varieties of style adapted to the matter, of the figures of speech,[4] of the rhythm and the prosody of the sentence, of the management of voice and gesture, were taught as carefully under Romulus Augustulus as they were when rhetoric was a practical art. And the actual training of the rhetor's class-room remained the same also. The grammarian founded his teaching on the reading of an author. The rhetor cultivated his class by debate or declamation on a prescribed thesis.[5] The subjects set to illustrate and cultivate every species of style were historical, mythological, often purely fanciful and unreal.[6]   As time went

---

[1] Sen. *Ep.* 106, 12.

[2] Mart. Cap. v. 427.

[3] Tisias appears in the train of the armed and stately goddess Rhetoric in Mart. Cap. v. 434; cf. Cic. *de Or.* i. 20 ; Quintil. iii. 1, 8 ; Luc. *Pseudolog.* 30.

[4] Mart. Cap. v. *passim.*

[5] Mommsen, iii. 443, 444 (Eng. Trans.) ; Nettleship, *Essays*, 2nd

series p. 88.

[6] Juv. vii. 150 ; x. 166 :

i, demens, et saevas curre per Alpes, ut pueris placeas, et declamatio fias.

S. Jerome had gone through the exercise, *Com. ad Gal.* lib. i. c. 2, aliquoties cum adolescentulus Romae controversias declamarem, et ad vera certamina fictis me litibus exercerer, currebam ad tribunalia judicum . . .

on, the ingenuity of the master was more and more
taxed to provide stimulating themes for his class.   More
and more the world of reality was left behind; master
and pupil were no longer guided by the necessities óf actual
life, by the force which controls all genuine and living
rhetoric, the wish to persuade the wills of men who have
to act.   The audience whom the rhetor had in view was
no longer the jury or the public assembly, but a gathering
of cultivated and perhaps rather *blasés* people, who came,
not to learn what they ought to do, but to be pleased by
a display of mental agility, or pomp and ingenuity of style.
The more trivial or fanciful the subject, the greater the
opportunity for the aspirant to rhetorical fame.   To speak
with equal skill and force for or against any proposition,
to put a single hackneyed thought in many different
lights, to invest commonplace situations with an air of
novelty by new and ingenious turns of phrase, these
were the objects of the rhetorical training.   The school
of rhetoric had become a place where the art of style, of
writing and speaking well according to the prevailing
taste, on any subject, was communicated.   Rhetoric
came to represent quite as much a habit of mind as the
rules of a definite art.   And as a mental tendency,
although it harmonised well with the social system of
the Lower Empire, it had disastrous effects on intellectual
progress.[1]   Indeed, it made progress impossible.   Under
such a system of education, any true conception of
science, as a domain at once limited and capable of
indefinite expansion, was lost.   The pupil's gaze was
fixed on a few models of unsurpassable excellence.   The
memory was exercised from the earliest youth on mythological fancies which had long ceased to be believed,
and brilliancies of figure and phrase, which were the
peculiar expression of individual genius or of the mental
attitude of a long past age.   The secrets of nature moved

[1] Boissier, *La Fin du Pag.* i. p. 221.

no curiosity, the great events of the most momentous
period in history excited only a languid interest.   The
true son of Rome was the man who believed in her past,
who was an adept in the mysteries of a discipline which
bound together cultivated men of all races under her
sway, who had a tranquil faith that to-morrow would be
as yesterday, and that the human spirit could subsist
for ever on the stores of ancient wisdom and industry.
Such an atmosphere, untroubled or unrefreshed by any
current blowing from the future, is indeed the congenial
air of despotism and caste; it is fatal to any germs of
the love of truth or of freedom.

If a man wished to characterise in a single word the
bad side of education and literature in the fifth century,
" servility " would probably be the most apt and truthful.
The whole tendency of the school training was to make
writers slavish imitators of inimitable models, to load the
memory instead of stimulating the reason and imagination.   When an author was praised, he was praised as
having rivalled or distanced Homer or Pindar, Horace or
Virgil;[1] he was never praised for having opened new
vistas to thought, or for having revealed new powers of
expression in language.   And the servile imitation of
ancient genius harmonised well with the Oriental prostration which had so long prevailed before the person of the
Emperor.[2]   The intellectual training of the Roman schools
conspired with the imperial despotism to produce a habit
of abject submission to authority, which was fatal to
originality and progress.   The finished product of these

---

[1] For specimens of this *v.* Auson.
Ep. xvii.; Sym. *Ep.* i. 14, hoc tuum
carmen libris Maronis adjungo;
Apoll. Sid. *Carm.* xxiii. 452; *Ep.*
viii. 11, subtilis, aptus, instructus,
quaque mens stilum ferret elo-
quentissimus, prorsus ut eum jure
censeres post Horatianos et Pindari-
cos cygnos gloriae pennis evolatu-
rum.   The climax is reached in the
Ep. (iv. 3) to Mam. Claudianus, §§
6, 7, in which every peculiar gift
of Greek or Roman genius, pagan
or Christian, is attributed to
Claudianus, from Pythagoras to S.
Ambrose.

[2] Réville, *Rel. zu Rom. unter den
Sev.* p. 31; Merivale, vi. p. 43.

two combined influences is seen in the literature of panegyric, a department in which the facile and exuberant rhetoric of Gaul attained a bad pre-eminence.   The great masters of this degraded art in the last age of the Western Empire were, with the exception of Claudian, the products of the Gallic schools.   The province, which was the last refuge of Graeco-Roman culture, furnished also the most glaring examples of its debasement. Ausonius and Sidonius Apollinaris stand, the one at the beginning, the other at the end of the period with which this work is chiefly occupied.   Both men owed their elevation to their literary skill and facility, and both have left us striking examples of the abuse of that power. in fulsome adulation of the chiefs of the State.

In his *Actio Gratiarum* for his elevation by Gratian to the consulship, Ausonius has probably surpassed all rivals in the art of self-abasement.   He exhausts his sufficiently copious vocabulary in the attempt to find epithets for Gratian's virtues.   Ausonius no longer wonders at the poetic licence which describes the universe as "full of God."[1]   By the unmerited favour of the Emperor he has attained a distinction which the less fortunate statesmen of old days had to win by humiliating themselves before the sovereign people.   Ausonius is thankful, beyond words to express, that for him the Roman people, the knights, the Senate, the whole machinery of free election, are summed up in the single word of an Emperor.[2] Even in his own domain of letters he must acknowledge the overwhelming superiority of his pupil.   The brief and conventional phrases in which Gratian designated him for the consulship are, to the taste of his tutor, a

---

[1] Auson. *Grat. Act.* i. 5, aedes enim locis omnibus; nec jam miramur licentiam poetarum qui omnia Deo plena dixerunt.

[2] *Ib.* iii. 13, Romanus populus, Martius Campus, equester ordo, rostra, ovilia, senatus, curia, unus mihi omnia Gratianus; cf. ix. 44, valete modo classes populi et urbanarum tribuum praerogativae, et centuriae jure vocatae.

masterpiece of eloquence, transcending all models of the past.[1] Every word of the imperial utterance is turned over with rapturous admiration, and the ancient pedagogue actually confesses that his pupil's Latinity is far beyond his own powers![2] It would be difficult to match the eager baseness of this self-humiliation.

It would probably be also hard to produce anything more absurd than the pomp of conventional mythology, of victories without fruit and prophecies without fulfilment, with which, three generations later, Sidonius seemed to mock the impotence of phantom emperors. We have seen that these poems when sifted furnish some grains of fact to the historian. But what a mass of rubbish and insincerity has to be dug away before the fact is reached! The poet has a genuine feeling of admiration for his father-in-law Avitus, and a genuine love of Auvergne; but the country gentleman of Auvergne, even when raised to the purple by the support of the Visigoths, is made somewhat ridiculous by the pedantic exaggeration of his panegyrist. Rome, staggering under the weight of her destiny,[3] appears before the throne of Olympus to beg for a champion in her troubles. Cannot Gaul furnish a chief to rival the glory of Trajan?[4] Avitus, the choice of the heavenly powers, is painted as the real victor in the Catalaunian plains,[5] without whom Aetius would have been helpless, the diplomatist endowed with a magical power over the triumphant Gothic chiefs of Bordeaux. His influence is the only barrier against their advance.[6] When Avitus comes as envoy, Theodoric professes that his mere wishes are law to the Goths, and

[1] Auson. *Grat. Act.* iv. 19.

[2] *Ib.* x. 49, quis haec verba docuit? Ego tam propria et tam Latina nescivi. The words referred to are the simple formula, "te Consulem designavi et declaravi et priorem nuncupavi."

[3] Apoll. Sid. *Carm.* vii. 53: summo satis obruta fato invideo abjectis.

[4] Apoll. Sid. *Carm.* vii. 116.
[5] *Ib.* vii. 328-350.
[6] *Ib.* vii. 342: et populis Geticis sola est tua gratia limes.

laments the one blot on his great ancestor's fame, his capture of Rome.[1]   The old warrior from the Danube, on the news of his approach, drops the sword he has been whetting for fresh bloody raids, and bitterly laments that he must now return to the ploughshare.[2] The poem ends with a glowing prophecy of Rome renewing her youth under the leadership of Avitus.[3] Within a year Avitus, disgraced by his vices, and flung off by a German master of the Empire, was fleeing for shelter to the shrine of S. Julian of Auvergne.[4]

The Panegyric on Anthemius displays perhaps less sincerity and more extravagance than that on Avitus. Avitus after all represented the national feeling of Gaul and the military force of the Visigothic kings.   Anthemius owed his position to the fact that he was son-in-law of Marcian and nominee of Leo.   It was not a very digni- fied position, even if we forget the fact that it was held on sufferance at the will of Ricimer.   But the poet uses alike the splendours of mythology and the very weakness of Rome to exalt the Emperor.   The goddess of Rome, at the entreaty of Italy and the god of the Tiber, betakes herself to the glittering palace of the Dawn to ask for Anthemius as the protector of her feeble age.[5]   The glories of his ancestors in Eastern diplomacy and war are celebrated as if they had dominated the realms of Alexander. The omens which heralded his birth were even more marvellous than those which ushered a Cyrus, an Alexander, or a Julius Caesar into the world.   The order of nature forsook its fixed course in honour of such

---

[1] Apoll. Sid. *Carm.* vii. 505 :
    abolere
quae noster peccavit avus, quem fuscat id
    unum,
quod te, Roma, capit . . .

[2] *Ib.* vii. 411.

[3] *Ib.* vii. 597 :
en princeps faciet juvenescere major,
quam pueri fecere senem.

[4] Greg. Tur. *Hist. Fr.* ii. 11,

basilicam sancti Juliani Arverni martyris cum multis muneribus expetivit : sed impleto in itinere vitae cursu, obiit, delatusque ad Brivatensem vicum (Brioude), ad pedes antedicti martyris est sepul- tus. Cf. Greg. Tur. *de Mirac. S. Jul.* c. i.

[5] Apoll. Sid. *Carm.* ii. 406.

an event. Honey and oil flowed in rivers. The fields waved with unsown harvests. Lilies and roses defied the rigours of winter. As a boy Anthemius performed miracles of strength or valour in war or the chase. Not less wonderful were his attainments as a young student.[1] He had a complete mastery of every Greek philosopher from Thales to Aristotle, and of the whole range of Latin literature from Plautus to Quintilian. The Dawn goddess yields to the prayer of Rome, and reminds her that she had sent Memnon to help her Trojan ancestors. It is an unfortunate reminiscence. Neither Troy nor Rome owed much to their champions from the East, and both had a tragic end.[2]

But panegyric was not offered to the emperors only. The members of every literary clique burnt incense to one another, and both secular and Christian literature are tainted with the vice of gross and insincere adulation.[3] It is difficult to understand how men, often of great talent, and always widely read in the really great authors of Greece and Rome, could lavish on some versifying friend, whom the great judge has condemned to oblivion, epithets of admiration which a sober criticism would hardly apply to Virgil or Pindar.[4] We are accustomed to regard as provincial the habit of reckless and extravagant eulogy of commonplace performance. But the greatest offenders in the fourth and fifth centuries were men of the world as well as trained scholars. Yet neither their knowledge of men nor of books had given

---

[1] Apoll. Sid. *Carm.* ii. 156 *sqq.*

[2] *Ib.* ii. 521 :

> prior hinc ego Memnona misi.

Cf. Pind. *Ol.* ii. 150.

[3] In the letters of Sidonius probably the grossest specimens of this sort of flattery are iv. 3 ; viii. 10, 11, 13 ; ix. 3 ; ix. 7, non extat ad praesens vivi hominis oratio, quam peritia tua non sine labore transgredi queat ac supervadere (addressed to S. Remi). Cf. Faust. *Ep.* viii. xvi. ; Ruric, *Ep.* i. 1, 3, 4, 16.

[4] The examples of this flattery are too frequent to be quoted. As a specimen cf. the extravagant eulogy of Lampridius of Bordeaux (Apoll. Sid. *Ep.* viii. 11), or the glorification of the literary circle at Narbonne (*Carm.* xxiii.).

them the sanity, the sense of proportion, the discrimin-
ating tact of genuine criticism.   That a crowd of clever
men, carefully trained in literature, and many of them
devoting a great deal of their time to its cultivation,
should be so wanting either in sincerity or in literary
sense, is a most startling phenomenon.   The causes of it
are to be sought partly in the want of a career for energy
and ambition, and partly in the exaggerated importance
attached to mere style, apart from ideas and matter.
The ambitious senator, conscious of great powers, had no
field for their display except that of literary composition.
He could not win fame as a soldier or as a statesman;
and he tried to satisfy his craving for it by imitations of
Virgil or Statius, or by curiously elaborated epistles, to
win the applause of posterity.[1] He might have little real
knowledge, and less fertility and originality of thought;
but his early training had given him a facility of expression or imitation which seemed to triumph over the
meagreness of any subject.[2] Living in close intimacy
with men moulded by the same powerful tradition and
condemned to the same sterile life as himself, the man,
who might in other days have commanded armies or composed a great history, frittered away his talents on fugitive pieces cast in the conventional mould, and was led
by the applause of a clique into imagining himself one of
the immortals.   Occasionally you may find a man like
Symmachus who has formed a true estimate of his own
poverty of intellect;[3] yet this makes him all the more
earnest in the cultivation of mere style; and, however

---

[1] Apoll. Sid. *Ep.* i. 1, 1, praecipis
. . . ut si quae epistolae paulo poli-
tiores varia occasione fluxerunt,
omnes retractatis exemplaribus
enucleatisque uno volumine inclu-
dam ; cf. viii. 16.

[2] This is expressed frankly by
Sidonius (*Ep.* viii. 10), nam moris
est eloquentibus viris ingeniorum
facultatem negotiorum probare diffi-

cultatibus, et illic stilum peritum
quasi quendam fecundi pectoris
vomerem figere, ubi materiae sterilis
argumentum velut arida caespitis
macri glaeba jejunat ; cf. the same
idea in Ruric, *Ep.* i. 4, sicuti in
jejuno atque otioso caespite magis
strenuitas cultoris apparet, etc.

[3] Sym. *Ep.* iv. 27, 28.

modest about his own powers he may be, he will be
capable of placing the *Moselle* of Ausonius in the same
rank as the poems of Virgil.[1]   To judge by the letters of
Sidonius, the crowd of literary people in Southern Gaul
must have been enormous, and of all their productions
hardly a fragment has come down to us.   Yet among
these obscure and forgotten poetasters and declaimers a
considerable number are represented not only as equal or
even superior to some great master, but as actually, by a
miracle of versatility, combining the varied genius of
them all.   There is a poem of Sidonius addressed to Consentius,[2] a cultivated magnate of Narbonne, which, for
sheer lawless recklessness of flattery, could probably not
be matched.   Magnus, the father of Consentius, is compared with every great name in Greek or Roman literature.   Thales, we are told, and the wise men of Greece,
might have listened to the wisdom of Magnus with
amazement.[3]   In geometry Euclid would have had difficulty in following in his track.   In music the bard of
Thrace, or Phoebus himself, would have to yield him the
palm.   In dramatic competition Sophocles, Euripides, and
Menander would vainly contend with him.   Homer and
Herodotus against such a rival would hardly keep their
pride of place.[4]   The long line of Latin authors from
Plautus to Martial would fare no better than the Greeks.
One is almost ashamed to transcribe these absurdities.
Hardly less outrageous is the adulation addressed to
Mamertus Claudianus, who had dedicated his work *De
Statu Animae* to Sidonius.   It is difficult to believe that
the writer of such a letter could have read or understood
the treatise.   Certainly, were such compliments offered

[1] Sym. *Ep.* i. 14, ita dii me probabi-
lem praestent ut ego hoc tuum carmen
libris Maronis adjungo.   Ausonius
more than returns the compliment
in *Ep.* xvii., quis ita ad enthyme-
mata Demosthenis, aut opulentiam
Tullianam, aut proprietatem nostri

Maronis accedat ? cf. *Ep.* xix. Paul-
ino.
[2] Apoll. Sid *Carm.* xxiii.
[3] *Ib.* xxiii. 101.
[4] *Ib.* xxiii. 134 :

primos vix poterant locos tueri
torrens Herodotus tonans Homerus.

to a philosophic writer of our time, they would be regarded as an insult or a bad joke. Not a word is said of the theory of the soul developed by Claudianus. But he is praised in the most hyberbolical and absurd fashion for his endless beauties of style, and for an absolutely irreconcilable diversity of gifts.[1] In a severe and heavy disquisition, on a highly abstract subject, Sidonius finds all the varied power or peculiar charm of Orpheus and Archimedes, of Plato and Vitruvius, of Pythagoras and Demosthenes, of Hortensius and Fabius Cunctator, Cato and Caesar, and all the special arts in controversy of the Christian fathers. It is as difficult to conceive the vanity which could accept such flattery, as the pedantic bad taste which could offer it. The truth seems to be that all the great names familiar in the schools were, by a depraved mannerism, employed, just as the machinery of exploded mythology was employed, on all occasions, to give false dignity to a commonplace theme. The names of gods and the names of great poets or philosophers were stage-properties handed on through the school tradition from one generation to another. If you wanted to express admiration for anything or anybody, the schoolmaster had provided the correct conventional forms in which the eulogium should be delivered. The gods were no longer believed in ; probably some of the authors referred to were no longer, or not often read. But culture was a worship of the models of the pagan past, a conventional discipline, weighing on the human mind with the over-whelming authority of a thousand years of unbroken tradition. The classical inspiration was so divine that all its forms of expression, the mere names of its great adepts, were consecrated for ever as the symbols of an unapproachable perfection. Sidonius, by reason of his unconscious barbarisms, and perverse contortions and in-genuities, is removed *toto caelo* from Cicero, from Pliny,

---

[1] Apoll. Sid. *Ep.* iv. 3

even from Symmachus. Yet Sidonius is praised by Mamertus Claudianus as the "restorer of ancient eloquence,"[1] and he regarded himself as writing in an unadorned and simple style.[2] It is this worship of past excellence, and uncritical judgment of what has been formed by inept imitation of the past, which is the most curious characteristic of fifth century literature. There never was an age which was at once so devoted to the cultivation of mere style, and which fell so far short of the ideal.

The faith in the power of mere words, skilfully used, according to the rules of ancient experience, was the literary faith of that age. And the ambition to survive the wreck of time as a master of studied and telling phrase is probably its highest ambition. Even a great saint and ascetic like S. Jerome, penetrated, if any man ever was, with the thought of the nothingness of all earthly glory in the view of the solemn realities of the life to come, cannot shake off the passion, inspired by memories of the class-room of Donatus, to live in the admiration of coming ages. He concludes his famous consolation to Paula,[3] on the death of her daughter Blaesilla, with words which show how little the isolation and self-discipline of the cell at Bethlehem had prevailed to extinguish the passion for literary fame. The name of Blaesilla, he says, will travel everywhere with the works of Jerome, and will have an immortality like theirs. On the death of Paula, Jerome wrote a long and enthusiastic narrative of a life which was, even in that age, remarkable

---

[1] Veteris reparator eloquentiae. See the dedication of the treatise *de Statu Animae.*

[2] *Ep.* viii. 16, nos opuscula sermone condidimus arido, exili, certe maxima ex parte vulgato (cf. Sym. *Ep.* v. 85). He contrasts his simplicity with a fashionable taste for verba Saliaria vel Sibyllina vel Sabinis abusque Curibus accita (*Ep.* viii. 16) ; cf. Auson. *Prof. Burd.* xxii. for a similar taste.

[3] Hieron. *Ep.* 39, § 7, quocunque sermonis nostri monumenta pervenerint, illa cum meis opusculis peregrinabitur. . . . Brevis vitae spatium aeterna memoria compensabit.

for absolute self-renunciation and abandonment of worldly
rank and wealth.[1]   The passionate sincerity of S. Jerome
is evident in every line of a piece which is full of the
romance of asceticism.   Yet he cannot, at the close,
refrain from recording the fact that he composed it in two
short sittings, without any attempt at elegance of style,[2]
while he has a perfect confidence that he has left a monument of Paula which no length of time will ever efface.[3]
We should be guilty of no injustice to Sidonius in thinking that he rated his own compositions quite as high as
he did those of Mamertus Claudianus or Lampridius.   He
certainly makes no secret of the fact that his letters were
really intended for the future,[4] and that he is anxious
about his fate on what he calls the " sea of fame."   And
that he thinks his fate depends entirely on his style is
clear from the letter addressed to Constantius, to whom
the work was entrusted.   He describes it as marked by
" pagana simplicitas," so different from the affected
archaic style, modelled on Saliarian or Sibylline verses,
which would need some priest of the ancient days to interpret.   Yet Sidonius is nothing if he is not a stylist.
We know that he carefully revised his letters before publishing them, and that he asked his friends to help him
in giving them the final polish.[5]

It is difficult indeed for us, with our severer ideas of
truth, to understand the encomiums which were lavished
by his contemporaries on the poems and letters of
Sidonius.[6]   It is hard to believe that these well-read

[1] Hieron. *Ep.* 108, § 30, testis est
Jesus, ne unum quidem nummum
ab ea filiae derelictum.

[2] *Ib.* § 32, hunc tibi librum ad
duas lucubratiunculas dictavi unde
et inculta oratio . . .

[3] *Ib.* § 32, quod nulla destruere
possit vetustas.

[4] Apoll. Sid. *Ep.* i. 1 ; cf. viii. 1.

[5] *Ib.* i. 1, omnibus retractatis
exemplaribus enucleatisque. The

letters were published in four re-
lays : (1) bk. i. at the instance of
Constantius ; (2) bks. ii.-vii. dedicated to the same friend ; (3) bk.
viii. at the request of Petronius of
Arles ; (4) bk. ix. at the request of
Firminus ; Sid. *Ep.* i. 1 ; iv. 10 ;
vii. 18 ; viii. 1 ; ix. 1.   Cf. Germain's *Apoll. Sid.* p. 72.

[6] See these collected in Germain's
Apoll. Sid. p. 112.

people really regarded him as worthy of a place beside
Homer and Virgil.[1] Yet it is certain that from the day
when he won, by his Panegyric on Avitus, a statue in
the forum, he was, except by a few snarling critics,
admitted to be the foremost man of letters in Gaul, the
best and greatest representative of the old classical
tradition.[2] His reputation lasted unobscured all through
the Middle Ages, and, to judge by the number of editions
of him, continued long after the invention of printing.
The modern scholar, whose taste has been formed on
classical models, is revolted by his affectations, his
perverse and barbarous ingenuity, his tasteless fondness
for extravagant verbal effects. Yet we should remember
that this is only the final and natural result of the
idolatry of mere style in an age without ideas or any
healthy intellectual movement; an age in which all the
stress of discipline was laid on the memory and the
imitative powers; an age in which men, expecting
nothing new in matter or thought, had a morbid craving
for fresh sensations in style, and would tolerate and even
applaud any surprise of exaggeration or ingenuity within
the conventional limits set by the schools. And the
critic inclined to be severe to Sidonius should remember
that he not only represents a debased form of culture
which grew inevitably out of the past, but that he was
with all his force stemming a rapid movement of decline.
However he may flatter his literary friends, it is clear
that many of his class were falling away from the ideal
of the lettered noble which Sidonius was constantly holding up to his contemporaries.[3] Some were becoming
absorbed in farming and hunting;[4] others were having
their Latinity corrupted by association with the Germans.

---

[1] Apoll. Sid. *Ep.* v. 17, mihi
assignas quae vix Maroni aut
Homero competenter accommo-
darentur.

[2] *Ib.* ix. 16. Cf. viii. 1.

[3] *Ib.* v. 11, viii. 2. solum erit
posthac nobilitatis indicium litteras
nosse.

[4] *Ib.* viii. 8.

A still larger number probably succumbed to mere sloth.[1]
There must have been many living in the seclusion of
a great estate, surrounded by luxury, with no stimulus
of public and unselfish interests, and cut off for long
intervals from friends and equals by the roving bands of
invaders, who lost their taste for literature and sank
into something like the mental torpor of the mediaeval
baron.

This failure of mental energy, which overwhelmed a
section of the educated class, affected to a certain extent
even those members of it who retained some energy and
literary ambition.   The want of sustained power is a
marked feature in the secular writers of that age.   If we
put aside the greater theological writings, there is no
evidence of the spirit to conceive, or the energy to
execute, any literary work on a great scale.   It does
not indeed surprise us that in an age of starched conventionality the notes of the higher poetry should be
silent; but that no considerable historical work should
have been produced causes some astonishment.   There
was surely much in the convulsions of the third century,
in the conflicts of religion in the fourth, in the ominous
appearance of the Northern peoples upon the scene, and
the startling calamities of the fifth century, to rouse
some one among the host of literary devotees to emulate
the work of Tacitus, or even of Ammianus.   Once or
twice we hear of some one who had a faint idea of
writing a history; Symmachus, for instance, had among
his friends a group of three brothers, belonging to a
literary circle at Trèves, one of whom seems to have
thought of composing a history of Gaul.[2]   But the
history was probably never written.   Sidonius had, at

[1] Apoll. Sid. *Ep.* ii. 10, 1, tantum
increbuit multitudo desidiosorum,
ut nisi vel paucissimi quique meram
linguae Latiaris proprietatem de
trivialium barbaris morum robigine
vindicaveritis, eam brevi abolitam
defleamus interemptamque; sic
omnes nobilium sermonum purpurae
per incuriam vulgi decolorabuntur.
[2] Sym. *Ep.* iv. 18.

the suggestion of Prosper,[1] bishop of Orleans, begun a
narrative of the war with Attila and the siege of Orleans,
for which, through his connection with Avitus and the
great leaders of that time, he must have had the most
authentic materials. But he soon gave up the project.
In a letter to Leo, the Secretary of State to the Visigothic
king, he gives his reasons at some length for not undertaking the composition of a historical work.[2] Leo, with
his eloquence, his vast practical knowledge of public
affairs, and a great position which raised him above the
fear of criticism, might fairly hope for fame as a writer
of history;[3] but Sidonius feels himself shut out from
this field, partly by his clerical profession, vowed to
humility, and concerned with the future rather than the
present, partly by his want of health and vigour;[4] but,
evidently in the main, from a fear of publishing the
truth about persons of power and influence.[5] Sidonius
may refer either to influential Roman nobles or to the
German chiefs, who were kept well informed of what
was said about them, and who were evidently sensitive to
Roman opinion. The nearest approach to historical composition which Sidonius ever made was in his Panegyrics.
And in his treatment of the relations of the Goths to the

[1] Apoll. Sid. *Ep.* viii. 15.

[2] *Ib.* iv. 22.

[3] *Ib.* iv. 22, tu cui praeter elo-
quentiam singularem, scientiae
ingentis magna opportunitas. . . .
Quique praestanti positus in cul-
mine non necesse habet vel sup-
primere verum vel concinnare
mendacium. On the Roman conception of history even in the best
times cf. H. Nettleship, *Lectures
and Essays*, 2nd series, p. 67.

[4] Apoll. Sid. *Ep.* iv. 22, postremo
languor impedimento, etc.

[5] *Ib.* iv. 22, turpiter falsa, peri-
culose vera dicuntur. Est enim
hujusmodi thema, in quo bonorum
si facias mentionem, modica gratia
paratur, si notabilium, maxuma

offensa. Cf. Hieron. *Chron.* Praef.
ad fin., quo fine (*i.e.* 378) contentus
reliquum temporis Gratiani et
Theodosii latioris historiae stilo
reservavi, *non quo de viventibus
timuerim libera et vere scribere . . .
sed quoniam, dibacchantibus adhuc
in terra nostra barbaris, incerta
sunt omnia;* Plin. *Ep.* v. 8, 12,
vetera et scripta aliis? parata in-
quisitio sed onerosa collatio. In-
tacta et nova? Gravis offensa,
levis gratia. (Quoted by Peter,
*Geschichtl. Litt. über die Röm.
Kaiserzeit*, ii. 191.) Peter has a
good chapter on the influence of
rhetoric on history, ii. 179 *sqq.* ; cf.
H. Nettleship, *Lectures and Essays*,
2nd series, p. 67.

Empire in the eulogy of Avitus, and of the relations of East and West in the poem on Anthemius, he shows that he keenly realised the delicate task which awaited any contemporary historian of that stormy time.   To these considerations we may add the reticence as to the prospects of the Empire which patriotic pride seemed to impose on Romans.   Enthusiastic Christians like Orosius or Salvianus, from different points of view, and with varying objects, discussed the import of the great changes which were passing before their eyes.   But the man who belonged more to the old Roman world than to the detached society of the Church shrank from examining them with an open-eyed scrutiny.   His faith in the destiny of Rome, in the stability of the ancient order and culture, had all the force of a religion, and he instinctively turned away from the spectacle of illusions which seemed to be vanishing in gloom.   The conception of history as a truthful record of fact had for ages been progressively depraved by the influence of the rhetorical school, and the events of the fifth century did not offer a tempting field even for the most audacious rhetoric.

Whatever the causes may have been, there is no work of the fifth century which, either in matter or in form, can pretend to the name of history.   Instead of it we inherit only some jejune chronicles, arid in style, and often ludicrously capricious in their selection of events deemed worthy of narration, occasionally rousing a curiosity which they never satisfy.   The Chronicle of Prosper of Aquitaine,[1] which, down to the year 378, is founded on S. Jerome's version of Eusebius, professes to give the history of the world from the birth of Seth to the taking of Rome by the Vandals in 455.   It is difficult to conceive the attitude of the writer's mind, the method on which he conducted his studies, or the

[1] Gennad. *de Scrip. Eccl.* c. 84 ; Ebert, *Lit. des Mittelalt.* i. 441. In some MSS. the chronicle comes down only to 445, or even 435 ; Peter, *Geschichtl. Litt.* ii. 381.

principle which guided him in his selection of events. In the first part of the work there is the strangest jumble of detached and often uninteresting facts, taken at random from the annals of Persia, Palestine, Greece, and Rome, without any sense of proportion or relative importance. The most momentous periods or crises are omitted, or dismissed in a single perfunctory phrase. The reign of Xerxes, for example, is casually, and rather inaccurately, mentioned as contemporaneous with the lives of Sophocles and Euripides.[1] The Persian invasion is not alluded to ; the age of Pericles is an utter blank. Not a single event of the Peloponnesian war is recorded. With a lordly disregard of chronology and the practical side of human affairs, Empedocles, Zeno, Parmenides, Heraclitus, Hippocrates, and Socrates are allowed to have that great age to themselves. The reign of Alexander and the campaigns of Caesar in Gaul are only honoured by a couple of lines,[2] while many lines are given to obscure Hebrew pontiffs, and to the vicissitudes of the chosen people. When we come to the period in which Prosper must have been personally interested, and for which he is solely responsible, the disproportion becomes even more startling.[3] The great incursions of Alaric and Radagaisus, the capture of Rome, and the Vandal occupation of Africa, are recorded with rather less emphasis than the apparition of a dove-shaped meteor which blazed for thirty days,[4] or the incredible abstinence of an Egyptian monk, or the feuds of John Chrysostom and Theophilus of Alexandria. It is only fair, however, to say that the interest of Prosper in his own province sheds here and there a ray of light on that dim period in

---

[1] Xerxes regnat annis XX. quo tempore Sophocles et Euripides clari habebantur.

[2] Caesar Rhenum transiens Germanos vastat, Gallias subigit.

[3] Prosp. *Chron.* pt. ii. *ad init.*, nos quae consecuta sunt adjicere curavimus.

[4] It might have been thought equally interesting to an ecclesiastic that in this very year was issued the great edict of Theodosius against pagan sacrifices, *C. Th.* xvi. 10, 12.

which the Visigoths were making themselves masters of Southern Gaul.[1]   The same provincial patriotism is even more strongly marked in the Chronicle of the Gallician bishop Idatius.   Although Idatius had made a pilgrimage to the Holy Places in his youth,[2] and represented his province as an envoy to Aetius, he shows less interest in the general history of the Empire than his brother chronicler. Yet, in spite of its provoking brevity, the work of Idatius gives some welcome glimpses of the career of the Visigoths in Gaul, of the ravages of the Vandal fleets, of the campaigns of Theodoric against the Sueves in Spain, and of the sufferings of that unfortunate province from the hordes who swept across it.   The mind of Idatius is full of the horrors of famine and slaughter which he must have often witnessed.   There is a strange pathos in his brief record of the misery which has found no other voice.

Prosper and Idatius, however, do not belong to the circle, the literary tone of which we have been trying to describe.   We should have been thankful if any of the friends of Symmachus or Sidonius had left us even such scrappy and unconnected jottings on the great events through which they lived.   Whatever faults of style and execution the earnest Christian writers of that time may offer to criticism, it is always to be remembered to their credit that they were occupied with living interests and ideas, while the semi-pagan men of the world were toying with mythological fancies, and feeding one another's vanity with tricks and surprises of style.   The defects of secular literature can nearly all be traced to barrenness of thought and absence of sincerity and love of truth ; and these again were the direct result of a school training, the whole aim of which was to turn out imitators and

---

[1] Cf. Prosp. *Chron.* ad a. 412, 419, 426, 436, 439.

[2] Idat. *Chron.* Praef. He remembered having seen S. Jerome : quem (Hieronymum) quodam tempore propriae peregrinationis in supradictis regionibus adhuc infantulus vidisse me certus sum.   The pilgrimage was probably about 407 ; cf. Ebert, i. p. 443.

masters of striking phrase. Symmachus and Sidonius
were often quite conscious that they had nothing to say,
or that the subject was slight and trivial; but the man
who had been trained to find arguments for or against
the marriage of a Vestal,[1] or to describe the feelings of
Thetis as she gazed on the corpse of Achilles, cared for
his subject only as a stimulus to ingenuity, a field for
exhibiting his skill in phrase-making.[2] The poorer and
more commonplace the theme, the more tempting the
chance for rhetorical display.

In poetry the poverty of imagination was to some
extent concealed, or supplemented, by the lavish employment of mythological scenery. Claudian, it is true, had
real poetic gifts; yet from taste or policy[3] he does not
shrink from the startling incongruity of enthroning
Theodosius, the champion of the Church, among the
Olympian gods,[4] or of inviting Serena, who was execrated
by all true pagans for appropriating the necklace on the
holy image of the great goddess, to preside as another
Juno at the nuptials of another Orpheus.[5] But his
Christian contemporaries or later imitators are as pagan
in their imagery, without his pagan attachments. S.
Paulinus had torn himself from the semi-pagan society of
Aquitaine, to lead a life of austerity and prayer. And
his shocked and afflicted friend Ausonius reproaches him
with his faithlessness to old ties by an appeal to the
mythical types of loyal friendship, Theseus and Pirithous,

[1] Ennod. *Dict.* xvi. (*Corp. Scrip. Eccl.* p. 471).

[2] *Ib.* xxv. There is a more curious subject in *Dict.* xx., "in eum qui in lupanari statuam Miner-vae locavit." For the effect of *declamatio* on fictitious themes *v.* H. Nettleship, *Lectures and Essays*, 2nd series, pp. 112, 113; cf. Peter, *Geschichtl. Litt.* ii. 206.

[3] Orosius, vii. 35, styles him poeta quidem eximius sed paganus

pervicacissimus. Cf. Rauschen, *Jahrbücher*, p. 555, on the question of Claudian's attitude to Christian-ity; Claudian. *Carm. Pasch.* and *Epigr. in Jacobum*; Ozanam, *Civ. au Vme Siècle*, i. 300.

[4] *De Sext. Cons. Honor.* 101 :
felix ille parens qui te securus Olympum succedente petit.

[5] Claud. *Ep.* ii. 34 :
sed quod Threicio Juno placabilis Orpheo, hoc poteris votis esse, Serena, meis.

Pylades and Orestes, Nisus and Euryalus.[1]   The Christian
Sidonius did not scruple to use to the uttermost the
wealth of ancient pagan imagination to aid his own
rather barren fancy.   The machinery of his Panegyrics
on Christian Emperors is all borrowed from the pagan
past.   The cradles of Anthemius and Avitus are surrounded with omens of their future greatness of the
antique kind.[2]   The Rome which receives or claims them
as her rulers seems for the moment to be the Rome of
the early Caesars, still true to her ancient gods.   One
would never gather from such pieces that the religion of
Jupiter and Mars and Venus had been for generations
lying crushed under penal edicts, and that to offer a
grain of incense on the old altars, or to screen the superstitious votary, might be punished with confiscation, exile,
or even with death.[3]   Yet there is a showy insincerity
about the mythological ornament of Sidonius which to
the critical eye saves him from any imputation of believing in the gods whom he uses for poetic effect.   Claudian
after all is a real poet; he is a posthumous child of the
great age, and has something of its fire and manner; but
the mythological pomp of Sidonius belongs to the same
order of taste as the sham Gothic of Strawberry Hill, or
the Daphnis and Chloe, the Damon and Cupid, of Gay
or Prior.   It is lavished with a frenzy of pedantry on
subjects which by contrast render it only ridiculous.
Pontius Paulinus had built himself a sumptuous country
seat on the banks of the Garonne, fortified with impreg-
nable walls, and arranged with all that could minister to
luxurious or fastidious taste.   Sidonius is not satisfied
with describing it simply as he had seen it.   Its splendour
must be made the subject of prophecy.[4]   Ages before the
Burgus of Leontius was built, Bacchus is described as

[1] Auson. *Ep.* xxiv. 34.   [3] *C. Th.* xvi. 10, 12, and 13.
[2] Apoll. Sid. *Carm.* vii. 165; ii.   [4] Apoll. Sid. *Carm.* xxii. 101 *sqq.*
105.

returning from his conquest of the East, seated on his car drawn by tigers, and escorted by fauns and satyrs. He was travelling through the air in triumph to Thebes, when he was met by Phoebus, and urged to turn his course from the city, where his godhead had been flouted by Pentheus, to that spot in the distant West where the vision of the god of prophecy saw the stately towers of Paulinus already rising in the future.

Down to the end of the century, marriages in Christian families were still celebrated by an epithalamium in the old pagan manner. Sidonius has left two of these pieces, in which his taste is probably seen at its worst. In one of these, Venus is summoned by her son to visit the home of the bride in the West.[1] On the shores of Corinth the goddess is found asleep in her temple, gorgeous with many-coloured marbles, and all the precious stones known to the ancients. Venus, after a eulogy on the beauty of Iberia, which the goddess confesses might have won the prize in the famous contest on Mount Ida, obeys the call of her son. She makes her journey in the orthodox fashion, sailing through the air on a car of crystal and gold, drawn by her swans, while her train is swelled by the Graces, Flora, Pomona, the Egyptian Osiris, and the noisy rout of Bacchus. The bridegroom, in whose honour this belated pagan song was composed, was that Ruric who, descended from the great Anician house,[2] some years afterwards took the vow of renunciation, and became bishop of Limoges. He probably lived to see the great battle in the plains of Poitiers, in which a son of his friend Sidonius rode at the head of the nobles of Auvergne, who were fighting in the Visigothic cause against the victorious Franks.[3]

---

[1] *Carm.* xi.
[2] See the epitaph by Fortunatus, quoted in Krusch's *Praef. Ruric. Ep.* p. lxii.

[3] Greg. Tur. *Hist. Fr.* ii. c. 37, maximus ibi (in campo Vogladense) tunc Arvernorum populus, qui cum Apollinare venerat, et primi

Not less incongruous is the epithalamium composed for the wedding of Polemius.[1] In this poem the bridegroom is a philosopher, and the patron goddess is no longer Venus but Minerva, who is seen hastening to Attica, clad in all her traditional armour, her shield covered with scenes from the war with the Giants. The poet carries us to a stately temple in Attica,[2] in which are gathered all the sages and philosophers known, by name at least, in the Gallic schools. The young Platonist is found seated among this august company, receiving the compliments of the Academy.[3] On another side are displayed the works of embroidery which are dear to the virgin goddess ; among them a robe in whose texture are figured a host of legendary monsters, which are enumerated like the beasts in a menagerie.[4] And the bride is discovered working into a mantle of victory for her father, a veteran of the Spanish wars,[5] the tales of Penelope's web, of Orpheus and Eurydice, and, strange subject for Christian maiden's thoughts, the legends of the many amours of the king of the gods.[6] Minerva, with the help of Plato, overcomes the philosophic indifference of Polemius to wedlock, and the pair are united in the hope that, favoured by the harmonious sisters, the marriage may give the world another Plato ![7] Sidonius, soon after the composition of this piece, became a bishop, and resolved to abandon the cultivation of pagan poetry as inconsistent with his sacred profession.[8] One could have wished that the renunciation had been made a little sooner.

(plurimi?) qui erant ex senatoribus corruerunt. For the site of this battle *v.* Jacobs, *Géographie de Grégoire de Tours*, pp. 142 *sqq.*

[1] *Carm.* xv.

[2] *Ib.* v. 36 *sqq.*

[3] *Ib.* v. 121.

[4] *Ib.* v. 141.

[5] *Ib.* v. 155.

[6] *Ib.* xv. 175.

[7] *Ib.* v. 191.
incipies iterum parvum mihi ferre Platona.

[8] *Ep.* ix. 12, 1 ; Germain's *Apoll. Sid.* pp. 39 and 69. He wrote, however, some verses after he became bishop ; cf. *Ep.* ix. 13 ; ix. 15 ; vii. 17 ; iv. 11.

The abuse of mythological ornament was only one result of a depravation of literary feeling which is quite as marked in the prose as in the poetry of the age. Indeed, in mere style and structure, it might be maintained that the prose is more tasteless and corrupt than the poetry. Sidonius recognised in theory that prose style should be less luxuriant,[1] and he was under the delusion that he wrote a prose of severe simplicity. Yet nearly every form of exaggerated and misplaced artifice, which criticism has observed in his verse,[2] can be discovered in the letters of Sidonius, and of many of his contemporaries. Alliteration and assonance,[3] pompous periphrasis taking the place of simple expression of ordinary fact, antithesis without real contrast, similarity of sound with no similarity of sense,[4] outrageous hyperbole, and the most excruciating puns [5]—all these vices were cultivated by Sidonius, with a melancholy waste of effort. The curious student must read Sidonius himself to appreciate the perverse elaboration of his style. It stares at us from every page. No translation could give even the faintest conception of the ingenious torture to which the Latin language has been subjected by this devotee of the past. Nor was Sidonius peculiar in these faults of style. It is true that in him the combined literary vanity and search for piquant phrase at any cost, which characterised his class, were seconded by a talent and facility which were then unrivalled, and almost universally admired.[6] But we may be sure that the shadowy crowd of poets and orators, whom he has saved from oblivion

---

[1] *Ep.* viii. 16, 3, in hoc stilo cui non urbanus lepos inest, sed pagana simplicitas . . . Nos opuscula sermone condidimus arido exili, certe maxima ex parte vulgato.

[2] Fertig, *Apoll. Sid. und seine Zeit,* iii. p. 17.

[3] For the worst specimens cf. *Ep.* viii. 7, § 2 ; i. 5, § 6 ; *Carm.* xxiii.

44 ; *Ep.* i. 8, § 2 ; viii. 3, 4.

[4] *Carm.* xxiii. 480 :
sedulitas sodalitasque.

[5] *Ep.* iv. 18, 5, perpetuo durent culmina Perpetui.

[6] Mamert. Claud. *Praef. de. Statu Animae* ; Gennad. *de Scrip. Eccl.* c. 92 ; cf. Germain, p. 112.

by his extravagant eulogies, pleased him by the very faults which he cultivated so assiduously in himself. And in imitators of his style, such as Ruric of Limoges,[1] we find in degenerate form the same ill-aimed literary ambition, and vicious elaboration of the commonplace, which are at the root of the faults of Sidonius.

Sidonius as a stylist is not a solitary eccentric; he is the most complete and elaborate product of a worn-out system of education, and of a society which had spent its force and was living in a world of ghosts and illusions. The very titles of " magnanimitas," " sublimitas," " celsitudo tua," [2] given by friends to one another in ordinary intercourse, reveal an age which cared for forms and words rather than for the sincerity of fact. Trained to believe that delicate manipulation of language for the purpose of striking effect was the great end of education, and that the very poverty of matter offered a finer opportunity for display of rhetorical art, men came to care nothing about fact and truth, or even the solid thoughts of the great writers whom they devotedly studied. Condemned to a sterile and monotonous existence, with no wholesome ambition or saving practical interest, the clever man of the world found his only intellectual stimulus in surprises and sensational effects of style, and the morbid appetite for novelty and piquancy stimulated fresh efforts of perverted ingenuity, and drew taste farther and farther from the beaten path of simple expression. By an inevitable Nemesis, these idolaters of mere style ended in writing a barbarous jargon, which even some of the adepts could hardly interpret.[3]

The adepts in the precious style in the latter half of the fifth century were countless. The Visigoth and Vandal did not much disturb their futile enthusiasm. In

---

[1] Cf. the affected modesty of style in Ruric, *Ep.* i. 4 ; ii. 18, §5.
[2] *Ib.* i. 3, § 1 ; i. 6, § 1 ; i. 10, § 1.

[3] *Ib.* ii. 26, § 3, ita prae obscuritate dictorum non accendit ingenium. So Petrarch found Sidonius hard reading (Germain, p. 79).

cities which were again and again beleaguered by Gothic armies, men calmly amused themselves with their imitations of Pindar and Virgil and Pliny, their declamatory displays, their childish sport with " versus echoici et recurrentes." [1] The poems and letters of Sidonius are often extolled as a storehouse of information as to the literary history of his time ; and for the spirit of it they are invaluable. But the modern can only scan the long array of forgotten names and ephemeral reputations with a languid interest or a pathetic sense of the vanity of provincial fame. The brilliant clique at Narbonne,[2] jurists, poets, philosophers, were doubtless very pleasant and interesting to one another. They had the pride of thinking that a Leo combined an unrivalled legal lore with a lyric power which might have challenged Horace or Pindar,[3] that a Magnus possessed all the depth and acumen of the greatest Greek thinkers, and could contend on equal terms in their separate fields with Sophocles and Menander, with Homer and Virgil, with Herodotus and Sallust ; [4] that the lyrics of Consentius were destined to charm posterity.[5] Vienne boasted to have in Supaudus a rhetorician who had the genius of the great age of Gallic rhetoric, the copiousness of Delphidius, the art of Agroecius, the energy of Alcimus. Secundinus, equally ready in celebrating in verse a wedding or an exploit of the chase, was famed for the skill and veiled severity with which he avenged the murder of Chilperic and his queen by Gundobald.[6] Bordeaux had still a worthy successor to the generation of Ausonius in the brilliant yet melancholy figure of Lampridius. There was none of his literary friends to whom Sidonius was more

---

[1] Apoll. Sid. *Ep.* viii. 11, § 5. See an example of the versus recurrens, *i.e.* which can be read either backwards or forwards, in *Ep.* ix. 14, § 4 :

    Roma tibi subito motibus ibit amor.

[2] *Carm.* xxiii.
[3] *Ib.* v. 446.
[4] *Ib.* v. 97.
[5] *Ep.* viii. 4.
[6] *Ib.* v. 10, § 3 ; v. 8 ; cf. Sirmond, p. 57.

devoted, or of whom perhaps he has left so vivid a portrait. Lampridius was hot-headed, imprudent, and the slave of superstition.   He was perhaps not unkindly, but he was a difficult friend, who showed his better side to the gentle and tolerant bishop of Auvergne.   Sidonius exhausts even his repertory of eulogy in the effort to do justice to the boundless range of Lampridius' accomplishments.   He was an accomplished orator; he could compose with equal readiness on any subject, in any species of verse, from the most weighty to the most frivolous.   Epic or elegiac, tragic, bucolic or fescennine, were all alike to his miraculous facility.   He was probably the last pagan man of letters in the West.   A troop of African diviners came to Bordeaux, and, on a study of his constellation, foretold the very day and hour of his death.   On the fated day the paragon of Gallic culture perished ignominiously by the hands of his slaves.

Many another orator or poet, who then enjoyed a short-lived fame, we must leave to slumber on in the pages of Sidonius.   We are now wandering in a land of pale, silent shades.   Only one of all that company has in a fashion survived to tell us what manner of men they were.   It is perhaps ungrateful to him to part from our guide with only a recollection of the faults of the society which he has so faithfully described to us.   Like many another obscure generation, they performed their allotted part in shaping or guarding the future of humanity.   To preserve the tradition of its hard-won culture may be at times as necessary a task, though one not so striking to the imagination, as to be the pioneers in fresh conquests. And these now forgotten pedants, in a period of political convulsion and literary decadence, softened the impact of barbarism, and kept open for coming ages the access to the distant sources of our intellectual life.

INDEX

Aetius, his campaigns against Franks, Burgundians, and Goths, 290, 325; his death, 335

Albinus, Publilius Caeonius, a pagan pontiff, father of Laeta, S. Jerome's reference to, 14, 128

Algasia, of Cahors, writes to S. Jerome about Biblical difficulties, 185

Ambrose, S., a friend of Symmachus, opposes the restoration of the altar of Victory, 22; his influence with Theodosius, 31

Ammianus Marcellinus, his career and religious opinions, 120; his severe judgment of Roman character in his time, 121 *sqq.*

Anthemius, his connections and accession, 339; Panegyric of Sidonius on, 340, 341

Apollinares, the, literary efforts of, 389 n. 3

Apostasy, frequent in the reign of Gratian, 13; laws against, from 381 to 396, 33

Apuleius, his description of the worship of Isis; 85 *sqq.*; exponent of Platonism, 98; his works emended by Sallustius, 155

Army, difficulty of recruiting, 235; desertion frequent, 236, 237; slaves enrolled, 237; barbarian corps and officers, 292, 295 *sqq.*; superiority of Roman troops to the invaders, 288

Arvandus, a corrupt governor, intrigues with the Visigoths, and is tried at Rome, 330

Asceticism, made men indifferent to civil duty, 11; its severe judgments of contemporary morality, 118; impulse given to, by S.

Martin, 180; Sidonius' reverence for, 221; pagan asceticism, 79, 81, 84, 88; Christian asceticism stimulated by S. Athanasius, 124 n. 2; ascetic ideal of S. Jerome, 126

Attalus, Priscus, his origin, character, and accomplishments, a friend of Libanius, his elevation to the purple, 25; baptized by an Arian bishop, 44; relies on divination, 52

Augustine, S., his correspondence with Volusianus, 14; with Longinianus the pagan philosopher, with Lampadius on fatalism, 15; attacks the doctrine of daemons, 51; the commencement of the *City of God,* 64; how it deals with doubts as to the capture of Rome, 65; devoted to astrology in his youth, 7 n. 2; his attitude to ancient culture, 387

Ausonius, his attitude to Christianity, 6; a friend of Probus, 23; his flattery of Symmachus, 157; his elevation in the reign of Gratian, 158, 159; influences the Emperor to improve the position of professors, 159, 402; his personal character and career, 168, 169, 172 n. 2; his grandfather and father, 170; his female relatives, 171, 172; his social position, 174; his dislike of town life, 175; country life in his time, 175-177; the extent of his estate at Bazas, 201; his wife, Attusia Lucana Sabina, died early, 171-173; his description of the Moselle, 289; his correspondence with S. Paulinus of Nola, 396; his flattery of Gratian, 429

Avitus, Sidonius marries his daughter,

Ecdicius, son of Avitus, and brother-in-law of Sidonius, his charity, 191 ; his gallant defence of Auvergne against the Goths, 217, 364

Education, its unchanging character, 391 *sqq.* ; provision for, under the Empire, 399 *sqq.* ; privileges of teachers, 400 ; their payment, 402, 403 ; their social position, 403 *sqq.* ; the great schools of Gaul, 406 *sqq.* ; favourite authors in the fifth century, 419, 421

Ennodius, an account of, his *Dictiones*, 391

Epiphanius of Pavia, his mission to Euric, 366

Eugenius, his character and support of the pagan reaction, 35

Euric, his character and aggressive policy, 363 ; attacks Auvergne, 364 ; his persecution of Catholics, 367 ; yet uses Catholic administrators, 368

Famine, after the death of Gratian, 30 ; fear of, in the Gildonic war, 148 ; in Gaul relieved by Ecdicius and Bishop Patiens, 191, 218, 381 ; fears of, at Rome in the end of the fourth century, 148

Faustus, bishop of Riez, a semi-Pelagian, 220 ; his controversy with Mam. Claudianus, 220, 414

Flavianus, Virius Nicomachus, his career and character, 19 ; takes part in the pagan reaction under Eugenius, 20, 35 ; his estates restored, 20 ; Pretorian prefect in 391, 31 ; one of the characters in the *Saturnalia* of Macrobius, his learning, 154, 155

Gladiatorial shows, attraction of, even for the refined, 54 ; defended by good men, and exhibited by the best emperors, 55 ; not finally abolished till 404, 56 ; Symmachus procures Saxon gladiators for his son's games, but they kill one another, 159

Gold, appreciation of, in the later Empire, 261, 261 n. 5

Governors, fail to execute the orders of the Emperor, 37 ; favour heretics, 19 n. 7 ; slackness of, in enforcing anti-pagan laws, 37 ; liable to be

tampered with, 270 ; rules for their conduct laid down, 270 ; intrigue with the barbarians, 330, 362

Grammar, the meaning of, 417 *sqq.* ; defects of the study in the Roman schools, 423

Greek, the study of, in Gaul, its decline, 416

Hedibia, a correspondent of S. Jerome, connection of her family with the worship of Belen, 184

Hellenism, its attitude to Christianity, 6, 394

Heraclian, his cruelty, 160 ; the murderer of Stilicho, his treatment of the refugees in 410, 308

History, Protadius, a friend of Symmachus, proposes to write a history of Gaul, 155 ; Sidonius urged to write a history of the wars of Attila, 440 ; history in the fifth century, why not written on an extended scale, 441

Innocent, bishop of Rome, permits the Tuscan diviners to perform their rites, 49

Inns, few and bad, 205

Invasions, of the third and fourth centuries, 287, 288 ; of the fifth century, 288; invaders not dreaded by Roman troops, 290 ; had no common purpose nor hatred of Rome, 291 ; numbers of, in the third century, 287 ; in the fifth, 299 ; varieties of character and religion among, 300, 301 ; horrors of the invasion of Gaul, 316

Isis, temple of, 42 B.C., at Rome, 78 ; her functions, her ritual, and priesthood, 79 ; her rites publicly celebrated at Rome in 394, 36

Jerome, S., his feeling to the pagan Albinus, 14 ; to Praetextatus, 11 n. 1, 18 ; his life at Rome, his friendship with women of the aristocracy, 124 ; a satirist as well as an ascetic, 125 ; his pictures of female extravagance and vanity, 129 ; of female licence, 134, 135 ; of clerical impostors, 133 ; his immense influence, 182, 183 ; his letters on Biblical interpretation to Hedibia and Algasia, 184, 185 ;

Richomer, a Frank, friend of Symmachus, his paganism, 21

Rome, awe of, felt by the barbarians, belief in her eternity, 61 ; ancient religion of, its character, 75, 95 ; seldom visited by the emperors in the fourth century, 146 ; Claudian's faith in, 45 ; the mob of Rome, its vices, 122 ; disturbed state of, during the Gildonic war, 147 ; its hereditary corporations, 232, 233 ; the corn-supply, 234 ; faith in, shaken by Alaric's capture, 305 ; damage done by Alaric probably exaggerated, 309 ; faith of Rutilius Namatianus in, 311, 312 ; aspect of, in 467, 332

Rutilius Namatianus, his official career, his return to Gaul in 416, 46 ; the paganism of, and his attitude to Christianity and the Jews, 47, 48 ; his hatred of Stilicho, 47 ; his faith in Rome, 310

Sallustius, son of Flav. Sall., Cos. 363, his estates in Spain, 150 ; emended the text of Apuleius, 155

Salvianus, on the attractions of the circus and the theatre, 58 ; his life and career, 137 ; the subject of the *De Gubernatione Dei*, 137 *sqq.* ; his hatred of avarice and theatrical displays, 138, 139 ; his picture of universal immorality in Aquitaine, 140 ; doubts as to its accuracy, 141 ; on the invasions, 318 ; on the miseries of the poor, 320 ; despairs of the Empire, 322

Saxons, sent for by Symmachus to fight as gladiators, 151 ; feeling of Symmachus about their fate, 159 ; pirates, 327

Senate, the majority of, pagan in the reign of Theodosius, 4, 29, 37 ; the position of, under the later emperors, 145 ; part of Stilicho's policy to consult the Senate, 40, 145 ; consulted on the war with Gildo, 147 ; the senatorial class of the later Empire, their burdens and privileges, 249 n. 1 and 2 ; the senatorial estate a refuge for broken men, 262, 263 ; low public morality of the senatorial class, 271, 272 ; their relations with the barbarians, 372 *sqq.* ; the wealth

of the senatorial class, 149 ; extent and organisation of estates in Gaul, 201 ; country house life described, 176, 205 *sqq.*; general character of senatorial class, 211 ; devotion to letters, 156, 449

Serena, takes the necklace from the image of Magna Mater in the presence of the last Vestal, 36 ; her accomplishments and influence, 164

Sidonius, Caius Sollius Apollinaris, date of his birth, 187 n. 1 ; his ancestors, 187 ; married a daughter of Avitus, publication of his letters, 188 ; concerned chiefly with his own order, 192, his style, 193, 323, 437 ; date of his episcopate, 214 n. 1 ; range of his friendships, 195 ; his ideal of the Roman noble, 196 *sqq.*; his fear of literary decadance, 200 ; his reverence for the ascetic life, 221 ; his friendship with the monk Abraham, 222 ; his knowledge of the times, 324, 325 ; his pictures of the barbarians, 326 *sqq.*; knows the court of Theodoric II., 327, 328 ; takes part in Gallic movements, 328 ; his journey to Rome in 467, 331 *sqq.*; relations with Arvandus, 330 ; his Panegyric on Anthemius, 334 ; his Panegyric on Avitus, 335 ; his defence of Auvergne, 364 ; his imprisonment, 368 ; his stay at Bordeaux, 369 ; his flattery of the Visigothic court, 370 ; restoration to his diocese, 371

Slavery, feeling towards, expressed in the *Saturnalia* of Macrobius, 162 ; dangerous influence of slaves, 129 ; German slaves in every household, 297

Stilicho, left guardian of the sons of Theodosius, his supposed commission, 40, 41 ; suspected by both Christians and pagans, calumnies against, 42 ; revives the importance of the Senate, 145 ; repairs the walls of Rome, 303 ; his courage, 304

Style, in the fifth century a mere "jargon of experts," 157 ; aristocracy of Gaul devoted to, 211, 449

Sulpicius Severus, his *Life of S. Martin*, 181

MERIDIAN BOOKS

17 Union Square West, New York 3, New York

Titles listed here are not necessarily available in the British Empire.

Titles listed here are not necessarily available in the British Empire.

MERIDIAN BOOKS

17 Union Square West, New York 3, New York

If you have enjoyed this book, you will want these titles of related interest. Ask your bookseller for them.

ART AND MUSIC

M7   THE PHILOSOPHY OF MODERN ART *by Herbert Read*

M8   CREATIVE INTUITION IN ART AND POETRY *by Jacques Maritain*

M18   NEW DIRECTIONS 15. International Issue

M33   VISION AND DESIGN *by Roger Fry*. Illustrations

M38   THE ESSENCE OF LAUGHTER *by Charles Baudelaire*

M40   ITALIAN PAINTERS OF THE RENAISSANCE *by Bernard Berenson*. Illustrations

M44   GOTHIC ARCHITECTURE AND SCHOLASTICISM *by Erwin Panofsky*. Illustrations

ML2   A DICTIONARY OF CLASSICAL ANTIQUITIES *by Oskar Seyffert*. Illustrations. Meridian Library

ML8   A HISTORY OF AESTHETIC *by Bernard Bosanquet*. Meridian Library

M30   BERLIOZ AND HIS CENTURY *by Jacques Barzun*

M36   THE FORMS OF MUSIC *by Donald Francis Tovey*

DRAMA AND THEATER

M6   THE PLAYWRIGHT AS THINKER *by Eric Bentley*

M41   SIGHTS AND SPECTACLES: Theater Chronicles *by Mary McCarthy*

M43   THE WHEEL OF FIRE *by G. Wilson Knight*

MG4   MY LIFE IN ART *by Constantin Stanislavski*. Meridian Giant

MG5   THE ROMANTIC AGONY *by Mario Praz*. Meridian Giant

MG10   FILM FORM AND THE FILM SENSE *by Sergei Eisenstein*. Meridian Giant

LA10   RELIGIOUS DRAMA 1: Five modern religious dramas. Living Age Original

LA20   RELIGIOUS DRAMA 2: Medieval English mystery and morality plays. *Edited by E. Martin Browne*

CLASSICS

M9   OUTLINES OF THE HISTORY OF GREEK PHILOSOPHY *by Eduard Zeller*

M23   BYZANTINE CIVILIZATION *by Steven Runciman*

MG3   PROLEGOMENA TO THE STUDY OF GREEK RELIGION *by Jane Harrison.* Meridian Giant

MG7   PLATO: THE MAN AND HIS WORK *by A. E. Taylor.* Meridian Giant

ML1   ROMAN SOCIETY FROM NERO TO MARCUS AURELIUS *by Samuel Dill.* Meridian Library

ML2   A DICTIONARY OF CLASSICAL ANTIQUITIES *by Oskar Seyffert*

ML8   A HISTORY OF AESTHETIC *by Bernard Bosanquet*

ML10 ROMAN SOCIETY IN THE LAST CENTURY OF THE WESTERN EMPIRE *by Samuel Dill.* Meridian Library

HISTORY AND HISTORICAL THEORY

M4   IMPERIALISM AND SOCIAL CLASSES *by Joseph Schumpeter*

M9   OUTLINES OF THE HISTORY OF GREEK PHILOSOPHY *by Eduard Zeller*

M12   ESSAYS ON FREEDOM AND POWER *by Lord Acton*

M17   HISTORY AS THE STORY OF LIBERTY *by Benedetto Croce*

M23   BYZANTINE CIVILIZATION *by Steven Runciman*

M35   THE MAKING OF EUROPE *by Christopher Dawson*

M37   THE VARIETIES OF HISTORY: From Voltaire to the Present. *Edited by Fritz Stern*

M42   MOHAMMED AND CHARLEMAGNE *by Henri Pirenne*

M49   RENAISSANCE OF THE 12TH CENTURY *by C. H. Haskins*

M52   CIVILIZATION ON TRIAL *and* THE WORLD AND THE WEST *by Arnold Toynbee*

M53   RELIGION AND CULTURE *by Christopher Dawson*

M57   DEBATES WITH HISTORIANS *by Pieter Geyl*

MG2   MEDIEVAL PANORAMA *by G. G. Coulton.* Meridian Giant

MG8   FRANCE AGAINST HERSELF *by Herbert Luethy.* Meridian Giant

MG14 CHINESE CIVILIZATION *by Marcel Granet.* Meridian Giant

MG15 THE ORIGINS OF TOTALITARIANISM *by Hannah Arendt.* Second enlarged edition. Meridian Giant

MG17 THE MAN OF THE RENAISSANCE *by Ralph Roeder.* Meridian Giant.

ML1   ROMAN SOCIETY FROM NERO TO MARCUS AURELIUS *by Samuel Dill.* Meridian Library

ML6   PROLEGOMENA TO THE HISTORY OF ANCIENT ISRAEL *by Julius Wellhausen.* Meridian Library

Titles listed here are not necessarily available in the British Empire.

MERIDIAN BOOKS

17 Union Square West, New York 3, New York

If you have enjoyed this book, you will want these titles of related interest. Ask your bookseller for them.

LITERATURE AND CRITICISM

Titles listed here are not necessarily available in the British Empire.

LIVING AGE BOOKS

Published by MERIDIAN BOOKS INC.
17 Union Square West, New York 3, New York

LIVING AGE BOOKS, an inexpensive paperbound series, contains works of proven merit on history, art, literature, theology and Biblical studies, as they illuminate the development of Christian tradition in the West.

Titles listed here are not necessarily available in the British Empire.